MACHINE LEARNING

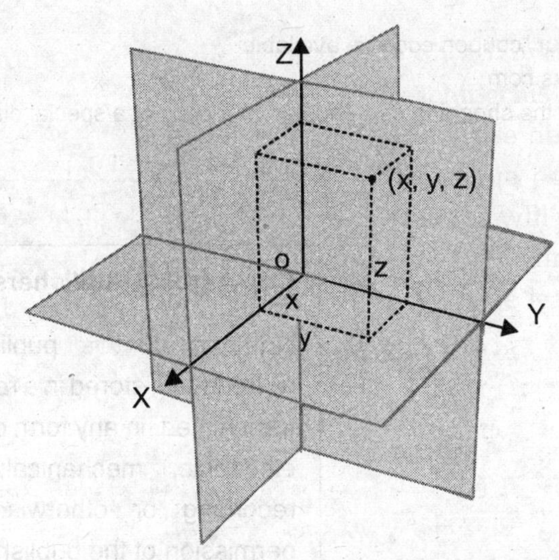

Er. V.K. JAIN

BE, M.Tech, FIE, FIETE, MISHRAE

Charted Engineer, Author, Visiting / Guest Faculty and

MEP Consultant Engineer Intelligent Services Consultants (MEP)

KHANNA BOOK PUBLISHING CO. (P) LTD.

Publisher, of Science, Technology and Engineering Books

4C/4344, Ansari Road, Darya Ganj, New Delhi-110002

Phone: 011-23244447-48 **Mobile:** +91-99109 09320

E-mail: contact@khannabooks.com

Website: www.khannabooks.com

Dear Readers,

To prevent the piracy, this book is secured with HIGH SECURITY HOLOGRAM on the front title cover. In case you don't find the hologram on the front cover title, please write us to at contact@khannabooks.com or whatsapp us at +91-99109 09320 and avail special gift voucher for yourself.

Specimen of Hologram on front Cover title:

Moreover, there is a SPECIAL DISCOUNT COUPON for you with EVERY HOLOGRAM.

How to avail this SPECIAL DISCOUNT:

Step 1: Scratch the hologram
Step 2: Under the scratch area, your "coupon code" is available
Step 3: Logon to www.khannabooks.com
Step 4: Use your "coupon code" in the shopping cart and get your copy at a special discount
Step 5: Enjoy your reading!

ISBN: 978-93-86173-66-9

Machine Learning
by V.K. Jain

First Edition: 2018
Reprint: 2024, **2026**

To view complete list of books,
Please scan the QR Code:

Published by:
Khanna Book Publishing Co. (P) Ltd.
CIN: U22110DL1998PTC095547

Visit us at: **www.khannabooks.com**
Write us at: **contact@khannabooks.com**

Printed in India.

PREFACE

"The human condition is plagued with a labyrinth of shortcomings, frailties and limitations that hinder man from reaching his fullest potential. Therefore, it only makes sense that we find ourselves at the next phase in human evolution where restricted man merges with the infinite possibilities of hyper-evolving technologies. This techno-human transmutation will prove to be 'the' quantum leap in human progression. The harmonization of technologically extending oneself, consciousness, artificial intelligence and machine learning will reverse the failures of genetic predisposition and limitation."

—James Scott, Senior Fellow, Institute for Critical Infrastructure Technology

Machine learning is perhaps the hottest thing in Silicon Valley right now, especially deep learning. We have Google's class on TensorFlow, which teaches you everything you need to know to work in Silicon Valley's top companies. The reason why it is so hot is because it can take over many repetitive, mindless tasks. It'll make doctors better doctors, and lawyers better lawyers and it makes cars drive themselves. I find this incredibly exciting. For example, when you're booking a taxi, you're shown how much the trip would cost. Or when you're on the trip, you're shown the path the taxi would take to reach your destination. All of that, is ***machine learning!***

While booking a ride on Uber, you're always told the amount of time the trip would take and how much it would cost. Machine learning helps obtain this information.

"Every day, we create 2.5 quintillion bytes of data so much that 90% of the data in the world today has been created in the last two years alone.

The ability to take data, to be able to understand it, to process it, to extract value from it, to visualize it, to communicate it's going to be a at the professional level.

Machine Learning employs techniques and theories drawn from many fields within the broad areas of mathematics, statistics, information science, and computer science, in particular from the sub-domains of machine learning, classification, cluster analysis, data mining, databases, and visualization.

The overall goal of the book is to provide a broad understanding of various faces of Machine Learning environment in an integrated manner.

While composing this book my intention was not to introduce a collection of new techniques and protocols, but rather to selectively present techniques from those currently available in the public domain.

Computer science has the greatest drawback of non-standardization of the stuff, not only of its software but in courseware also. A vast amount of curriculum exists at different levels of various Universities. As such I have tried to include all desired courseware from the syllabi for different levels.

The various facades of computer science are changing its attributes with such a fast speed that it's very difficult to keep track of latest development and it's a great task to get aware with the latest happenings in the field. Therefore in presenting the state-of-the art text ware, immense help had been sought by the author from various literature forms who in turn expresses his gratitude to the authors of the works from where information has been derived.

I am to acknowledge with great sense of gratitude to Mrs. Heera Jain and Anurag Jain Director NICT (Vikas Marg Branch) and my publisher M/s Khanna Publishing House.

Author

CONTENTS

Unit **1**

SUPERVISED LEARNING (REGRESSION/CLASSIFICATION)

Learning Objectives and Outcome

At the end of this unit the reader will be able to grasp ;

- Machine Learning Concept
- Basic methods: Distance-based methods, Nearest-Neighbours, Decision Trees, Naive Bayes 1
- Linear models: Linear Regression, Logistic Regression, Generalized Linear Models
- Support Vector Machines, Nonlinearity and Kernel Methods
- Beyond Binary Classification: Multi-class/Structured Outputs, Ranking

1.1 INTRODUCTION TO MACHINE LEARNING

Machine learning is a subfield of artificial intelligence (AI). The goal of machine learning generally is to understand the structure of data and fit that data into models that can be understood and utilized by people.

Although machine learning is a field within computer science, it differs from traditional computational approaches. In traditional computing, algorithms are sets of explicitly programmed instructions used by computers to calculate or problem solve. Machine learning algorithms instead allow for computers to train on data inputs and use statistical analysis in order to output values that fall within a specific range. Because of this, machine learning facilitates computers in building models from sample data in order to automate decision-making processes based on data inputs.

Any technology user today has benefitted from machine learning. Facial recognition technology allows social media platforms to help users tag and share photos of friends. Optical character recognition (OCR) technology converts images of text into movable type. Recommendation engines, powered by machine learning, suggest what movies or television shows to watch next based on user preferences. Self-driving cars that rely on machine learning to navigate may soon be available to consumers.

Machine learning is a continuously developing field. Because of this, there are some considerations to keep in mind as you work with machine learning methodologies, or analyze the impact of machine learning processes.

Machine learning is a term closely associated with data science. It refers to a broad class of methods that revolve around data modeling to :

(1) *Supervised Learning* to algorithmically make predictions, and

(2) *Unsupervised Learning* to algorithmically decipher patterns in data.

Another categorization of machine learning tasks arises when one considers the desired output of a machine-learned system:[5]:3

- In **classification**, inputs are divided into two or more classes, and the learner must produce a model that assigns unseen inputs to one or more (multi-label classification) of these classes. This is typically tackled in a supervised way. Spam filtering is an example of classification, where the inputs are email (or other) messages and the classes are "spam" and "not spam".
- In **regression**, also a supervised problem, the outputs are continuous rather than discrete.
- In **clustering**, a set of inputs is to be divided into groups. Unlike in classification, the groups are not known beforehand, making this typically an unsupervised task.We shall read about this in unit 2.
- **Density** estimation finds the distribution of inputs in some space.
- **Dimensionality reduction simplifies** inputs by mapping them into a lower-dimensional space. Topic modeling is a related problem, where a program is given a list of human language documents and is tasked to find out which documents cover similar topics.

1.1.1 Supervised Machine learning for Making Predictions

Core concept is to use tagged data to train predictive models. *Tagged data* means observations where ground truth is already known. *Training models* means automatically characterizing tagged data in ways to predict tags for unknown data points. E.g. a credit card fraud detection model can be trained using a historical record of tagged fraud purchases. The resultant model estimates the likelihood that any new purchase is fraudulent. Common methods for training models range from basic regressions to complex neural nets. All follow the same paradigm known as *supervised learning*.

1.1.2 Un Supervised Machine learning for Pattern Discovery

Another modeling paradigm known as *unsupervised learning* tries to surface underlying patterns and associations in data when no existing ground truth is known (i.e. no observations are tagged). Within this broad category of methods, the most commonly used are clustering techniques, which algorithmically detect what are the natural groupings that exist in a data set. For example, clustering can be used to programmatically learn the natural customer segments in a company's user base. Other unsupervised methods for mining underlying characteristics include: principal component analysis, hidden markov models, topic models, and more.

Not all machine learning methods fit neatly into the above two categories. For example, collaborative filtering is a type of recommendations algorithm with elements related to both supervised and unsupervised learning. Contextual bandits are a twist on supervised learning where predictions get adaptively modified on-the-fly using live feedback.

This wide-ranging breadth of machine learning techniques comprise an important part of the data science toolbox. It is up to the data scientist to figure out which tool to use in different circumstances (as well as how to use the tool correctly) in order to solve analytically open-ended problems.

1.2 TYPES OF MACHINE LEARNING ALGORITHMS

Machine learning is used to predict, categorize, classify, finding polarity, etc from the given datasets and concerned with minimizing the error. Machine Learning is always algorithm based and basic machine learning algorithms can be classified as

(1) Supervised Learning

(2) Unsupervised learning

(3) Reinforcement Learning

1.3 SUPERVISED LEARNING

It is used for structured dataset. It analyzes the training data and generates function which will be used for other datasets. It is **Machine learning for making predictions** – Core concept is to use tagged data to train predictive models. *Tagged data* means observations where ground truth is already known. *Training models* means automatically characterizing tagged data in ways to predict tags for unknown data points. For example a credit card fraud detection model can be trained using a historical record of tagged fraud purchases. The resultant model estimates the likelihood that any new purchase is fraudulent. Common methods for training models range from basic regressions to complex neural nets. All follow the same paradigm known as *supervised learning*.

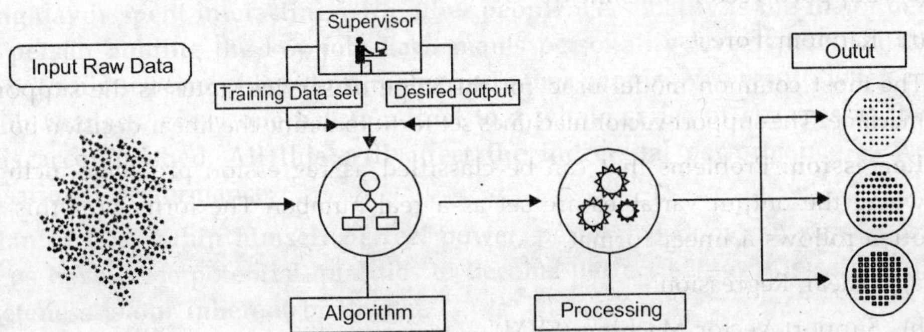

Fig. 1.1: Supervised LearningProcess

Before we go into the technical details regarding supervised learning, it is imperative to give a brief and simplistic overview that can be understood by all readers, regardless of their experience in this growing field.

With supervised learning, you feed the output of your algorithm into the system. This means that in supervised learning, the machine already knows the output of the algorithm before it starts working on it or learning it. A basic example of this concept would be a student learning a course from an instructor. The student knows what he/she is learning from the course.

With the output of the algorithm known, all that a system needs to do is to work out the steps or process needed to reach from the input to the output. The algorithm is being taught through a training data set that guides the machine. If the process goes haywire and the algorithms come up with results completely different than what should be expected, then the training data does its part to guide the algorithm back towards the right path.

Supervised Machine Learning currently makes up most of the ML that is being used by systems across the world. The input variable (x) is used to connect with the output variable (y) through the use of an algorithm. All of the input, the output, the algorithm, and the scenario are being provided by humans. We can understand supervised learning in an even better way by looking at it through three types of problems which we shall explore further in various sections of this book..

(1) Classification: Classification problems categorize all the variables that form the output. Examples of these categories formed through classification would include demographic data such as marital status, sex, or age. It is often used for sentimental analysis or finding polarity. It is used to classify objects. For example- If any mail is received, then this algorithm helps to classify whether the received mail is spam or not. It is also used to categorize objects like name of persons in same category who live in same area.

(a) Naïve Bayes

(b) Logistic Regression

(c) Decision Trees

(d) K-Nearest Neighbors

(e) Support Vector Machines

(f) Random Forests

The most common model used for this type of service status is the support vector machine. The support vector machines set forth to define the linear decision boundaries.

(2) Regression: Problems that can be classified as regression problems include types where the output variables are set as a real number. The format for this problem often follows a linear format.

(a) Linear Regression

(b) Support Vector Maching (SVM)

(3) Cluctering

(a) Machines Clustering

(b) K-Means Clustering

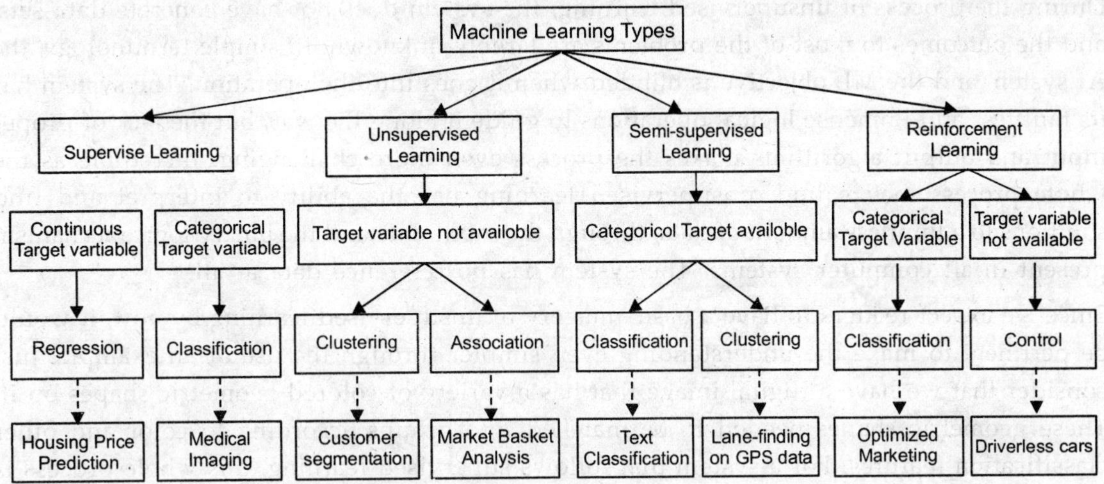

1.4 UNSUPERVISED LEARNING

It is used for raw datasets. Its main task is to convert raw data to structured data. In today's world there is a huge amount of raw data in ever field. Even the computer generates log files which are in the form of raw data. Therefore it's the most important part of machine learning. It consists of **machine learning for pattern discovery** – Another modeling paradigm known as *unsupervised learning* tries to surface underlying patterns and associations in data when no existing ground truth is known (i.e. no observations are tagged). Within this broad category of methods, the most commonly used are clustering techniques, which algorithmically detect what are the natural groupings that exist in a data set. For example, clustering can be used to programmatically learn the natural customer segments in a company's user base. Other unsupervised methods for mining underlying characteristics include: principal component analysis, hidden markov models, topic models, and more.

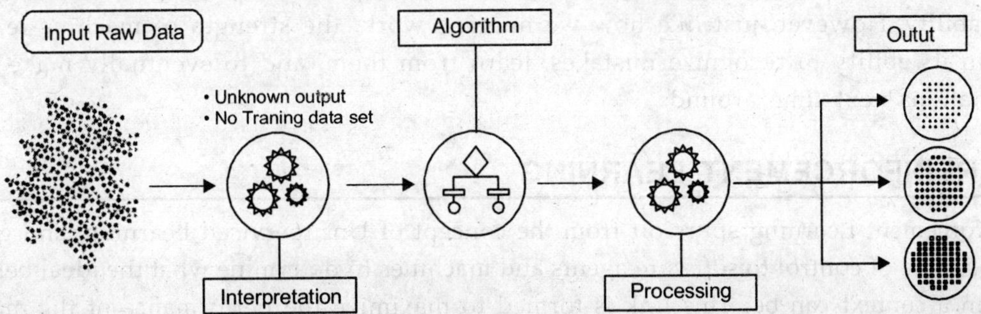

Fig. 1.2: Unsupervised Learning Process

The concept of unsupervised learning is not as widespread and frequently used as supervised learning. In fact, the concept has been put to use in only a limited amount of applications as of yet.

During the process of unsupervised learning, the system does not have concrete data sets, and the outcomes to most of the problems are largely unknown. In simple terminology, the AI system and the ML objective is blinded when it goes into the operation. The system has its faultless and immense logical operations to guide it along the way, but the lack of proper input and output algorithms makes the process even more challenging. Incredible as the whole process may sound, unsupervised learning has the ability to interpret and find solutions to a limitless amount of data, through the input data and the binary logic mechanism present in all computer systems. The system has no reference data at all.

Since we expect readers to have a basic imagery of unsupervised learning by now, it would be pertinent to make the understanding even simpler through the use of an example. Just consider that we have a digital image that has a variety of colored geometric shapes on it. These geometric shapes needed to be matched into groups according to color and other classification features. For a system that follows supervised learning, this whole process is a bit too simple. The procedure is extremely straightforward, as you just have to teach the computer all the details pertaining to the figures. You can let the system know that all shapes with four sides are known as squares, and others with eight sides are known as octagons, etc. We can also teach the system to interpret the colors and see how the light being given out is classified.

However, in unsupervised learning, the whole process becomes a little trickier. The algorithm for an unsupervised learning system has the same input data as the one for its supervised counterpart (in our case, digital images showing shapes in different colors).

Once it has the input data, the system learns all it can from the information at hand. In fact, the system works by itself to recognize the problem of classification and also the difference in shapes and colors. With information related to the problem at hand, the unsupervised learning system will then recognize all similar objects, and group them together. The labels that it will give to these objects will be designed by the machine itself. Technically, there are bound to be wrong answers, since there is a certain degree of probability. However, just like how we humans work, the strength of machine learning lies in its ability to recognize mistakes, learn from them, and to eventually make better estimations next time around.

1.5 REINFORCEMENT LEARNING

Reinforcement Learning spurs off from the concept of Unsupervised Learning, and gives a high sphere of control to software agents and machines to determine what the ideal behavior within a context can be. This link is formed to maximize the performance of the machine in a way that helps it to grow. Simple feedback that informs the machine about its progress is required here to help the machine learn its behavior.

Reinforcement Learning is not simple, and is tackled by a plethora of different algorithms. As a matter of fact, in Reinforcement Learning an agent decides the best action based on the current state of the results.

The growth in Reinforcement Learning has led to the production of a wide variety of algorithms that help machines learn the outcome of what they are doing. Since we have a basic understanding of Reinforcement Learning by now, we can get a better grasp by forming a comparative analysis between Reinforcement Learning and the concepts of Supervised and Unsupervised Learning that we have studied in detail before.

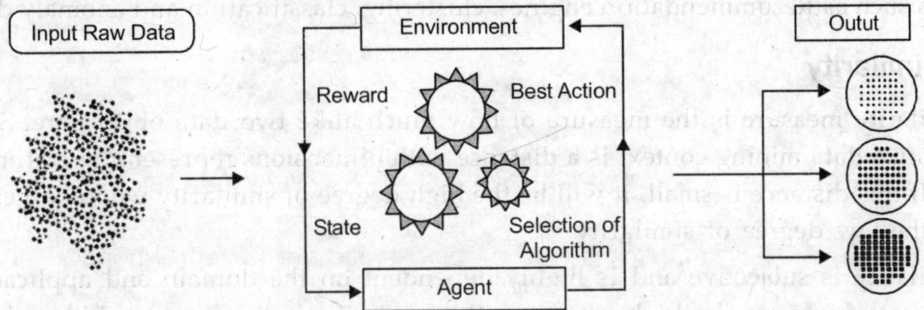

Fig. 1.3: Reinforcement Learning Process

Not all machine learning methods fit neatly into the above three categories. For example, collaborative filtering is a type of recommendations algorithm with elements related to both supervised and unsupervised learning. Contextual bandits are a twist on supervised learning where predictions get adaptively modified on-the-fly using live feedback.

1.6 CLASSIFICATION OF MACHINE LEARNING CONCEPT

(a) Basic methods:
   (1) Distance-based methods,
   (2) Nearest-Neighbours,
   (3) Decision Trees,
   (4) Naive Bayes 1
(b) Linear Models
   (1) Linear Regression,
   (2) Logistic Regression,
   (3) Generalized Linear Models
(c) Support Vector Machines, : Nonlinearity and Kernel Methods
(d) Beyond Binary Classification: Multi-class/Structured Outputs, Ranking

1.7 DISTANCE BASED MACHINE LEARNING METHODS

Distance-based algorithms are machine learning algorithms that classify queries by computing distances between these queries and a number of internally stored exemplars. Exemplars that are closest to the query have the largest influence on the classification assigned to the query.

The buzz term similarity distance measure has got a wide variety of definitions among the math and data mining practitioners. As a result, those terms, concepts and their usage went way beyond the head for the beginner, Who started to understand them for the very first time.

Before going to explain different similarity distance measures let me explain the effective key term similarity in data mining. This similarity is the very basic building block for activities such as Recommendation engines, clustering, classification and anomaly detection.

1.7.1 Similarity

The similarity measure is the measure of how much alike two data objects are. Similarity measure in a data mining context is a distance with dimensions representing features of the objects. If this distance is small, it will be the high degree of similarity where large distance will be the low degree of similarity.

The similarity is subjective and is highly dependent on the domain and application. For example, two fruits are similar because of color or size or taste. Care should be taken when calculating distance across dimensions/features that are unrelated. The relative values of each element must be normalized, or one feature could end up dominating the distance calculation. Similarity are measured in the range 0 to 1 [0,1].

Two main consideration about similarity:

Similarity = *1* if $X = Y$ (Where X, Y are two objects)

Similarity = *0* if $X \neq Y$

That's all about similarity let's drive to five most popular similarity distance measures.

1.7.2 Euclidean space

Euclidean space encompasses the 3 nos. two-dimensional Euclidean planes perpendicular to each other and the three-dimensional space of Euclidean geometry,

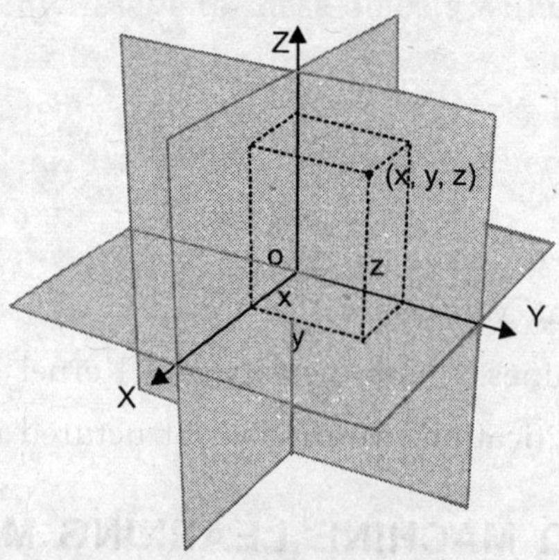

Euclidean 3rd Space

Every point in three-dimensional Euclidean space is determined by three coordinates. Euclidean space can, as one possible choice of representation, be modeled using Cartesian coordinates. In this case, the Euclidean space is then modeled by the real coordinate space (R^n)

of the same dimension. In one dimension, this is the real line; in two dimensions, it is the Cartesian plane; and in higher dimensions it is a coordinate space with three or more real number coordinates

(1) Euclidean Distance

Euclidean distance is the most common use of distance. In most cases when people said about distance, they will refer to Euclidean distance. Euclidean distance is also known as simply distance. When data is dense or continuous, this is the best proximity measure.

The Euclidean distance between two points is the length of the path connecting them. The Pythagorean theorem gives this distance between two points.

Euclidean distance implementation in python

```
#!/usr/bin/env python


from math import*

def euclidean_distance(x,y):

    return sqrt(sum(pow(a-b,2) for a, b in zip(x, y)))

print euclidean_distance([0,3,4,5],[7,6,3,-1])
```

The output shall be:

```
9.74679434481
[Finished in 0.0s]
```

(2) Manhattan Distance

Manhattan distance is a metric in which the distance between two points is the sum of the absolute differences of their Cartesian coordinates. In a simple way of saying it is the total suzm of the difference between the x-coordinates and y-coordinates.

Suppose we have two points A and B if we want to find the Manhattan distance between them, just we have, to sum up, the absolute x-axis and y–axis variation means we have to find how these two points A and B are varying in X-axis and Y-axis. In a more mathematical way of saying Manhattan distance between two points measured along axes at right angles.

In a plane with p_1 at (x_1, y_1) and p_2 at (x_2, y_2).

Manhattan distance = $|x_1 - x_2| + |y_1 - y_2|$

This Manhattan distance metric is also known as Manhattan length, rectilinear distance, L_1 distance or L_1 norm, city block distance, Minkowski's L_1 distance, taxi-cab metric, or city block distance.

Manhattan distance implementation in python:

```
#!/usr/bin/env python

from math import*

def manhattan_distance(x,y):

    return sum(abs(a-b) for a,b in zip(x,y))

print manhattan_distance([10,20,10],[10,20,20])
```

The outpus shall be :

```
10
[Finished in 0.0s]
```

(3) Minkowski distance:

The Minkowski distance is a generalized metric form of Euclidean distance and Manhattan distance.

$$d^{MKD}(i, J) = \lambda\sqrt{\sum_{b-0}^{n-1} | y_{i,k} - y_{j,k} |^{\lambda}}$$

In the equation, d^{MKD} is the Minkowski distance between the data record *i* and *j*, *k* the index of a variable, n the total number of variables y and ë the order of the Minkowski metric. Although it is defined for any *ë* > 0, it is rarely used for values other than 1, 2 and".

The way distances are measured by the Minkowski metric of different orders between two objects with three variables (In the image it displayed in a coordinate system with *x*, *y*, *z*-axes).

Synonyms of Minkowski:

Different names for the Minkowski distance or Minkowski metric arise from the order:

$\lambda = 1$ is the Manhattan distance. Synonyms are L1-Norm, Taxicab or City-Block distance. For two vectors of ranked ordinal variables, the Manhattan distance is sometimes called Foot-ruler distance.

$\lambda = 2$ is the Euclidean distance. Synonyms are L2-Norm or Ruler distance. For two vectors of ranked ordinal variables, the Euclidean distance is sometimes called Spear-man distance.

λ = " is the Chebyshev distance. Synonyms are Lmax-Norm or Chessboard distance

reference.

Minkowski distance implementation in python:

```
#!/usr/bin/env python


from math import*
from decimal import Decimal

def nth_root(value, n_root):

    root_value = 1/float(n_root)
    return round (Decimal(value) ** Decimal(root_value),3)

def minkowski_distance(x,y,p_value):

    return nth_root(sum(pow(abs(a-b),p_value) for a,b in zip(x, y)),p_value)

print minkowski_distance([0,3,4,5],[7,6,3,-1],3)
```

The output shall be:

```
8.373
[Finished in 0.0s]
```

1.8 K-NEAREST NEIGHBOR (KNN)

K-nearest neighbor classifier is one of the introductory supervised classifier, which every data science learner should be aware of. Fix & Hodges proposed K-nearest neighbor classifier algorithm in the year of 1951 for performing pattern classification task.

For simplicity, this classifier is called as Knn Classifier. To be surprised k-nearest neighbor classifier mostly represented as Knn, even in many research papers too. Knn address the pattern recognition problems and also the best choices for addressing some of the classification related tasks.

The simple version of the K-nearest neighbor classifier algorithms is to predict the target label by finding the nearest neighbor class. The closest class will be identified using the distance measures like Euclidean distance

The k-nearest neighbor algorithm is a pattern recognition model that can be used for classification as well as regression. Often abbreviated as k-NN, the k in k-nearest neighbor is a positive integer, which is typically small. In either classification or regression, the input will consist of the k closest training examples within a space.

We will focus on k-NN classification. In this method, the output is class membership. This will assign a new object to the class most common among its k nearest neighbors. In the case of k = 1, the object is assigned to the class of the single nearest neighbor.

Let's look at an example of k-nearest neighbour. In the diagram below, there are blue diamond objects and orange star objects. These belong to two separate classes: the diamond class and the star class.

When a new object is added to the space — in this case a green heart — we will want the machine learning algorithm to classify the heart to a certain class.

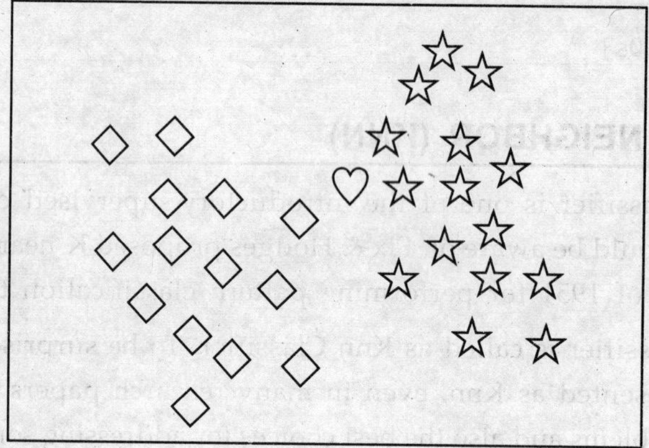

When we choose k = 3, the algorithm will find the three nearest neighbors of the green heart in order to classify it to either the diamond class or the star class.

In our diagram, the three nearest neighbors of the green heart are one diamond and two stars. Therefore, the algorithm will classify the heart with the star class.

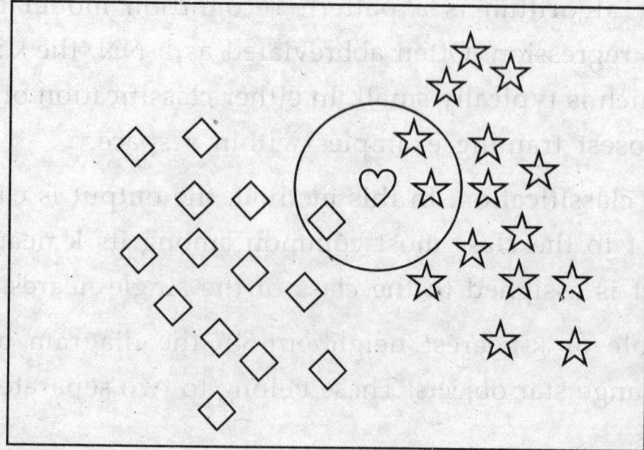

Among the most basic of machine learning algorithms, k-nearest neighbor is considered to be a type of "lazy learning" as generalization beyond the training data does not occur until a query is made to the system.

1.8.1 KNN for Classification

In pattern recognition, the KNN algorithm is a method for classifying objects based on closest training examples in the feature space. KNN is a type of instance-based learning, or lazy learning where the function is only approximated locally and all computation is deferred until classification. The KNN is the fundamental and simplest classification technique when there is little or no prior knowledge about the distribution of the data This rule simply retains the entire training set during learning and assigns to each query a class represented by the majority label of its k-nearest neighbors in the training set.

The Nearest Neighbor rule (NN) is the simplest form of KNN when K = 1. In this method each sample should be classified similarly to its surrounding samples. Therefore, if the classification of a sample is unknown, then it could be predicted by considering the classification of its nearest neighbor samples. Given an unknown sample and a training set, all the distances between the unknown sample and all the samples in the training set can be computed. The distance with the smallest value corresponds to the sample in the training set closest to the unknown sample.

Therefore, the unknown sample may be classified based on the classification of this nearest neighbor.

Figure 1.4 shows the KNN decision rule for K= 1 and K= 4 for a set of samples divided into 2 classes. In Figure 1.4(a), an unknown sample is classified by using only one known sample; in Figure 1.4(b) more than one known sample is used. In the last case, the parameter K is set to 4, so that the closest four samples are considered for classifying the unknown one.

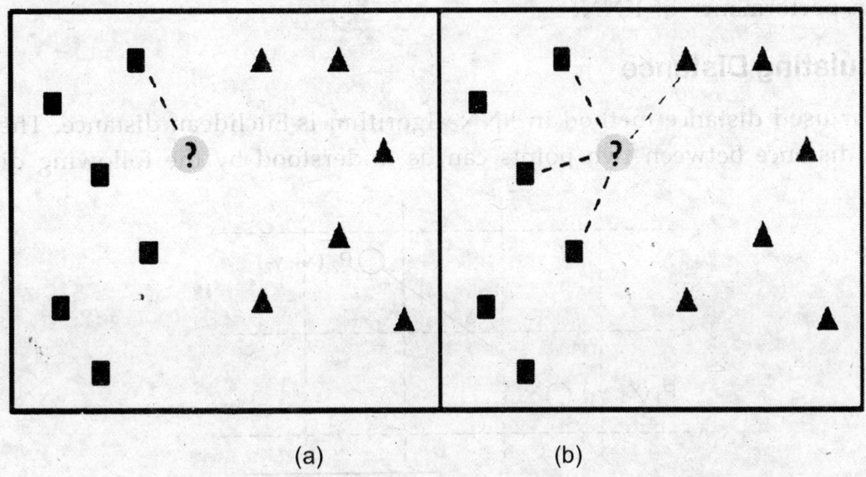

Fig. 1.4: (a) The 1-NN decision rule: the point ? is assigned to the class on the left; (b) the KNN

Three of them belong to the same class, whereas only one belongs to the other class. In both cases, the unknown sample is classified as belonging to the class on the left. Figure 1.5 provides a sketch of the KNN algorithm. Figure 1.4 (a) The 1-NN decision rule: the point? is assigned to the class on the left; (b) the KNN decision rule, with K= 4: the point ? is assigned to the class on the left as well.

```
for all the unknown samples UnSample(i)
        for all the known samples Sample(j)
                compute the distance between
UnSamples(i) and Sample(j)
        end for
        find the k smallest distances
        locate the corresponding samples
Sample(jl),...,Sample(jk)
        assign UnSample(i) to the class which
appears more frequently
end for
```

Fig. 1.5: The KNN algorithm.

The performance of a KNN classifier is primarily determined by the choice of K as well as the distance metric applied. The estimate is affected by the sensitivity of the selection of the neighborhood size K, because the radius of the local region is determined by the distance of the Kth nearest neighbor to the query and different K yields different conditional class probabilities. If K is very small, the local estimate tends to be very poor owing to the data sparseness and the noisy, ambiguous or mislabeled points. In order to further smooth the estimate, we can increase K and take into account a large region around the query. Unfortunately, a large value of K easily makes the estimate over smoothing and the classification performance degrades with the introduction of the outliers from other classes. To deal with the problem, the related research works have been done to improve the classification performance of KNN. How to select a suitable neighborhood size K is a key issue that largely affects the classification performance of KNN.

1.8.2 Calculating Distance

Most popular used distance method in kNN algorithm is Euclidean distance. The formula to calculate distance between two points can be understood by the following diagram.

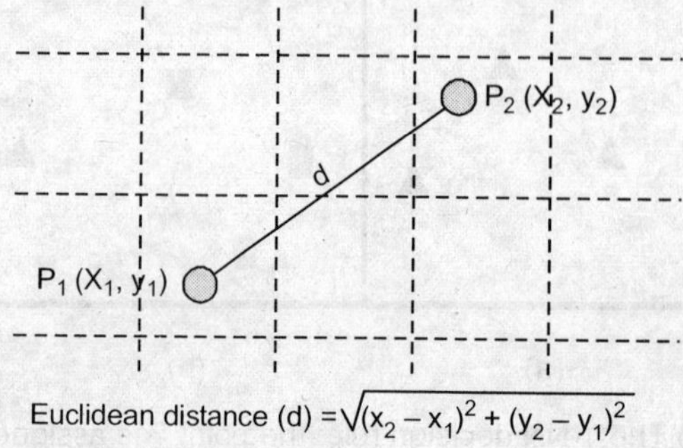

Euclidean distance $(d) = \sqrt{(x_2 - x_1)^2 + (y_2 - y_1)^2}$

Fig. 1.6: Euclidean Distance

For example to Calculate Distance between Two Points say A(fac_1 = 6, fac_2 = 4) and B(fac_1 = 3, fac_2 = 7), we can use the above mentioned formula and calculate the distance as shown below:

$$A(facl = 6, fac2 = 4), B(facl = 3, fac2 = 7)$$

$$\text{dist}(A,B) = \sqrt{(6-3)^2 + (7-4)^2}$$

$$\text{dist}(A,B) = \sqrt{9+9}$$

$$\text{dist}(A,B) = 4.2$$

1.8.3 kNN Classification Using R Programing

Before starting with the kNN implementation using R, I would like to discuss two Data Normalization/Standardization techniques.

Min-Max Normalization:

This process transforms a feature value in such a way that all of its values falls in the range of 0 and 1. Formula to do so is below:

$$X_{new} = \left.\frac{x - \min(x)}{\max(x) - \min(x)}\right]^{\text{Min–Max}}_{\text{Normalization}}$$

Z-Score Standardization:

This process subtracts the mean value of feature 'x' and divides it with the standard deviation of 'x'. Formula is shown below:

$$X_{new} = \left.\frac{x - \min(x)}{\text{std.der}(x)}\right]^{\text{Z–Score}}_{\text{Standardization}}$$

Example 1.1 Using Iris DataSet Classify the species.

We are going to use the Iris Dataset, this dataset contains Sepal Length, Sepal Width, Petal Length, Petal Width and Species. The sepal and petal length and width are real-valued and species (categorical) can assume three different categories: Iris Setosa, Iris Virginica and Versicolor. Our goal here is to predict the species using a classifier.

Data Set Information:

This is perhaps the best known database to be found in the pattern recognition literature. Fisher's paper is a classic in the field and is referenced frequently to this day. (See Duda & Hart, for example.) The data set contains 3 classes of 50 instances each, where each class refers to a type of iris plant. One class is linearly separable from the other 2; the latter are NOT linearly separable from each other.

Iris Data Set

Data Set Characteristics:	Multivariate	Number of Instances:	150	Area:	Life
Attribute Characteristics:	Real	Number of Attributes:	4	Date Donated	1988-07-01
Associated Tasks:	Classification	Missing Values?	No	Number of Web Hits	1710909

  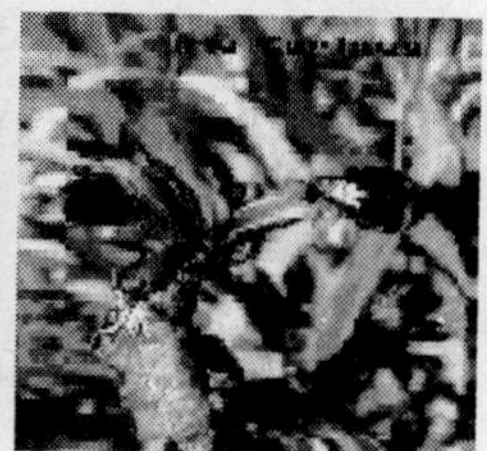

Enter following code in R-console.

```
iris_data <- read.csv(url("http://archive.ics.uci.edu/ml/machine-learning-databases/iris/iris.data"), header = FALSE, stringsAsFactors = FALSE)
names(iris_data) <- c("Sepal.Length", "Sepal.Width", "Petal.Length", "Petal.Width", "Species")
str(iris_data)
table(iris_data$Species)
```

Following output shall be displayed.

```
R Console

You are welcome to redistribute it under certain conditions.
Type 'license()' or 'licence()' for distribution details.

R is a collaborative project with many contributors.
Type 'contributors()' for more information and
'citation()' on how to cite R or R packages in publications.

Type 'demo()' for some demos, 'help()' for on-line help, or
'help.start()' for an HTML browser interface to help.
Type 'q()' to quit R.

> iris_data <- read.csv(url("http://archive.ics.uci.edu/ml/machine-learning-dat$
> names(iris_data) <- c("Sepal.Length", "Sepal.Width", "Petal.Length", "Petal.W$
> str(iris_data)
'data.frame':   150 obs. of  5 variables:
 $ Sepal.Length: num  5.1 4.9 4.7 4.6 5 5.4 4.6 5 4.4 4.9 ...
 $ Sepal.Width : num  3.5 3 3.2 3.1 3.6 3.9 3.4 3.4 2.9 3.1 ...
 $ Petal.Length: num  1.4 1.4 1.3 1.5 1.4 1.7 1.4 1.5 1.4 1.5 ...
 $ Petal.Width : num  0.2 0.2 0.2 0.2 0.2 0.4 0.3 0.2 0.2 0.1 ...
 $ Species     : chr  "Iris-setosa" "Iris-setosa" "Iris-setosa" "Iris-setosa" .$
> table(iris_data$Species)

    Iris-setosa Iris-versicolor  Iris-virginica
             50              50              50
> |
```

The last line after > is Output of the Table() function.

To Normalize the data use the following function.

```
normalize <- function(x)
{
  return((x-min(x))/max(x)-min(x))
}
iris_n <- as.data.frame(lapply(iris_data[1:4], normalize))
Now Create Training and Test Data Set.
set.seed(1234)
ind <- sample(2, nrow(iris), replace=TRUE, prob=c(0.67, 0.33))
iris_train <- iris[ind==1, 1:4]
iris_test <- iris[ind==2, 1:4]
iris_train_labels <- iris[ind==1, 5]
iris_test_labels <- iris[ind==2, 5]
Load Class Package and Call knn() function to build the model.
library(class)
iris_test_pred<-knn(train=iris_train,
test=iris_test,cl=iris_train_labels,k=3)
```

To evaluate the model, Use CrossTable() function in "gmodels" package.

```
library(gmodels)
CrossTable(x=iris_test_labels, y=iris_test_pred, prop.chisq = FALSE)
```

Output:

```
Total Observations in Table:  40

                 | iris_test_pred
iris_test_labels |     setosa | versicolor |  virginica | Row Total |
-----------------|------------|------------|------------|-----------|
          setosa |         12 |          0 |          0 |        12 |
                 |      1.000 |      0.000 |      0.000 |     0.300 |
                 |      1.000 |      0.000 |      0.000 |           |
                 |      0.300 |      0.000 |      0.000 |           |
-----------------|------------|------------|------------|-----------|
      versicolor |          0 |         12 |          0 |        12 |
                 |      0.000 |      1.000 |      0.000 |     0.300 |
                 |      0.000 |      0.923 |      0.000 |           |
                 |      0.000 |      0.300 |      0.000 |           |
-----------------|------------|------------|------------|-----------|
       virginica |          0 |          1 |         15 |        16 |
                 |      0.000 |      0.062 |      0.938 |     0.400 |
                 |      0.000 |      0.077 |      1.000 |           |
                 |      0.000 |      0.025 |      0.375 |           |
-----------------|------------|------------|------------|-----------|
    Column Total |         12 |         13 |         15 |        40 |
                 |      0.300 |      0.325 |      0.375 |           |
-----------------|------------|------------|------------|-----------|
```

As you can see from the table above the model make one error mistake of predicting as versicolor instead of virginica, whereas rest all the predicted correctly.

Since the Data contains only 150 observations, the model makes only one mistake. There may be more mistakes in Huge Data. In that case we need to try using different approach like instead of min-max normalization use Z-Score standardization and also vary the values of k to see the impact on accuracy of predicted result.

1.8.4 Selection Of The Optimal Neighborhood Size K

As for KNN, the small training sample size can greatly affect the selection of the optimal neighborhood size K and the degradation of the classification performance of KNN is easily produced by the sensitivity of the selection of K. Generally speaking, the classification results are very sensitive to two aspects: the data sparseness and the noisy, ambiguous or mislabeled points if K is too small, and many outliers within the neighborhood from other classes if K is too large. From a theoretical point of view, the classification performance of KNN is determined by the estimate of the conditional class probabilities of the query in a local region of the data space, which is determined by the distance of the Kth nearest neighbor to the query. So the classification performance is very sensitive to the selected value of K. Furthermore, the simplest majority voting of combining the class labels for KNN can be a problem if the nearest neighbors vary widely over their distances and the closer ones more reliably indicate the class of the query object. With the goal of addressing the sensitivity issue of different choices of the neighborhood size K, some weighted voting methods have been developed for KNN. It has been shown in when the points are not uniformly distributed; predetermining the value of K becomes difficult. Generally, larger values of K are more immune to the noise presented, and make boundaries smoother between classes. As a result, choosing the same (optimal) K becomes almost impossible for different applications.

1.8.5 KNN for Regression

The same method can be used for regression, by simply assigning the property value for the object to be the average of the values of its K nearest neighbors. It can be useful to weight the contributions of the neighbors, so that the nearer neighbors contribute more to the average than the more distant ones.

Regression problems are concerned with predicting the outcome of a dependent variable given a set of independent variables. To start with, we consider the schematic shown above in Figure 3, where a set of points (green squares) are drawn from the relationship between the independent variable x and the dependent variable y (red curve). Given the set of green objects (known as examples) we use the KNN method to predict the outcome of X (also known as query point) given the example set (green squares).

To begin with, let's consider the 1-nearest neighbor method as an example. In this case we search the example set (green squares) and locate the one closest to the query point X. For this particular case, this happens to be x_4. The outcome of x_4 (i.e., y_4) is thus then taken to be the answer for the outcome of X (i.e.Y). Thus for -nearest neighbor we can write $Y = y_4$

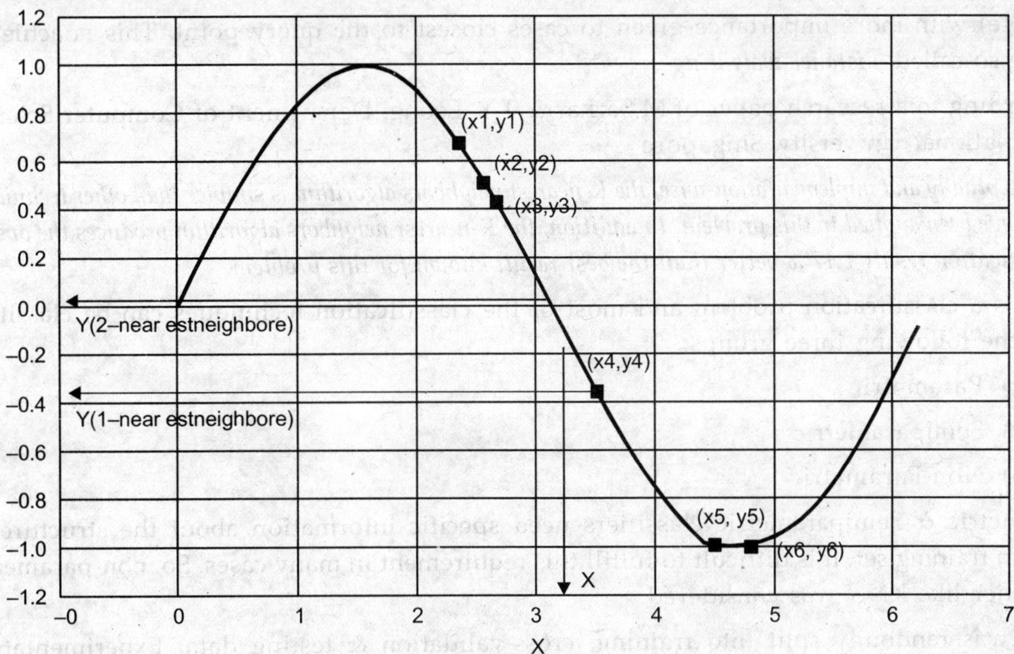

Fig. 1.7: the KNN decision rule for regression

For the next step, let's consider the -nearest neighbor method. In this case, we locate the first two closest points to X , which happen to be y_3 and y_4. Taking the average of their outcome, the solution for is then given by:

$$Y = \frac{y_3 + y_4}{2}$$

The above discussion can be extended to an arbitrary number of nearest neighbours K. To summarize, in a KNN method, the outcome Y of the query point X is taken to be the average of the outcomes of its K nearest neighbors.

1.8.6 Nearest Neighbor Predictions

After selecting the value of K, you can make predictions based on the KNN examples. For regression, KNN prediction is the average of the K nearest neighbors outcome:

$$y = \frac{1}{K}\sum_{i=1}^{k} y_i$$

where is y_1 the i th case of the examples sample and y is the prediction (outcome) of the query point. In contrast to regression, in classification problems,

KNN predictions are based on a voting scheme in which the winner is used to label the query. So far we have discussed KNN analysis without paying any attention to the relative distance of the K nearest examples to the query point. In other words, we let the K neighbours have equal influence on predictions irrespective of their relative distance from the query point. An alternative approach is to use arbitrarily large values of (if not the entire prototype sample) with more importance given to cases closest to the query point. This is achieved using so-called *'distance weighting'*.

According to a research paper of M.Sarkar & T.Y. Leong, Department of Computer Science, The National University Singapore

"Conceptually and implementation-wise, the K-nearest neighbors algorithm is simpler than other techniques that have been applied to this problem. In addition, the K-nearest neighbors algorithm produces the overall classification result 1.17% better than the best result known for this problem."

This is a classification problem and most of the classification techniques can be classified into the following three groups:

(1) Parametric

(2) Semiparametric

(3) Non-Parametric

Parametric & Semiparametric classifiers need specific information about the structure of data in training set. It is difficult to fulfill this requirement in many cases. So, non-parametric classifier like KNN was considered.

Data was randomly split into training, cross-validation & testing data. Experimentation was done with the value of K from K = 1 to 15. With KNN algorithm, the classification result of test set fluctuates between 99.12% and 98.02%. The best performance was obtained when K is 1.

1.8.7 Advantages of K-nearest neighbors algorithm

(1) Knn is simple to implement.

(2) Knn executes quickly for small training data sets.

(3) performance asymptotically approaches the performance of the Bayes Classifier.

(4) Don't need any prior knowledge about the structure of data in the training set.

(5) No retraining is required if the new training pattern is added to the existing training set.

Thus KNN has several main advantages: simplicity, effectiveness, intuitiveness and competitive classification performance in many domains. It is Robust to noisy training data and is effective if the training data is large.

1.8.8 Limitation to K-nearest neighbors algorithm

(1) When the training set is large, it may take a lot of space.

(2) For every test data, the distance should be computed between test data and all the training data. Thus a lot of time may be needed for the testing.

(3) KNN can have poor run-time performance when the training set is large. It is very sensitive to irrelevant or redundant features because all features contribute to the similarity and thus to the classification. By careful feature selection or feature weighting, this can be avoided.

(4) Distance based learning is not clear which type of distance to use and which attribute to use to produce the best results.

(5) Computation cost is quite high because we need to compute distance of each query instance to all training samples.

1.8.9 Applications of KNN

KNN is a versatile algorithm and is used in a huge number of fields. Let us take a look at few uncommon and non trivial applications.

(1) Nearest Neighbor based Content Retrieval

This is one the fascinating applications of KNN – Basically we can use it in Computer Vision for many cases – You can consider handwriting detection as a rudimentary nearest neighbor problem. The problem becomes more fascinating if the content is a video – given a video find the video closest to the query from the database – Although this looks abstract, it has lot of practical applications – Eg : Consider **ASL** (American Sign Language) . Here the communication is done using hand gestures.

So lets say if we want to prepare a dictionary for ASL so that user can query it doing a gesture. Now the problem reduces to find the (possibly k) closest gesture(s) stored in the database and show to user. In its heart it is nothing but a KNN problem.

(2) Gene Expression

This is another cool area where many a time, KNN performs better than other state of the art techniques . In fact a combination of KNN-SVM is one of the most popular techniques there.

(3) Protein-Protein interaction and 3D structure prediction

Graph based KNN is used in protein interaction prediction. Similarly KNN is used in structure prediction.

(4) Text mining

The KNN algorithm is one of the most popular algorithms for text categorization or text mining. Some of the most recent works on this topic are for instance. Different numbers of nearest neighbors are used for different classes in this approach, rather than a fixed number across all classes. In this way, the only parameter that needs to be chosen by the user when using KNN, the K value, becomes less sensible and hence it does not need to be carefully chosen as in the standard algorithm. Indeed, the probability that an unknown sample belongs to a class is computed by using only some top Kn nearest neighbors for that class. The Kn value is derived from K according to the size of the corresponding class in the training set. This modified KNN was efficient and less sensible to the K values when applied to text mining problems.

(5) Agriculture

In general, KNN is applied less than other data mining techniques in agriculture related fields. It has been applied, for instance, for simulating daily precipitations and other weather variables. Another interesting application is the evaluation of forest inventories and for estimating forest variables. In these applications, satellite imagery is used, with the aim of mapping the land cover and land use with few discrete classes. The other applications of the k-NN method in agriculture include climate forecasting and estimating soil water parameters.

(6) Finance

Data mining as a process of discovering useful patterns and correlations has its own niche in financial modeling. Similar to other computational methods almost every data mining method and technique has been used in financial modeling. An incomplete list includes a variety of linear and nonlinear models multi-layer neural networks, k-means and hierarchical clustering, k-nearest neighbors, decision tree analysis, regression (logistic regression, general multiple regression), ARIMA, principal component analysis, and Bayesian learning. Stock market forecasting is one of the most core financial tasks of KNN. Stock market forecasting includes uncovering market trends, planning investment strategies, identifying the best time to purchase the stocks, and what stocks to purchase. Some of other applications of KNN in finance are mentioned below:

Forecasting stock market: Predict the price of a stock, on the basis of company performance measures and economic data. The other cases may be:

(1) Currency exchange rate
(2) Bank bankruptcies
(3) Understanding and managing financial risk
(4) Trading futures
(5) Credit rating
(6) Loan management
(7) Bank customer profiling
(8) Money laundering analyses

(7) Medicine

Predict whether a patient, hospitalized due to a heart attack, will have a second heart attack. The prediction is to be based on demographic, diet and clinical measurements for that patient.

Estimate the amount of glucose in the blood of a diabetic person, from the infrared absorption spectrum of that person's blood.

Identify the risk factors for prostate cancer,based on clinical and demographic variables.

The KNN algorithm has been also applied for analyzing micro-array gene expression data, where the KNN algorithm has been coupled with genetic algorithms, which are used as a search tool.

Other applications include the prediction of solvent accessibility in protein molecules, the detection of intrusions in computer systems, and the management of databases of moving objects such as computer with wireless connections.

1.9 CLASSIFICATIONS

The block diagram of classification model is shown in Fig. 1.5.

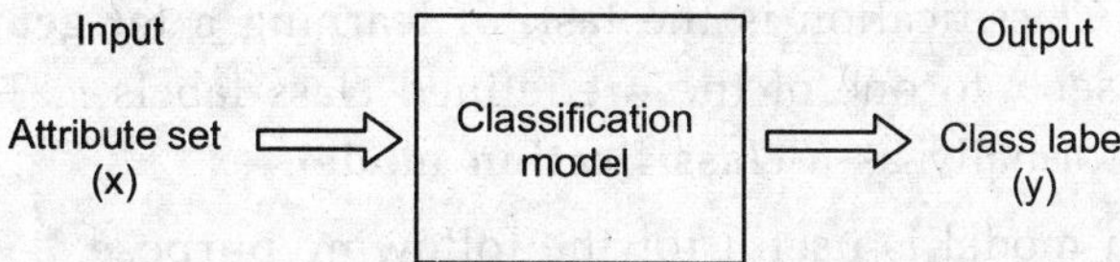

Fig. 1.5: Classification as the task of mapping an input attribute set X into its class label y.

The input data for a classification task is a collection of records. Each record, also known as an instance or example, is characterized by a tuple (x. y). where x is the attribute set and *y* is a special attribute, designated as the Class label (also known as category or target attribute).

Table 1.1 shows a sample data set used tor classifying vertebrates into one of the following categories: mammal, bird, fish, reptile, or amphibian.

Table 1.1

Name	Body Temperature	Skin Cover	Gives Birth	Aquatic Creature	Acrial Creature	Has Legs	Hiber-nates	Class Label
human	warm-blooded	hair	yes	no	no	yes	no	mammal
python	cold-blooded	scales	no	no	no	no	yes	reptile
salnion	cold-blooded	scales	no	yes	no	no	no	fish
whale	warm-blooded	hair	yes	yes	no	no	no	mammal
frog	cold- blooded	none	no	semi	no	yes	yes	amphibian
komodo dragon	cold-blooded	scales	no	no	no	yes	no	reptile
bar	warm-blooded	hair	yes	no	yes	yes	yes	mammal
pigeon	warm-blooded	feathers	no	no	yes	yes	no	bird
cat	warm-blooded	fur	yes	no	no	yes	no	mammal
leopard shark	cold-blooded	scales	yes	yes	no	no	no	fish
turtle	cold-blooded	scales	no	semi	no	yes	no	reptile
penguin	warm-blooded	feathers	no	semi	no	yes	no	bird
poreupine	warm-blooded	quills	yes	no	no	yes	yes	mammal
eel	cold-blooded	scales	no	yes	no	no	no	fish
salamander	cold-blooded	none	no	semi	no	yes	yes	amphiblan

The attribute set includes properties of a vertebrate such as its body temperature, skin cover, method of reproduction. ability to fly, and ability to live in water. Although the attributes presented in Table 4.1 are mostly discrete, the attribute set can also contain continuous features. The class label, on the other hand, must be a discrete attribute. This is a key characteristic that distinguishes classification from **regression**, a predictive modeling task in which y is a continuous attribute. Let us explore some terms:

(1) Classification Classification is the task of learning a **tar-get function** f that maps each attribute set x to one of the predefined class labels y. The target function is also known informally as a **classification model.**

A classification model is useful for the following purpose.

(2) Descriptive Modeling A classification model can serve as an explanatory tool to distinguish between objects of different classes. Fot example, it would be useful—for both biologists and others—to have a descriptive model that summarizes the data shown in Table 4.1 and explains what features define a vertebrate as mammal, reptile, bird, fish, or amphibian.

(3) Predictive Modeling A classification model cab also be used to predict the class label of unknown records. As shown in Figure 4.2, a classification model can be treated as a black box that automatically assigus a class label when presented with the attribute set of an unknown record. Suppose we are given the following characteristics of a creatue known as a gila monster:

Name	Body Temperature	Skin Cover	Gives Birth	Aquatic Creature	Acrial Creature	Has Legs	Hiber-nates	Class Label
gila monster	cold-blooded	scales	no	no	no	yes	yes	?

We can use a classification model built from the data set shown in Table 4.1 to determine the class to which the creature belongs.

Classification techniques are most suited for predicting or describing data sets with binary or nominal categories. They are less effective for ordinal categories (e.g., to classify a person as a member of high-, medium-, or low-ineome group) because they do not consider the implicit order among the categories. Other forms of relationships, such as the subchkss-superclass relationships among categories (e.g., humans and apes are primates, which in turn, is a subclass of mammals) are also ignored.

General Approach to Solving a Classification Problem

A classification techique (or classifier) is a systematic approach to building classification models from an input data set, Examples include decision free classifiers, rule-based classifiers, neural networks, support vector machines, and naive Bayes classifiers. Each technique employs a **learning algorithm** to idenfify a model that best fits the retationship between the attribute set, and class label of the input data. The model generated by a learning algorithm should both fit the inpul data well and correctly predict the class labels of records it has never seen, before. Therefore, a key objective of the learning algorithm is to build models with good generalization capability; i.e., models that accurately predict the class label of previously unknown records.

Figure 1.6 Shows a general approach for solving classification problems. First, a training set consisting of records whose class labels are known must be provided. The training set is used to build a classification model, which is subsequently applied to the **test set,** which consists of records with unknown class labels.

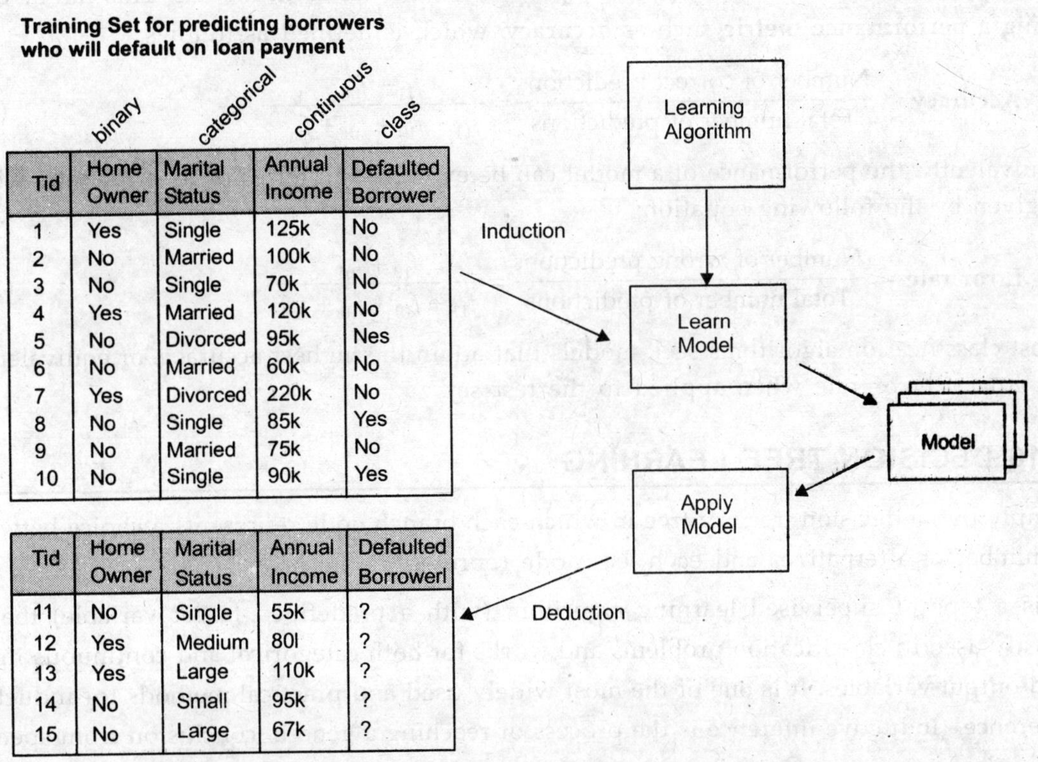

Tid	Home Owner	Marital Status	Annual Income	Defaulted Borrower
1	Yes	Single	125k	No
2	No	Married	100k	No
3	No	Single	70k	No
4	Yes	Married	120k	No
5	No	Divorced	95k	Nes
6	No	Married	60k	No
7	Yes	Divorced	220k	No
8	No	Single	85k	Yes
9	No	Married	75k	No
10	No	Single	90k	Yes

Tid	Home Owner	Marital Status	Annual Income	Defaulted Borrowerl
11	No	Single	55k	?
12	Yes	Medium	80l	?
13	Yes	Large	110k	?
14	No	Small	95k	?
15	No	Large	67k	?

Fig. 1.6: General approach for buiding a classification model.

1.9.1 Confusion Matrix

Evaluation of the performance of a classification model is based on the counts of test records correctly and incorrectly predicted by the model. These counts are tabulated in a table known as a confusion **matrix.** Table 1.2 depict the confusion matrix for a binary classification problem.

Table 1.2 Confusion matrix lor a 2-class problem.

		Predicted Class	
		Class = 1	Class = 0
Actual Class	Class = 1	f_{11}	f_{10}
	Class = 0	f_{01}	f_{00}

Each entry f_{ij} in this table denotes number of records from class *i*, predicted of class *j*. For instance, f_{01} is the number of records from class 0 incorrectly predicted as class 1. Based on the entries in the confusion matrix, the total number of correct predictions made by the model is $(f_{11} + f_{00})$ and the total number of incorrect predictions is $(f_{10} + f_{01})$.

Although a confusion matrix provides the information needed to determine how well a classification model performs, summarizing this information with a single number would make it more convenient to compare the performance of different models. This can be done using a **performance metric** such as **accuracy,** which is defined as follows:

$$\textbf{Accuracy} = \frac{\text{Number of correct predictions}}{\text{Total number of predictions}} = \frac{f_{11} + f_{00}}{f_{11} + f_{10} + f_{01} + f_{00}}. \qquad (1.1)$$

Equivalently, the performance of a model can be expressed in terms of its **error rate,** which is given by the following equation:

$$\textbf{Error rate} = \frac{\text{Number of wrong predictions}}{\text{Total number of predictions}} = \frac{f_{10} + f_{01}}{f_{11} + f_{10} + f_{01} + f_{00}} \qquad (1\text{-}2)$$

Most classification algorithms seek models that attain the highest accuracy, or equivalently, the lowest error rate when applied to the test set.

1.10 DECISION TREE LEARNING

Simply put, a decision tree is a tree in which each branch node represents a choice between a number of alternatives and each leaf node represents a decision.

It is a type of supervised learning algorithm (with a predefined target variable) that is mostly used in classification problems and works for both categorical and continuous input and output variables. It is one of the most widely used and practical methods for inductive inference. (Inductive inference is the process of reaching a general conclusion from specific examples.)

Decision trees learn and train themselves from given examples and predict for unseen circumstances. The following is the block diagram of decision tree learning method.

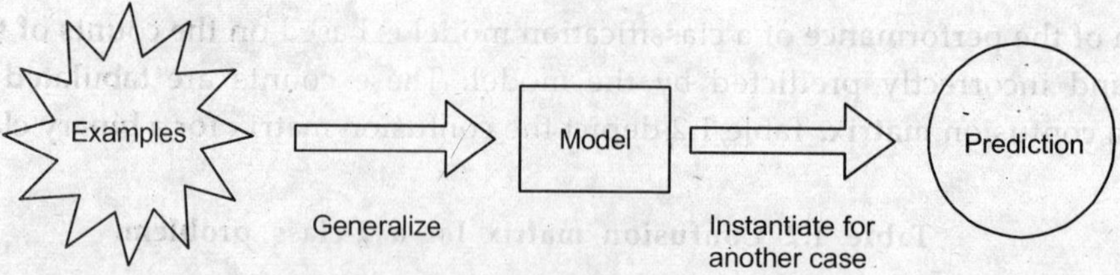

Fig. 1.7: Block Diagram of Decision Tree Model

A graphical representation of a sample decision tree could be:

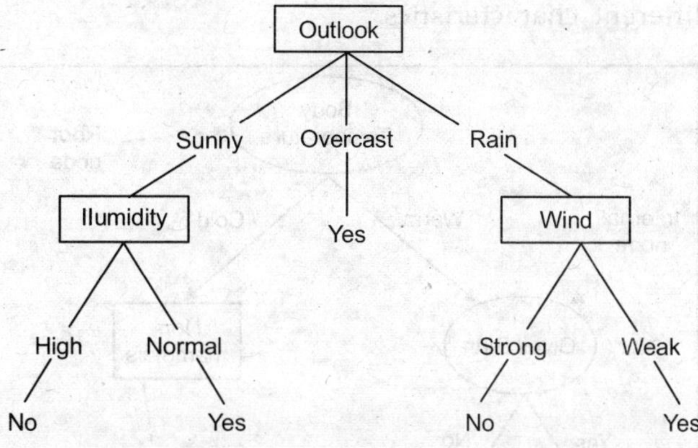

Fig. 1.8: Decision Tree

1.10.1 Woring of a Decision Tree

To illustrate how classification with a decision tree works, consider a simpler version of the vertebrate classification problem described in the previous section. Instead of classifying the vertebrates into five distinct groups of species, we assign them to two categories: mammals and non~manirnais.

Suppose a new species is discovered by scientists. How can we tell whether it is a mammal or a non-mammal? One approach is to pose a series oi questions about the characteristics of the species. The first question we may ask is whether the species is cold or wann-biooded. If it is cold-blooded, then it is definitely not a mammal. Otherwise, it is either a bird or a mammal. In the latter case, we need to ask a follow-up question: Do the females of the species give birth to their young? Those that do give birth are definitely mammals, while those that do not are likely to be non-mammals (with the exception of egg-laying mammals such as the platypus and spiny anteater).

The previous example illustrates how we can solve a classification problem by asking a series of carefully craftcd questions about the attributes of the test record. Each time we receive an answer, a follow-up question is asked until we reach a conclusion about the class label of the record. The series of questions and their possible answers can be organized in the form of a decision tree, which is a hierarchical structure consisting of nodes and directed edges. Figure 1.9 shows the decision tree for the mammal classification problem. The tree has three types of nodes:

- **A root node** that has no incoming edges and zero or more outgoing edges.
- **Internal nodes,** each of which has exactly one incoming edge and two or more outgoing edges.
- **Leaf** or **Terminal** nodes, each of which has exactly one incoming edge and no outgoing edges.

In a decision tree, each leaf node is assigned a class label. The non-terminal nodes. which include the root and other internal nodes contain attribute test conditions to separate records that have different characteristics.

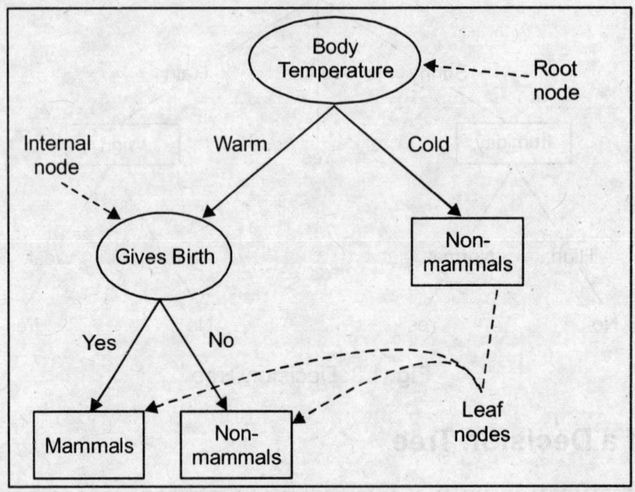

Fig. 1.9: A decision Tree Example for Mammal Classification Sample Problem

For example, the root node shown in Figure 1.10 uses the attribute body Temperature to separate warm-blooded from cold-blooded vertebrates. Since all cold-blooded vertebrates are non-mammals, a leaf nod,e labeled Non-mammals is created as the right child of the root node. If the vertebrate is warm-blooded, a subsequent attribute. Gives Birth, is used to distinguish mammals from other warm-blooded creatures, which are mostly birds.

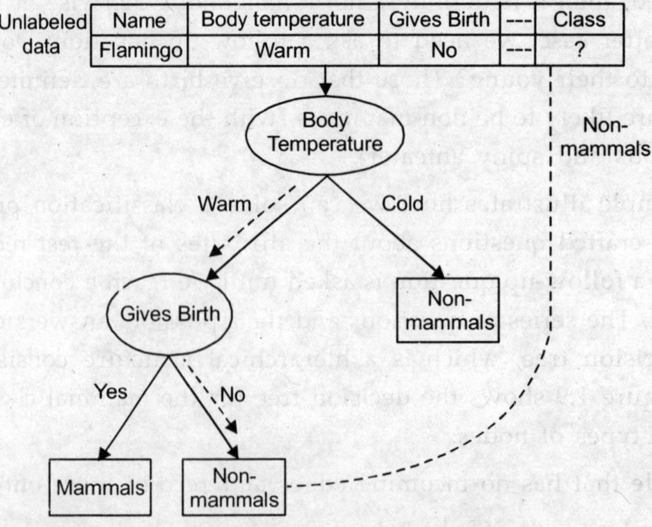

Fig. 1.10: Classifying an unlabeled vertebrate. The dashed lines represent the outcomes of applying various attribute test conditions on the unlabeled vertebrate. The vertebrate is eventually assigned to the Non-mammal Class.

Classifying a test record in straightforward once a decision tree has been constructed. Starting from the root node, we apply the test condition to the record and follow the appropriate branch based on the outcome of the test. This will lead us either to another internal node, for which-a new test condition is applied, or to a leaf node. The class label associated with the leaf node is then assigned to the record, As an illustration. Figure 1.10 traces the path in the decision tree that is used to predict the class label of a flamingo. The path terminates at a leaf node labeled Non-mammals.

1.10.2 How to Build a decision Tree

In Principle, there are exponentially many decision trees that can be constructed from a given set of attributes. While some of the trees are more accurate than others finding the optinial tree is computationally infesible beeause of the exponential size of the search space. Nevertheless, efficient algorithms have been developed to induce a reasonably accurate, albeit suboptimal, decision tree in a reasonable amount of time, These algorithms nsually employ a greedy strategy that grows a decision tree by making a series of locally optimum decistion about which attrbute to use for partitioning the data. One such algorithm is hunt's algorithm, which is the hasis of many existing decision tree induction algorithms. Including ID3, C4.5, and CART. This section presents a high-level discussion of Hunt's algorithm and illustrates some of its design issues.

Hunt's Algorithm

In Hunt's algorithm, a deeision tree is grown in a recursive fashion by partitioning the training records successively purer subsets. Let D_t be the set of training records that are associated with node t and $y = \{y_1, y_2\ldots., y_c\}$ be the class labels. The following is a recursive definition of Hunt's algorithm.

Step 1: If all the records in D_t belong to the same class y_t, then t is a leaf node labeled as y_t.

Step 2: If D_t, contains records that belong to more than one class, an attribute test condition is selected to partition the records into smaller subsets. A child node is created for each outcome of the test condition and the reconds in D_t, are distributed to the children based on the outcomes. The algorithm is then recursively applied to each child node.

To illustrate low the algorithm works, consider the problem of predicting whether a loan applicant will repay her loan obligations or become delinquent, subsequently defaulting on her loan. A training set for this problem can be constructed by examining the records of previous borrowers. In the example shown in Figure 1.11 each record contains the personal information of a borrower along with a class habel indicating whether the borrower has defaulted on loan payments.

	binary	categorical	continuous	class
Tid	Home Owner	Marital Status	Annual Income	Defaulted Borrower
1	Yes	Single	125k	No
2	No	Married	100k	No
3	No	Single	70k	No
4	Yes	Married	120k	No
5	No	Divorced	95k	Nes
6	No	Married	60k	No
7	Yes	Divorced	220k	No
8	No	Single	85k	Yes
9	No	Married	75k	No
10	No	Single	90k	Yes

Fig. 1.11: Training set for predicting borrowers who will default on loan payments.

The initial tree for the classification problem contains a single node with class label defaulted = No (See Figure 1.12 (a)), Which means that most of the borrowers successfully repaid their loans. The tree, however, need to be refined since the root node contains records from both classes. The records are subsrquently divided into smaller subsets based on the outcomes of the home owner test condition, as shown in Figure 1.12b). The justification for choosing this attribute test condition will be discussed later. For new, will assume that this is the best criterion for splitting the data at this point. Hunt's algorithm is then applied recursively to each child of the root node. From the training set given in Figure 1.11 notice that al borrowers who home owners successfully repaid their loans. The left child of the root is therefore a leaf node labeled defaulted = No (see figure 1.12b). For the right child, we need to continue applying the reersive step of Hunt's algorithm until all the records belong to the same class. The trees resulting from each recursive step are shown in Figures 1.12(c) and (d).

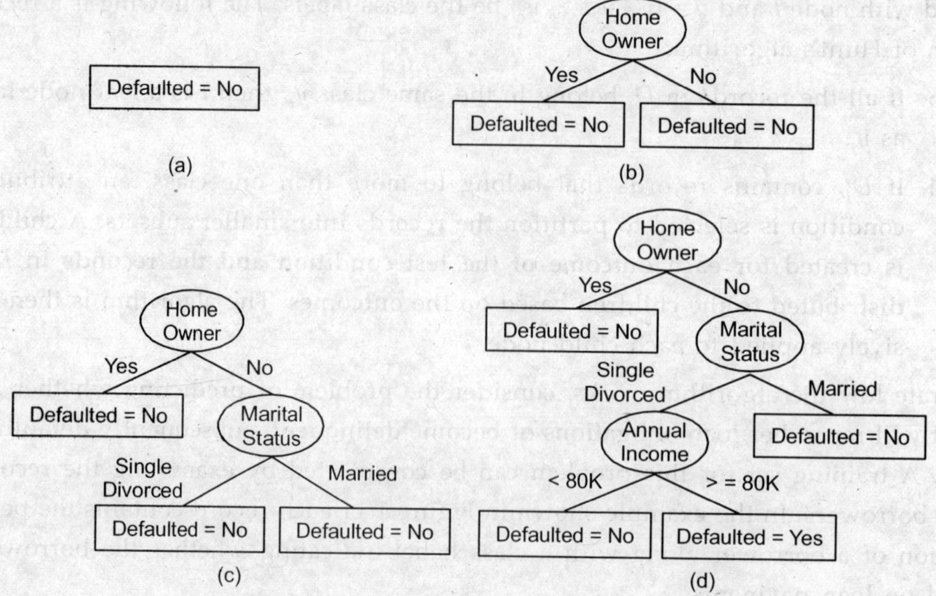

Fig. 1.12: Hunt's algonithm for inducing decision trees.

Hunt's algorithm will work if every combination of attribute values is prresent in the training data and each combination has a unique class label. These assumptions are too stringent for use in most practical situations. Additional conditions are needed to handle the following cases:

(1) It is possible for some of the child nodes created in Step 2 to be empty; i.e. there are no records associated with these nodes. This cab happen if none of the training records havethe combination of attribute values associated with such nodes. In this case the node is declared a leaf node with the same class label as the majority class of training records associated with its parent node.

(2) In Step 2, if all the records associated with D_1 have idential attribute value (except for the class label), then it is not possible to split these records any further. In this case, the node is declared a leaf node with the same class label as the majority class of training records associated with this node.

Design Issues of Decision Tree Induction

A learning algorithm of inducing trees must address the following two issues.

(1) **How should the training records be split?** Each recursive step of the tree-growing process must select an attribute test condition to divide the records into smaller subsets. To implement this step, the algorithm must provide a method for specifying the test condition for different attribute types as well as an objective measure for evaluating the goodness of each test condition.

(2) **How should the splitting procedure step?** A stopping conditions is needed to treminate a node until either all the reecords belong to the same class or all the records have identiecal attribute values. Althought both conditions are sufficient to stop any decision tree induction algorithm, other criteria can be imposed to allow the tree-growing procedure to terminate earlier. The advantages of early termination will be discussed later in Section 4.4.5.

1.10.3 Methods for Expressing Attribute Test Conditions

Decision tree induction algorithms must provide a method for expressing an attribute test condition and its corresponding outecomes for different attribute types.

(a) Binary Attributes—The test condition for a binary attribute generates two potential outcomes, as shown in Figure 1.13.

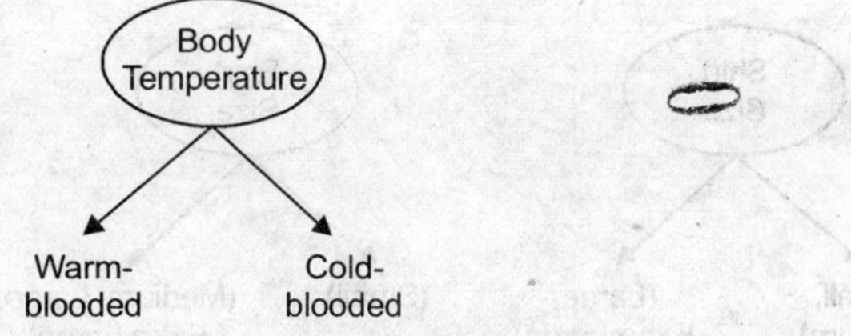

Fig. 1.13: EST condition for binary attributes.

(b) Nominal Attributes—Since a nominal attribute can have many values. Its test condition can be expressed in two wavs, as shown in Figure 1.14. For a multhvay split (Figure 1.14(a)). the number of outcomes depends on the number of distinct values *for* the corresponding attribute,. For example, if an attribute such as marital status hits three distinct values- single, married. or divorced—its test condition will produce a three-way split. On the other hand, some decision tree algorithms, such as GAHT. produce only binary splits by considering all 2^{k-1}–l ways of creating a binary partition of k attribute values. (Figure 1.14(b)) illustrates three different ways of grouping the attribute for marital status into two subsets.

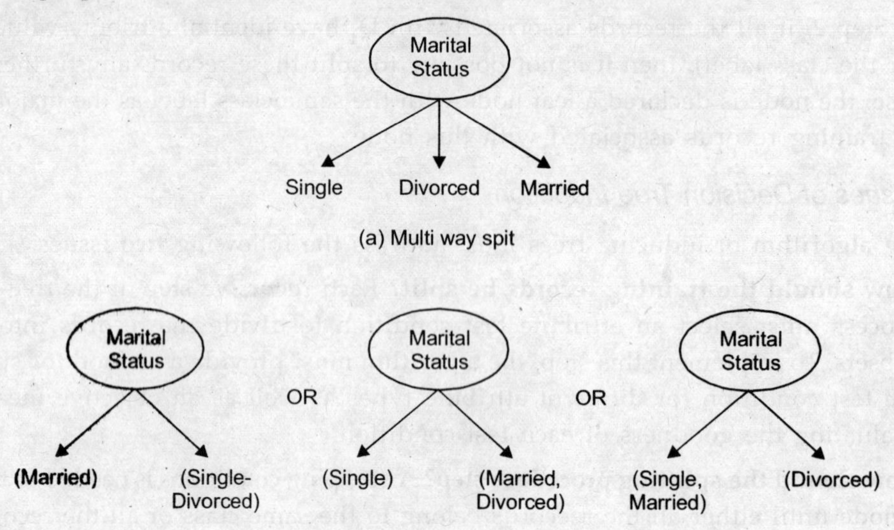

Fig. 1.14: Test conditions for nominal attributes

(c) Ordinal At tributes—Ordinal attributes can also produce binary or multiway splits. Ordinal attribute values can be grouped as long as the grouping does not violate the order property of the attribute values, Figure 1.15 illustrates various ways of splitting training traning records based on the Shirt Size attribute. The groupings shown in Figures 1.15(a) and (b) preserve the order among the attribute values, whereas the grouping shown in Figure 1.15(c) violates this property because it combines the attribute values Small and Large into the same partition while Medium and Extra Large are combined into another partition.

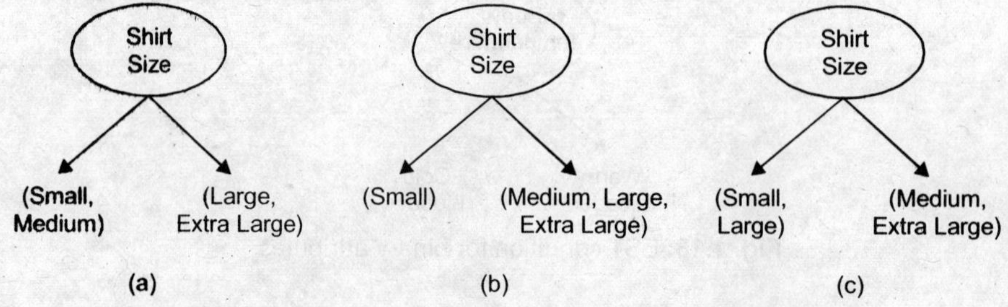

Fig. 1.15: Different ways of grouping ordinal attribute values.

(d) Continous Attributes—For continuous attributes, the test condition cab be expressedas a comparison test ($A < v$) or ($A \geq v$) with binary outcomes, or a range query with outcomes of the form $v_i \leq A < v_i + 1$, for i = 1, ..., k. The difference between these approaches is shown in Figure 1.16 For the binary ease, the decision tree algorithm must consider all possible split positions v, and it selects the one that produces the best protition. For the multiway split, the algorithm must consider all possible ranges of continuous values.

After discretzation, a new ordinal value will be assigned to each discretized interval. Adjacent intervals can also be aggregated into wider ranges as long as the order property is preserved.

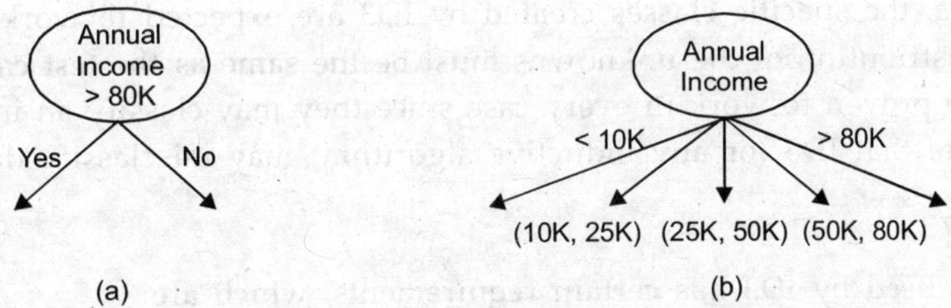

Fig. 1.16: Test condition for continuous attributes

1.10.4 ID3 Classification Algorithm

Very simply, ID3 builds a decision tree from a fixed set of examples. The resulting tree is used to classify future samples. The example has several attributes and belongs to a class (like yes or no). The leaf nodes of the decision tree contain the class name whereas a non-leaf node is a decision node. The decision node is an attribute test with each branch (to another decision tree) being a possible value of the attribute. ID3 uses information gain to help it decide which attribute goes into a decision node. The advantage of learning a decision tree is that a program, rather than a knowledge engineer, elicits knowledge from an expert.

Introduction

J. Ross Quinlan originally developed ID3 at the University of Sydney. He first presented ID3 in 1975 in a book, *Machine Learning*, vol. 1, no. 1. ID3 is based off the Concept Learning System (CLS) algorithm. The basic CLS algorithm over a set of training instances C:

Step 1: If all instances in C are positive, then create YES node and halt.

If all instances in C are negative, create a NO node and halt.

Otherwise select a feature, F with values v1, ..., vn and create a decision node.

Step 2: Partition the training instances in C into subsets C1, C2, ..., Cn according to the values of V.

Step 3: apply the algorithm recursively to each of the sets Ci.

Note, the trainer (the expert) decides which feature to select.

ID3 improves on CLS by adding a feature selection heuristic. ID3 searches through the attributes of the training instances and extracts the attribute that best separates the given examples. If the attribute perfectly classifies the training sets then ID3 stops; otherwise it recursively operates on the n (where n = number of possible values of an attribute) partitioned subsets to get their "best" attribute. The algorithm uses a greedy search, that is, it picks the best attribute and never looks back to reconsider earlier choices.

Discussion

ID3 is a nonincremental algorithm, meaning it derives its classes from a fixed set of training instances. An incremental algorithm revises the current concept definition, if necessary, with a new sample. The classes created by ID3 are inductive, that is, given a small set of training instances, the specific classes created by ID3 are expected to work for all future instances. The distribution of the unknowns must be the same as the test cases. Induction classes cannot be proven to work in every case since they may classify an infinite number of instances. Note that ID3 (or any inductive algorithm) may misclassify data.

Data Description

The sample data used by ID3 has certain requirements, which are:

(1) Attribute-value description - the same attributes must describe each example and have a fixed number of values.

(2) Predefined classes - an example's attributes must already be defined, that is, they are not learned by ID1.

(3) Discrete classes - classes must be sharply delineated. Continuous classes broken up into vague categories such as a metal being "hard, quite hard, flexible, soft, quite soft" are suspect.

(4) Sufficient examples - since inductive generalization is used (i.e. not provable) there must be enough test cases to distinguish valid patterns from chance occurrences.

Attribute Selection

How does ID3 decide which attribute is the best? A statistical property, called information gain, is used. Gain measures how well a given attribute separates training examples into targeted classes. The one with the highest information (information being the most useful for classification) is selected. In order to define gain, we first borrow an idea from information theory called entropy. Entropy measures the amount of information in an attribute.

Entropy

In information theory, entropy is a measure of the uncertainty about a source of messages. It gives us the degree of disorganization in our data.

Given a collection S containing positive and negative examples of some target concept, the entropy of S relative to this boolean classification is:

$$Entropy(S) \equiv pe \log_2 p_\oplus - p_\oplus \log_2 p_\oplus$$

Here, p+ and p– are the proportion of positive and negative examples in S.

Consider this entropy function relative to a boolean classification, as the proportion of positive examples p+ varies between 0 and 1.

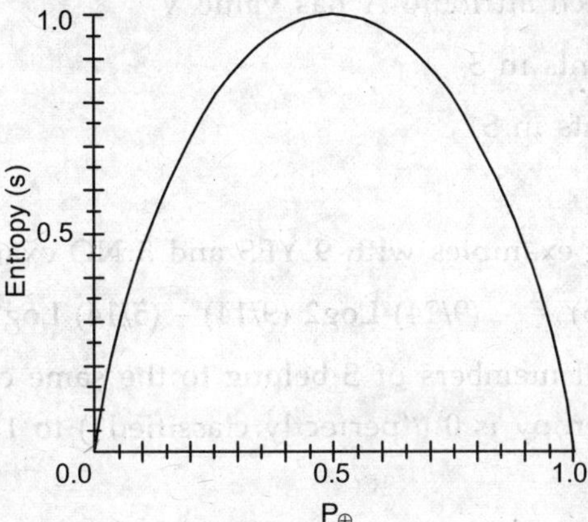

Notice that the entropy is 0 if all members of S belong to the same class. For example, if all members are positive (p+ = 1), then p- is 0, and Entropy(S) = -1. log2(1) – 0. log2 0 = -1. 0 – 0. log2 0 = 0.

The entropy is 1 when the collection contains an equal number of positive and negative examples. If the collection contains unequal numbers of positive and negative examples, the entropy is between 0 and 1.

Information Gain

It measures the expected reduction in entropy. It decides which attribute goes into a decision node. To minimize the decision tree depth, the attribute with the most entropy reduction is the best choice!

More precisely, the information gain Gain(S, A) of an attribute A relative to a collection of examples S is defined as:

$$\text{Gain (S,A)} = \underbrace{Entropy(S)}_{\text{orignal entropy of } S} - \underbrace{\sum_{v \in values(A)} \frac{|S_v|}{|S|}.Entropy(S)}_{\text{relative entropy of } S}$$

In above equation:

- **S** = Each value v of all possible values of attribute A
- **Sv** = Subset of S for which attribute A has value v
- **|Sv|** = Number of elements in Sv
- **|S|** = Number of elements in S

Gain(S, A) is information gain of example set S on attribute A is defined as

$$\text{Gain(S, A)} = \text{Entropy(S)} - \Sigma\ ((|S_v| / |S|) * \text{Entropy}(S_v))$$

Where:

Σ is each value v of all possible values of attribute A

S_v = subset of S for which attribute A has value V

$|S_v|$ = number of elements in S_v

$|S|$ = number of elements in S

Example 1.2

If S is a collection of 14 examples with 9 YES and 5 NO examples then

$$\text{Entropy}(S) = -(9/14)\ \text{Log2}\ (9/14) - (5/14)\ \text{Log2}\ (5/14) = 0.940$$

Notice entropy is 0 if all members of S belong to the same class (the data is perfectly classified). The range of entropy is 0 ("perfectly classified") to 1 ("totally random").

Example 1.3

Suppose S is a set of 14 examples in which one of the attributes is wind speed. The values of Wind can be *Weak* or *Strong*. The classification of these 14 examples are 9 YES and 5 NO. For attribute Wind, suppose there are 8 occurrences of Wind = Weak and 6 occurrences of Wind = Strong. For Wind = Weak, 6 of the examples are YES and 2 are NO. For Wind = Strong, 3 are YES and 3 are NO. Therefore

$$\begin{aligned} \text{Gain}(S,\text{Wind}) &= \text{Entropy}(S)-(8/14)*\text{Entropy}(\text{Sweak}) - (6/14)*\text{Entropy}(\text{Sstrong}) \\ &= 0.940 - (8/14)*0.811 - (6/14)*1.00 \\ &= 0.048 \end{aligned}$$

$$\text{Entropy}(S_{weak}) = -(6/8)*\log2(6/8) - (2/8)*\log2(2/8) = 0.811$$

$$\text{Entropy}(S_{strong}) = -(3/6)*\log2(3/6) - (3/6)*\log2(3/6) = 1.00$$

For each attribute, the gain is calculated and the highest gain is used in the decision node.

Example of ID3

Suppose we want ID3 to decide whether the weather is amenable to playing baseball. Over the course of 2 weeks, data is collected to help ID3 build a decision tree (see table 1).

The target classification is "should we play baseball?" which can be yes or no.

The weather attributes are outlook, temperature, humidity, and wind speed. They can have the following values:

outlook = {sunny, overcast, rain}

temperature = {hot, mild, cool}

humidity = {high, normal}

wind = {weak, strong}

Examples of set S are:

Day	Outlook	Temperature	Humidity	Wind	Play ball
D1	Sunny	Hot	Hight	Weak	No
D2	Sunny	Hot	Hight	Weak	No
D3	Overcast	Hot	Hight	Weak	Yes
D4	Rain	Mild	Hight	Weak	Yes
D5	Rain	Cool	Normal	Weak	Yes
D6	Rain	Cool	Normal	Strong	No
D7	Overcast	Cool	Normal	Strong	Yes
D8	Sunny	Mild	Hight	Weak	No
D9	Sunny	Cool	Normal	Weak	Yes
D10	Rain	Mild	Normal	Weak	Yes
D11	Sunny	Mild	Normal	Strong	Yes
D12	Overcast	Mild	Hight	Strong	Yes
D13	Overcast	Hot	Normal	Weak	Yes
D14	Rain	Mild	Hight	Strong	No

We need to find which attribute will be the root node in our decision tree. The gain is calculated for all four attributes:

$$\text{Gain}(S, \text{Outlook}) = 0.246$$

$$\text{Gain}(S, \text{Temperature}) = 0.029$$

$$\text{Gain}(S, \text{Humidity}) = 0.151$$

$$\text{Gain}(S, \text{Wind}) = 0.048 \text{ (calculated in example 2)}$$

Outlook attribute has the highest gain, therefore it is used as the decision attribute in the root node.

Since Outlook has three possible values, the root node has three branches (sunny, overcast, rain). The next question is "what attribute should be tested at the Sunny branch node?" Since we=92ve used Outlook at the root, we only decide on the remaining three attributes: Humidity, Temperature, or Wind.

$$S_{sunny} = \{D1, D2, D8, D9, D11\}$$

$$= 5 \text{ examples from table 1 with outlook = sunny}$$

$$\text{Gain}(S_{sunny}, \text{Humidity}) = 0.970$$

$$\text{Gain}(S_{sunny}, \text{Temperature}) = 0.570$$

$$\text{Gain}(S_{sunny}, \text{Wind}) = 0.019$$

Humidity has the highest gain; therefore, it is used as the decision node. This process goes on until all data is classified perfectly or we run out of attributes.

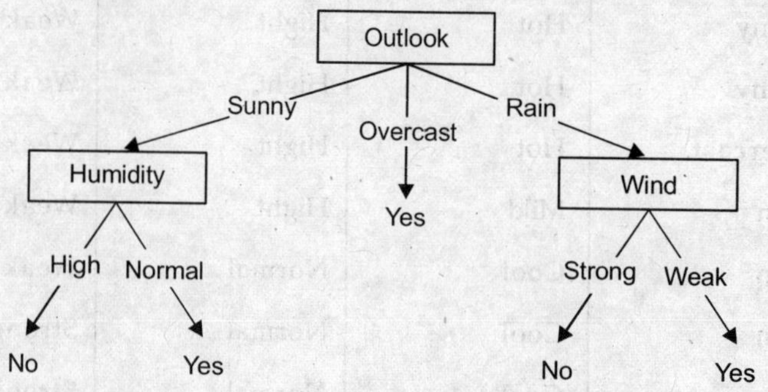

The final decision = tree

The decision tree can also be expressed in rule format:

IF outlook = sunny AND humidity = high THEN playball = no

IF outlook = rain AND humidity = high THEN playball = no

IF outlook = rain AND wind = strong THEN playball = yes

IF outlook = overcast THEN playball = yes

IF outlook = rain AND wind = weak THEN playball = yes

ID3 has been incorporated in a number of commercial rule-induction packages. Some specific applications include medical diagnosis, credit risk assessment of loan applications, equipment malfunctions by their cause, classification of soybean diseases, and web search classification.

Conclusion

The discussion and examples given show that ID3 is easy to use. Its primary use is replacing the expert who would normally build a classification tree by hand. As industry has shown, ID3 has been effective.

Decision tree learning uses a decision tree (as a predictive model) to go from observations about an item (represented in the branches) to conclusions about the item's target value (represented in the leaves). It is one of the predictive modelling approaches used in statistics, data mining and machine learning. Tree models where the target variable can take a discrete set of values are called classification trees; in these tree structures, leaves represent class labels and branches represent conjunctions of features that lead to those class labels. Decision trees where the target variable can take continuous values (typically real numbers) are called regression trees.

A decision tree is a simple representation for classifying examples. For this section, assume that all of the input features have finite discrete domains, and there is a single target feature called the "classification". Each element of the domain of the classification is called a class.

Decision tree is a type of supervised learning algorithm (having a pre-defined target variable) that is mostly used in classification problems.

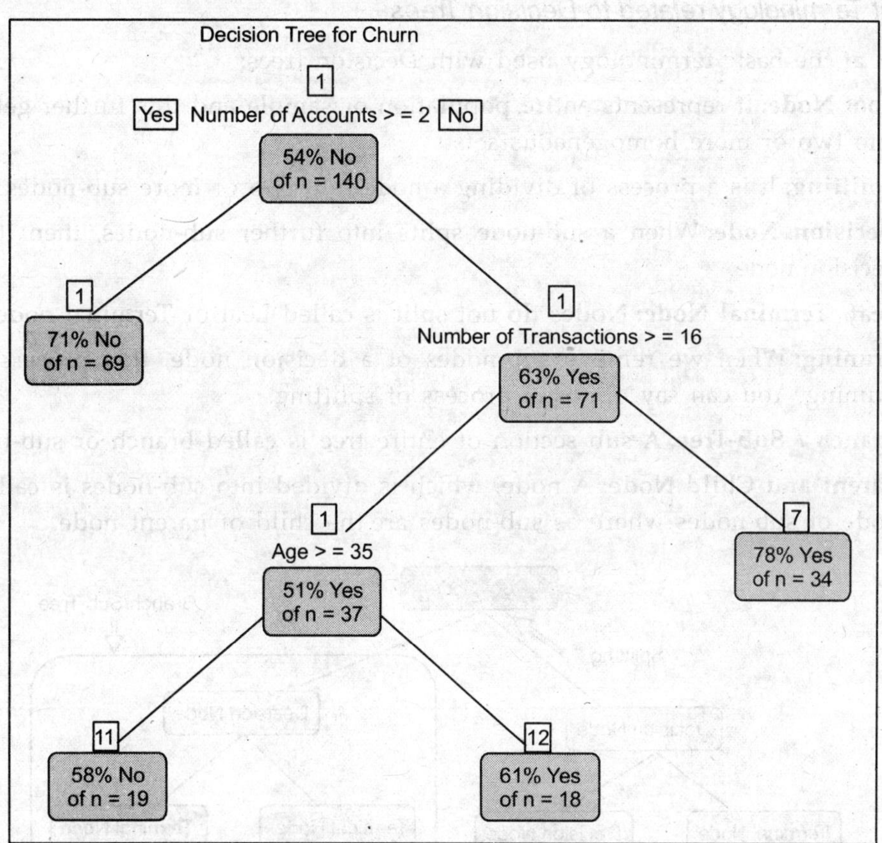

It works for both categorical and continuous input and output variables. In this technique, we split the population or sample into two or more homogeneous sets (or sub-populations) based on most significant splitter/differentiator in input variables.

Types of Decision Trees

Types of decision tree is based on the type of target variable we have. It can be of two types:

(1) Categorical Variable Decision Tree: Decision Tree which has categorical target variable then it called as categorical variable decision tree. Example:- In above scenario of student problem, where the target variable was "Student will play cricket or not" i.e. YES or NO.

(2) Continuous Variable Decision Tree: Decision Tree has continuous target variable then it is called as Continuous Variable Decision Tree.

Example:- Let's say we have a problem to predict whether a customer will pay his renewal premium with an insurance company (yes/no). Here we know that income of customer is a significant variable but insurance company does not have income details for all customers. Now, as we know this is an important variable, then we can build a decision tree to predict customer income based on occupation, product and various other variables. In this case, we are predicting values for continuous variable.

Important Terminology related to Decision Trees

Let's look at the basic terminology used with Decision trees:

1. **Root Node:** It represents entire population or sample and this further gets divided into two or more homogeneous sets.
2. **Splitting:** It is a process of dividing a node into two or more sub-nodes.
3. **Decision Node:** When a sub-node splits into further sub-nodes, then it is called decision node.
4. **Leaf/ Terminal Node:** Nodes do not split is called Leaf or Terminal node.
5. **Pruning:** When we remove sub-nodes of a decision node, this process is called pruning. You can say opposite process of splitting.
6. **Branch / Sub-Tree:** A sub section of entire tree is called branch or sub-tree.
7. **Parent and Child Node:** A node, which is divided into sub-nodes is called parent node of sub-nodes where as sub-nodes are the child of parent node.

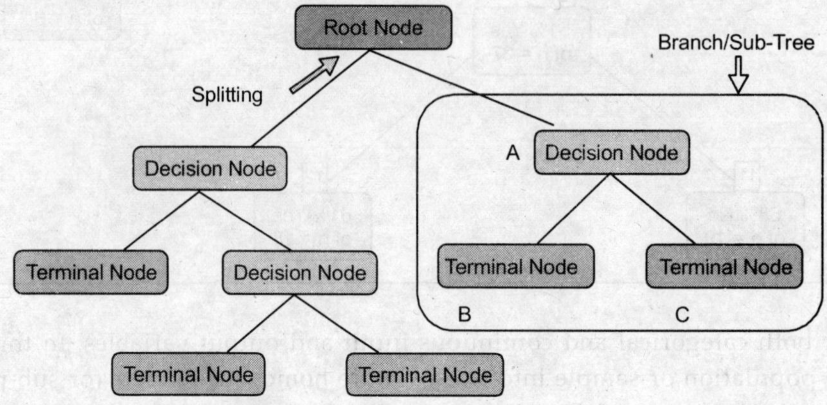

Note:- A is parent node of B and C.

These are the terms commonly used for decision trees. As we know that every algorithm has advantages and disadvantages, below are the important factors which one should know.

Examples of use of decision tress is "predicting an email as spam or not spam, predicting of a tumor is cancerous or predicting a loan as a good or bad credit risk based on the factors in each of these. Generally, a model is created with observed data also called training data. Then a set of validation data is used to verify and improve the model. R has packages which are used to create and visualize decision trees. For new set of predictor variable, we use this model to arrive at a decision on the category (yes/No, spam/not spam) of the data. The R package "party" is used to create decision trees.

Install Party Package

Use the below command in R console to install the package. You also have to install the dependent packages if any.

```
install.packages("party")
```

The package "party" has the function ctree() which is used to create and analyze decison tree.

Syntax

The basic syntax for creating a decision tree in R is "

```
ctree(formula, data)
```

Following is the description of the parameters used "

- formula is a formula describing the predictor and response variables.
- data is the name of the data set used.

Input Data

We will use the R in-built data set named readingSkills to create a decision tree. It describes the score of someone's readingSkills if we know the variables "age","shoesize","score" and whether the person is a native speaker or not.

Here is the sample data.

```
> library(party)
>
> # Print some records from data set readingSkills.
> print(head(readingSkills))
  nativeSpeaker age shoeSize    score
1           yes   5 24.83189 32.29385
2           yes   6 25.95238 36.63105
3            no  11 30.42170 49.60593
4           yes   7 28.66450 40.28456
5           yes  11 31.88207 55.46085
6           yes  10 30.07843 52.83124
```

Example 1.4

We will use the **ctree**() function to create the decision tree and see its graph.

```
# Load the party package. It will automatically load other dependent
packages.
library(party)
# Create the input data frame.
input.dat <- readingSkills[c(1:105),]
# Give the chart file a name.
png(file = "decision_tree.png")
# Create the tree.
  output.tree <- ctree(
  nativeSpeaker ~ age + shoeSize + score,
  data = input.dat)
```

```
# Plot the tree.
plot(output.tree)
# Save the file.
dev.off()
```

When we execute the above code, it produces the following result."

```
R Console
> # Load the party package. It will automatically load other dependent packages.
> library(party)
>
> # Create the input data frame.
> input.dat <- readingSkills[c(1:105),]
>
> # Give the chart file a name.
> png(file = "decision_tree.png")
>
> # Create the tree.
>   output.tree <- ctree(
+   nativeSpeaker ~ age + shoeSize + score,
+   data = input.dat)
>
> # Plot the tree.
> plot(output.tree)
> # Save the file.
> dev.off()
null device
          1
> |
```

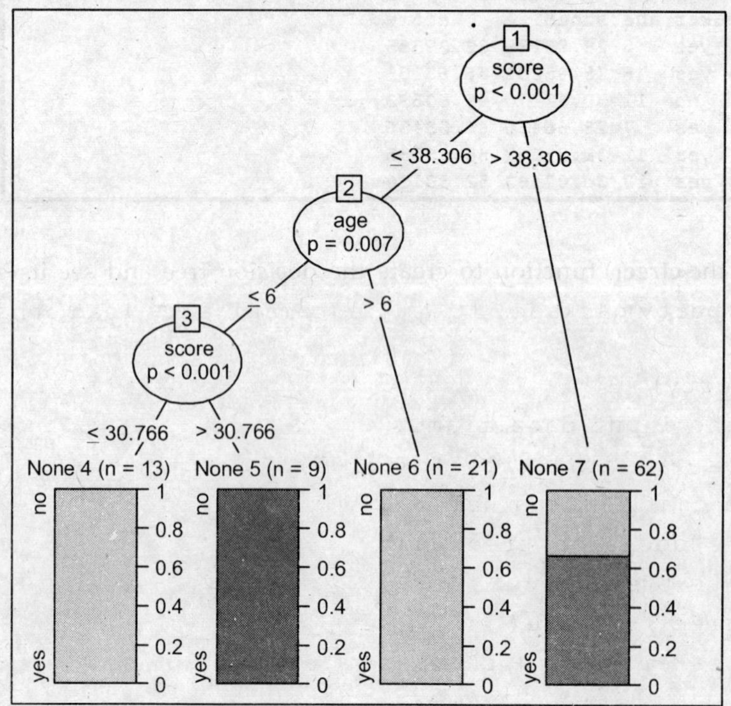

Conclusion

From the decision tree shown above we can conclude that anyone whose readingSkills score is less than 38.3 and age is more than 6 is not a native Speaker.

Advantages

Decision trees are one of the most popular statistical techniques. The advantages of using R decision trees are as follows:

1. **Easy to Understand**: Decision tree output is very easy to understand even for people from non-analytical background. It does not require any statistical knowledge to read and interpret them. Its graphical representation is very intuitive and users can easily relate their hypothesis.
2. **Useful in Data exploration:** Decision tree is one of the fastest way to identify most significant variables and relation between two or more variables. With the help of decision trees, we can create new variables / features that has better power to predict target variable.. It can also be used in data exploration stage. For example, we are working on a problem where we have information available in hundreds of variables, there decision tree will help to identify most significant variable.
3. **Less data cleaning required:** It requires less data cleaning compared to some other modeling techniques. It is not influenced by outliers and missing values to a fair degree.
4. **Data type is not a constraint:** It can handle both numerical and categorical variables.
5. **Non Parametric Method:** Decision tree is considered to be a non-parametric method. This means that decision trees have no assumptions about the space distribution and the classifier structure.
6. You can understand the results which express as explicit conditions on the original variables. IT staff can program the resulting model, and the execution is faster when this model applies to new individuals. Since the calculations consist of numeric comparisons or inclusion tests depending on whether an individual is a quantitative or qualitative model.
7. The presence of extreme individuals can not affect the Decision trees. These can be isolated in small nodes and do not affect the classification as a whole.
8. Decision trees can deal with missing data. CHAID treats all missing values of a variable as a category which can either remain isolated or can be merged with another category.
9. Some trees such as CART and C5.0 allow variables of all types to handle directly. For example Continuous, discrete and qualitative variables.
10. A decision tree provides a visual interpretation of a situation for decision making. So the use of decision trees enhances communication. Branches of the decision tree represent all factors that are important in decision making.

Disadvantages

The disadvantages of using R decision trees are as follows

1. **Over fitting:** Over fitting is one of the most practical difficulty for decision tree models. This problem gets solved by setting constraints on model parameters and pruning (discussed in detailed below).
2. **Not fit for continuous variables**: While working with continuous numerical variables, decision tree looses information when it categorizes variables in different categories.
3. The definition of the nodes at level n + 1 is dependent on the definition of level n. If the condition at level n is true, then only condition at level n+1 will be true.
4. The tree detects local, not global, optima. It evaluates all the independent variables sequentially, not simultaneously. The choice of a division for a node at a certain level of the tree is never revised subsequently. This may be troublesome, particularly as some trees (CART) make biased choices.
5. The modification of a single variable may change the whole tree if this variable is located near the top of the tree. This results in a lack of robustness. You can overcome it by resampling, in which one can construct the trees on many successive samples and can aggregate by a vote or a mean. But this will lead to losing the simplicity and readability of the model, which are the advantages of decision trees. For example, an individual item has all categories of a group A except the value of a variable that splits the tree. In this case, a variable is misclassified in another group as the tree has tested this particular variable

Applications of Decision Trees

Following are the common areas for applying decision trees:

- **Direct Marketing** – While the marketing of products and services, business should track products and services offered by the competitors as it identifies the best combination of products and marketing channels that target specific sets of consumers.
- **Customer Retention** – Decision trees helps organizations keep their valuable customers and get new ones by providing good quality products, discounts, and gift vouchers. These can also analyze buying behaviors of the customers and know their satisfaction levels.
- **Fraud Detection** – Fraud is a major problem for many industries. Using classification tree, a business can detect frauds beforehand and can drop fraudulent customers.
- **Diagnosis of Medical Problems** – Classification trees identifies patients who are at risk of suffering from serious diseases such as cancer and diabetes.

2. Regression Trees vs Classification Trees

We all know that the terminal nodes (or leaves) lies at the bottom of the decision tree. This means that decision trees are typically drawn upside down such that leaves are the the bottom & roots are the tops (shown on next page).

Both the trees work almost similar to each other, let's look at the primary differences & similarity between classification and regression trees:

1. Regression trees are used when dependent variable is continuous. Classification trees are used when dependent variable is categorical.
2. In case of regression tree, the value obtained by terminal nodes in the training data is the mean response of observation falling in that region. Thus, if an unseen data observation falls in that region, we'll make its prediction with mean value.
3. In case of classification tree, the value (class) obtained by terminal node in the training data is the mode of observations falling in that region. Thus, if an unseen data observation falls in that region, we'll make its prediction with mode value.
4. Both the trees divide the predictor space (independent variables) into distinct and non-overlapping regions. For the sake of simplicity, you can think of these regions as high dimensional boxes or boxes.
5. Both the trees follow a top-down greedy approach known as recursive binary splitting. We call it as 'top-down' because it begins from the top of tree when all the observations are available in a single region and successively splits the predictor space into two new branches down the tree. It is known as 'greedy' because, the algorithm cares (looks for best variable available) about only the current split, and not about future splits which will lead to a better tree.
6. This splitting process is continued until a user defined stopping criteria is reached. For example: we can tell the the algorithm to stop once the number of observations per node becomes less than 50.

7. In both the cases, the splitting process results in fully grown trees until the stopping criteria is reached. But, the fully grown tree is likely to overfit data, leading to poor accuracy on unseen data. This bring 'pruning'. Pruning is one of the technique used tackle overfitting. We'll learn more about it in following section.

1. How does a tree decide where to split?

The decision of making strategic splits heavily affects a tree's accuracy. The decision criteria is different for classification and regression trees.

Decision trees use multiple algorithms to decide to split a node in two or more sub-nodes. The creation of sub-nodes increases the homogeneity of resultant sub-nodes. In other words, we can say that purity of the node increases with respect to the target variable. Decision tree splits the nodes on all available variables and then selects the split which results in most homogeneous sub-nodes.

The algorithm selection is also based on type of target variables. Let's look at the four most commonly used algorithms in decision tree:

Gini Index

Gini index says, if we select two items from a population at random then they must be of same class and probability for this is 1 if population is pure.

1. It works with categorical target variable "Success" or "Failure".
2. It performs only Binary splits
3. Higher the value of Gini higher the homogeneity.
4. CART (Classification and Regression Tree) uses Gini method to create binary splits.

Steps to Calculate Gini for a split

1. Calculate Gini for sub-nodes, using formula sum of square of probability for success and failure (p^2 + q^2).
2. Calculate Gini for split using weighted Gini score of each node of that split

Example: – Referring to example used above, where we want to segregate the students based on target variable (playing cricket or not). In the snapshot below, we split the population using two input variables Gender and Class. Now, I want to identify which split is producing more homogeneous sub-nodes using Gini index.

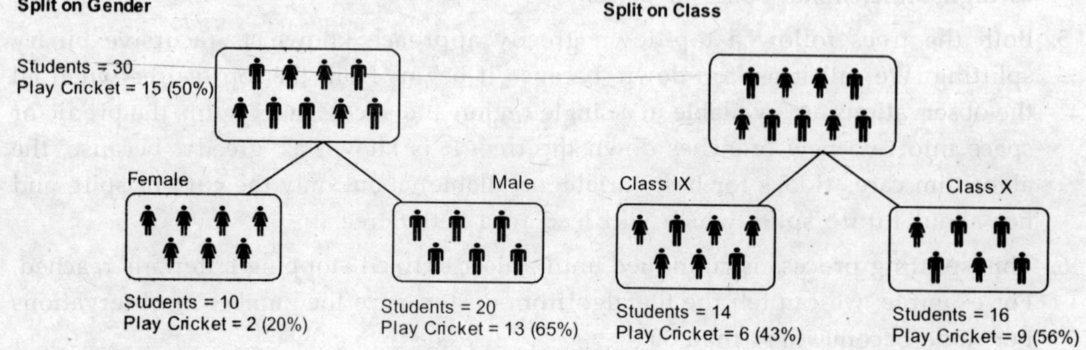

Split on Gender:

1. Calculate, Gini for sub-node Female = (0.2)*(0.2) + (0.8)*(0.8) = 0.68
2. Gini for sub-node Male = (0.65)*(0.65) + (0.35)*(0.35) = 0.55
3. Calculate weighted Gini for Split Gender = (10/30)*0.68 + (20/30)*0.55 = **0.59**

Similar for Split on Class:

1. Gini for sub-node Class IX = (0.43)*(0.43) + (0.57)*(0.57) = 0.51
2. Gini for sub-node Class X = (0.56)*(0.56) + (0.44)*(0.44) = 0.51
3. Calculate weighted Gini for Split Class = (14/30)*0.51 + (16/30)*0.51 = **0.51**

Above, you can see that Gini score for *Split on Gender* is higher than *Split on Class,* hence, the node split will take place on Gender.

Chi-Square Test

It is an algorithm to find out the statistical significance between the differences between sub-nodes and parent node. We measure it by sum of squares of standardized differences between observed and expected frequencies of target variable.

1. It works with categorical target variable "Success" or "Failure".
2. It can perform two or more splits.
3. Higher the value of Chi-Square higher the statistical significance of differences between sub-node and Parent node.
4. Chi-Square of each node is calculated using formula,
5. Chi-square = ((Actual – Expected)^2 / Expected)^1/2
6. It generates tree called CHAID (Chi-square Automatic Interaction Detector)

Steps to Calculate Chi-square for a split:

1. Calculate Chi-square for individual node by calculating the deviation for Success and Failure both
2. Calculated Chi-square of Split using Sum of all Chi-square of success and Failure of each node of the split

Example: Let's work with above example that we have used to calculate Gini.

Split on Gender:

1. First we are populating for node Female, Populate the actual value for **"Play Cricket"** and **"Not Play Cricket"**, here these are 2 and 8 respectively.
2. Calculate expected value for **"Play Cricket"** and **"Not Play Cricket"**, here it would be 5 for both because parent node has probability of 50% and we have applied same probability on Female count(10).
3. Calculate deviations by using formula, Actual – Expected. It is for **"Play Cricket"** (2 – 5 = –3) and for **"Not play cricket"** (8 – 5 = 3).

4. Calculate Chi-square of node for "**Play Cricket**" and "**Not Play Cricket**" using formula with formula, = **((Actual – Expected)^2 / Expected)^1/2**. You can refer below table for calculation.
5. Follow similar steps for calculating Chi-square value for Male node.
6. Now add all Chi-square values to calculate Chi-square for split Gender.

Node	Play Cricket	Not Play Cricket	Total	Expected Play Cricket	Expected Not Play Cricket	Deviation Play Cricket	Deviation Not Play Cricket	Chi-Square	
								Play Cricket	Not Play Cricket
Female	2	8	10	5	5	-3	3	1.34	1.34
Male	13	7	20	10	10	3	-3	0.95	0.95
							Total Chi-Square	4.58	

Split on Class:

Perform similar steps of calculation for split on Class and you will come up with below table.

Node	Play Cricket	Not Play Cricket	Total	Expected Play Cricket	Expected Not Play Cricket	Deviation Play Cricket	Deviation Not Play Cricket	Chi-Square	
								Play Cricket	Not Play Cricket
IX	6	8	14	7	7	-1	1	0.38	0.38
X	9	7	16	8	8	1	-1	0.35	0.35
							Total Chi-Square	1.46	

Above, you can see that Chi-square also identify the Gender split is more significant compare to Class.

Information Gain:

Look at the image below and think which node can be described easily. I am sure, your answer is C because it requires less information as all values are similar. On the other hand, B requires more information to describe it and A requires the maximum information. In other words, we can say that C is a Pure node, B is less Impure and A is more impure.

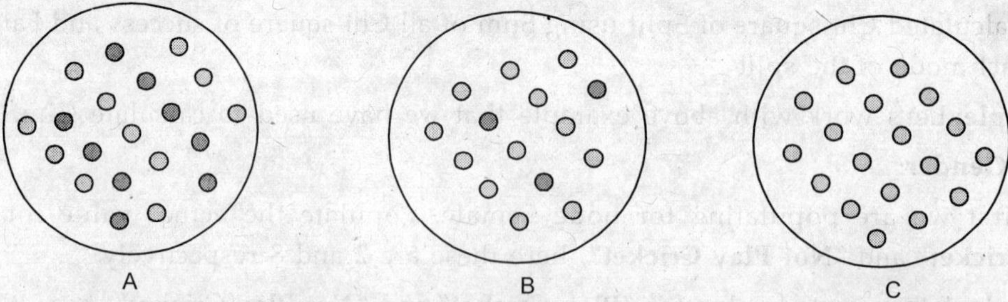

Now, we can build a conclusion that less impure node requires less information to describe it. And, more impure node requires more information. Information theory is a measure to define this degree of disorganization in a system known as Entropy. If the sample is completely homogeneous, then the entropy is zero and if the sample is an equally divided (50% – 50%), it has entropy of one.

Entropy can be calculated using formula: Entropy = – p log2p – q log2q

Here p and q is probability of success and failure respectively in that node. Entropy is also used with categorical target variable. It chooses the split which has lowest entropy compared to parent node and other splits. The lesser the entropy, the better it is.

Steps to calculate entropy for a split:

1. Calculate entropy of parent node
2. Calculate entropy of each individual node of split and calculate weighted average of all sub-nodes available in split.

Example 1.5: Let's use this method to identify best split for student example.

1. Entropy for parent node = – (15/30) log2 (15/30) – (15/30) log2 (15/30) = **1**. Here 1 shows that it is a impure node.
2. Entropy for Female node = – (2/10) log2 (2/10) – (8/10) log2 (8/10) = 0.72 and for male node, – (13/20) log2 (13/20) – (7/20) log2 (7/20) = **0.93**
3. Entropy for split Gender = Weighted entropy of sub-nodes = (10/30)*0.72 + (20/30)*0.93 = **0.86**
4. Entropy for Class IX node, – (6/14) log2 (6/14) – (8/14) log2 (8/14) = 0.99 and for Class X node, – (9/16) log2 (9/16) – (7/16) log2 (7/16) = 0.99.
5. Entropy for split Class = (14/30)*0.99 + (16/30)*0.99 = **0.99**

Above, you can see that entropy for *Split on Gender* is the lowest among all, so the tree will split on *Gender*. We can derive information gain from entropy as **1 – Entropy.**

Reduction in Variance

Till now, we have discussed the algorithms for categorical target variable. Reduction in variance is an algorithm used for continuous target variables (regression problems). This algorithm uses the standard formula of variance to choose the best split. The split with lower variance is selected as the criteria to split the population:

$$\text{Variance} = \frac{\Sigma(X-\bar{X})^2}{n}$$

Above X-bar is mean of the values, X is actual and n is number of values.

Steps to calculate Variance:

1. Calculate variance for each node.
2. Calculate variance for each split as weighted average of each node variance.

Example 1.6: Let's assign numerical value 1 for play cricket and 0 for not playing cricket. Now follow the steps to identify the right split:

1. Variance for Root node, here mean value is (15*1 + 15*0)/30 = 0.5 and we have 15 one and 15 zero. Now variance would be ((1 – 0.5)^2 + (1 – 0.5)^2 + ...15 times+ (0 – 0.5)^2 + (0 – 0.5)^2 +...15 times) / 30, this can be written as (15*(1 – 0.5)^2 + 15*(0 – 0.5)^2) / 30 = **0.25**

2. Mean of Female node = (2*1 + 8*0)/10 = 0.2 and Variance = (2*(1 – 0.2)^2 + 8*(0 – 0.2)^2) / 10 = 0.16
3. Mean of Male Node = (13*1 + 7*0)/20 = 0.65 and Variance = (13*(1 – 0.65)^2 + 7*(0 – 0.65)^2) / 20 = 0.23
4. Variance for Split Gender = Weighted Variance of Sub-nodes = (10/30)*0.16 + (20/30) *0.23 = **0.21**
5. Mean of Class IX node = (6*1 + 8*0)/14 = 0.43 and Variance = (6*(1 – 0.43)^2 + 8*(0 – 0.43)^2) / 14 = 0.24
6. Mean of Class X node = (9*1 + 7*0)/16 = 0.56 and Variance = (9*(1 – 0.56)^2 + 7*(0 – 0.56)^2) / 16 = 0.25
7. Variance for Split Gender = (14/30)*0.24 + (16/30) *0.25 = **0.25**

Above, you can see that Gender split has lower variance compare to parent node, so the split would take place on *Gender* variable.

Until here, we learnt about the basics of decision trees and the decision making process involved to choose the best splits in building a tree model. As I said, decision tree can be applied both on regression and classification problems. Let's understand these aspects in detail.

Key parameters of tree modeling and avoiding over-fitting in decision trees

Overfitting is one of the key challenges faced while modeling decision trees. If there is no limit set of a decision tree, it will give you 100% accuracy on training set because in the worse case it will end up making 1 leaf for each observation. Thus, preventing overfitting is pivotal while modeling a decision tree and it can be done in 2 ways:

(1) Setting constraints on tree size

(2) Tree pruning

We will discuss both in very brief.

Setting Constraints on Tree Size

This can be done by using various parameters which are used to define a tree. First, lets look at the general structure of a decision tree:

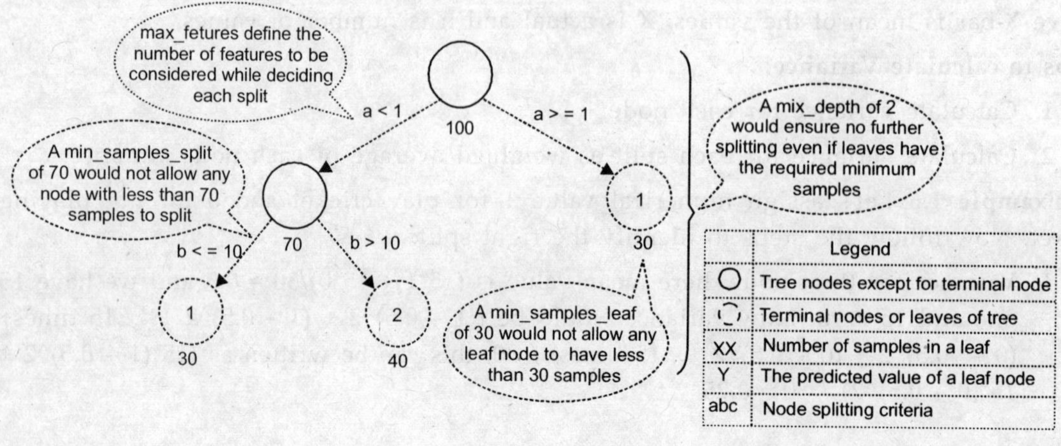

The parameters used for defining a tree are further explained below. The parameters described below are irrespective of tool. It is important to understand the role of parameters used in tree modeling. These parameters are available in R & Python.

1. **Minimum samples for a node split**
   - Defines the minimum number of samples (or observations) which are required in a node to be considered for splitting.
   - Used to control over-fitting. Higher values prevent a model from learning relations which might be highly specific to the particular sample selected for a tree.
   - Too high values can lead to under-fitting hence, it should be tuned using CV.
2. **Minimum samples for a terminal node (leaf)**
   - Defines the minimum samples (or observations) required in a terminal node or leaf.
   - Used to control over-fitting similar to min_samples_split.
   - Generally lower values should be chosen for imbalanced class problems because the regions in which the minority class will be in majority will be very small.
3. **Maximum depth of tree (vertical depth)**
   - The maximum depth of a tree.
   - Used to control over-fitting as higher depth will allow model to learn relations very specific to a particular sample.
   - Should be tuned using CV.
4. **Maximum number of terminal nodes**
   - The maximum number of terminal nodes or leaves in a tree.
   - Can be defined in place of max_depth. Since binary trees are created, a depth of 'n' would produce a maximum of 2^n leaves.
5. **Maximum features to consider for split**
   - The number of features to consider while searching for a best split. These will be randomly selected.
   - As a thumb-rule, square root of the total number of features works great but we should check upto 30 – 40% of the total number of features.
   - Higher values can lead to over-fitting but depends on case to case.

Tree-Based Models

Recursive partitioning is a fundamental tool in data mining. It helps us explore the stucture of a set of data, while developing easy to visualize decision rules for predicting a categorical (classification tree) or continuous (regression tree) outcome. This section briefly describes CART modeling, conditional inference trees, and random forests.

CART Modeling via rpart

Classification and regression trees (as described by Brieman, Freidman, Olshen, and Stone) can be generated through the rpart package. Detailed information on rpart is available in An Introduction to Recursive Partitioning Using the RPART Routines. The general steps are provided below followed by two examples.

(1) Grow the Tree

To grow a tree, use

rpart(*formula*, data=, method=,control=) where

formula	is in the format *outcome ~ predictor1 + predictor2 + predictor3* + ect.
data =	specifies the data frame
method =	**"class"** for a classification tree **"anova"** for a regression tree
control =	optional parameters for controlling tree growth. For example, control = rpart.control (minsplit = 30, cp = 0.001) requires that the minimum number of observations in a node be 30 before attempting a split and that a split must decrease the overall lack of fit by a factor of 0.001 (cost complexity factor) before being attempted.

(2) Examine the results

The following functions help us to examine the results.

printcp(*fit*)	display cp table
plotcp(*fit*)	plot cross-validation results
rsq.rpart(*fit*)	plot approximate R-squared and relative error for different splits (2 plots). labels are only appropriate for the "anova" method.
print(*fit*)	print results
summary(*fit*)	detailed results including surrogate splits
plot(*fit*)	plot decision tree
text(*fit*)	label the decision tree plot
post(*fit*, file =)	create postscript plot of decision tree

In trees created by **rpart( )**, move to the **LEFT** branch when the stated condition is true (see the graphs below).

1. prune tree

Prune back the tree to avoid overfitting the data. Typically, you will want to select a tree size that minimizes the cross-validated error, the **xerror** column printed by **printcp( )**.

Prune the tree to the desired size using

prune(*fit*, cp=)

Specifically, use **printcp( )** to examine the cross-validated error results, select the complexity parameter associated with minimum error, and place it into the **prune( )**function. Alternatively, you can use the code fragment

fit$cptable[which.min(fit$cptable[,"xerror"]), "CP"]

to automatically select the complexity parameter associated with the smallest cross-validated error. Thanks to HSAUR for this idea.

Classification Tree example

Let's use the data frame **kyphosis** to predict a type of deformation (kyphosis) after surgery, from age in months (Age), number of vertebrae involved (Number), and the highest vertebrae operated on (Start).

```
# Classification Tree with rpart
library(rpart)

# grow tree
fit <- rpart(Kyphosis ~ Age + Number + Start,
  method="class", data=kyphosis)

printcp(fit) # display the results
plotcp(fit) # visualize cross-validation results
summary(fit) # detailed summary of splits

# plot tree
plot(fit, uniform = TRUE,
  main="Classification Tree for Kyphosis")
text(fit, use.n = TRUE, all = TRUE, cex = .8)

# create attractive postscript plot of tree
post(fit, file = "c:/tree.ps",
  title = "Classification Tree for Kyphosis")
```

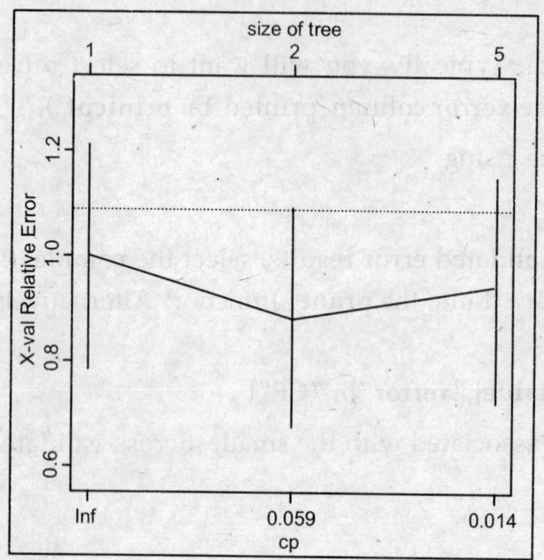

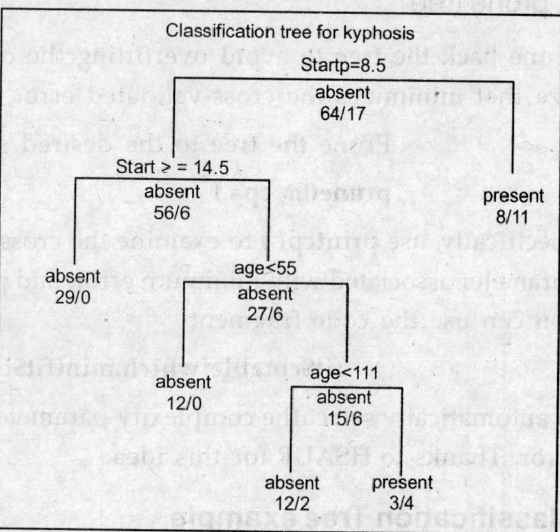

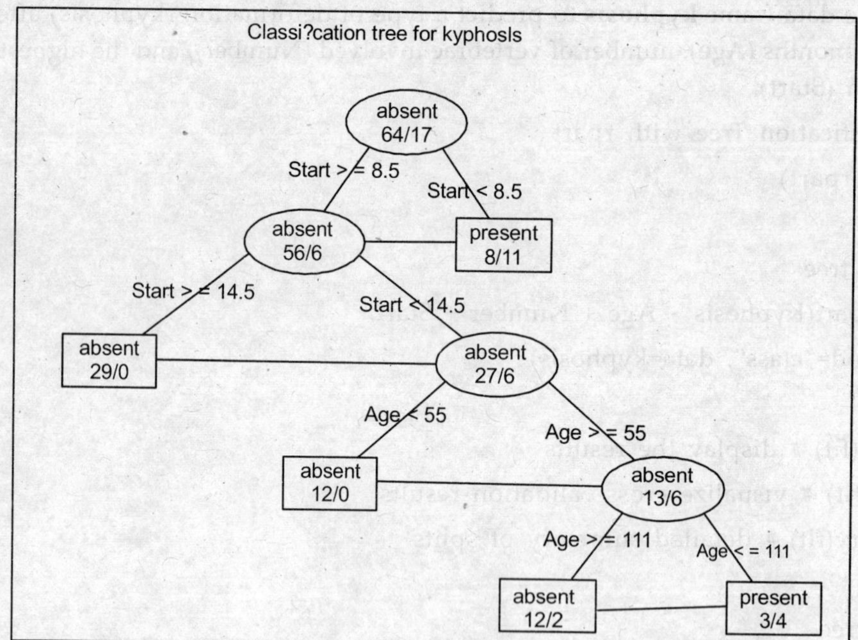

Tree Pruning Technique

The Tree Pruning technique of setting constraint is a greedy-approach. In other words, it will check for the best split instantaneously and move forward until one of the specified stopping condition is reached.

```
# prune the tree
pfit<- prune(fit, cp = fit$cptable[which.min(fit$cptable[,"xerror"]),"CP"])
# plot the pruned tree
plot(pfit, uniform = TRUE,
```

```
    main = "Pruned Classification Tree for Kyphosis")
text(pfit, use.n = TRUE, all = TRUE, cex = .8)
post(pfit, file = "c:/ptree.ps",
    title = "Pruned Classification Tree for Kyphosis")
```

The following are the outcomes:

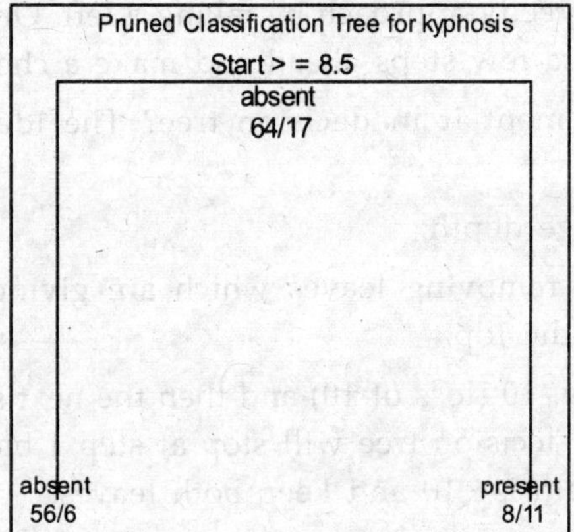

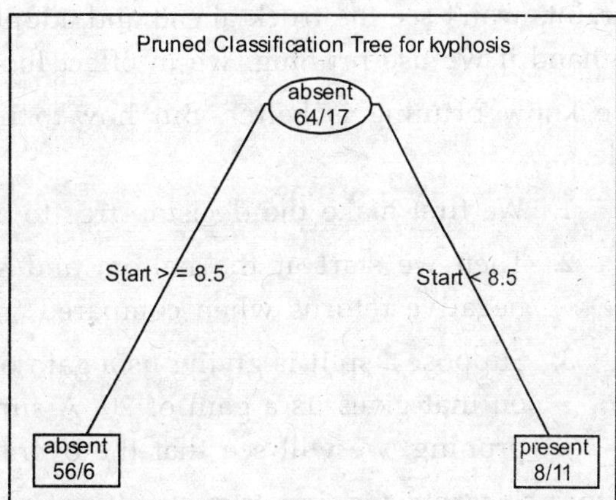

Tree Pruning

As discussed earlier, the technique of setting constraint is a greedy-approach. In other words, it will check for the best split instantaneously and move forward until one of the specified stopping condition is reached. Let's consider the following case when you're driving:

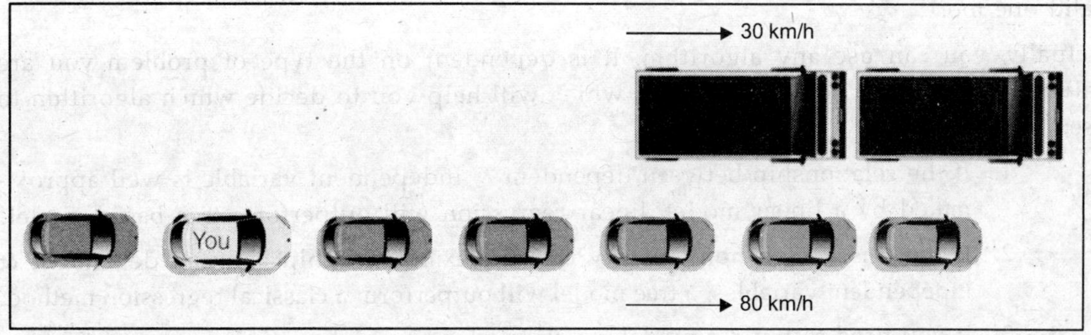

There are 2 lanes:

1. A lane with cars moving at 80km/h
2. A lane with trucks moving at 30km/h

At this instant, you are the yellow car and you have 2 choices:

1. Take a left and overtake the other 2 cars quickly
2. Keep moving in the present lane

Lets analyze these choice. In the former choice, you'll immediately overtake the car ahead and reach behind the truck and start moving at 30 km/h, looking for an opportunity to move back right. All cars originally behind you move ahead in the meanwhile. This would be the optimum choice if your objective is to maximize the distance covered in next say 10 seconds. In the later choice, you sale through at same speed, cross trucks and then overtake maybe depending on situation ahead. Greedy you!

This is exactly the difference between normal decision tree & pruning. A decision tree with constraints won't see the truck ahead and adopt a greedy approach by taking a left. On the other hand if we use pruning, we in effect look at a few steps ahead and make a choice.

So we know pruning is better. But how to implement it in decision tree? The idea is simple.

1. We first make the decision tree to a large depth.
2. Then we start at the bottom and start removing leaves which are giving us negative returns when compared from the top.
3. Suppose a split is giving us a gain of say -10 (loss of 10) and then the next split on that gives us a gain of 20. A simple decision tree will stop at step 1 but in pruning, we will see that the overall gain is +10 and keep both leaves.

Note that sklearn's decision tree classifier does not currently support pruning. Advanced packages like xgboost have adopted tree pruning in their implementation. But the library *rpart* in R, provides a function to prune. Good for R users!

5. Are tree based models better than linear models?

"If I can use logistic regression for classification problems and linear regression for regression problems, why is there a need to use trees"? Many of us have this question. And, this is a valid one too.

Actually, you can use any algorithm. It is dependent on the type of problem you are solving. Let's look at some key factors which will help you to decide which algorithm to use:

1. If the relationship between dependent & independent variable is well approximated by a linear model, linear regression will outperform tree based model.
2. If there is a high non-linearity & complex relationship between dependent & independent variables, a tree model will outperform a classical regression method.
3. If you need to build a model which is easy to explain to people, a decision tree model will always do better than a linear model. Decision tree models are even simpler to interpret than linear regression!

6. Working with Decision Trees in R and Python

For R users and Python users, decision tree is quite easy to implement. Let's quickly look at the set of codes which can get you started with this algorithm. For ease of use, I've shared standard codes where you'll need to replace your data set name and variables to get started.

For R users, there are multiple packages available to implement decision tree such as ctree, rpart, tree etc.

```
> library(rpart)
> x <- cbind(x_train,y_train)
# grow tree
> fit <- rpart(y_train ~ ., data = x,method="class")
> summary(fit)
#Predict Output
> predicted= predict(fit,x_test)
```

In the code above:

- y_train – represents dependent variable.
- x_train – represents independent variable
- x – represents training data.

For Python users, below is the code:

```
#Import Library
#Import other necessary libraries like pandas, numpy...
from sklearn import tree
#Assumed you have, X (predictor) and Y (target) for training data set and x_test(predictor) of test_dataset
# Create tree object
model = tree.DecisionTreeClassifier(criterion='gini') # for classification, here you can change the algorithm as gini or entropy (information gain) by default it is gini
# model = tree.DecisionTreeRegressor() for regression
# Train the model using the training sets and check score
model.fit(X, y)
model.score(X, y)
#Predict Output
predicted = model.predict(x_test)
```

Applications of Decision Trees

Following are the common areas for applying decision trees:

- Direct Marketing – While the marketing of products and services, business should track products and services offered by the competitors as it identifies the best combination of products and marketing channels that target specific sets of consumers.
- Customer Retention – Decision trees helps organizations keep their valuable customers and get new ones by providing good quality products, discounts, and gift vouchers.

These can also analyze buying behaviors of the customers and know their satisfaction levels.

- Fraud Detection – Fraud is a major problem for many industries. Using classification tree, a business can detect frauds beforehand and can drop fraudulent customers.
- Diagnosis of Medical Problems – Classification trees identifies patients who are at risk of suffering from serious diseases such as cancer and diabetes.

Classification And Regression Tree (CART)

The term Classification And Regression Tree (CART) analysis is an umbrella term used to refer to both of the above procedures, first introduced by Breiman et al. Trees used for regression and trees used for classification have some similarities - but also some differences, such as the procedure used to determine where to split.

For general use, decision trees are employed to visually represent decisions and show or inform decision making. When working with machine learning and data mining, decision trees are used as a predictive model. These models map observations about data to conclusions about the data's target value.

The goal of decision tree learning is to create a model that will predict the value of a target based on input variables.

In the predictive model, the data's attributes that are determined through observation are represented by the branches, while the conclusions about the data's target value are represented in the leaves.

When "learning" a tree, the source data is divided into subsets based on an attribute value test, which is repeated on each of the derived subsets recursively. Once the subset at a node has the equivalent value as its target value has, the recursion process will be complete.

Let's look at an example of various conditions that can determine whether or not someone should go fishing. This includes weather conditions as well as barometric pressure conditions.

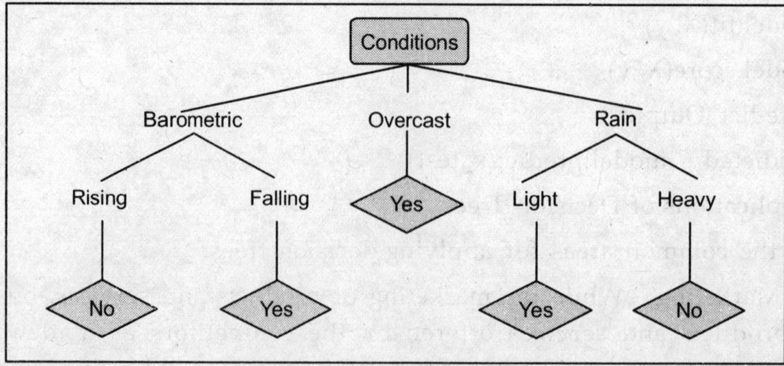

Fig. 1.17: Decision Tree

In the simplified decision tree above, an example is classified by sorting it through the tree to the appropriate leaf node. This then returns the classification associated with the particular leaf, which in this case is either a Yes or a No. The tree classifies a day's conditions based on whether or not it is suitable for going fishing.

A true classification tree data set would have a lot more features than what is outlined above, but relationships should be straightforward to determine. When working with decision tree learning, several determinations need to be made, including what features to choose, what conditions to use for splitting, and understanding when the decision tree has reached a clear ending.

Decision tree advantages

Amongst other data mining methods, decision trees have various advantages:

1. Simple to understand and interpret. People are able to understand decision tree models after a brief explanation. Trees can also be displayed graphically in a way that is easy for non-experts to interpret.
2. Able to handle both numerical and categorical data. Other techniques are usually specialised in analysing datasets that have only one type of variable. (For example, relation rules can be used only with nominal variables while neural networks can be used only with numerical variables or categoricals converted to 0-1 values.)
3. Requires little data preparation. Other techniques often require data normalization. Since trees can handle qualitative predictors, there is no need to create dummy variables.
4. Uses a white box model. If a given situation is observable in a model the explanation for the condition is easily explained by boolean logic. By contrast, in a black box model, the explanation for the results is typically difficult to understand, for example with an artificial neural network.
5. Possible to validate a model using statistical tests. That makes it possible to account for the reliability of the model.
6. Non-statistical approach that makes no assumptions of the training data or prediction residuals; e.g., no distributional, independence, or constant variance assumptions
7. Performs well with large datasets. Large amounts of data can be analysed using standard computing resources in reasonable time.
8. Mirrors human decision making more closely than other approaches. This could be useful when modeling human decisions/behavior.
9. Robust against co-linearity, particularly boosting
10. In built feature selection. Additional irrelevant feature will be less used so that they can be removed on subsequent runs.

Limitations

1. Trees do not tend to be as accurate as other approaches.
2. Trees can be very non-robust. A small change in the training data can result in a big change in the tree, and thus a big change in final predictions.
3. The problem of learning an optimal decision tree is known to be NP-complete under several aspects of optimality and even for simple concepts.Consequently, practical decision-tree learning algorithms are based on heuristics such as the greedy algorithm where locally-optimal decisions are made at each node. Such algorithms cannot guarantee to return the globally-optimal decision tree. To reduce the greedy effect of local-optimality some methods such as the dual information distance (DID) tree were proposed.
4. Decision-tree learners can create over-complex trees that do not generalize well from the training data. (This is known as overfitting. Mechanisms such as pruning are necessary to avoid this problem (with the exception of some algorithms such as the Conditional Inference approach, that does not require pruning.
5. There are concepts that are hard to learn because decision trees do not express them easily, such as XOR, parity or multiplexer problems. In such cases, the decision tree becomes prohibitively large. Approaches to solve the problem involve either changing the representation of the problem domain (known as propositionalization) or using learning algorithms based on more expressive representations (such as statistical relational learning or inductive logic programming).
6. For data including categorical variables with different numbers of levels, information gain in decision trees is biased in favor of those attributes with more levels. However, the issue of biased predictor selection is avoided by the Conditional Inference approach, a two-stage approach, or adaptive leave-one-out feature selection.

1.11 NAIVE BAYES

Naive Bayes is a simple technique for constructing classifiers: models that assign class labels to problem instances, represented as vectors of feature values, where the class labels are drawn from some finite set. It is not a single algorithm for training such classifiers, but a family of algorithms based on a common principle: all naive Bayes classifiers assume that the value of a particular feature is independent of the value of any other feature, given the class variable. For example, a fruit may be considered to be an apple if it is red, round, and about 10 cm in diameter. A naive Bayes classifier considers each of these features to contribute independently to the probability that this fruit is an apple, regardless of any possible correlations between the color, roundness, and diameter features.

What makes a naive Bayes classifier naive is its assumption that all attributes of a data point under consideration are independent of each other. A classifier sorting fruits into apples and oranges would know that apples are red, round and are a certain size, but would not assume all these things at once. Oranges are round too, after all.

For some types of probability models, naive Bayes classifiers can be trained very efficiently in a supervised learning setting. In many practical applications, parameter estimation for naive Bayes models uses the method of maximum likelihood; in other words, one can work with the naive Bayes model without accepting Bayesian probability or using any Bayesian methods.

Despite their naive design and apparently oversimplified assumptions, naive Bayes classifiers have worked quite well in many complex real-world situations. In 2004, an analysis of the Bayesian classification problem showed that there are sound theoretical reasons for the apparently implausible efficacy of naive Bayes classifiers. Still, a comprehensive comparison with other classification algorithms in 2006 showed that Bayes classification is outperformed by other approaches, such as boosted trees or random forests.

An advantage of naive Bayes is that it only requires a small number of training data to estimate the parameters necessary for classification.

A naive Bayes classifier uses probability theory to classify data. Naive Bayes classifier algorithms make use of Bayes' theorem. The key insight of Bayes' theorem is that the probability of an event can be adjusted as new data is introduced.

A naive Bayes classifier is not a single algorithm, but a family of machine learning algorithms that make uses of statistical independence. These algorithms are relatively easy to write and run more efficiently than more complex Bayes algorithms.

The most popular application is spam filters. A spam filter looks at email messages for certain key words and puts them in a spam folder if they match.Despite the name, the more data it gets, the more accurate a naive Bayes classifier becomes, such as from a user flagging email messages in an inbox for spam.

It is a classification technique based on Bayes' Theorem with an assumption of independence among predictors. In simple terms, a Naive Bayes classifier assumes that the presence of a particular feature in a class is unrelated to the presence of any other feature. For example, a fruit may be considered to be an apple if it is red, round, and about 7.5 Centimeter (3 inches) in diameter. Even if these features depend on each other or upon the existence of the other features, all of these properties independently contribute to the probability that this fruit is an apple and that is why it is known as 'Naive'.

Naive Bayes model is easy to build and particularly useful for very large data sets. Along with simplicity, Naive Bayes is known to outperform even highly sophisticated classification methods.

1.11.1 Bayes Theorem

Bayes theorem provides a way of calculating posterior probability $P(c|x)$ from $P(c)$, $P(x)$ and $P(x|c)$. Look at the equation below:

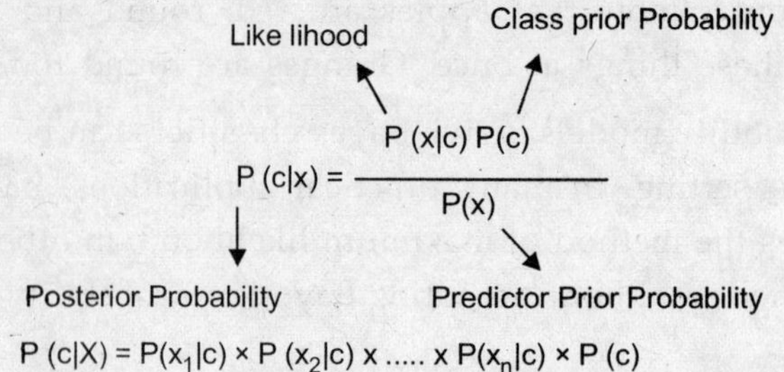

$$P(c|X) = P(x_1|c) \times P(x_2|c) \times \ldots \times P(x_n|c) \times P(c)$$

In above equation:

1. *P*(*c*|*x*) is the posterior probability of *class* (c, *target*) given *predictor* (x, *attributes*).
2. *P*(*c*) is the prior probability of *class*.
3. *P*(*x*|*c*) is the likelihood which is the probability of *predictor* given *class*.
4. *P*(*x*) is the prior probability of *predictor*.

1.11.2 How Naive Bayes algorithm works?

Let's presume a training data set of weather and corresponding target variable 'Play' (suggesting possibilities of playing). Now, we need to classify whether players will play or not, based on weather condition. Let's follow the below steps to perform it.

Step 1: Convert the data set into a frequency table

Step 2: Create Likelihood table by finding the probabilities like Overcast probability = 0.29 and probability of playing is 0.64.

Weather	Play
Sunny	No
Overcast	Yes
Rainy	Yes
Sunny	Yes
Sunny	Yes
Overcast	Yes
Rainy	No
Rainy	No
Sunny	Yes
Rainy	Yes
Sunny	No
Overcast	Yes
Overcast	Yes
Rainy	No

Frequency Table		
Weather	No	Yes
Overcast		4
Rainy	3	2
Sunny	2	3
Grand Total	5	9

Likelihood table				
Weather	No	Yes		
Overcast		4	= 4/14	0.29
Rainy	3	2	= 5/14	0.36
Sunny	2	3	= 5/14	0.36
All	5	9		
	= 5/14	= 9/14		
	0.36	0.64		

Step 3: Now, use Naive Bayesian equation to calculate the posterior probability for each class. The class with the highest posterior probability is the outcome of prediction.

Example 1.7: To find out whetherkollowing statement is true "Players will play if weather is sun.?

We can solve it using above discussed method of posterior probability.

P(Yes | Sunny) = P(Sunny | Yes)*P(Yes) / P (Sunny)

Here we have *P (Sunny | Yes) = 3/9 = 0.33, P(Sunny) = 5/14 = 0.36, P(Yes) = 9/14 = 0.64*

Now, P *(Yes | Sunny) = 0.33*0.64 / 0.36 = 0.60,* which has higher probability.

Naive Bayes uses a similar method to predict the probability of different class based on various *attributes*. This algorithm is mostly used in text classification and with problems having multiple classes.

1.11.3 Pros and Cons of Naive Bayes?

Pros:

1. It is easy and fast to predict class of test data set. It also perform well in multi class prediction
2. When assumption of independence holds, a Naive Bayes classifier performs better compare to other models like logistic regression and you need less training data.
3. It perform well in case of categorical input variables compared to numerical variable(s). For numerical variable, normal distribution is assumed (bell curve, which is a strong assumption).

Cons:

1. If categorical variable has a category (in test data set), which was not observed in training data set, then model will assign a 0 (zero) probability and will be unable to make a prediction. This is often known as *"Zero Frequency"*. To solve this, we can use the smoothing technique. One of the simplest smoothing techniques is called Laplace estimation.
2. On the other side naive Bayes is also known as a bad estimator, so the probability outputs from predict_*proba* are not to be taken too seriously.
3. Another limitation of Naive Bayes is the assumption of independent predictors. In real life, it is almost impossible that we get a set of predictors which are completely independent.

1.11.4 Applications of Naive Bayes Algorithms

(a) Frequentist and Bayesian methods

There are at least two different ways of considering uncertainty, resulting in two different classes of methods for inference, decision, and other statistical questions. These are called frequentist and Bayesian methods. Some people prefer frequentist methods, while others prefer Bayesian methods.

Frequentists interpret a probability as a statistical average across many independent realizations (law of large numbers). Bayesians interpret it as a degree of belief (no need for many realizations). The Bayesian interpretation is very useful when only a single trial is considered. In addition, Bayesian theory takes into account our prior knowledge about a random process. This prior probability distribution is updated into a posterior distribution as we get more and more data.

Both frequentist and Bayesian methods have their advantages and disadvantages. For instance, one could say that frequentist methods might be easier to apply than Bayesian methods, but more difficult to interpret.

(b) Real time Prediction

Naive Bayes is an eager learning classifier and it is sure fast. Thus, it could be used for making predictions in real time.

1. **Multi class Prediction:** This algorithm is also well known for multi class prediction feature. Here we can predict the probability of multiple classes of target variable.
2. **Text classification/ Spam Filtering/ Sentiment Analysis:** Naive Bayes classifiers mostly used in text classification (due to better result in multi class problems and independence rule) have higher success rate as compared to other algorithms. As a result, it is widely used in Spam filtering (identify spam e-mail) and Sentiment Analysis (in social media analysis, to identify positive and negative customer sentiments)
3. **Recommendation System:** Naive Bayes Classifier and Collaborative Filteringtogether builds a Recommendation System that uses machine learning and data mining techniques to filter unseen information and predict whether a user would like a given resource or not.

1.11.5 Building a Basic Model using Naive Bayes in Python

Again, scikit learn (python library) will help here to build a Naive Bayes model in Python. There are three types of Naive Bayes model under scikit learn library:

1. **Gaussian:** It is used in classification and it assumes that features follow a normal distribution.
2. **Multinomial:** It is used for discrete counts. For example, let's say, we have a text classification problem. Here we can consider bernoulli trials which is one step further and instead of "word occurring in the document", we have "count how often word occurs in the document", you can think of it as "number of times outcome number x_i is observed over the n trials".
3. **Bernoulli:** The binomial model is useful if your feature vectors are binary (i.e. zeros and ones). One application would be text classification with 'bag of words' model where the 1s & 0s are "word occurs in the document" and "word does not occur in the document" respectively.

Based on your data set, you can choose any of above discussed model. Below is the example of Gaussian model.

(a) Python Code

```
#Import Library of Gaussian Naive Bayes model from sklearn.naive_bayes
import GaussianNB
import numpy as np
#assigning predictor and target variables
x= np.array([[-3,7],[1,5], [1,2], [-2,0], [2,3], [-4,0], [-1,1],
[1,1], [-2,2], [2,7], [-4,1], [-2,7]])
Y = np.array([3, 3, 3, 3, 4, 3, 3, 4, 3, 4, 4, 4])
#Create a Gaussian Classifier
model = GaussianNB()
# Train the model using the training sets
model.fit(x, y)
#Predict Output
predicted= model.predict([[1,2],[3,4]])
print predicted
```

Output: ([3,4])

(b) R Code:

```
require(e1071) #Holds the Naive Bayes Classifier
Train <- read.csv(file.choose())
Test <- read.csv(file.choose())
#Make sure the target variable is of a two-class classification
problem only
levels(Train$Item_Fat_Content)
model <- naiveBayes(Item_Fat_Content~., data = Train)
class(model)
pred <- predict(model,Test)
table(pred)
```

Above, we looked at the basic Naive Bayes model, you can improve the power of this basic model by tuning parameters and handle assumption intelligently. Let's look at the methods to improve the performance of Naive Bayes Model. I'd recommend you to go through this document for more details on Text classification using Naive Bayes.

1.11.6 Improving the power of Naive Bayes Model

Here are some tips for improving power of Naive Bayes Model:

1. If continuous features do not have normal distribution, we should use transformation or different methods to convert it in normal distribution.

2. If test data set has zero frequency issue, apply smoothing techniques "Laplace Correction" to predict the class of test data set.
3. Remove correlated features, as the highly correlated features are voted twice in the model and it can lead to over inflating importance.
4. Naive Bayes classifiers has limited options for parameter tuning like alpha=1 for smoothing, fit_prior=[True|False] to learn class prior probabilities or not and some other options .
5. You might think to apply some *classifier combination technique like* ensembling, bagging and boosting but these methods would not help. Actually, "ensembling, boosting, bagging" won't help since their purpose is to reduce variance. Naive Bayes has no variance to minimize.

1.12 LINEAR REGRESSION

It is the most well known and popular algorithm in machine learning and statistics. This model will assume a linear relationship between the input and the output variable. It is represented in the form of linear equation which has a set of inputs and a predictive output. Then it will estimate the values of coefficient used in the representation.

In ML, we have a set of input variables (x) that are used to determine the output variable (y). A relationship exists between the input variables and the output variable. The goal of ML is to quantify this relationship.

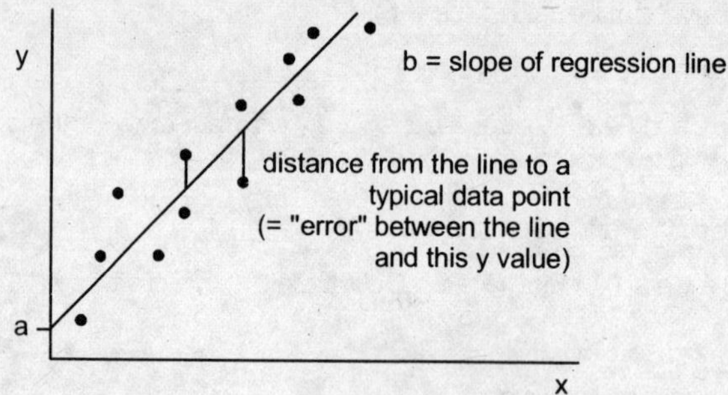

Fig. 1.18: Linear Regression is represented as a line in the form of y = a + bx.

In Linear Regression, the relationship between the input variables (x) and output variable (y) is expressed as an equation of the form y = a + bx. Thus, the goal of linear regression is to find out the values of coefficients a and b. Here, a is the intercept and b is the slope of the line.

Figure 1.18 shows the plotted x and y values for a dataset. The goal is to fit a line that is nearest to most of the points. This would reduce the distance ('error') between the y value of a data point and the line.

The overall idea of regression is to examine two things:

(1) does a set of predictor variables do a good job in predicting an outcome (dependent) variable?

(2) Which variables in particular are significant predictors of the outcome variable, and in what way do they–indicated by the magnitude and sign of the beta estimates–impact the outcome variable?

These regression estimates are used to explain the relationship between one dependent variable and one or more independent variables. The simplest form of the regression equation with one dependent and one independent variable is defined by the formula y = c + b*x, where y = estimated dependent variable score, c = constant, b = regression coefficient, and x = score on the independent variable.

Simple linear regression is a statistical method that allows us to summarize and study relationships between two continuous (quantitative) variables:

One variable, denoted x, is regarded as the predictor, explanatory, or independent variable.

The other variable, denoted y, is regarded as the response, outcome, or dependent variable.

Because the other terms are used less frequently today, we'll use the "predictor" and "response" terms to refer to the variables encountered in this course. The other terms are mentioned only to make you aware of them should you encounter them in other arenas. Simple linear regression gets its adjective "simple," because it concerns the study of only one predictor variable. In contrast, multiple linear regression, which we study later in this course, gets its adjective "multiple," because it concerns the study of two or more predictor variables.

1.12.1 Types of Relationships

Before proceeding, we must clarify what types of relationships we won't study in this course, namely, deterministic (or functional) relationships. Here is an example of a deterministic relationship.

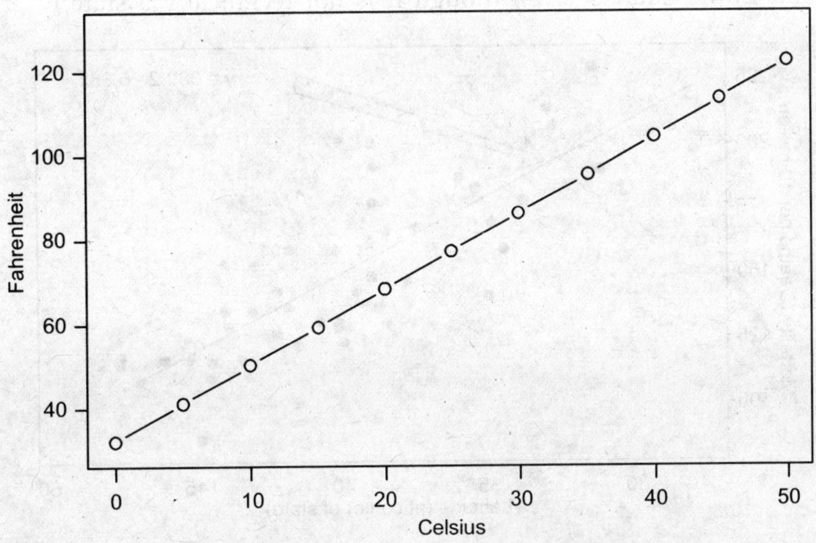

Fig. 1.19: Linear Regression between Fahrenheit vs Celsius plot

Note that the observed (x, y) data points fall directly on a line. As you may remember, the relationship between degrees Fahrenheit and degrees Celsius is known to be:

$$\text{Fahr} = 1.8 \ \text{Cels} + 32$$

That is, if you know the temperature in degrees Celsius, you can use this equation to determine the temperature in degrees Fahrenheit exactly.

Here are some examples of other deterministic relationships that students from previous semesters have shared:

1. Circumference = $\pi \times$ diameter
2. Hooke's Law: $Y = \alpha + \beta X$, where Y = amount of stretch in a spring, and X = applied weight.
3. Ohm's Law: $I = V/r$, where V = voltage applied, r = resistance, and I = current.
4. Boyle's Law: For a constant temperature, $P = \alpha/V$, where P = pressure, α = constant for each gas, and V = volume of gas.

For each of these deterministic relationships, the equation exactly describes the relationship between the two variables. This course does not examine deterministic relationships. Instead, we are interested in statistical relationships, in which the relationship between the variables is not perfect.

Here is an example of a statistical relationship. The response variable y is the mortality due to skin cancer (number of deaths per 10 million people) and the predictor variable x is the latitude (degrees North) at the center of each of 49 states in the U.S. (skincancer.txt) (The data were compiled in the 1950s, so Alaska and Hawaii were not yet states. And, Washington, D.C. is included in the data set even though it is not technically a state.)

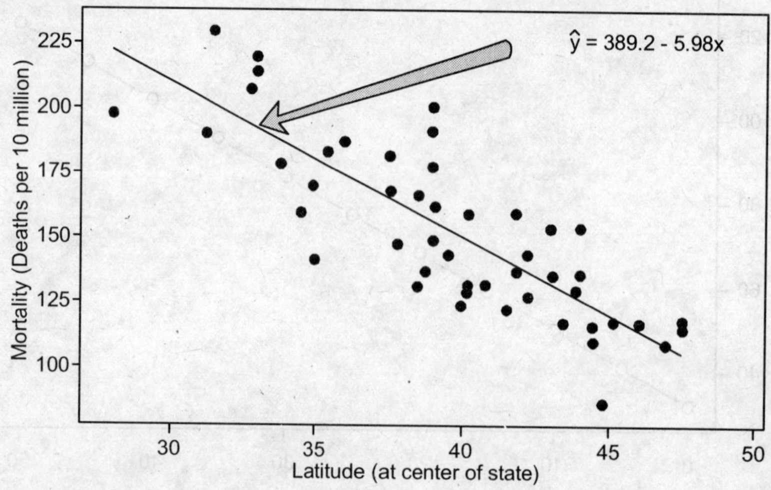

Fig. 1.20: Skin Cancer Vs State Latitude Plot

You might anticipate that if you lived in the higher latitudes of the northern U.S., the less exposed you'd be to the harmful rays of the sun, and therefore, the less risk you'd have of death due to skin cancer. The scatter plot supports such a hypothesis. There appears to be a negative linear relationship between latitude and mortality due to skin cancer, but the relationship is not perfect. Indeed, the plot exhibits some "trend," but it also exhibits some "scatter." Therefore, it is a statistical relationship, not a deterministic one.

Linear Regression using R Programming

To demonstrate How Linear Regression can be applied using R, wem are going to consider two case studies: One Case Study will involve analysis of the algorithm on data created by me and other analysis will be on Iris Dataset.

Case Study 1: Predicting Height of the person based on Weight.

Step 1: Create the data in R

Enter the following code in R-Console:

```
weight<-c(150,180,140,128,133,152,131)
height<-c(62,84,55,52,54,63,53)
```

Step 2: Build Model using lm() function

Again add following code in R-Console:

```
model <- lm(height~weight)
print(model)
```

Step3: Predict Weight based on new Height value using model build in the previous step

Enter the following code in R-Console:

```
test <- data.frame(weight=165)
result <- predict(model,test)
print(result)
       1
72.83109
```

You can see that out model predicted the height of the person as 72.83 for input weight of 165.

We can also see the result in a graphical form using plot function as shown below:

plot (height, weight, col = "red", main = "Example of Linear Regression", abline (lm(weight ~ height)), cex = 1.3, pch = 16, xlab = "Weight", ylab = "Height")

```
R Console
> weight<-c(150,180,140,128,133,152,131)
> height<-c(62,84,55,52,54,63,53)
> model <- lm(height~weight)
> print(model)

Call:
lm(formula = height ~ weight)

Coefficients:
(Intercept)       weight
   -28.7640       0.6157

> test <- data.frame(weight=165)
> result <- predict(model,test)
> print(result)
       1
72.83109
> plot(height,weight,col = "red",main = "Example of Linear Regression",abline(l$
> |
```

Above code shall output following plot :

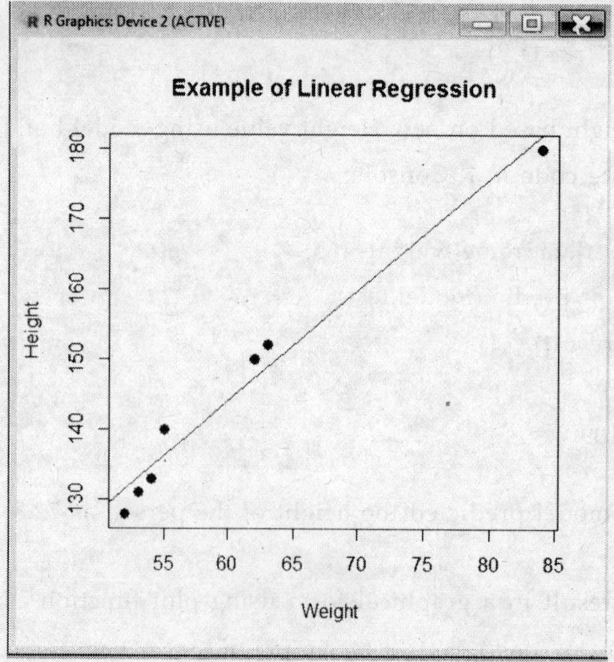

Example 1.8 : Perform Linear Regression on Iris Dataset. To demonstrate the use of Linear Regression in a dataset I am going to consider two variables Petal Length and Petal Width.

Predicted attribute: class of iris plant.

This is an exceedingly simple domain.

This data differs from the data presented in Fishers article (identified by Steve Chadwick, spchadwick '@' espeedaz.net). The 35th sample should be: 4.9,1.1,1.5,0.2,"Iris-setosa" where the error is in the fourth feature. The 38th sample: 4.9,1.6,1.4,0.1,"Iris-setosa" where the errors are in the second and third features.

Step1: Build Linear Regression Model on the Length and Width Column

Enter the following code in R-Console:

```
model.iris <- lm(Petal.Length~Petal.Width, data=iris)
```

Step2: Predicting the Length of Petal based on the Width of the Petal

Enter the following code in R-Console:

```
predict(model.iris, newdata=data.frame(Petal.Width = 0.5))
```

Step3: Plot Graph

Enter the following code in R-Console:

```
plot (iris$Petal.Width, iris$Petal.Length,col = "blue",main = "Example
of Linear Regression on Iris Data",abline(model.iris),cex = 1.3,pch
= 16,xlab = "Petal width",ylab = "Petal Length")
```

```
R Console
> model.iris <- lm(Petal.Length~Petal.Width, data=iris)
> predict(model.iris, newdata=data.frame(Petal.Width=0.5))
       1
2.198528
> plot(iris$Petal.Width, iris$Petal.Length,col = "blue",main = "Example of Line$
> |
```

Output:

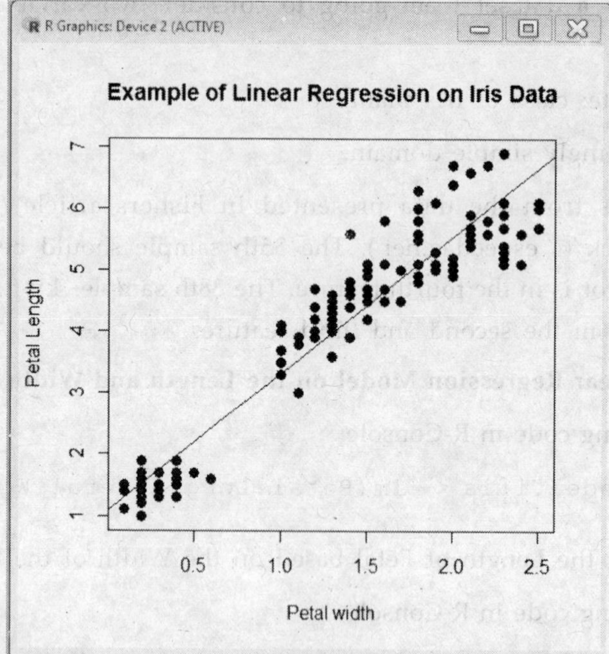

Multiple Regression

Multiple Regression is an extension of Linear Regression technique. In Linear Regression Value of one unknown variable is predicted with one known variable. Extending the capability of Linear Regression, if the value of unknown variable if predicted using values of two or more unknown variable then it is called as Multiple Regression analysis.

Multiple Regression – Mathematical Formula

In multiple regression there are more than one predictor variable and one response variable, relation of the variables is shown below:

$Y = a + b^1x^1 + b^2x^2 + \ldots\ldots\ldots b^nx^n$, Where Y is response, $a\ldots\ldots b^n$ are coefficients and $x^1\ldots\ldots x^n$ are predictor variables.

Multiple Regression using R Programming

For this example on Multiple Regression Analysis using R Programming, I am going to use mtcars dataset and we will see How the Model is built for two and three predictor variables.

Example 1.9: Establishing Relationship between "mpg" as response variable and "disp", "hp" as predictor variables.

Step1: Load the required data

```
data <- mtcars[,c("mpg","disp","hp")]##From this command
we are creating new data variable with all rows and only
required columns
head(data)
```

	mpg	disp	hp
Mazda RX4	21.0	160	110
Mazda RX4 Wag	21.0	160	110
Datsun 710	22.8	108	93
Hornet 4 Drive	21.4	258	110
Hornet Sportabout	18.7	360	175
Valiant	18.1	225	105

Step2: Build Model using lm() function

```
model <- lm(mpg~disp + hp, data = data)
summary(model)
```

As you can see in the summary output shown above, we have got the intercept value which is the value of 'a' in the equation and coefficients of "disp" and "hp" are –0.030346 and –0.024840 respectively. Therefore the regression analysis equation will be:

mpg = 30.735904 + (–0.030346)disp + (–0.024840)hp

Using the above equation we can predict the value of mpg based on disp and hp.

Step3: Predicting the output.

```
predict(model, newdata = data.frame(disp=140, hp=80))
```

Predicted Output Mileage is 24.50022

If you enter the values of disp and hp in the equation derived above you will get the same output.

Plotting the Regression:

```
plot(model)
```

```
> data <- mtcars[,c("mpg","disp","hp")]##From this command we are creating new $
> head(data)
                   mpg disp  hp
Mazda RX4         21.0  160 110
Mazda RX4 Wag     21.0  160 110
Datsun 710        22.8  108  93
Hornet 4 Drive    21.4  258 110
Hornet Sportabout 18.7  360 175
Valiant           18.1  225 105
> model <- lm(mpg~disp+hp, data=data)
> summary(model)

Call:
lm(formula = mpg ~ disp + hp, data = data)

Residuals:
    Min      1Q  Median      3Q     Max
-4.7945 -2.3036 -0.8246  1.8582  6.9363
```

```
Coefficients:
             Estimate Std. Error t value Pr(>|t|)
(Intercept) 30.735904   1.331566  23.083  < 2e-16 ***
disp        -0.030346   0.007405  -4.098 0.000306 ***
hp          -0.024840   0.013385  -1.856 0.073679 .
Signif. codes:  0 '***' 0.001 '**' 0.01 '*' 0.05 '.' 0.1 ' ' 1

Residual standard error: 3.127 on 29 degrees of freedom
Multiple R-squared:  0.7482,    Adjusted R-squared:  0.7309
F-statistic: 43.09 on 2 and 29 DF,  p-value: 2.062e-09

> predict(model, newdata = data.frame(disp=140, hp=80))
       1
24.50022
> plot(model)
Waiting to confirm page change...
Waiting to confirm page change...
Waiting to confirm page change...
Waiting to confirm page change...
> |
```

Output:

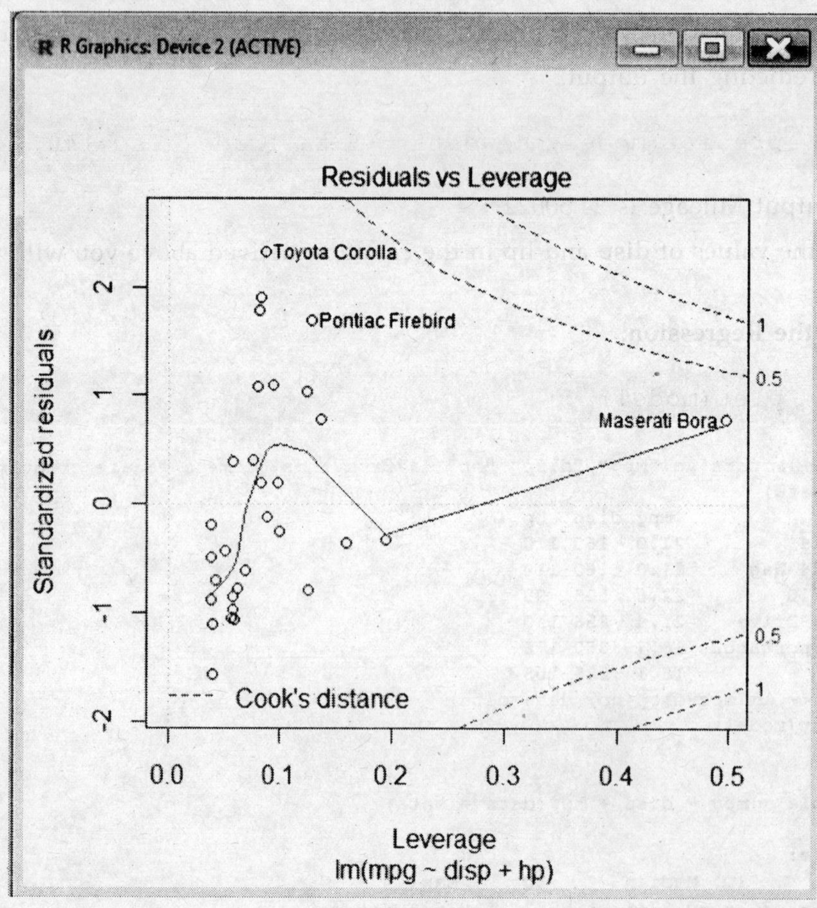

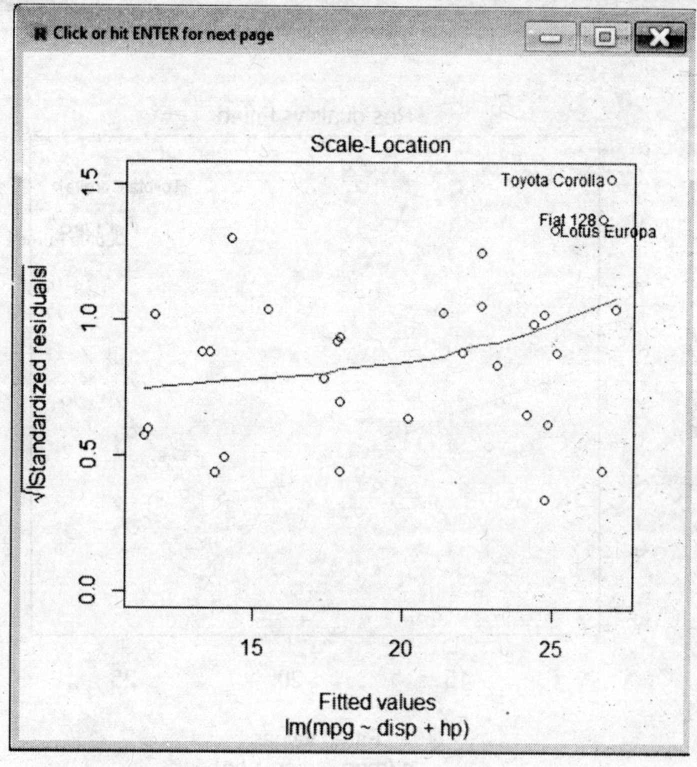
Click or hit ENTER for next page
Scale-Location
Toyota Corolla
Fiat 128
Lotus Europa
√|Standardized residuals|
Fitted values
lm(mpg ~ disp + hp)

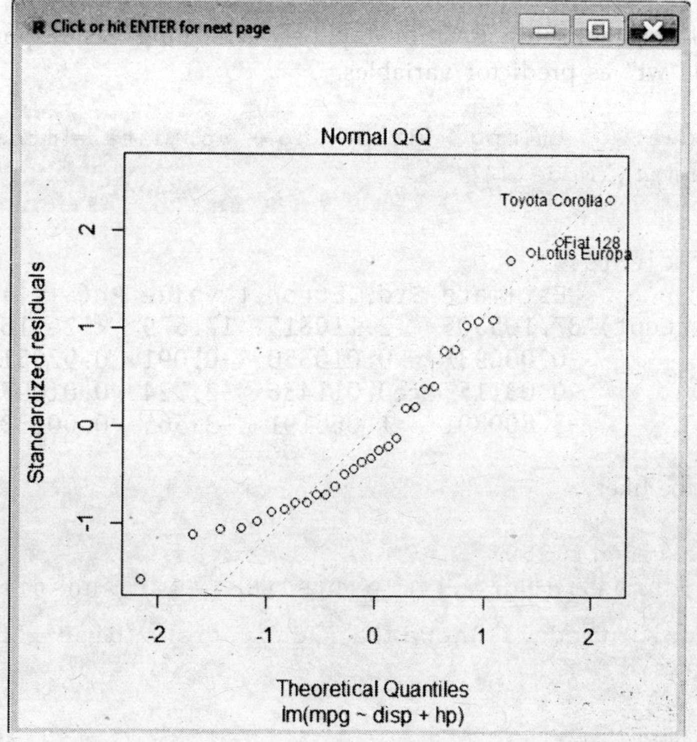
Click or hit ENTER for next page
Normal Q-Q
Toyota Corolla
Fiat 128
Lotus Europa
Standardized residuals
Theoretical Quantiles
lm(mpg ~ disp + hp)

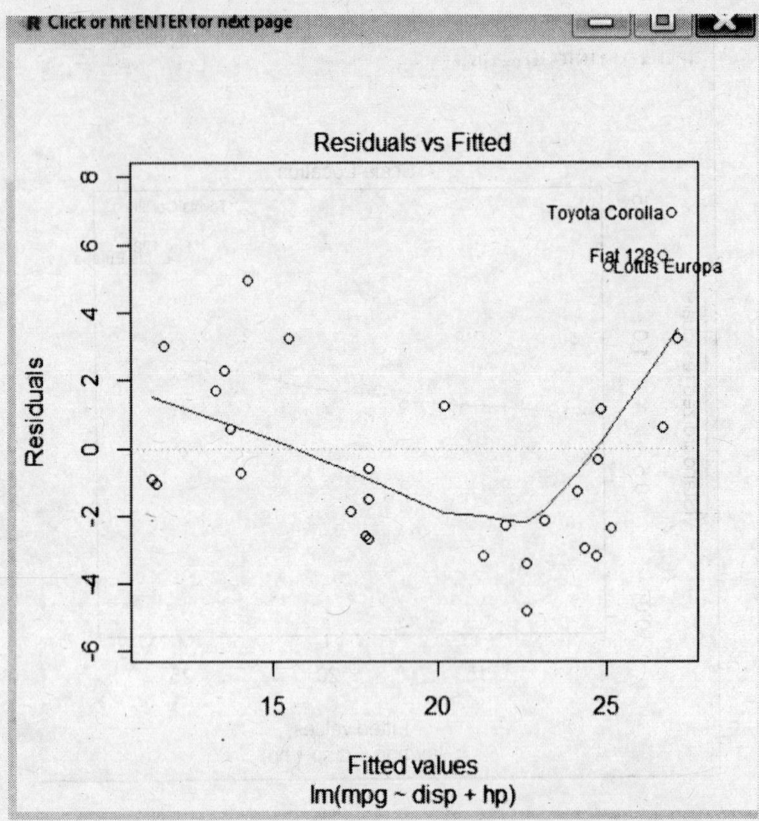

Example 1.10 : Establishing Relationship between "mpg" as response variable and "disp", "hp" and "wt" as predictor variables.

```
model1 <- lm(mpg ~ disp + hp + wt, data = mtcars)
summary(model1)
```

```
Coefficients:
             Estimate Std. Error t value Pr(>|t|)
(Intercept) 37.105505   2.110815  17.579  < 2e-16 ***
disp        -0.000937   0.010350  -0.091  0.92851
hp          -0.031157   0.011436  -2.724  0.01097 *
wt          -3.800891   1.066191  -3.565  0.00133 **
```

Equation will be like:

```
mpg = 37.105505
+ (-0.000937)disp + (-0.031157)hp + (-1.800891)wt
predict(model1, newdata = data.frame(disp = 160, hp = 100,
wt = 2.5))
```

Predicted Output Mileage is 24.3377

How to Compare Different Model on Regression Analysis

To compare model, use anova() function.

```
anova(model, model1)
```

R Console

```
> model1 <- lm(mpg~disp+hp+wt, data=mtcars)
> summary(model1)

Call:
lm(formula = mpg ~ disp + hp + wt, data = mtcars)

Residuals:
   Min     1Q Median     3Q    Max
-3.891 -1.640 -0.172  1.061  5.861

Coefficients:
             Estimate Std. Error t value Pr(>|t|)
(Intercept) 37.105505   2.110815  17.579  < 2e-16 ***
disp        -0.000937   0.010350  -0.091  0.92851
hp          -0.031157   0.011436  -2.724  0.01097 *
wt          -3.800891   1.066191  -3.565  0.00133 **
---
Signif. codes:  0 '***' 0.001 '**' 0.01 '*' 0.05 '.' 0.1 ' ' 1

Residual standard error: 2.639 on 28 degrees of freedom
Multiple R-squared:  0.8268,     Adjusted R-squared:  0.8083
F-statistic: 44.57 on 3 and 28 DF,  p-value: 8.65e-11

> predict(model1, newdata = data.frame(disp=160, hp=100, wt=2.5))
      1
24.3377
> anova(model, model1)
Analysis of Variance Table

Model 1: mpg ~ disp + hp
Model 2: mpg ~ disp + hp + wt
  Res.Df    RSS Df Sum of Sq      F   Pr(>F)
1     29 283.49
2     28 194.99  1    88.503 12.709 0.001331 **
---
Signif. codes:  0 '***' 0.001 '**' 0.01 '*' 0.05 '.' 0.1 ' ' 1
> |
```

1.12.2 Best Fitting Line

Since we are interested in summarizing the trend between two quantitative variables, the natural question arises—"what is the best fitting line?" At some point in your education, you were probably shown a scatter plot of (x, y) data and were asked to draw the "most appropriate" line through the data. Even if you weren't, you can try it now on a set of heights (x) and weights (y) of 10 students as given below as a sample. Looking at the plot below, which line—the solid line or the dashed line—do you think best summarizes the trend between height and weight?

Ht (inches)	wt (pounds)
63	127
64	121
66	142
69	157
69	162
71	156
71	169
72	165
73	181
75	208

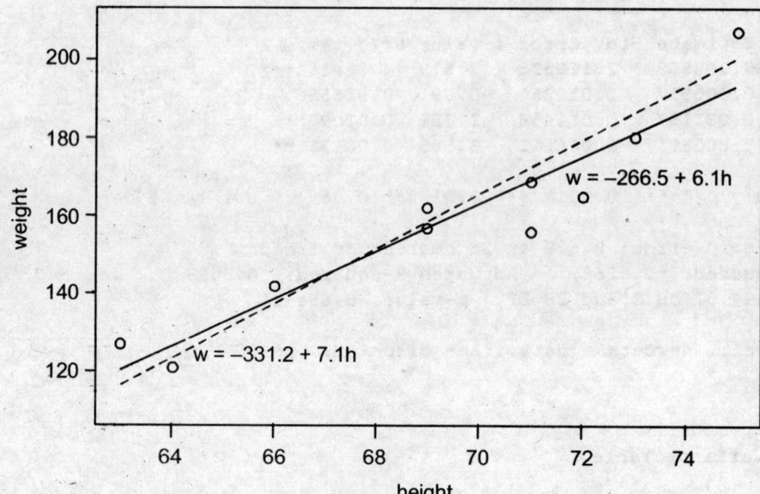

Fig. 1.21: Trying to plot best fitted line

Let us consider the equation for best Fitting line:

The equation for the best fiting line is.

$$y_1 = b_0 + b_1x_i$$

Where

y_i denotes the observed response for experimental unit t

x_1 denotes the predictor value for experimental unit i

y_i is the predicted response (or fitted value) for experimental unit i

Then,

Ancdentally, recall that an 'experimental unit' is the object or person on which the measurment is made. In our height and weight example the experimental units are students.

Let's my cut the notation on our example with the trend summarized by the line u = –266.53 + 6.1376 h. (Note that this line is just a more precise version of the alove solid line w= –266.5 + 6.1h) The first data point in the list indicates that student 1 is 63 inches tall and weighs 127 pounds. That is x_1 = 63 and y_1 = 127. Do your see this point on the plor? If we know this student's height but not his or her weight we could use the equation of the line to predict his or her weight. We'd predict the student's weight to be 266.53 + 6.1376(63) or 120.1 pounds. That is, y_1 = 120. Clearly, our prediction wouldn't be perfectly correct—if has some 'prediction error' (or 'resdual error'). In fact, the size of its prediction error is 127-120.1 or 6.9 pounds.

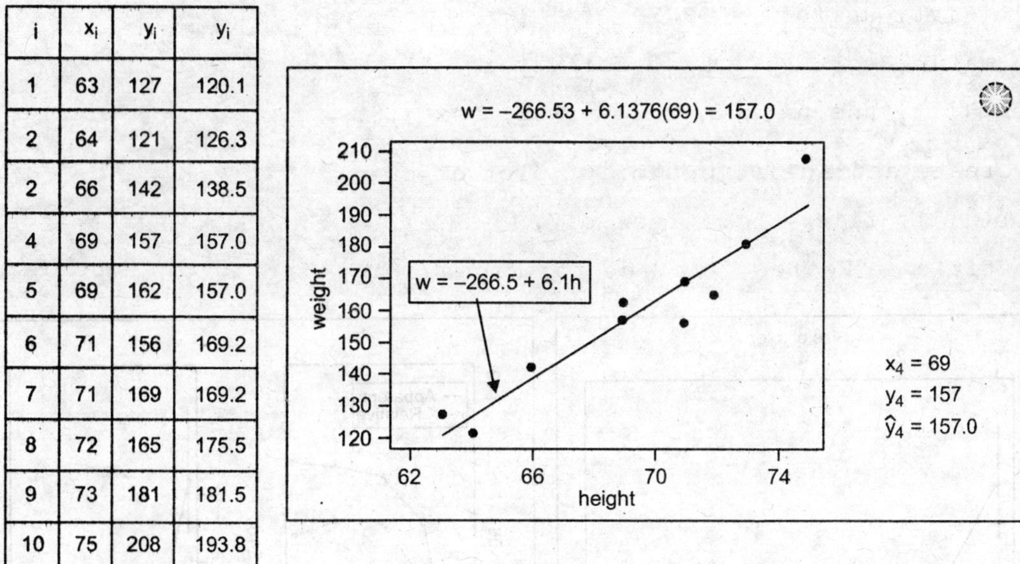

i	x_i	y_i	y_i
1	63	127	120.1
2	64	121	126.3
2	66	142	138.5
4	69	157	157.0
5	69	162	157.0
6	71	156	169.2
7	71	169	169.2
8	72	165	175.5
9	73	181	181.5
10	75	208	193.8

Fig. 1.22: Prediction Error

From above we can realise that the size of the prediction error depends on the data point. If we didn't know the weight of student 5, the equation of the line would predict *his or her* weight to be –266.53 + 6.1376(69) or 157 pounds. The size of the prediction error here is 162-157, or 5 pounds.

Regression Tree example

In this example we will predict car mileage from price, country, reliability, and car type. The data frame is **cu.summary**.

```
# Regression Tree Example
library(rpart)

# grow tree
fit <- rpart(Mileage~Price + Country + Reliability + Type,
   method="anova", data=cu.summary)
```

```
printcp(fit) # display the results
plotcp(fit) # visualize cross-validation results
summary(fit) # detailed summary of splits
# create additional plots
par(mfrow = c(1,2)) # two plots on one page
rsq.rpart(fit) # visualize cross-validation results
# plot tree
plot(fit, uniform = TRUE,
   main="Regression Tree for Mileage ")
text(fit, use.n=TRUE, all = TRUE, cex =.8)
# create attractive postcript plot of tree
post(fit, file = "c:/tree2.ps",
   title = "Regression Tree for Mileage ")
```

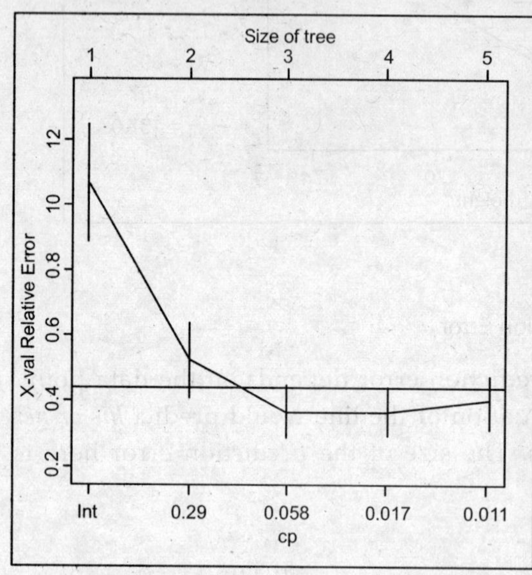

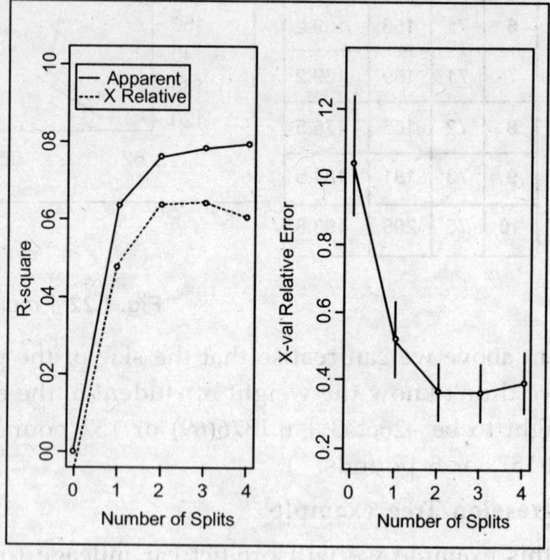


```
# prune the tree
pfit<- prune(fit, cp=0.01160389) # from cptable

# plot the pruned tree
plot(pfit, uniform=TRUE,
  main="Pruned Regression Tree for Mileage")
text(pfit, use.n=TRUE, all=TRUE, cex=.8)
```

```
post(pfit, file = "c:/ptree2.ps",
  title = "Pruned Regression Tree for Mileage")
```

It turns out that this produces the same tree as the original.

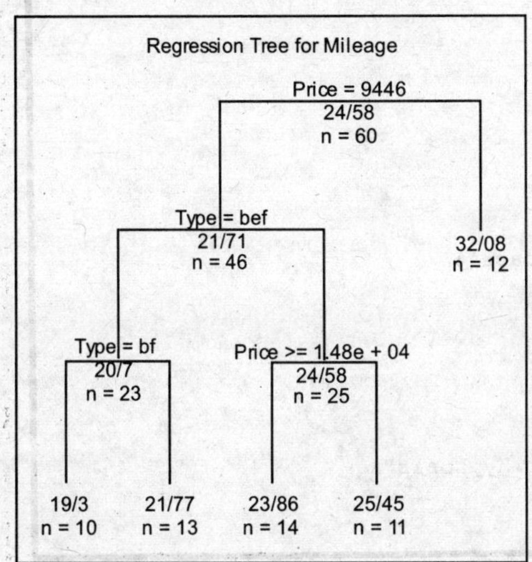

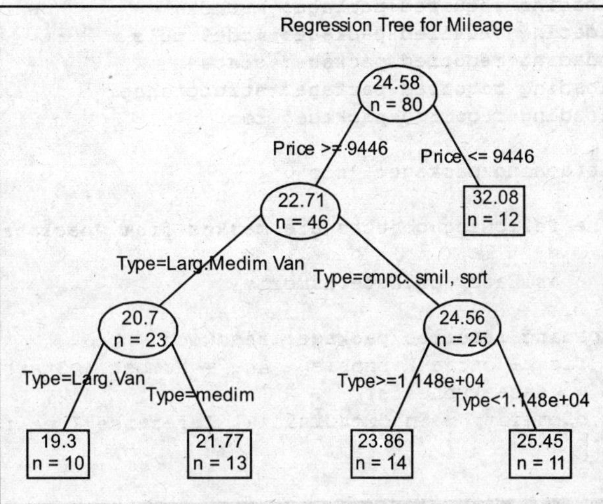

Conditional inference trees via party

The party package provides nonparametric regression trees for nominal, ordinal, numeric, censored, and multivariate responses. party: A laboratory for recursive partitioning, provides details.

You can create a regression or classification tree via the function

ctree(*formula*, data=)

The type of tree created will depend on the outcome variable (nominal factor, ordered factor, numeric, etc.). Tree growth is based on statistical stopping rules, so pruning should not be required.

The previous two examples are re-analyzed below.

```
# Conditional Inference Tree for Kyphosis
library(party)
fit <- ctree(Kyphosis ~ Age + Number + Start,
  data=kyphosis)
plot(fit, main="Conditional Inference Tree for Kyphosis")
```

R Console

```
> # Conditional Inference Tree for Kyphosis
> library(party)
Loading required package: grid
Loading required package: mvtnorm
Loading required package: modeltools
Loading required package: stats4
Loading required package: strucchange
Loading required package: zoo

Attaching package: 'zoo'

The following objects are masked from 'package:base':

    as.Date, as.Date.numeric

Loading required package: sandwich
> fit <- ctree(Kyphosis ~ Age + Number + Start,
+    data=kyphosis)
> plot(fit, main="Conditional Inference Tree for Kyphosis")
> |
```

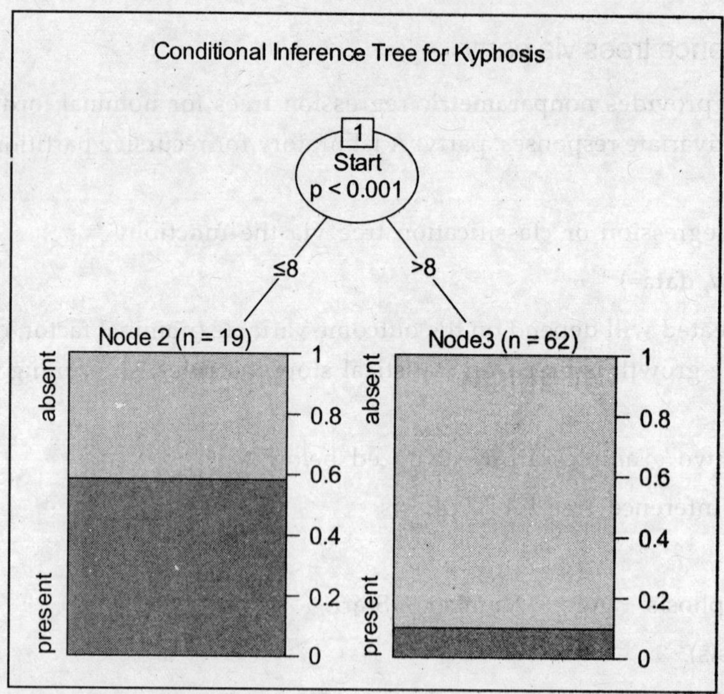


```
# Conditional Inference Tree for Mileage
library(party)
fit2 <- ctree(Mileage~Price + Country + Reliability + Type,
   data=na.omit(cu.summary))
```

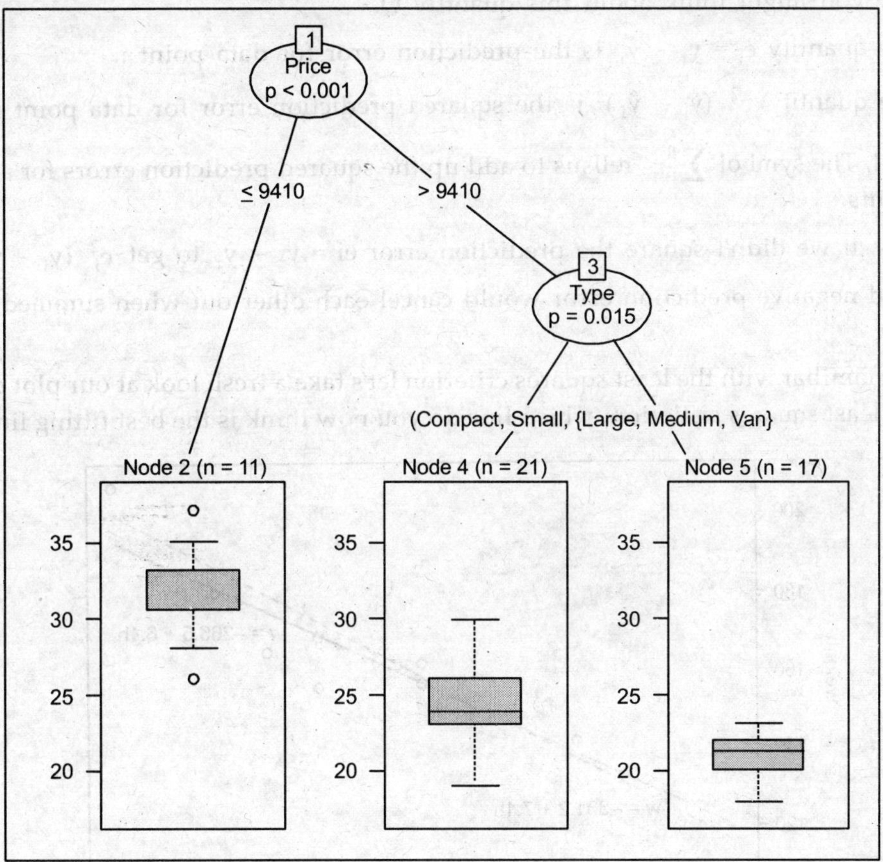

1.12.3 Least Squares Criterion

In general, when we use $\hat{y}_i = b_0 + b_i x_i$ to predict the actual response y_i, we make a prediction error (or residual error) of size:

$$e_i = y_i - \hat{y}_i$$

A line thatfits the data 'best' will be one for which then prediction errors—one for each abserved data point — are as small as possible in some overall sense. One way to achieve this goal is to invoke the 'least squares criterion' which says to 'minimize the sum of the squared prediction errors.' That is:

- The equation of the best fitting line is $\hat{y}_i = b_0 + b_1 x_i$
- We just need to find the values b_0 that make the sum of the squared prediction errors the smallest it can be.
- That is we need to find the values b_0 and b_1 that minimize:

$$Q = \sum_{t=1}^{n} (y_i - \hat{y}_i)^2$$

Here's how you might think about this quantity Q.

- The quantity $e_i = y_i - \hat{y}_i$ is the prediction error for data point i.
- The quantity e_i^2 $(y_i - \hat{y}_i)^2$ is the squared prediction error for data point i.
- And, The symbol $\sum_{i=1}^{n}$ tellsus to add up the squared prediction errors for all n data points.

Incidentally, if we didn't square the prediction error ei = yi – $\hat{y}_i$ to get e_i^2 $(y_i - \hat{y}_i)^2$, the positive and negative prediction error would cancel each other out when summed, always yielding 0.

Now, being familiar with the least squares criterion let's take a fresh look at our plot again. In light of the least squares critierion, which line do you now think is the best fitting line?

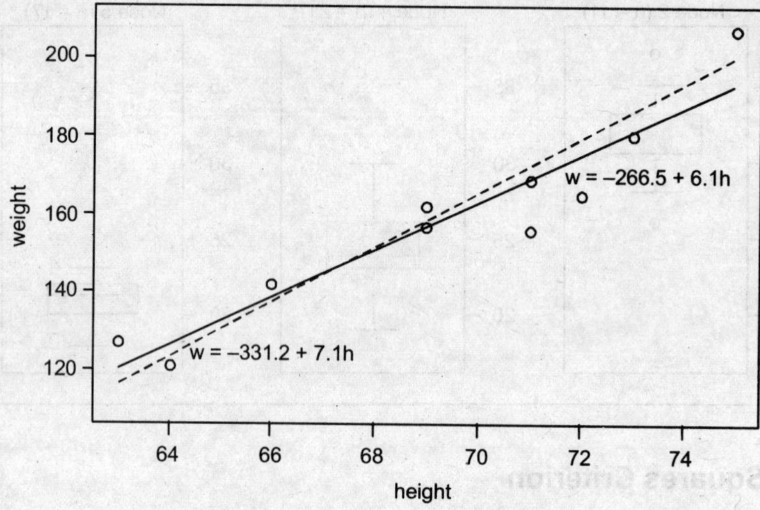

Fig. 1.23: Finding out bestfitting Line with Least Squares Criterion

1.12.4 Implementation of Least Squares Criterion

Let explore how we did! The following two side-by-side tables illustrate the implementation of the least squares criterion for the two lines up for consideration — the dashed line and the solid line.

Let us find out based on the least squares criterion, which equation best summarizes the data? The sum of the squared prediction errors is 766.5 for the dashed line, while it is only 597.4 for the solid line. Therefore, of the two lines, the solid line, w = –266.53 + 6.1376h, best summarizes the data. But, is this equation guaranteed to be the best fitting line of all of the possible lines we didn't even consider? Of course not!

The Least Squares Method is a statistical procedure for using sample data to find the value of the estimated regression equation. The Least Squares Method was proposed by Carl Friedrich Gauss, who was born in the year 1777 and died in 1855. The Least Squares Method is still widely used.

w = -331.2 + 7.1 h (the dashed line)						**w = -266.53 + 6.1376 h** (the solid line)					
i	x_i	y_i	$\hat{y}_i$	$(y_i - \hat{y}_i)$	$(y_i - \hat{y}_i)^2$	i	x_i	y_i	$\hat{y}_i$	$(y_i - \hat{y}_i)$	$(y_i - \hat{y}_i)^2$
1	63	127	116.1	10.9	118.81	1	63	127	120.139	6.8612	47.076
2	64	121	123.2	-2.2	4.84	2	64	121	126.276	-5.2764	27.840
3	66	142	137.4	4.6	21.16	3	66	142	138.552	3.4484	11.891
4	69	157	158.7	-1.7	2.89	4	69	157	156.964	0.0356	0.001
5	69	162	158.7	3.3	10.89	5	69	162	156.964	5.0356	25.357
6	71	156	172.9	-16.9	285.61	6	71	156	169.240	-13.2396	175.287
7	71	169	172.9	-3.9	15.21	7	71	169	169.240	-0.2396	0.057
8	72	165	180.0	-15.0	225.00	8	72	165	175.377	-10.3772	107.686
9	73	181	187.1	-6.1	37.21	9	73	181	181.515	-0.5148	0.265
10	75	208	201.3	6.7	44.89	10	75	208	193.790	14.2100	201.924
					766.5						**597.4**

1.12.5 Least Square Regression Line

If we used the above approach for finding the equation of the line that minimizes the sum of the squared prediction errors, we'd have our work cut out for us. We'd have to implement the above procedure for an infinite number of possible lines that is clearly, an impossible task! Fortunately, somebody has done some dirty work for us by figuring out formulas for the **intercept** b_0 and the **slope** b_1 for the equation of the line that minimizes the sum of the squared prediction errors.

The formulas are determined using methods of calculus. We minimize the equation for the sum of the squared prediction errors:

The formulas are determined using methods of calculus. We minimize the equation for the sum of the squared prediction errors:

$$Q = \sum_{i=1}^{n} (y_i - (b_0 + b_1 x_1))^2$$

(that is, take the derivative with respect to b_0 and b_1, set to 0, and solve for b_0 and b_1) and get the 'Least squares estimates' for b_0 and b_1: $b_0 = \bar{y} - b_1 \bar{x}$ and:

$$b_1 = \frac{\sum_{i-1}^{n} (x_i - \bar{x})(y_i - \bar{y})}{\sum_{i-1}^{n} (x_i - \bar{x})^2}$$

Because the formulas for b_0 and b_1 are derived using the least squares criterion, the resulting equation — $\hat{y} = b_0 + b_1x_i$ – is often refered to as the 'least squares regresslon line.' or simply the 'least squares line'. It is also sometimes called the 'estimated regression equation' Incidentally. note that in deriving the above formulas, we made no assumptions about the data other than that they follow some sort of linear trend.

We cab see from these formulas that the least squares line passes through $(\bar{x}, \bar{y})$, since when x = x, then $y = b_0 + b_i\bar{x} = \bar{y} - b_1\bar{x} + b_1\bar{x} = \bar{y}$.

In practics, you won't really need to worry about the formulas for b_0 and b_1. Instead, you are going to let statistical software. such as minitab, find least squares lines for you. But, we can still learn something from the formulas — for b_1 in particular.

If you study the formula for the slope b_1:

$$b_1 = \frac{\sum_{i-1}^{n}(x_i - \bar{x})(y_i - \bar{y})}{\sum_{i-1}^{n}(x_i - \bar{x})^2}$$

You see that the denominator is necessrily positive since it only involves sunming positive terms. Therefore, the sign of the slope b_1 is dolely determined by the mumerator. The numerator tellsus, for each data, to sum up the product of twodistances—the distance of the x-value from the mean of all of the x-values and the distance of the y-value from the mean of all of the y-values.

1.12.6 Uses of *Linear Regression*

Three major uses for regression analysis are

(1) determining the strength of predictors,

(2) forecasting an effect, and

(3) trend forecasting.

First, the regression might be used to identify the strength of the effect that the independent variable(s) have on a dependent variable. Typical questions are what is the strength of relationship between dose and effect, sales and marketing spending, or age and income.

Second, it can be used to forecast effects or impact of changes. That is, the regression analysis helps us to understand how much the dependent variable changes with a change in one or more independent variables. A typical question is, "how much additional sales income do I get for each additional $1000 spent on marketing?"

Third, regression analysis predicts trends and future values. The regression analysis can be used to get point estimates. A typical question is, "what will the price of gold be in 6 months?"

1.13 LOGISTIC REGRESSION

Linear regression predictions are continuous values (rainfall in cm),logistic regression predictions are discrete values (whether a student passed/failed) after applying a transformation function.

Logistic regression is best suited for binary classification (datasets where y = 0 or 1, where 1 denotes the default class. Example: In predicting whether an event will occur or not, the event that it occurs is classified as 1. In predicting whether a person will be sick or not, the sick instances are denoted as 1). It is named after the transformation function used in it, called the logistic function $h(x) = 1/ (1 + e^{x})$, which is an S-shaped curve.

In logistic regression, the output is in the form of probabilities of the default class (unlike linear regression, where the output is directly produced). As it is a probability, the output lies in the range of 0 – 1. The output (y-value) is generated by log transforming the x-value, using the logistic function $h(x) = 1/ (1 + e^{-x})$. A threshold is then applied to force this probability into a binary classification.

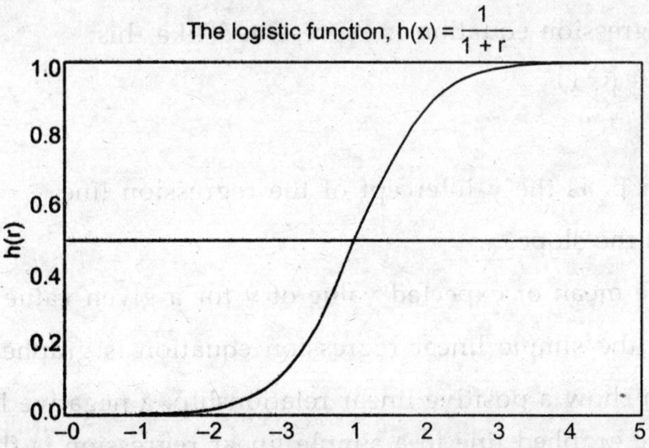

Fig. 1.24: Logistic Regression to determine if a tumour is malignant or benign. Classified as malignant if the probability h(x)>= 0.5.

In Figure 1.26, to determine whether a tumour is malignant or not, the default variable is y=1 (tumour= malignant) ; the x variable could be a measurement of the tumour, such as the size of the tumour. As shown in the figure, the logistic function transforms the x-value of the various instances of the dataset, into the range of 0 to 1. If the probability crosses the threshold of 0.5 (shown by the horizontal line), the tumour is classified as malignant.

The logistic regression equation $P(x) = e^\wedge(b_0 + b_1{}^*x) / (1 + e^\wedge(b_0 + b_1{}^*x))$ can be transformed into $\ln(p(x) / 1 - p(x)) = b_0 + b1^*x$.

The goal of logistic regression is to use the training data to find the values of coefficients b_0 and b_1 such that it will minimize the error between the predicted outcome and the actual outcome. These coefficients are estimated using the technique of Maximum Likelihood Estimation.

1.14 LINEAR REGRESSION MODELS

Linear regression models are used to show or predict the relationship between two variables or factors. The factor that is being predicted (the factor that the equation solves for) is called the dependent variable. The factors that are used to predict the value of the dependent variable are called the independent variables.

Good data does not always tell the complete story. Regression analysis is commonly used in research as it establishes that a correlation exists between variables. In simple linear regression, each observation consists of two values. One value is for the dependent variable and one value is for the independent variable.

1.14.1 Multiple Regression Analysis

When two or more independent variables are used in regression analysis, the model is no longer a simple linear one.

(a) Simple Linear Regression Model

The simple linear regression equation is represented like this:

$$E(y) = (\beta_0 + \beta_1 x)$$

Where

Parameter β_0 is the y intercept of the regression line.

And β_1 is the slope.

E(y) is the mean or expected value of y for a given value of x.

Needless to say that the simple linear regression equation is graphed as a straight line.

A regression line can show a positive linear relationship, a negative linear relationship, or no relationship. If the graphed line in a simple linear regression is flat (not sloped), there is no relationship between the two variables. If the regression line slopes upward with the lower end of the line at the y intercept (axis) of the graph, and the upper end of line extending upward into the graph field, away from the x intercept (axis) a positive linear relationship exists. If the regression line slopes downward with the upper end of the line at the y intercept (axis) of the graph, and the lower end of line extending downward into the graph field, toward the x intercept (axis) a negative linear relationship exists.

The graph of the estimated simple regression equation is called the ***estimated regression line.***

Important Note: Regression analysis is not used to interpret cause-and-effect relationships between variables. Regression analysis can, however, indicate how variables are related or to what extent variables are associated with each other.

In so doing, regression analysis tends to make salient relationships that warrant a knowledgeable researcher taking a closer look.

There are several types of linear regression analyses available to researchers.

(1) Simple linear regression: 1 dependent variable (interval or ratio), 1 independent variable (interval or ratio or dichotomous)

(2) Multiple linear regression: 1 dependent variable (interval or ratio), 2 + independent variables (interval or ratio or dichotomous)

(3) Logistic regression: 1 dependent variable (dichotomous), 2 + independent variable(s) (interval or ratio or dichotomous)

(4) Ordinal regression 1 dependent variable (ordinal), 1 + independent variable(s) (nominal or dichotomous)

(5) Multinominal regression: 1 dependent variable (nominal), 1 + independent variable(s) (interval or ratio or dichotomous)

(6) Discriminant analysis: 1 dependent variable (nominal), 1 + independent variable(s) (interval or ratio)

When selecting the model for the analysis, an important consideration is model fitting. Adding independent variables to a linear regression model will always increase the explained variance of the model (typically expressed as R^2). However, overfitting can occur by adding too many variables to the model, which reduces model generalizability. Occam's razor describes the problem extremely well – a simple model is usually preferable to a more complex model. Statistically, if a model includes a large number of variables, some of the variables will be statistically significant due to chance alone

1.15 SUPPORT VECTOR MACHINE (SVM)

SVM is a supervised machine learning algorithm which can be used for both **classification** or **regression** challenges. However, it is mostly used in classification problems. In this *algorithm*, we plot each data item as a point in *n-dimensional space* (where n is number of features you have) with the value of each feature being the value of a particular coordinate. Then, we perform *classification* by finding the *hyper-plane* (in two dimensional space it is a classifier line, mostly strait) that differentiate the two classes (groups of data) very well (vide Figure 1.25).

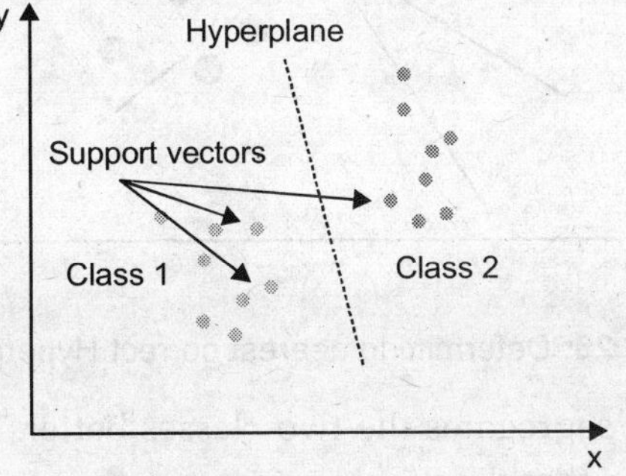

Fig. 1.25: Support Vectors

Support Vectors are simply the co-ordinates of individual observation. Support Vector Machine is a frontier which best segregates the two classes (hyper-plane/ line).

Fig. 1.20 describes the process of segregating the two classes with a hyper-plane.

You can use a support vector machine (SVM) when your data has exactly two classes. An SVM classifies data by finding the best hyperplane that separates all data points of one class from those of the other class. The *best* hyperplane for an SVM means the one with the largest *margin* between the two classes. Margin means the maximal width of the slab parallel to the hyperplane that has no interior data points.

The *support vectors* are the data points that are closest to the separating hyperplane; these points are on the boundary of the slab. The following figure illustrates these definitions, with + indicating data points of type 1, and – indicating data points of type –1.

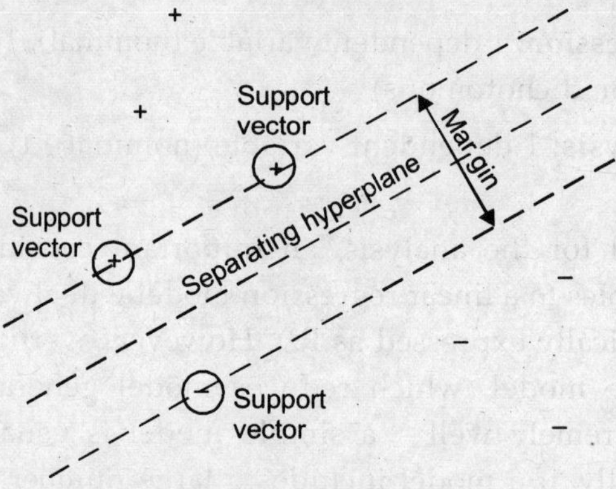

1.15.1 Determining the right hyper-plane

Case-1: Here, we have three hyper-planes (A, B and C) segregation two distinct data groups to classification star and circle.

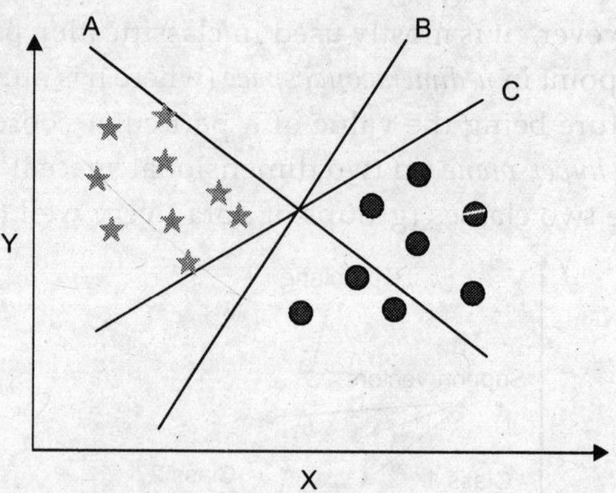

Fig. 1.26: Determining nearest correct Hyperplane

Select the hyper-plane which segregates the two classes better. In this scenario, hyper-plane "B" is best option among the three.

Case-2: In this case three hyper-planes (A, B and C) are seemingly segregating the classes well, and we have to identify the right hyper-plane?

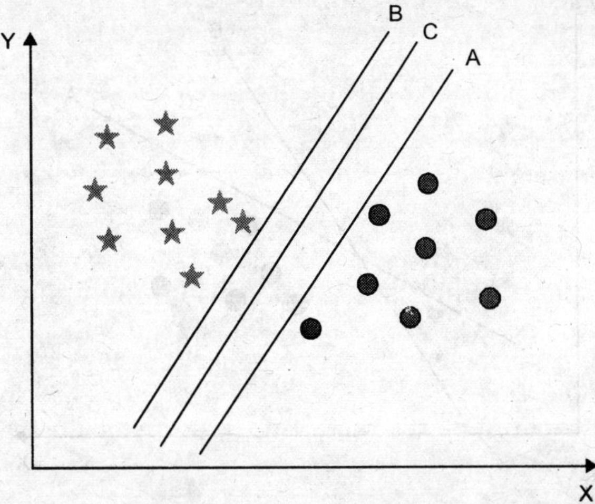

Fig. 1.27: Determining best among bettert Hyperplanes

We have to use technique of optimizing the distances between group of points of either of the class and classifier hyperplane This distance is called as **Margin**. Let's look at Figure 1.28.

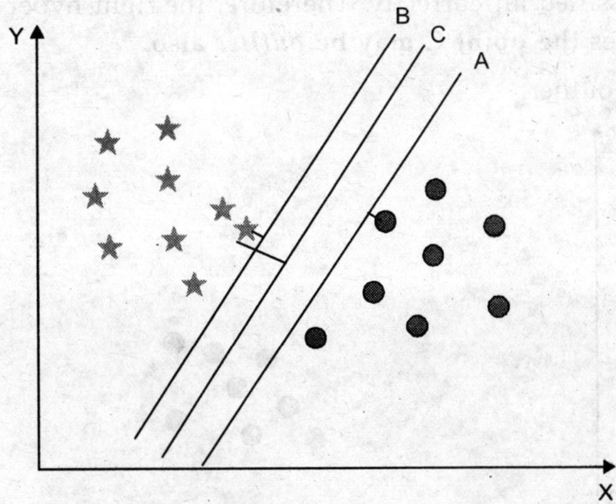

Fig. 1.28: Margin between a point (i.e. a data instance) Desired Hyperplane

From figure 1.28 we can realise that you the margin for hyper-plane C is high as compared to both A and B. Hence, the right hyper-plane is C. Another lightning reason for selecting the hyper-plane with higher margin is *robustness*. If we select a hyper-plane having low margin then there is high chance of miss-classification.

Case-3: Figure 1.39

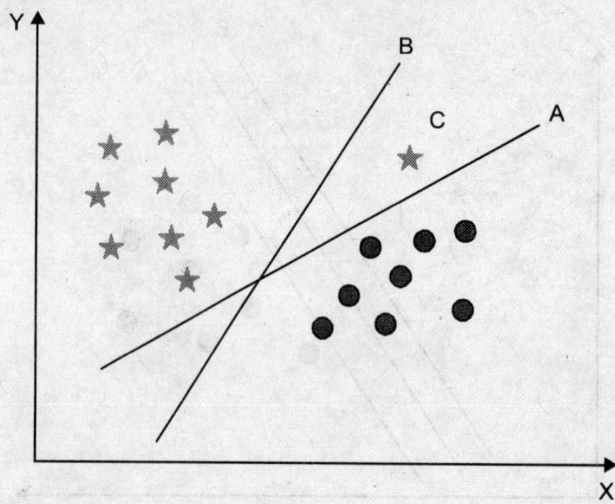

Fig. 1.29: Choosing the Hyperplane after correct data group classification

Adopt the procedure as earlier but carefully to identify the right hyper-plane Some of us may tend to select the hyp er-plane **B** as it has higher margin compared to **A.** But, here is the catch, SVM selects the hyper-plane which classifies the classes accurately prior to maximizing *margin*. Here, hyper-plane B has a classification error as it forgot to include point C, and A has classified all correctly. Therefore, the right hyper-plane is **A. But keep in mind that some times the point C may be *outlier* also.**

Case-4 : Example with outlier

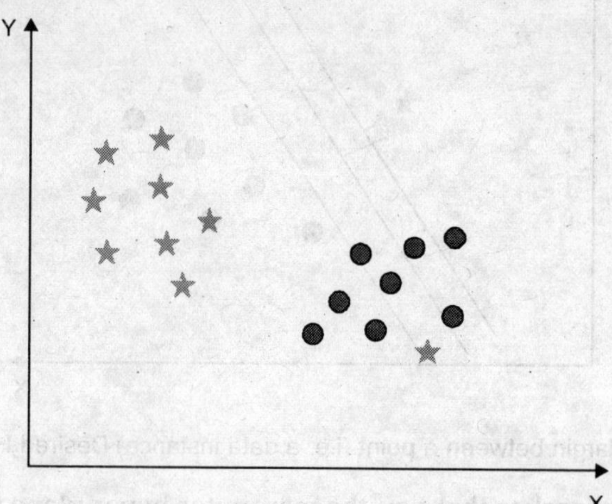

Fig. 1.30: Case with an outlier posing problem of misclassification

In Figure 1.30 the programmer may be unable to segregate the two classes using a straight line, as one of star lies in the territory of other(circle) class as an *outlier*.

One star at other end is like an outlier for star class. SVM has a feature to ignore outliers and find the hyper-plane that has maximum margin. AS such we can say, SVM is robust to outliers.

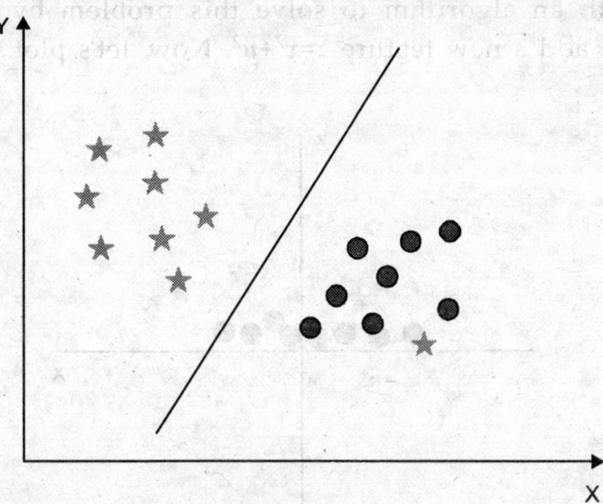

Fig. 1.31: SVM rejects the outlierand finds the appropriate hyperplane classifier

Case-5: Inter mixing classes of Data Set

In the scenario of Figure 1.31, the user is apparently at problem in putting up the linear hyper-plane between the two classes, so how does SVM classify these two classes? Till now, we have only looked at the linear hyper-plane.

Classifying data is a common task in machine learning. Suppose some given data points each belong to one of two classes, and the goal is to decide which class a new Data point will be in. In the case of support vector machines, a data point is viewed as a *p*-dimensional vector (a list of *p* numbers), and we want to know whether we can separate such points with *(p-1)*-dimensional hyperplane. This is called a **linear classifier.**

There are many hyperplanes that might classify the data. One reasonable choice as the best hyperplane is the one that represents the largest separation, or margin, between the two classes. So we choose the hyperplane so that the distance from it to the nearest data point on each side is maximized. If such a hyperplane exists, it is known as the maximum-margin hyperplane and the linear classifier it defines is known as a maximum margin classifier; or equivalently, the perceptron of optimal stability.

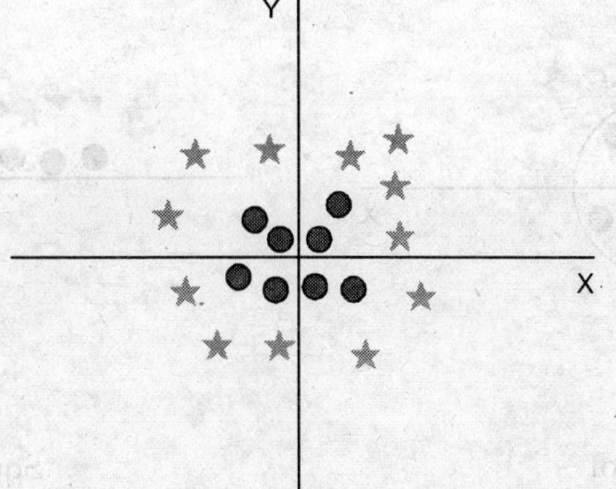

Fig. 1.32: Intermixing Classification

SVM is provided with an algorithm to solve this problem by introducing additional feature. Here, we will add a new feature $z=x^2+y^2$. Now, let's plot the data points on axis x and z:

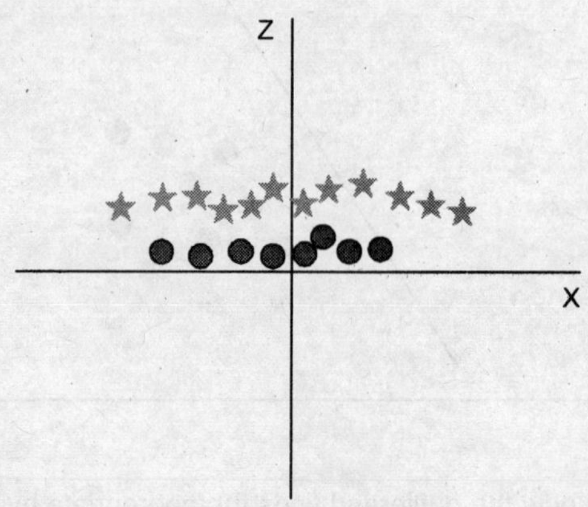

Fig. 1.33: Z-Plane method with square values

In above plot, points to consider are:

1. All values for z would be positive always because z is the squared sum of both x and y
2. In the original plot, red circles appear close to the origin of x and y axes, leading to lower value of z and star relatively away from the origin result to higher value of z.

In SVM, it is easy to have a linear hyper-plane between these two classes. SVM has a technique called the kernel trick. These are functions which takes low dimensional input space and transform it to a higher dimensional space i.e. it converts not separable problem to separable problem, these functions are called kernels. It is mostly useful in non-linear separation problem. Simply put, it does some extremely complex data transformations, then find out the process to separate the data based on the labels or outputs you've defined.

When we look at the hyper-plane in original input space it looks like a circle:

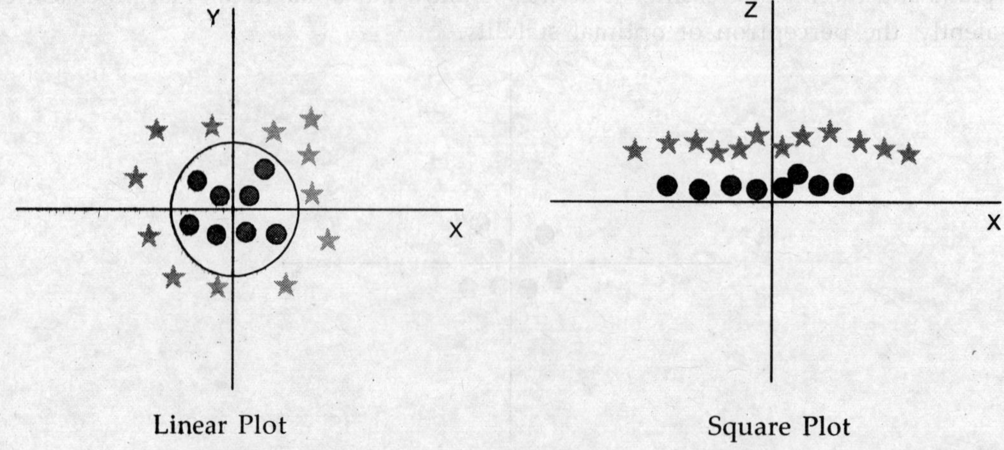

Fig. 1.34: Comparing Z-Plane method with square values

Now, let's look at the methods to apply SVM algorithm in a data science challenge.

Support Vector Machines (SVMs, as a part of machine learning, also support vector networks) are supervised learning models with associated learning algorithms that analyze data used for classification and regression analysis. Given a set of training examples say a cluster of data of one group, each marked as belonging to one or the other of two categories, an SVM training algorithm builds a model that assigns new examples to one category or the other, making it a non-probabilistic binary linear classifier.

1.15.2 Applications

SVMs can be used to solve various real world problems:

SVMs are helpful in text and hypertext categorization as their application can significantly reduce the need for labelled training instances in both the standard inductive and transductive settings.

Classification of images can also be performed using SVMs. Experimental results show that SVMs achieve significantly higher search accuracy than traditional query refinement schemes after just three to four rounds of relevance feedback. This is also true of image segmentation systems, including those using a modified version SVM that uses the privileged approach as suggested by Vapnik·

Hand-written characters can be recognized using SVM.

The SVM algorithm has been widely applied in the biological and other sciences. They have been used to classify proteins with up to 90% of the compounds classified correctly. Permutation tests based on SVM weights have been suggested as a mechanism for interpretation of SVM models· Support vector machine weights have also been used to interpret SVM models in the past· Posthoc interpretation of support vector machine models in order to identify features used by the model to make predictions is a relatively new area of research with special significance in the biological sciences.

1.15.3 Pros and Cons associated with SVM

- Pros:
  1. It works really well with clear margin of separation
  2. It is effective in high dimensional spaces.
  3. It is effective in cases where number of dimensions is greater than the number of samples.
  4. It uses a subset of training points in the decision function (called support vectors), so it is also memory efficient.
- Cons:
  1. It doesn't perform well, when we have large data set because the required training time is higher
  2. It also doesn't perform very well, when the data set has more noise i.e. target classes are overlapping

3. SVM doesn't directly provide probability estimates, these are calculated using an expensive five-fold cross-validation. It is related SVC method of Python scikit-learn library.

1.15.4 Issues with SVM

Potential drawbacks of the SVM include the following aspects:

1. Requires full labeling of input data
2. Uncalibrated class membership probabilities — SVM stems from Vapnik's theory which avoids estimating probabilities on finite data
3. The SVM is only directly applicable for two-class tasks. Therefore, algorithms that reduce the multi-class task to several binary problems have to be applied; see the multi-class SVM section.
4. Parameters of a solved model are difficult to interpret.

1.16 SOME DEFINITIONS

1.16.1 Training Data set

In machine learning, the study and construction of algorithms that can learn from and make predictions on data [a] is a common task. Such algorithms work by making data-driven predictions or decisions, [b] through building a mathematical model from input data. A training dataset is a dataset of examples used for learning, that is to fit the parameters (e.g., weights) of, for example, a classifier.

Most approaches that search through training data for empirical relationships tend to overfit the data, meaning that they can identify apparent relationships in the training data that do not hold in general.

The data used to build the final model usually comes from multiple datasets. In particular, three data sets are commonly used in different stages of the creation of the model.

The model is initially fit on a training dataset, [c] that is a set of examples used to fit the parameters (e.g. weights of connections between neurons in artificial neural networks) of the model. [d] The model (e.g. a neural net or a naive Bayes classifier) is trained on the training dataset using a supervised learning method (e.g. gradient descent or stochastic gradient descent). In practice, the training dataset often consist of pairs of an input vector and the corresponding answer vector or scalar, which is commonly denoted as the target. The current model is run with the training dataset and produces a result, which is then compared with the target, for each input vector in the training dataset. Based on the result of the comparison and the specific learning algorithm being used, the parameters of the model are adjusted. The model fitting can include both variable selection and parameter estimation.

Finally, the test dataset is a dataset used to provide an unbiased evaluation of a final model fit on the training dataset. [e] A test dataset is a dataset that is independent of the training dataset, but that follows the same probability distribution as the training dataset. If a model fit to the training dataset also fits the test dataset well, minimal overfitting has taken place (see figure below). A better fitting of the training dataset as opposed to the test dataset usually points to overfitting.

A test set is therefore a set of examples used only to assess the performance (i.e. generalization) of a fully specified classifier.

1.16.2 Mean Squared Error (MSE) Or Mean Squared Deviation (MSD

Mean squared error (MSE) or mean squared deviation (MSD) of an estimator (of a procedure for estimating an unobserved quantity) measures the average of the squares of the errors or deviations—that is, the difference between the estimator and what is estimated. MSE is a risk function, corresponding to the expected value of the squared error loss or quadratic loss. The difference occurs because of randomness or because the estimator doesn't account for information that could produce a more accurate estimate.

The MSE is a measure of the quality of an estimator—it is always non-negative, and values closer to zero are better.

Predictor

If $\hat{Y}$ is a vector of n predictions, and Y is the vector of observed values of the variable being predicted, then the within-sample MSE of the predictor is computed as:

$$\text{MSE} = \frac{1}{n}\sum_{i=1}^{n}(Y_i - \hat{Y}_i)^2$$

I.e., the MSE is the mean $\left(\frac{1}{n}\sum_{i=1}^{n}\right)$ of the squares of the errors $(Y_i - \hat{Y}_i)^2$. This is an easily computable quantity for a particular sample (and hence is sample-dependent).

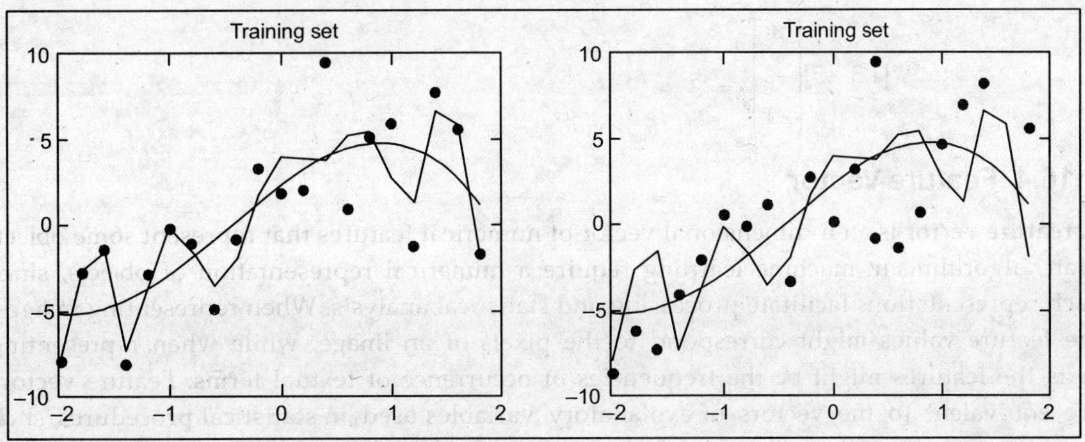

A training set (left) and a test set (right) from the same statistical population are shown as blue points. Two predictive models are fit to the training data. Both fitted models are plotted with both the training and test sets. In the training set, the MSE of the fit shown in orange is 4 whereas the MSE for the fit shown in green is 9. In the test set, the MSE for the fit shown in orange is 15 and the MSE for the fit shown in green is 13. The orange curve severely overfits the training data, since its MSE increases by almost a factor of four when comparing the test set to the training set. The green curve overfits the training data much less, as its MSE increases by less than a factor of 2.

1.16.3 Dot Product Algebraic definition

Algebraically, the dot product is the sum of the products of the corresponding entries of the two sequences of numbers.

The dot product of two vectors **a** = $[a_1, a_2, ..., a_n]$ and **b** = $[b_1, b_2, ..., b_n]$ is defined as:

$$a.b = \sum_{i=1}^{n} a_i b_i = a_1 b_1 + a_2 b_2 + ... + a_n b_n$$

where Σ denotes summation and n is the dimension of the vector space. For instance, in three-dimensional space, the dot product of vectors [1, 3, "5] and [4, "2, "1] is:

$$[1,3,-5] \cdot [4,-2,-1] = (1)(4) + (3)(-2) + (-5)(-1)$$
$$= 4 - 6 + 5$$
$$= 3$$

The dot product can also be written as:

$$a.b = a^T b.$$

Here, a^T means the transpose of a.

Using the above example, a 1 × 3 matrix (row vector) is multiplied by a 3 × 1 matrix (column vector) to get the result (1 × 1 matrix is obtained by matrix multiplication, which is a scalar):

$$[1\ 3\ -5]\begin{bmatrix} 4 \\ -2 \\ -1 \end{bmatrix} = 3$$

1.16.4 Feature Vector

A **feature vector** is an n-dimensional vector of numerical features that represent some object. Many algorithms in machine learning require a numerical representation of objects, since such representations facilitate processing and statistical analysis. When representing images, the feature values might correspond to the pixels of an image, while when representing texts the features might be the frequencies of occurrence of textual terms. Feature vectors are equivalent to the vectors of explanatory variables used in statistical procedures such as linear regression. Feature vectors are often combined with weights using a dot product in order to construct a linear predictor function that is used to determine a score for making a prediction.

1.16.5 Non-linearity and Kernel Methods

Linearity is rather special, and outside quantum mechanics no model of a real system is truly linear. Naturally, one wants the best of both worlds. So, if a problem is non-linear, instead of trying to fit a non-linear model, one can map the problem from the input space to a new (higher-dimensional) space (called the feature space) by doing a nonlinear transformation using suitably chosen basis functions and then use a linear model in the feature space. This is known as the 'kernel trick'.

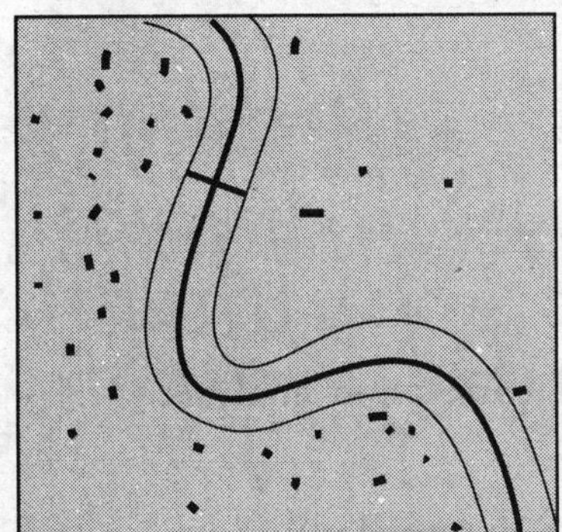

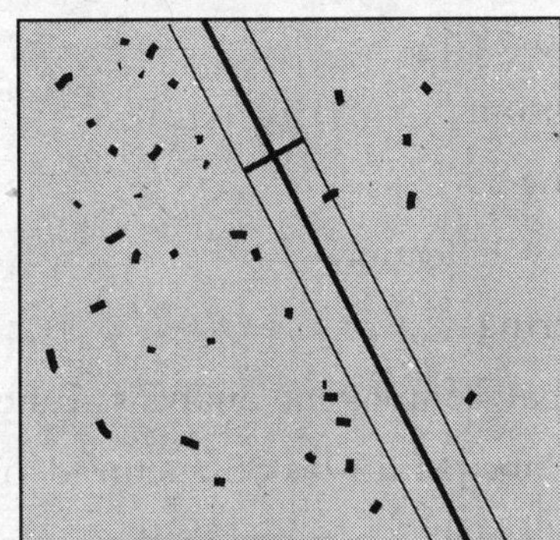

The non-linear model can be converted to linear by transforming an equation from its original domain into another domain by integral transform where it is manipulated and solved much more easily than in the original domain.

The linear model in the feature space corresponds to a non-linear model in the input space. This approach can be used in both classification and regression problems.

Algorithms capable of operating with kernels include the kernel perceptron, support vector machines (SVM), Gaussian processes, principal components analysis (PCA), canonical correlation analysis, ridge regression, spectral clustering, linear adaptive filters and many others.

Support Vector Machines are also the most well known learning systems based on kernel methods. The kernel representation of data amounts to a nonlinear projection of data into a high-dimensional space where it is easier to separate the two classes of data.

Kernel methods Key characteristics of kernel methods:

- **Embedding:** Inputs $x \in X$ from some input space X are embedded into a feature space F via a feature map $\phi : X \rightarrow F$, ϕ may be highly non-linear and F potentially very high-dimensional vector space.
- **Liner models:** are built for the patterns in the feature space (typically $w'\phi(x)$); efficient to find the optimal model, convex optimization.

- **Kernel trick:** Algonithms work with kernels, inner products of feature vectors k(x,z) = $\Sigma_j \phi_j$ (x)ϕ_j(z) rather than the explicit features ϕ(x); side-step the effciency problems of high-dimensionality
- **Regularized learning:** To avoid overfitting, large feature wefights are penalized, separation by large margin is favoured

Many data analysis algorithms can be 'kernelized', i.e. transformed to an equivalent form by replacing object descriptions (feature vectors) by pairwise similarities (kernels):

1. Classification
2. Regression
3. Ranking
4. Novelty detection
5. Clustering
6. Principal component analysis, canonical correlation analysis
7. Multi-label/Multi-task/Structured output

Informally, a kernel is a function that calculates the similarity between two objects, e.g.

1. two proteins
2. two images
3. two documents

- Xi $\in$ X and xj $\in$ X

  μ X = set of all proteins in the nature (finite set)

  μ X = all possible images (infinite set)

  μ X = all possible documents (infinite set)
- k: X x X $\rightarrow$ R

1.16.6 Kernel Methods for Classification and Regression

The term kernel is derived from a word that can be traced back to c. 1000 and originally meant a seed (contained within a fruit) or the softer (usually edible) part contained within the hard shell of a nut or stone-fruit Kernel methods have been widely used as a general strategy for simplifying data structure so that it becomes amenable to linear methods. Following the increasing popularity of support vector machines, kernel methods have been successfully applied to various machine learning problems and have established themselves as a computationally efficient approach to extract non-linearity or higher order moments from data.

Any kernel methods solution comprises two parts: a module that performs the mapping into the embedding or feature space and a learning algorithm designed to discover linear patterns in that space.

First of all, detecting linear relations has been the focus of much research in statistics and machine learning for decades, and the resulting algorithms are both well understood and efficient. Secondly, we will see that there is a computational shortcut which makes it possible to represent linear patterns efficiently in high-dimensional spaces to ensure adequate representational power. The shortcut is what we call a kernel function.

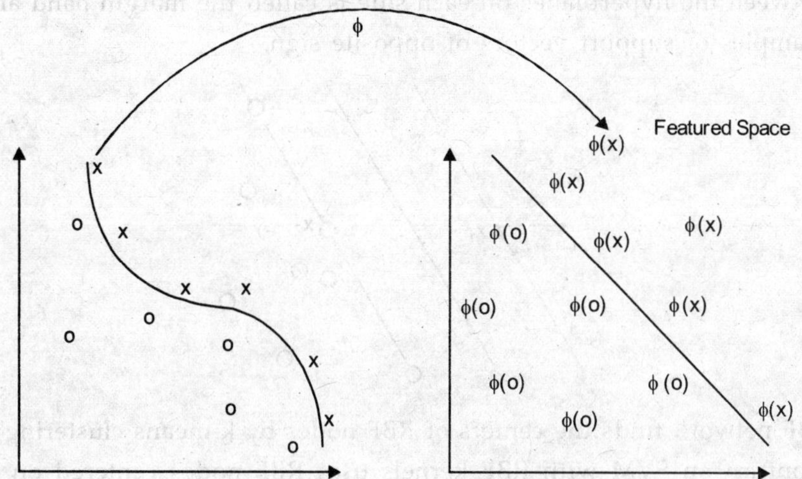

Fig. 1.35. The function ö embeds the data into a feature space where the nonlinear pattern now appears linear. The kernel computes inner products in the feature space directly from the inputs.

Direct kernel methods are a general-purpose and powerful data mining tool for predictive modeling, feature selection and visualization. Direct kernel methods are a generalized methodology to convert linear modeling tools into nonlinear regression models by applying the kernel transformation as a data pre-processing step.

Direct kernel methods transpire the powerful nonlinear modeling power of support vector machines in a straightforward manner to more traditional regression and classification algorithms. An additional advantage of direct kernel methods is that only linear algebra is required.

Definition. The kernel of a function f is the equivalence relation on the function's domain that roughly expresses the idea of 'equivalent as far as the function f can tell'. Definition 1 Let X and Y be sets and let f be a function from X to Y . Elements x_1 and x_2 of X are equivalent if $f(x_1)$ and $f(x_2)$ are equal, i.e. are the same element of Y.

Formally: if $f : X$ '! Y

$$\ker(f) = \{(x_1, x_2) \in X \times X : f(x_1) = f(x_2)\}.$$

Kernel Methods: Motivation Often we want to capture nonlinear patterns in the data Nonlinear Regression: Input-output relationship may not be linear Nonlinear Classification: Classes may not be separable by a linear boundary Linear models (e.g., linear regression, linear SVM) are not just rich enough Kernels: Make linear models work in nonlinear settings By mapping data to higher dimensions where it exhibits linear patterns Apply the linear model in the new input space Mapping a" changing the feature representation Note: Such mappings can be expensive to compute in general.

The margin is the perpendicular distance between the separating hyperplane and a hyperplane through the closest points (these are support vectors).

The region between the hyperplanes on each side is called the margin band and x_1 and x_2 and x_2 are examples of support vectors of opposite sign.

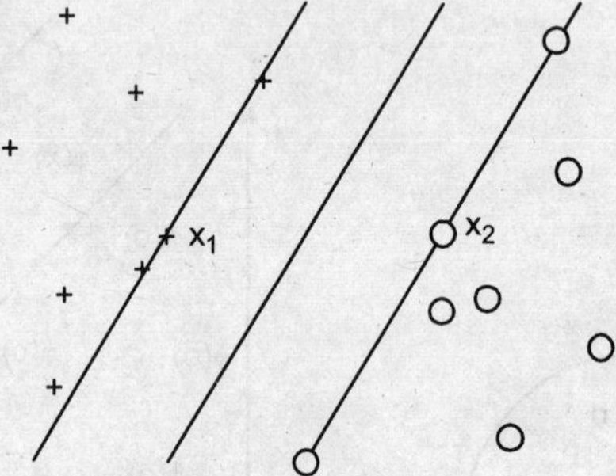

A classical RBF network finds the centers of RBF nodes by k-means clustering (marked by crosses). In contrast an SVM with RBF kernels uses RBF nodes centered on the support vectors (circled), i.e., the datapoints closest to the separating hyperplane (the vertical line illustrated).

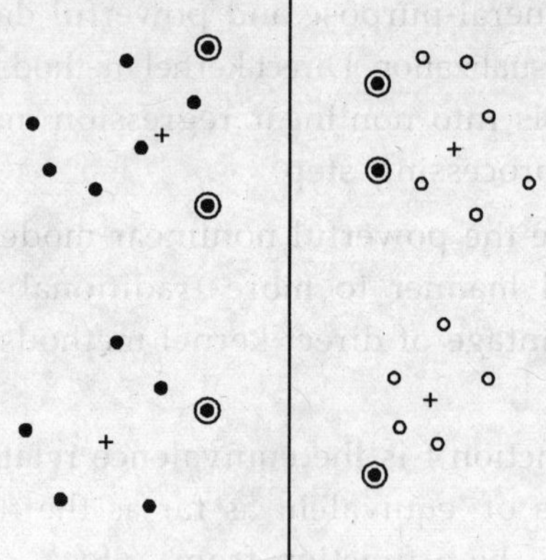

Kernel Ridge Regression

The Problem

Suppose we are given a set of T examples (x_1, y_1), $x_2, y_2)$,....., (x_T, y_T) , where xi ∈ R^n are signals and $y_i \in$ R are outcomes or labels. We want to find a dpendency between signals and outcomes and to be able to predict y given a new x. This problem is often referred to as the regression problem[1].

Let us start by restricting ourselves to linear dependencies of the form y = (w, x) = w'x, where $w \in R^n$, (., .) is the standard scalar product in R^n, and the prime stands for transposition (by default all vectors are assumed to be column vectors).

Non-linear Regression

Now let us try to extend the class of functions weuse and consider a wider class. Suppose that n = 1, i.e., all rs are numbers and we are interested in approximations be polynomials of degree 3, i.e., functions of the form $w_0 + w_1x + w_2x^2 + w_3x^3$. of couse we cab write down L(w) for this case, perform the differentiation and find the solution as we did before. However there is a simpler argument based on the dual form.

Let us map x into R^4 as follows: $x \to (1, x, x^2, x^3)$. Once we have done this, we can do linear regression on new 'long' signals. If we use the dual form, we do not even have to perform the transformations explicitly. Because we only need scalar products, we cabcompute all the necessary products $1 + x_1x_2 + x_1^2\, x_2^2 + x_1^3\, x_2^3$ and substitute them into thedual form formula.

Let us write down a formal generalisation. The signals x do not have to come from R^n any longer. Let them be drawn from some arbitary set[3] X. Suppose that we have a mapping ϕ : $x \to S$, where S is some vector space equipped with a scalar product (. , .) (dot-product space); the space S is sometimes referred to as the feature space. We can use ridge regression in the feature space. The prediction of ridge regression on a signal x can be written as

$$Y_{RR} = Y'(aI + K)^{-1}k,$$

where

$$K = \begin{pmatrix} K(x_1,x_1) & K(x_1,x_2) & \dots & K(x_1,x_T) \\ K(x_2,x_1) & K(x_2,x_2) & \dots & K(x_2,x_T) \\ \vdots & \vdots & \ddots & \vdots \\ K(x_T,x_1) & K(x_T,x_2) & \dots & K(x_T,x_T) \end{pmatrix}$$

and

$$K = \begin{pmatrix} K(x_1,x) \\ K(x_2,x) \\ \dots \\ K(x_T,x) \end{pmatrix};$$

the function $K : X^2 \to R$ is given by $K(x_1, x_2) = (\Phi(x_1), \Phi(x_2))$.

The space S does not have to be finite-dimensional. However since every vector space with a scalar product cab be embedded into a Hilbert space (see below for a definition) we can assume that it is Hilbert.

The transformation Φ is of no particular importance to us. Once we know the

K, we can perform regression with it.

Mappings and Kernels

It would be nice to have a characterisation of all K without a reference to Φ. A characterisation ofthis kind can be given.

It is easy to see that $K(x_1, x_2) = (\Phi(x_1), \Phi(x_2))$ has ths the following properties:

- It is symmetric: $K(x_1, x_2) = K(x_2, x_1)$ for all $x_1, x_2 \in X$: this following from the symmetry of the scalar product (. , .):
- It is *positiove semi-definite:* for every posotive integer T and every $x_1, x_2, \ldots, x_T \in X$: the matrix

$$K = \begin{pmatrix} K(x_{1,}x_1) & K(x_{1,}x_2) & \cdots & K(x_{1,}x_T) \\ K(x_{2,}x_1) & K(x_{2,}x_2) & \cdots & K(x_{2,}x_T) \\ \vdots & \vdots & \ddots & \vdots \\ K(x_{T,}x_1) & K(x_{T,}x_2) & \cdots & K(x_{T,}x_T) \end{pmatrix}$$

is positive semi-definite[4]; indeed, K is the Gram matrix of the images $\Phi(x_1), \Phi(x_2), \ldots, \Phi(x_T)$[5].

Surprisingle these two simple properties are fufficient. Let us call a function $K : X^2 \to R$ satisfying these two properties a *kernel*. Then the following theorem can be formulated.

Theorem 1. *For any set X a function $K : X_2 \to R$ is a kernel. i.e. it is symmetric and positive semi-definite, if and only if there is a mapping Φ from X into a hilbert space Hwith a scalar product (. , .) such that $K(x_1, x_2) = \Phi(x_1), \Phi(x_2)$ for all $x_1, x_2 \in X$:*

We proved the 'if' part when we defined kernels. The 'only if' part follows from the results of the nextsections, where we will show that the class of kernels coincides with the class of so called reproducting kernels.

An SVM model is a representation of the examples as points in space, mapped so that the examples of the separate categories are divided by a clear gap that is as wide as possible. New examples are then mapped into that same space and predicted to belong to a category based on which side of the gap they fall.

In addition to performing linear classification, SVMs can efficiently perform a non-linear classification using what is called the kernel trick, implicitly mapping their inputs into high-dimensional feature spaces.

Polynomial Kernel

Polynomial kernel is a kernel function commonly used with support vector machines

Definition

For degree-d polynomials, the polynomial kernel is defined as:

$$K(x, y) = (x^T y + c)^d$$

where x and y are vectors in the input space, i.e. vectors of features computed from training or test samples and *c e" 0* is a free parameter trading off the influence of higher-order versus lower-order terms in the polynomial. When $c = 0$, the kernel is called homogeneous. A further generalized polykernel divides $x^T y$ by a user-specified scalar parameter a.

where x and y are vectors in the input space, i.e. vectors of features computed from training or testsample and c > 0 is a free parameter trading off theinfluence of higher-order versus lower-order terms in the polynomial.when c = 0, the kernel is called homogeneous. (A further generalized polykernel divides $x^T y$ by a user-specified.

As a kernel, K corresponds to an inner product in a feature space based on some mapping φ.

$$K(x, y) = (\varphi(x), \varphi(y))$$

As a kernel, ***K*** corresponds to an inner product in a feature space based on some mapping ***φ***:

$$K(x, y) = (\varphi(x), \varphi(y))$$

The nature of *ö* can be seen from an example. Let ***d*** = 2, so we get the special case of the quadratic kernel. After using the multinomial theorem (twice—the outermost application is the binomial theorem) and regrouping,

$$k(x,y) = \left(\sum_{i-1}^{n} x_i y_i + c\right)^2 = \sum_{i-1}^{n}\left(x_i^2\right)\left(y_i^2\right) + \sum_{i-2}^{n}\sum_{j-1}^{i-1}\left(\sqrt{2}x_i x_j\right)\left(\sqrt{2}y_i y_j\right) + \sum_{i-1}^{n}\left(\sqrt{2c}x_i\right)\left(\sqrt{2c}y_i\right) + c^2$$

From this it follows that the feature map is given by:

$$\varphi(x) = (x_1^2, \ldots . x_1^2, \sqrt{2}x_n x_{n-1}, \ldots, \sqrt{2}x_n x_1, \sqrt{2}x_{n-1}x_{n-2}, \ldots, \sqrt{2}x_{n-1}x_1, \ldots, \sqrt{2}x_2 x_1, \sqrt{2c}x_n, \ldots, \sqrt{2c}x_1, c)$$

Practical use

Although the RBF kernel is more popular in SVM classification than the polynomial kernel, the latter is quite popular in natural language processing (NLP). The most common degree is d = 2 (quadratic), since larger degrees tend to overfit on NLP problems.

Various ways of computing the polynomial kernel (both exact and approximate) have been devised as alternatives to the usual non-linear SVM training algorithms, including:

1. full expansion of the kernel prior to training/testing with a linear SVM, i.e. full computation of the mapping ϕ as in polynomial regression;
2. basket mining (using a variant of the apriori algorithm) for the most commonly occurring feature conjunctions in a training set to produce an approximate expansion;
3. inverted indexing of support vectors.

   One problem with the polynomial kernel is that it may suffer from numerical instability: when $x^T y + c < 1$, K(x, y) = $x^T y + c)^d$. tends to zero with increasing ***d***, whereas when $x^T y + c > 1$, K(x, y) tends to infinity.

Advantages

- The kernel defines a similarity measure between two data points and thus allows one to incorporate prior knowledge of the problem domain.
- Most importantly, the kernel contains all of the information about the relative positions of the inputs in the feature space and the actual learning algorithm is

based only on the kernel function and can thus be carried out without explicit use of the feature space. The training data only enter the algorithm through their entries in the kernel matrix (a Gram matrix), and never through their individual attributes. Because one never explicitly has to evaluate the feature map in the high dimensional feature space, the kernel function represents a computational shortcut.

- The number of operations required is not necessarily proportional to the number of features.

1.17 BEYOND BINARY CLASSIFICATIONS: MULTICLASS OR MULTINOMIAL CLASSIFICATION

Multiclass or multinomial classification is the problem of classifying instances into one of three or more classes. (Classifying instances into one of the two classes is called binary classification.)

While some classification algorithms naturally permit the use of more than two classes, others are by nature binary algorithms; these can, however, be turned into multinomial classifiers by a variety of strategies.

1.17.1 Multinomial Logistic Regression

Multinomial logistic regression is a classification method that generalizes logistic regression to multiclass problems, i.e. with more than two possible discrete outcomes. That is, it is a model that is used to predict the probabilities of the different possible outcomes of a categorically distributed dependent variable, given a set of independent variables (which may be real-valued, binary-valued, categorical-valued, etc.

Multinomial logistic regression is used when the dependent variable in question is nominal (equivalently categorical, meaning that it falls into any one of a set of categories that cannot be ordered in any meaningful way) and for which there are more than two categories. Some examples would be:

1. Which major will a college student choose, given their grades, stated likes and dislikes, etc.?
2. Which blood type does a person have, given the results of various diagnostic tests?
3. In a hands-free mobile phone dialing application, which person's name was spoken, given various properties of the speech signal?
4. Which candidate will a person vote for, given particular demographic characteristics?
5. Which country will a firm locate an office in, given the characteristics of the firm and of the various candidate countries?

These are all statistical classification problems. They all have in common a dependent variable to be predicted that comes from one of a limited set of items that cannot be meaningfully ordered, as well as a set of independent variables (also known as features, explanators, etc.), which are used to predict the dependent variable. Multinomial logistic regression is a particular solution to the classification problem that assumes that a linear combination of the observed features and some problem-specific parameters can be used to determine the probability of each particular outcome of the dependent variable. The best values of the parameters for a given problem are usually determined from some training data (e.g. some people for whom both the diagnostic test results and blood types are known, or some examples of known words being spoken).

References

1. James Huddleston in Business 2 community web site article "5 Types of Big Data Analytics and How They Help Customer Success"
2. "Data collection". SearchCIO. TechTarget. Retrieved 20 December 2016.
3. "Which Data Collection Method Should I Choose?". B2B International. Retrieved 20 December 2016.
4. "How and Why Data Will Save Small Business". Small Business Trends Small Business Trends. LLC. Retrieved 20 December 2016.
5. "FAQ: Data Collection Requirements for Broker-Dealers". FINRA.org. Financial Industry Regulatory Authority, Inc. on behalf of the U.S. Securities and Exchange Commission (SEC). Retrieved 4 February 2017.
6. Data Collection and Analysis By Dr. Roger Sapsford, Victor Jupp ISBN 0-7619-5046-X
7. "Glossary of statistical terms: Population". Statistics.com. Retrieved 22 February 2016.
8. Weisstein, Eric W. "Statistical population". MathWorld.
9. Weisberg H.F (1992) Central Tendency and Variability, Sage University Paper Series on Quantitative Applications in the Social Sciences, ISBN 0-8039-4007-6 p.2
10. Ronald van Loon, Director Adversitement Machine Learning Explained: Understanding Supervised, Unsupervised, and Reinforcement Learning,Published on Published onJanuary 15, 2018
11. Anderson, D. R., Sweeney, D. J., and Williams, T. A. (2003). Essentials of Statistics for Business and Economics (3rd ed.) Mason, Ohio: Southwestern, Thompson Learning.
12. Sunil Ray , September 13, 2017 article " Understanding Support Vector Machine algorithm from examples (along with code)" available in www.analyticsvidhya.com/blog/2017/09/understaing-support-vector-machine-example-code/
13. Vapnik, Vladimir N.: Invited Speaker. IPMU Information Processing and Management 2014)
14. Barghout, Lauren. "Spatial-Taxon Information Granules as Used in Iterative Fuzzy-Decision-Making for Image Segmentation." Granular Computing and Decision-Making. Springer International Publishing, 2015. 285-318.

15. *DeCoste, Dennis (2002). "Training Invariant Support Vector Machines" (PDF). Machine Learning. 46: 161–190.*

16. Gaonkar, Bilwaj; Davatzikos, Christos; "Analytic estimation of statistical significance maps for support vector machine based multi-variate image analysis and classification"

17. Cuingnet, Rémi; Rosso, Charlotte; Chupin, Marie; Lehéricy, Stéphane; Dormont, Didier; Benali, Habib; Samson, Yves; and Colliot, Olivier; "Spatial regularization of SVM for the detection of diffusion alterations associated with stroke outcome", *Medical Image Analysis*, 2011, 15 (5): 729–737

18. Statnikov, Alexander; Hardin, Douglas; & Aliferis, Constantin; (2006); "Using SVM weight-based methods to identify causally relevant and non-causally relevant variables", *Sign*, 1, 4

19. Zhang, Harry. The Optimality of Naive Bayes (PDF). FLAIRS2004 conference.

20. Caruana, R.; Niculescu-Mizil, A. (2006). An empirical comparison of supervised learning algorithms. Proc. 23rd International Conference on Machine Learning. CiteSeerX 10.1.1.122.5901.

Unit 2

UNSUPERVISED LEARNING

Learning Objectives and Outcome

At the end of this unit the reader shall be able to understand :

- Clustering: K-means/Kernel K-means
- Dimensionality Reduction: PCA and kernel PCA
- Matrix Factorization and Matrix Completion
- Generative Models (mixture models and latent factor models)

2.1 UNSUPERVISED MACHINE LEARNING

As alreadt learnt in unit 1, Machine learning is a term closely associated with data science. It refers to a broad class of methods that revolve around data modelling to :

(1) *Supervised Learning* to algorithmically make predictions, and

(2) *Unsupervised Learning* to algorithmically decipher patterns in data.

In unsupervised learning only the data $x_1,.....,X_n \in R^N$., is given, i.e. the labels are missing. Standard questions of unsupervised learning are clustering, density estimation, and data description. The kernel trick cannot only be applied in supervised learning scenarios, but also for unsupervised learning, given that the base algorithm can be written in terms of scalar products.

Unsupervised learning tries to surface underlying patterns and associations in data when no existing ground truth is known (i.e. no observations are tagged). Within this broad category of methods, the most commonly used are clustering techniques, which algorithmically detect what are the natural groupings that exist in a data set. For example, clustering can be used to programmatically learn the natural customer segments in a company's user base. Other unsupervised methods for mining underlying characteristics include: principal component analysis, hidden markov models, topic models, and more.

2.2 INTRODUCTION TO CLUSTERING TECHNIQUES

Clustering is the process of examining a collection of "points," and grouping the points into "clusters" according to some distance measure. The goal is that points in the same cluster have a small distance from one another, while points in different clusters are at a large distance from one another.

It is very necessary to understand the notions of *distance measures and spaces*. The two major approaches to clustering – hierarchical and point-assignment – are to be defined. We then turn to a discussion of the "curse of dimensionality," which makes clustering in high-dimensional spaces difficult, but also, as we shall see, enables some simplifications if used correctly in a clustering algorithm.

2.2.1 Points, Spaces, and Distances

A dataset suitable for clustering is a collection of points, which are objects belonging to some space. In its most general sense, a space is just a universal set of points, from which the points in the dataset are drawn. However, we should be mindful of the common case of a Euclidean space, which has a number of important properties useful for clustering. In particular, a Euclidean space's points are vectors of real numbers. The length of the vector is the number of dimensions of the space. The components of the vector are commonly called coordinates of the represented points.

All spaces for which we can perform a clustering have a distance measure, giving a distance between any two points in the space.

The common Euclidean distance (square root of the sums of the squares of the differences between the coordinates of the points in each dimension) vide 1.5.2 of this book, serves for all Euclidean spaces, although we also mentioned some other options for distance measures in Euclidean spaces, including the Manhattan distance (sum of the magnitudes of the differences in each dimension) and the L"-distance (maximum magnitude of the difference in any dimension)

Example 2.1 : Classical applications of clustering often involve low-dimensional Euclidean spaces. For example, Fig. 2.1 shows height and weight measurements of dogs of several varieties. Without knowing which dog is of which variety, we can see just by looking at the diagram that the dogs fall into three clusters, and those clusters happen to correspond to three varieties. With small amounts of data, any clustering algorithm will establish the correct clusters, and simply plotting the points and "eyeballing" the plot will suffice as well.

Clustering can be considered the most important unsupervised learning problem; so, as every other problem of this kind, it deals with finding a structure in a collection of unlabeled data..

In this case we easily identify the 4 clusters into which the data can be divided; the similarity criterion is distance: two or more objects belong to the same cluster if they are "close" according to a given distance (in this case geometrical distance). This is called distance-based clustering.

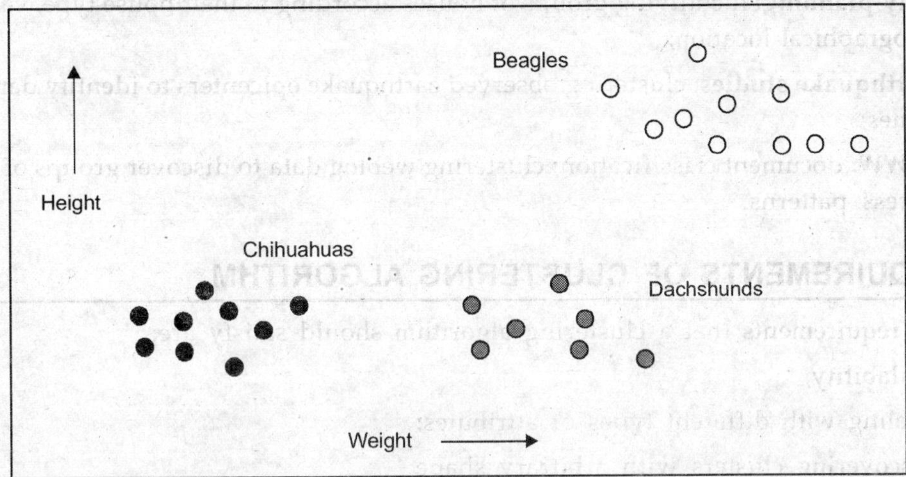

Fig. 2.1: Heights and weights of dogs taken from three varieties

Another kind of clustering is conceptual clustering: two or more objects belong to the same cluster if this one defines a concept common to all that objects. In other words, objects are grouped according to their fit to descriptive concepts, not according to simple similarity measures.

2.2.2 The Goals of using Clustering Methods

The goal behind using clustering method is to determine the intrinsic grouping in a set of *unlabeled data*. But how to decide what constitutes a good clustering? It can be shown that there is no absolute "best" criterion which would be independent of the final aim of the clustering. Consequently, it is the user which must supply this criterion, in such a way that the result of the clustering will suit their needs.

For instance, we could be interested in finding representatives for homogeneous groups (data reduction), in finding "natural clusters" and describe their unknown properties ("natural" data types), in finding useful and suitable groupings ("useful" data classes) or in finding unusual data objects (outlier detection).

2.3 POSSIBLE APPLICATIONS

Clustering algorithms can be applied in many fields, for instance:

1. **Marketing**: finding groups of customers with similar behavior given a large database of customer data containing their properties and past buying records;
2. **Biology**: classification of plants and animals given their features;
3. **Libraries**: book ordering;
4. **Insurance**: identifying groups of motor insurance policy holders with a high average claim cost; identifying frauds;

5. **City-planning**: identifying groups of houses according to their house type, value and geographical location;
6. **Earthquake studies**: clustering observed earthquake epicenters to identify dangerous zones;
7. **WWW:** document classification; clustering weblog data to discover groups of similar access patterns.

2.4 REQUIREMENTS OF CLUSTERING ALGORITHM

The main requirements that a clustering algorithm should satisfy are:

1. scalability;
2. dealing with different types of attributes;
3. discovering clusters with arbitrary shape;
4. minimal requirements for domain knowledge to determine input parameters;
5. ability to deal with noise and outliers;
6. insensitivity to order of input records;
7. high dimensionality;
8. interpretability and usability.

2.5 PROBLEMS ASSOCIATED WITH USING CLUSTERING TECHNIQUE

There are a number of problems with clustering. Among them:

1. current clustering techniques do not address all the requirements adequately (and concurrently);
2. dealing with large number of dimensions and large number of data items can be problematic because of time complexity;
3. the effectiveness of the method depends on the definition of "distance" (for distance-based clustering);
4. if an obvious distance measure doesn't exist we must "define" it, which is not always easy, especially in multi-dimensional spaces;
5. the result of the clustering algorithm (that in many cases can be arbitrary itself) can be interpreted in different ways.

2.6 TYPES OF CLUSTERING METHODS

They are different types of clustering methods, including:

1. **Partitioning methods.:** K means Centroid models: for example, the k-means algorithm represents each cluster by a single mean vector.
2. **Hierarchical clustering:** Connectivity models: for example, hierarchical clustering builds models based on distance connectivity.

3. Fuzzy clustering.
4. Density-based clustering.
5. Model-based clustering.
6. **Subspace models**: in bi-clustering (also known as co-clustering or two-mode-clustering), clusters are modelled with both cluster members and relevant attributes.
7. **Group models**: some algorithms do not provide a refined model for their results and just provide the grouping information.
8. **Graph-based models**: a clique, that is, a subset of nodes in a graph such that every two nodes in the subset are connected by an edge can be considered as a prototypical form of cluster. Relaxations of the complete connectivity requirement (a fraction of the edges can be missing) are known as quasi-cliques, as in the HCS clustering algorithm.
9. **Neural models**: the most well known unsupervised neural network is the self-organizing map and these models can usually be characterized as similar to one or more of the above models, and including subspace models when neural networks implement a form of Principal Component Analysis or Independent Component Analysis.

Clusterings can be roughly distinguished as:

- Hard clustering: each object belongs to a cluster or not
- Soft clustering (also: fuzzy clustering): each object belongs to each cluster to a certain degree (for example, a likelihood of belonging to the cluster)

2.7 CLUSTERING STRATEGIES

We can divide clustering algorithms into two groups that follow two fundamentally different strategies.

1. **Hierarchical** or agglomerative algorithms start with each point in its own cluster. Clusters are combined based on their "closeness," using one of many possible definitions of "close." Combination stops when further combination leads to clusters that are undesirable for one of several reasons. For example, we may stop when we have a predetermined number of clusters, or we may use a measure of compactness for clusters, and refuse to construct a cluster by combining two smaller clusters if the resulting cluster has points that are spread out over too large a region.
2. The other class of algorithms involve point assignment. Points are considered in some order, and each one is assigned to the cluster into which it best fits. This process is normally preceded by a short phase in which initial clusters are estimated. Variations allow occasional combining or splitting of clusters, or may allow points to be unassigned if they are outliers (points too far from any of the current clusters). Algorithms for clustering can also be distinguished by:

   (a) Whether the algorithm assumes a Euclidean space, or whether the algorithm works for an arbitrary distance measure. We shall see that a key distinction is that in a Euclidean space it is possible to summarize a collection of points by their centroid – the average of the points. In a non-Euclidean space, there is no notion of a centroid, and we are forced to develop another way to summarize clusters.

(b) Whether the algorithm assumes that the data is small enough to fit in main memory, or whether data must reside in secondary memory, primarily. Algorithms for large amounts of data often must take shortcuts, since it is infeasible to look at all pairs of points, for example. It is also necessary to summarize clusters in main memory, since we cannot hold all the points of all the clusters in main memory at the same time.

Machine Learning is one of the most recent and exciting technologies. You probably use it dozen of times a day without even knowing it. Machine Learning is a type of artificial intelligence that provides computers with an ability to learn without being explicitly programmed. It works on supervised and unsupervised learning models. Unlike supervised learning model, the unsupervised model of Machine Learning has no predefined groups under which you can distribute your data. You can find these groupings through clustering. I will explain it further through the following examples.

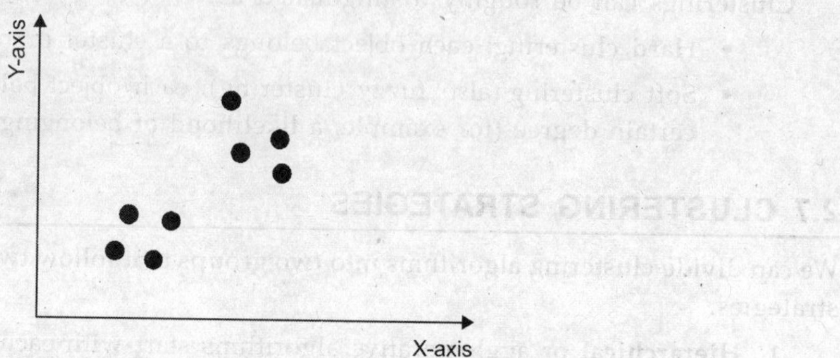

As you can see in this image, the data points are shown as blue dots. These data points do not have labels based on which you can differentiate them. You do not know anything about this data. So now the question is, can you find out any structure in this data? This problem can be solved using clustering technique. Clustering will divide this entire dataset under different labels (here called clusters) with similar data points into one cluster as shown in the graph given below. It is used as a very powerful technique for exploratory descriptive analysis.

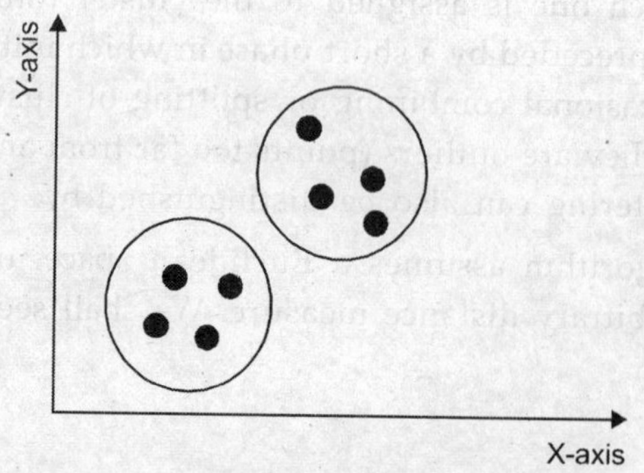

Here, the clustering technique has partitioned the entire data points into two clusters. The data points within a cluster are similar to each other but different from other clusters. For example, you have the data on symptoms of patients. Now, you can find out the name of a particular disease based on these symptoms.

Now, once you have understood what is clustering, let's look at different ways to achieve these clusters.

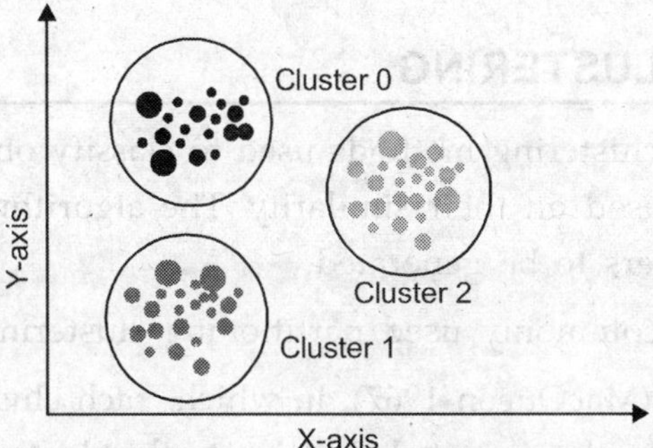

Exclusive Clustering: In exclusive clustering, an item belongs exclusively to one cluster, not several. In the image, you can see that data belonging to cluster 0 does not belong to cluster 1 or cluster 2. k-means clustering is a type of exclusive clustering.

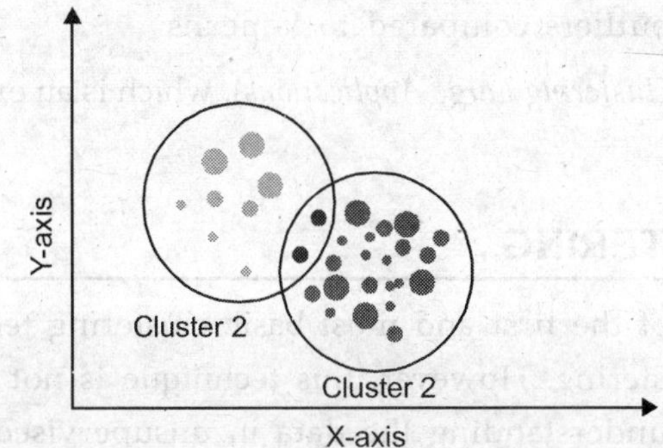

Overlapping Clustering: Here, an item can belong to multiple clusters with different degree of association among each cluster. Fuzzy C-means algorithm is based on overlapping clustering.

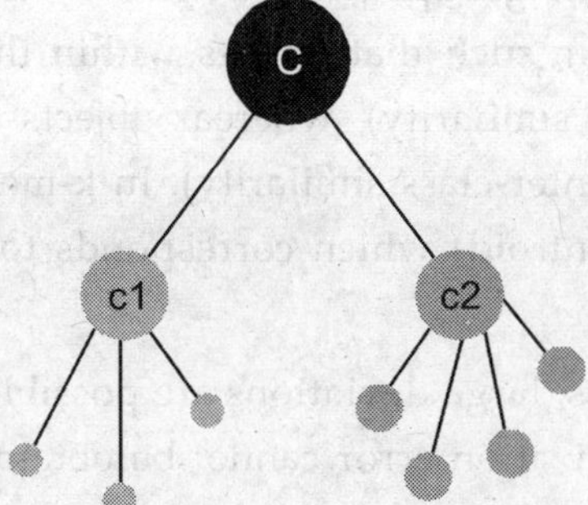

Hierarchical Clustering: In hierarchical clustering, the clusters are not formed in a single step rather it follows series of partitions to come up with final clusters. It looks like a tree as visible in the image.

While implementing any algorithm, computational speed and efficiency becomes a very important parameter for end results. So, I have explained k-means clustering as it works really well with large datasets due to its more computational speed and its ease of use.

2.8 PARTITIONING CLUSTERING

Partitioning clustering are clustering methods used to classify observations, within a data set, into multiple groups based on their similarity. The algorithms require the analyst to specify the number of clusters to be generated.

This chapter describes the commonly used partitioning clustering, including:

- **K-means clustering** (MacQueen 1967), in which, each cluster is represented by the center or means of the data points belonging to the cluster. The K-means method is sensitive to anomalous data points and outliers.
- **K-medoids clustering** or **PAM** (*Partitioning Around Medoids*, Kaufman & Rousseeuw, 1990), in which, each cluster is represented by one of the objects in the cluster. PAM is less sensitive to outliers compared to k-means.
- **CLARA algorithm** (*Clustering Large Applications*), which is an extension to PAM adapted for large data sets.

2.9 K-MEANS CLUSTERING

K-means clustering is one of the first and most basic clustering techniques whenever one thinks of unsupervised clustering. However, this technique is not just powerful, but also teaches the importance of understanding the data in unsupervised learning.

K-means clustering (MacQueen 1967) is the most commonly used unsupervised machine learning algorithm for partitioning a given data set into a set of k groups (i.e. k clusters), where k represents the number of groups pre-specified by the analyst. It classifies objects in multiple groups (i.e., clusters), such that objects within the same cluster are as similar as possible (i.e., high intra-class similarity), whereas objects from different clusters are as dissimilar as possible (i.e., low inter-class similarity). In k-means clustering, each cluster is represented by its center (i.e, centroid) which corresponds to the mean of points assigned to the cluster.

How- ever, for small sample sizes, large deviations are possible and over fitting might occur (see Figure 2.2). Then a generalization error cannot be obtained by simply minimizing the training error.

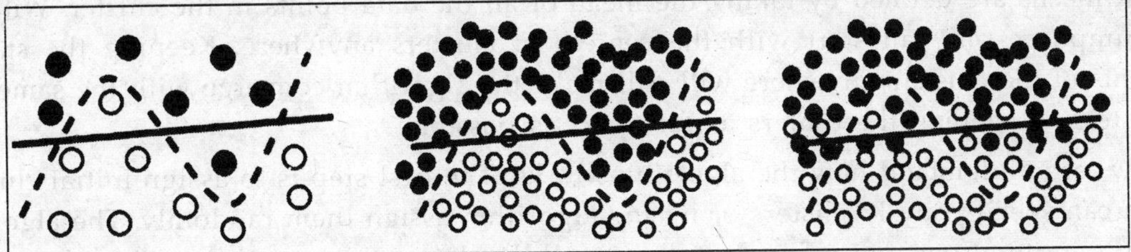

Fig. 2.2: Illustration of the over fitting dilemma: Given only a small sample (left) either, the solid or the dashed hypothesis might be true, the dashed one being more complex, but also having a smaller training error. Only with a large sample we are able to see which decision reflects the true distribution more closely. If the dashed hypothesis is correct the solid would under fit (middle); if the solid were correct the dashed hypothesis would over fit (right).

2.9.1 K-means basic ideas

The basic idea behind k-means clustering consists of defining clusters so that the total intra-cluster variation (known as total within-cluster variation) is minimized.

There are several k-means algorithms available. The standard algorithm is the Hartigan-Wong algorithm (Hartigan and Wong 1979), which defines the total within-cluster variation as the sum of squared distances Euclidean distances between items and the corresponding centroid:

$$W(C_k) = \sum_{x_1 \in C_k} (x_1 - \mu_k)^2$$

- x_i design a data point belonging to the cluster C_k
- μ_k is the mean value of the points assigned to the cluster C_k

Each observation (x_1) is assigned to a given cluster such that the sum of squares (SS) distance of the observation to their assigned cluster centers μ_k is a minimum.

We define the total within-cluster variation as follow:

$$\text{tot.withinss} = \sum_{k-1}^{k} W(C_k) = \sum_{k-1}^{k} \sum_{x_1 \in C_k} (x_1 - \mu_k)^2$$

The total within-cluster sum of square measures the compactness (i.e goodness) of the clustering and we want it to be as small as possible.

2.9.2 Assumptions and Process

To divide your dataset into clusters, one must define the criteria of a cluster and those make the assumptions for the technique. K-Means clustering method considers two assumptions regarding the clusters – first that the clusters are spherical and second that the clusters are of similar size. Spherical assumption helps in separating the clusters when the algorithm works on the data and forms clusters. If this assumption is violated, the clusters formed may not be what one expects. On the other hand, assumption over the size of clusters helps in deciding the boundaries of the cluster. This assumption helps in calculating the number of data points each cluster should have. This assumption also gives an advantage. Clusters in K-means are defined by taking the mean of all the data points in the cluster. With this assumption, one can start with the centers of clusters anywhere. Keeping the starting points of the clusters anywhere will still make the algorithm converge with the same final clusters as keeping the centers as far apart as possible.

Now let's understand how the algorithm works. The first step is to assign initial clusters. You can specify any K clusters or let the algorithm assign them randomly. The algorithm works in iterations and in every iteration, all the data points are then assigned to one of the clusters based on the nearest distance from the centers. After all points are assigned to one of the cluster, the cluster centers are now updated. The new centers are decided based on the centroid mean of all the points within the cluster. This is repeated, iteration after iteration until the there is no change in the cluster assignment of any of the data points but there are a lot of calculations which are not fixed in this algorithm. For example, one can decide how the distance for each data point from the cluster center is defined. All of us are familiar with the Euclidean distance. The algorithm is straightforward and easy to understand but using the technique is not as easy as it looks. Let's try out some examples in R.

k-means is an unsupervised technique which is used for raw datasets. It is used to classify objects based on attributes into k numbers of groups. Its main aim is to partition n items into k clusters. The main idea is to define k centers, for each cluster. This centered k should be placed in such a way that most accurate result will be obtained. This centered k plays an important role to get the accurate result.

k-means clustering is one of the simplest algorithms which uses unsupervised learning method to solve known clustering issues. k-means clustering require following two inputs.

1. k = number of clusters
2. Training set(m) = $\{x_1, x_2, x_3, \ldots\ldots\ldots, x_m\}$

Let's say you have an unlabeled data set like the one shown below and you want to group this data into clusters.

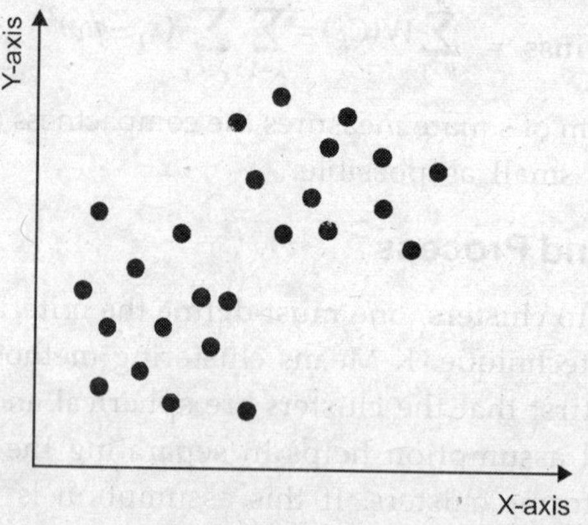

Now, the important question is how should you choose the optimum number of clusters? There are two possible ways for choosing the number of clusters.

(i) Elbow Method: Here, you draw a curve between WSS (within sum of squares) and the number of clusters. It is called elbow method because the curve looks like a human arm and the elbow point gives us the optimum number of clusters. As you can see that after the elbow point, there is a very slow change in the value of WSS, so you should take the elbow point value as the final number of clusters.

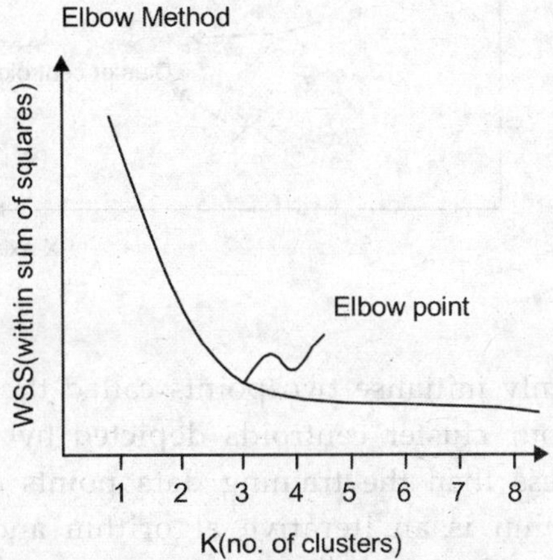

(ii) Purpose Based: You can run k-means clustering algorithm to get different clusters based on a variety of purposes. You can partition the data on different metrics and see how well it performs for that particular case. Let's take an example of marketing T-shirts of different sizes. You can partition the dataset into different number of clusters depending upon the purpose that you want to meet. In the following example, two different criteria, price and comfort has been used.

Let's see these two possibilities as shown in the image below.

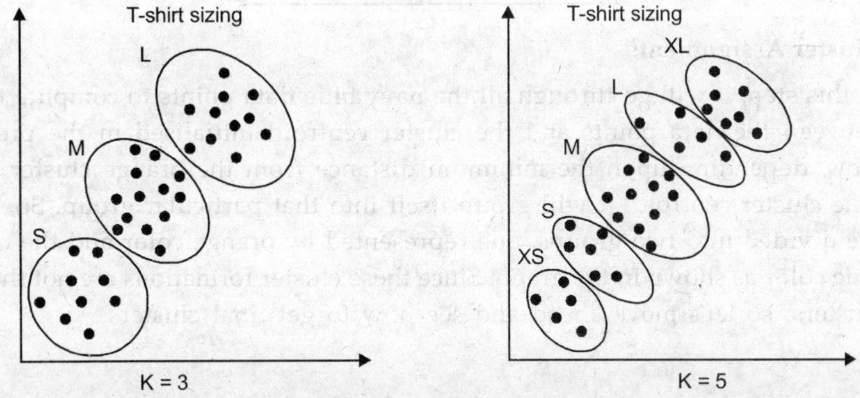

1. K=3: If you want to provide only 3 sizes (S, M, L) so that prices are cheaper, you will divide the data set into 3 clusters.
2. K=5: Now, if you want to provide more comfort and variety to your customers with more sizes (XS, S, M, L, XL), then you will divide the data set into 5 clusters.

Now, once we have the value of k with us, let's understand it's execution.

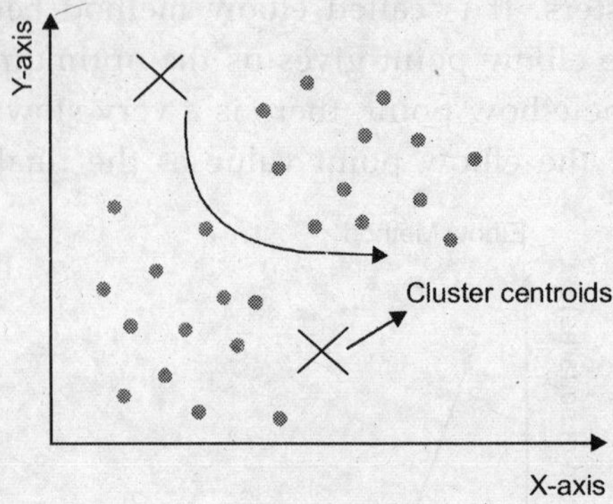

Initialisation

Firstly, you need to randomly initialise two points called the cluster centroids. Here, you need to make sure that your cluster centroids depicted by an orange and blue cross as shown in the image are less than the training data points depicted by navy blue dots. k-means clustering algorithm is an iterative algorithm and it follows next two steps iteratively. Once you are done with the initialization, let's move on to the next step.

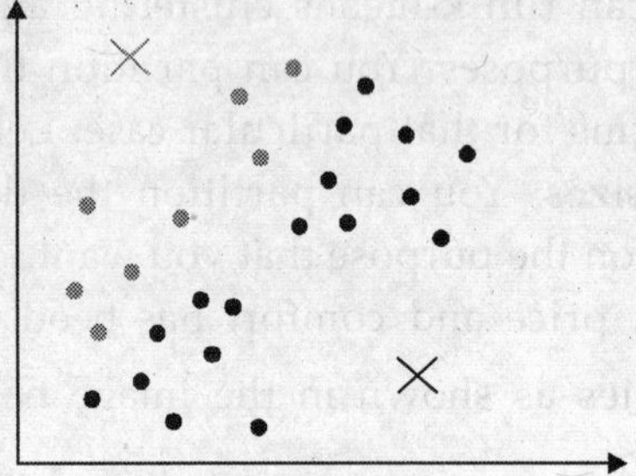

- **Cluster Assignment:**

  In this step, it will go through all the navy blue data points to compute the distance between the data points and the cluster centroid initialised in the previous step. Now, depending upon the minimum distance from the orange cluster centroid or blue cluster centroid, it will group itself into that particular group. So, data points are divided into two groups, one represented by orange color and the other one in blue color as shown in the graph. Since these cluster formations are not the optimised clusters, so let's move ahead and see how to get final clusters.

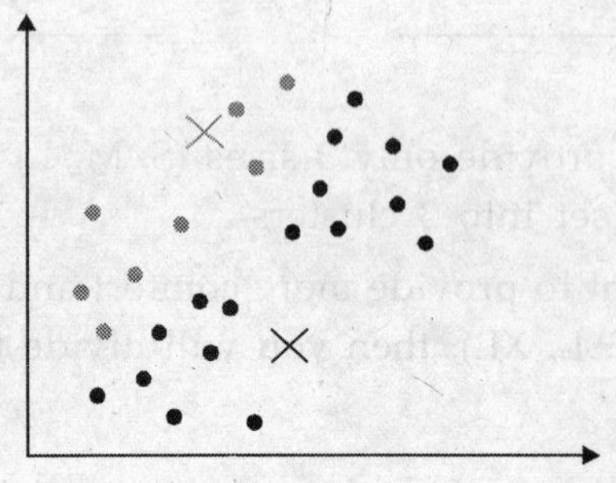

- **Move Centroid:**

  Now, you will take the above two cluster centroids and iteratively reposition them for optimization. You will take all blue dots, compute their average and move current cluster centroid to this new location. Similarly, you will move orange cluster centroid to the average of orange data points. Therefore, the new cluster centroids will look as shown in the graph. Moving forward, let's see how can we optimize clusters which will give us better insight.

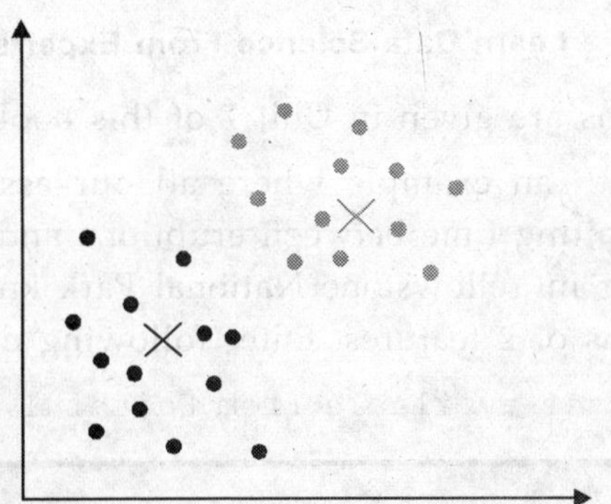

- **Optimization:**

  You need to repeat above two steps iteratively till the cluster centroids stop changing their positions and become static. Once the clusters become static, then k-means clustering algorithm is said to be converged.

- **Convergence:**

  Finally, k-means clustering algorithm converges and divides the data points into two clusters clearly visible in orange and blue. It can happen that k-means may end up converging with different solutions depending on how the clusters were initialised.

  As you can see in the graph below, the three clusters are clearly visible but you might end up having different clusters depending upon your choice of cluster centroids.

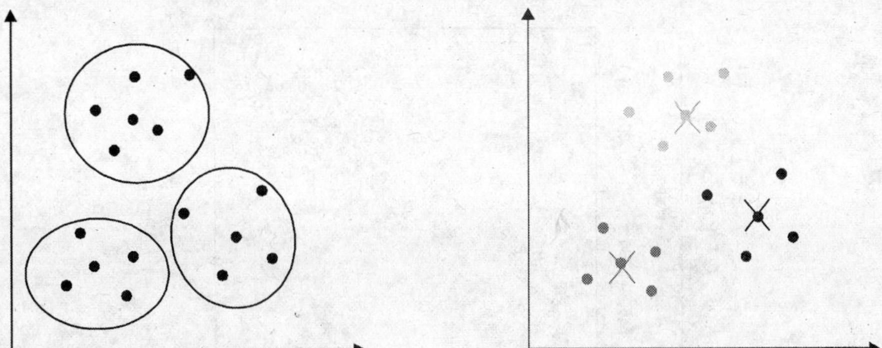

Below shown are some other possibilities of cluster partitioning based on the different choice of cluster centroids. You may end up having any of these groupings based on your requirements and the goal that you are trying to achieve.

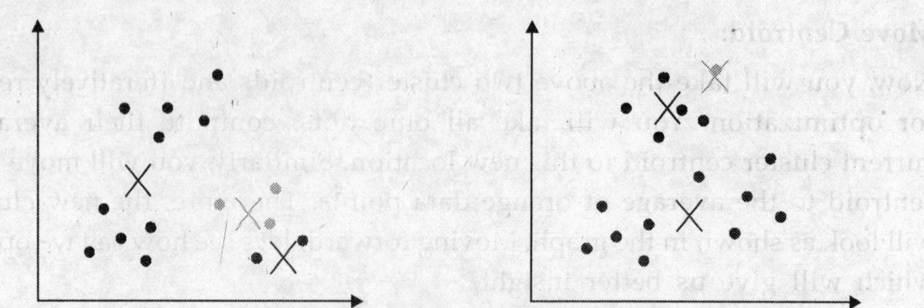

Learn Data Science From Experts

The R Programming lessons are given in Unit 7 of this book.

Example 2.1: We start with an example where all our assumptions hold. R includes a dataset about empirical waiting time between eruptions and the duration of the eruption for the Old Faithful geyser in Yellowstone National Park known as 'faithful'. The dataset consists of 272 observations of 2 features. Enter following data in R- Console

```
#Plotting  the dataset available from Faithful library plot(faithful)
```

Press Enter to see following visual :

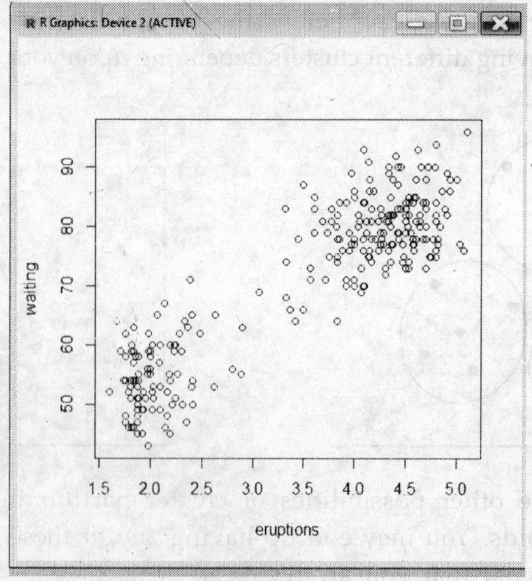

Observing the visual of dataset, two distinct clusters are seen. WE will now use the kmeans() function in R to form clusters.

Let's see how K-Means clustering works on the data

```
#Specify 2 centers
k_clust_start=kmeans(faithful,
centers=2)
#Plot the data using clusters
plot(faithful, col=k_
clust_start$cluster,pch=2)
```

R Console

```
> #Plotting  the dataset available from Faithful library
> plot(faithful)
> #Specify 2 centers
> k_clust_start=kmeans(faithful, centers=2)
> #Plot the data using clusters
> plot(faithful, col=k_clust_start$cluster,pch=2)
> |
```

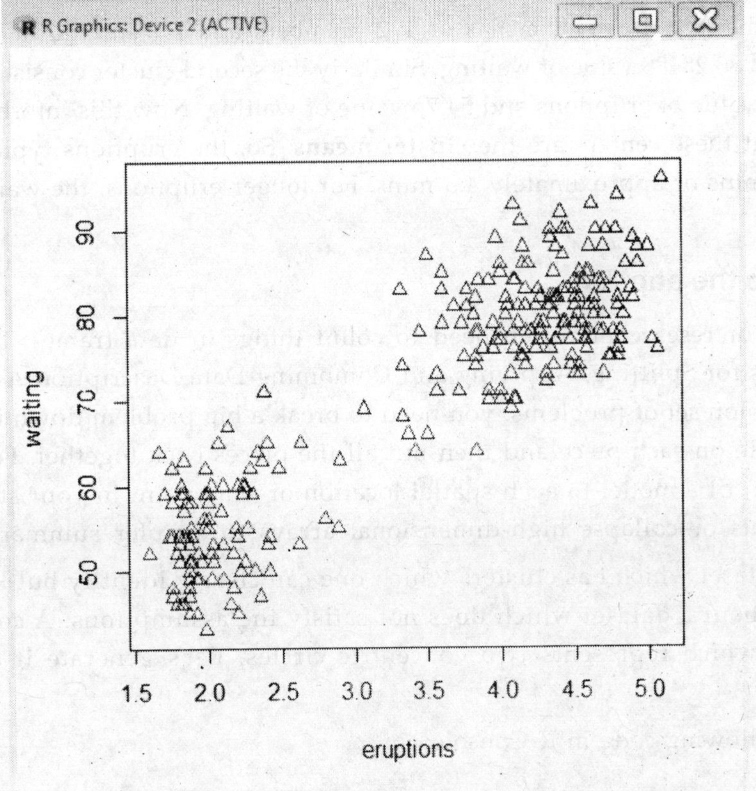

Being a small dataset, clusters are formed almost instantaneously but how do we see the clusters, their centers or sizes? The k_clust_start variable is used that contains information on both *centers* and the size of clusters. We will check them out by entering following code in R Console:

```
#Use the centers to find the cluster centers
k_clust_start$centers
```

```
> #Use the centers to find the cluster centers
> k_clust_start$centers
  eruptions  waiting
1   4.29793 80.28488
2   2.09433 54.75000
> |
```

We are given the details of centers of eruption clusters of data with their corresponding waiting interval:

Now enter following code in R Console:

```
> #Use the size to find the cluster sizes
> k_clust_start$size
[1] 172 100
> |
```

This means the first cluster consists of 172 members and is centered at 4.29793 value of eruptions and 80.28488 value of waiting. Similarly the second cluster consists of 100 members with 2.09433 value of eruptions and 54.75 value of waiting. Now this information is golden! We know that these centers are the **cluster means**. So, the eruptions typically happen for either ~2.09 mins or approximately 4.3 mins. For longer eruptions, the waiting time is also longer.

Getting into the depths

Programmer or researcher often need to count things in data frames. Package 'plyr' is a set of tools for Splitting, Applying and Combining Data Description A set of tools that solves a common set of problems: you need to break a big problem down into manageable pieces, operate on each piece and then put all the pieces back together. For example, you might want to fit a model to each spatial location or time point in your study, summarise data by panels or collapse high-dimensional arrays to simpler summary statistics

Imagine a dataset which has clusters which one can clearly identify but k-means cannot. I'm talking about a dataset which does not satisfy the assumptions. A common example is a dataset which represents two concentric circles. Let's generate it and see how it looks like.

Now enter following code in R Console:

```
#The following code will generate different plots for
library(plyr)
library(dplyr)
#Generate random data which will be first cluster
clust1 = data_frame(x = rnorm(200), y = rnorm(200))
#Generate the second cluster which will 'surround' ti
clust2 = data_frame(r = rnorm(200, 15, .5), theta = ri
                     x = r * cos(theta), y = r & sin(theta)
   dplyr : : select(x, y)
#combine the data
dataset_cirs = rbind(clust1, clust2)
#see the plot
plot(dataset_cir)
```

After entering data, press "Enter" key to see following visual on programming screen;

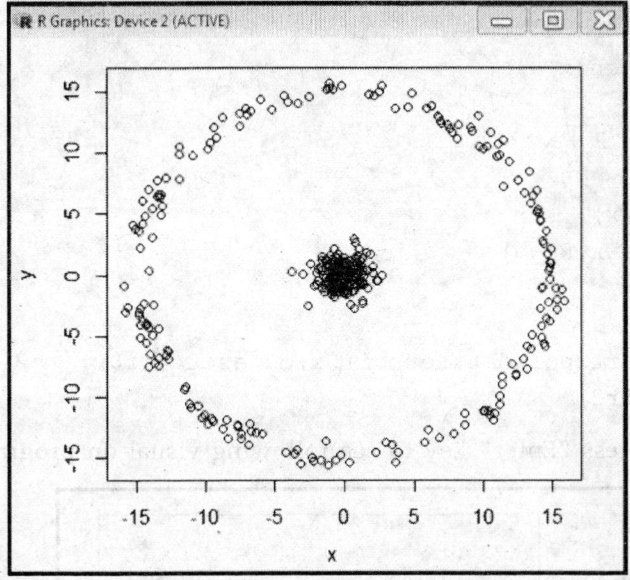

We are now able to see two distinct clusters – one in the middle and the other circling the first. However, this violates the assumption that the clusters are spherical. The inner data is spherical while the outer circle is not. Even though the clustering will not be good, let's see how does k-means perform on this data. Now enter following code in R Console:

```
#Fit the k-means model
k_clust_spher1=kmeans(dateset_cir, center=2)
#Plot the data and clusters
plot(dataset_cir, Col=k_clust_spher1Scluster, pch=2)
```

After entering data, press "Enter" key to see following visual on programming screen;

How do we solve this problem? There are clearly 2 clusters but k-means is not working well. A simple way in this case is to transform our data into polar format.

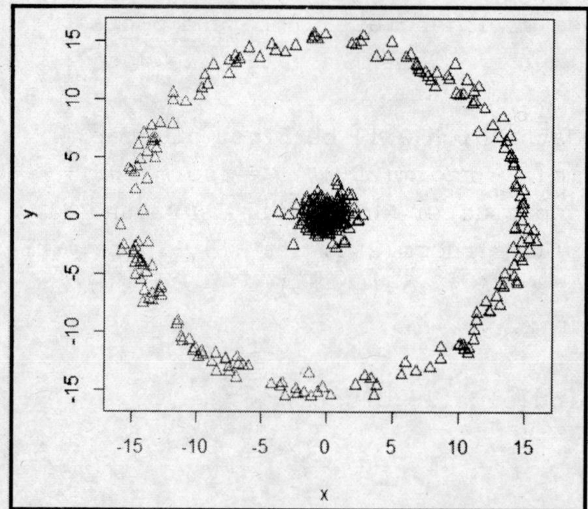

So we will convert it and plot it by entering following code in R Console:

```
#Using a function for transformation
cart2pol=function(x, y){
#This is r
   nwex=sqrt (x^2 + y^2)
#This is theta
   newy=atan(y/x)
   x_y=cbind(newx,newy)
   return(x_y)
}
dataset_cir2=cart2pol(dataset_cir$x,dataset_cir$y)
plot(dataset_cir2)
```

After entering data, press "Enter" key to see following visual on programming screen;

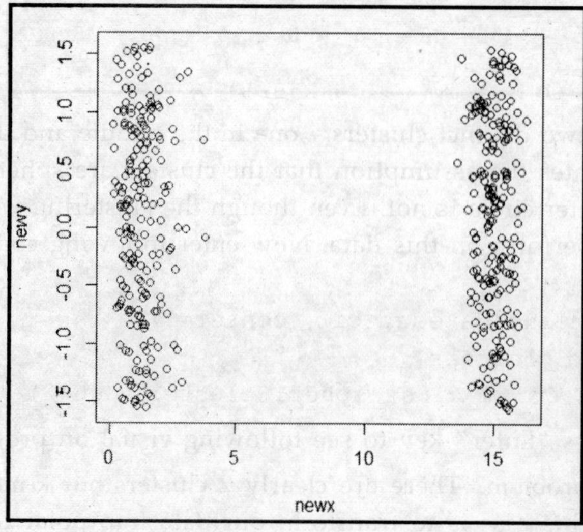

Now we run the k-means model on this data by entering following code in R Console:

```
k_clust_spher2=kmeans(dataset_cir2, centers=2)
#Plot the data and clusters
plot(dataset_cir2, col=k_clust_spher2$cluster,pch=2)
```

After entering data, press "Enter" key to see following visual on programming screen;

This time k-means algorithm works well and correctly transform the data. We can also view the clusters on the original data to double-check this by entering following code in R Console:

```
plot(dataset_cir,
col=k_clust_spher2$cluster,pch=2)
```

After entering data, press "Enter" key to see following visual on programming screen;

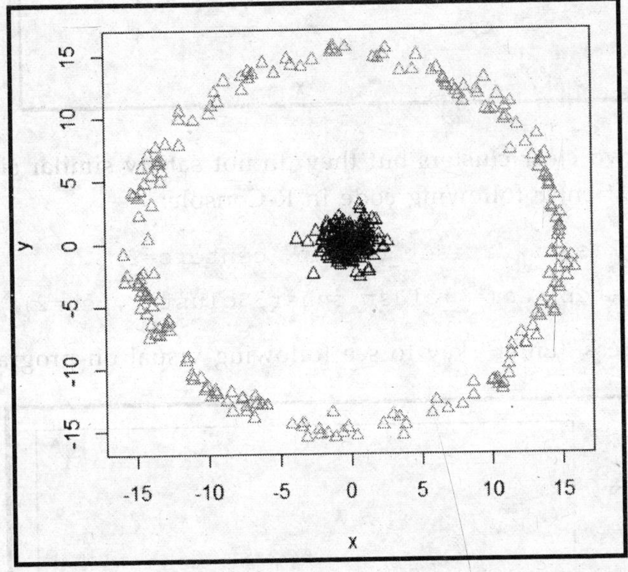

By transforming our data into polar coordinates and fitting k-means model on the transformed data, we fulfil the spherical data assumption and data is accurately clustered.

Now let's look at a data where the clusters are not of similar sizes. Similar size does not mean that the clusters have to be exactly equal. It simply means that no cluster should have 'too few' members. Just enter following code in R Console:

```
#Make the first cluster with 1000 random values
clust1 = data_frame(x = rnorm(1000), y = rnorm(1000))
#Keep 10 values together to make the second cluster
clust2=data_frame(x=c(5,5.1,5.2,5.3,5.4,5,5.1,5.2,5.3
#Combine the data
dataset_uneven=rbind(clust1,clust2)
plot(dataset_uneven)
```

After entering data, press "Enter" key to see following visual on programming screen;

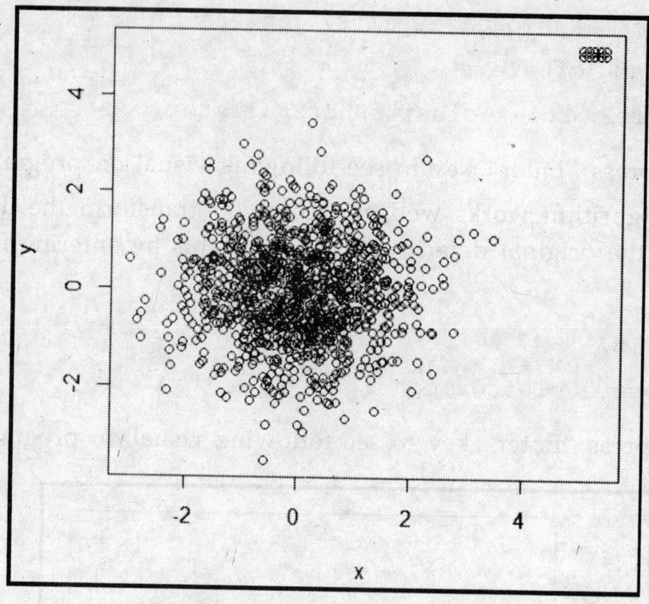

Here again, we have two clear clusters but they do not satisfy similar size requirement of k-means algorithm. Just enter following code in R Console:

```
k_clust_spher3=kmeans(dataset_uneven, centers=2)
plot(dataset_uneven, col=k_clust_spher3$cluster,pch=2)
```

After entering data, press "Enter" key to see following visual on programming screen;

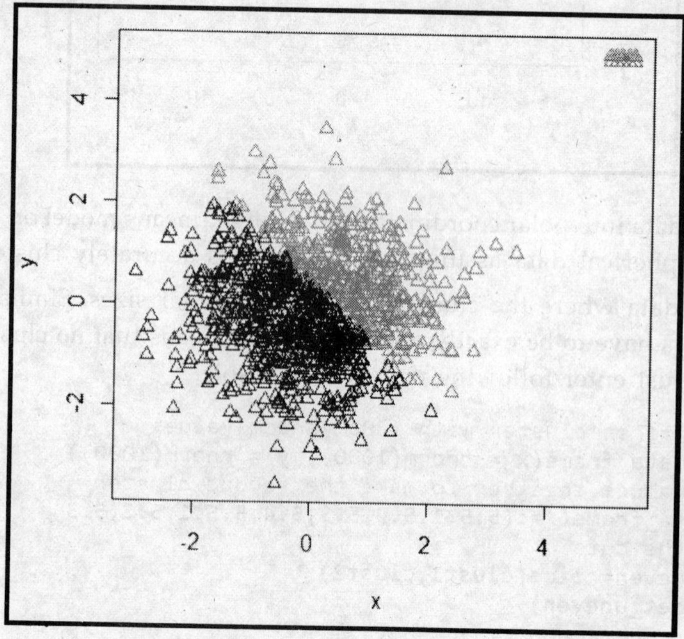

Why did this happen? K-means tries to minimize inter cluster and intracluster distance and create 'tight' clusters. In this process, it assigns some data points in the first cluster to the second cluster incorrectly. This makes the clustering inaccurate.

How to decide the value of K in data

The datasets I worked on in this article are all simple and it is easily to identify clusters by plotting them. However, complicated datasets do not have this luxury. The Elbow method is popular for finding a suitable value of 'K' for k-means clustering. This method uses SSE within groups for different values of k and plots them. Using this plot, we can choose the 'k' which shows an abrupt change in SSE, creating an 'elbow effect'. I will show an illustration on iris dataset using petal width and petal length. Just enter following code in R Console:

```
#Create a vector for storing the sse
sse=vector('numeric')
for(i in 2:15){
#k-means function in R has a feature withinss which
  sse[i-1]=sum(kmeans(iris[,3:4],centers=i)$withinss
}
#Converting the sse to a data frame and storing corr
sse=as.data.frame(sse)
sse$k=seq.int(2,15)
#Making the plot. This plot is also known as screepl
plot(sse$k,sse$sse,type="b")
```

After entering data, press "Enter" key to see following visual on programming screen;

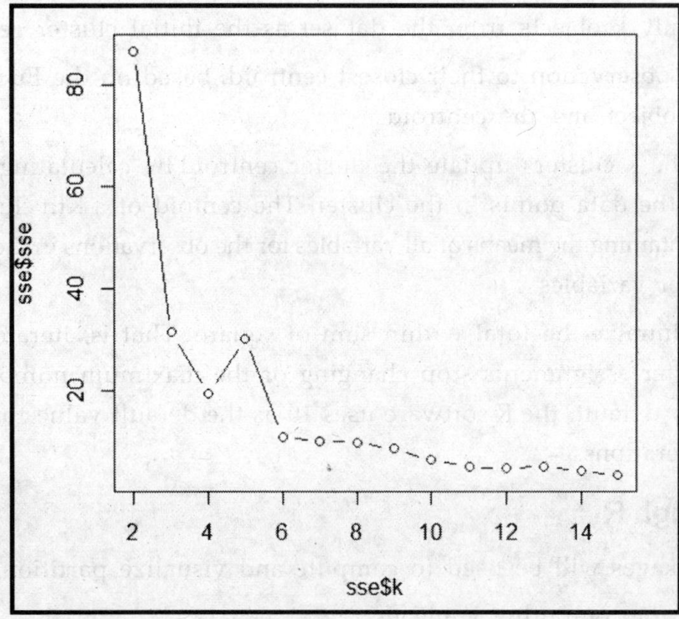

In this plot, the first elbow is formed at k=3. This method suggest that we should have 3 clusters for this data.

Example 2 Another example of K-means algorithm

We have learnt at the end of example 2.1, that the first step in using k-means clustering is to indicate the number of clusters (k) that will be generated in the final solution.

The algorithm starts by randomly selecting k objects from the data set to serve as the initial centers for the clusters. The selected objects are also known as cluster means or centroids.

Next, each of the remaining objects is assigned to it's closest centroid, where closest is defined using the Euclidean distance between the object and the cluster mean. This step is called "cluster assignment step". Note that, to use correlation distance, the data are input as z-scores.

After the assignment step, the algorithm computes the new mean value of each cluster. The term cluster "centroid update" is used to design this step. Now that the centers have been recalculated, every observation is checked again to see if it might be closer to a different cluster. All the objects are reassigned again using the updated cluster means.

The cluster assignment and centroid update steps are iteratively repeated until the cluster assignments stop changing (i.e until convergence is achieved). That is, the clusters formed in the current iteration are the same as those obtained in the previous iteration.

K-means algorithm can be summarized as follow:

1. Specify the number of clusters (K) to be created (by the analyst)
2. Select randomly k objects from the dataset as the initial cluster centers or means
3. Assigns each observation to their closest centroid, based on the Euclidean distance between the object and the centroid
4. For each of the k clusters update the cluster centroid by calculating the new mean values of all the data points in the cluster. The centoid of a Kth cluster is a vector of length p containing the means of all variables for the observations in the kth cluster; p is the number of variables.
5. Iteratively minimize the total within sum of square. That is, iterate steps 3 and 4 until the cluster assignments stop changing or the maximum number of iterations is reached. By default, the R software uses 10 as the default value for the maximum number of iterations.

(1) Example through R

The following R packages will be used to compute and visualize partitioning clustering:

- stats package for computing K-means
- cluster package for computing PAM and CLARA algorithms
- factoextra for beautiful visualization of clusters

First we will have to Install some relevant packages of R and then Load them for computation purpose by entering following code in R Console:

```
install.packages("factoextra")
install.packages("cluster")
install.packages("magrittr")
```

Load packages:

```
library("cluster")
library("factoextra")
library("magrittr")
```

(2) Data Preparation

- Demo data set: the built-in R dataset named USArrest
- Remove missing data
- Scale variables to make them comparable

Enter following code in R Console:

```
# Load  and prepare the data
data("USArrests")
my_data <- USArrests %>%
  na.omit() %>%           # Remove missing values (NA)
  scale()                 # Scale variables
# View the firt 3 rows
head(my_data, n = 3)
```

After entering data, press "Enter" key to see following visual on programming screen

```
R Console
> data("USArrests")      # Loading the data set
> df <- scale(USArrests) # Scaling the data
> # View the firt 3 rows of the data
> head(df, n = 3)
            Murder   Assault   UrbanPop         Rape
Alabama 1.24256408 0.7828393 -0.5209066 -0.003416473
Alaska  0.50786248 1.1068225 -1.2117642  2.484202941
Arizona 0.07163341 1.4788032  0.9989801  1.042878388
> |
```

(3) Required R packages and functions

The standard R function for k-means clustering is *kmeans*() [*stats* package], which simplified format is as follow:

kmeans (x, centers, iter.max = 10, nstart = 1)

where

- *x*: numeric matrix, numeric data frame or a numeric vector
- ***centers***: Possible values are the number of clusters (k) or a set of initial (distinct) cluster centers. If a number, a random set of (distinct) rows in x is chosen as the initial centers.
- ***iter.max***: The maximum number of iterations allowed. Default value is 10.
- ***nstart***: The number of random starting partitions when centers is a number. Trying nstart > 1 is often recommended.

To create a beautiful graph of the clusters generated with the *kmeans*() function, will use the *factoextra* package.

- Installing *factoextra* package as:

  install.packages("factoextra")

- Loading *factoextra*:

  library(factoextra)

(4) Estimating the optimal number of clusters

The k-means clustering requires the users to specify the number of clusters to be generated. One fundamental question is: How to choose the right number of expected clusters (k)?

There is a simple solution. The idea is to compute k-means clustering using different values of clusters k. Next, the wss (within sum of square) is drawn according to the number of clusters. The location of a bend (knee) in the plot is generally considered as an indicator of the appropriate number of clusters.

The R function *fviz_nbclust*() [in *factoextra* package] provides a convenient solution to estimate the optimal number of clusters. Enter following code at R-console:

```
library(factoextra)
fviz_nbclust(df, kmeans, method = "wss") +
  geom_vline(xintercept = 4, linetype = 2)
```

After entering data, press "Enter" key to see following visual on programming screen The plot above represents the variance within the clusters. It decreases as k increases, but it can be seen a bend (or "elbow") at k = 4. This bend indicates that additional clusters beyond the fourth have little value.. In the next section, we'll classify the observations into 4 clusters.

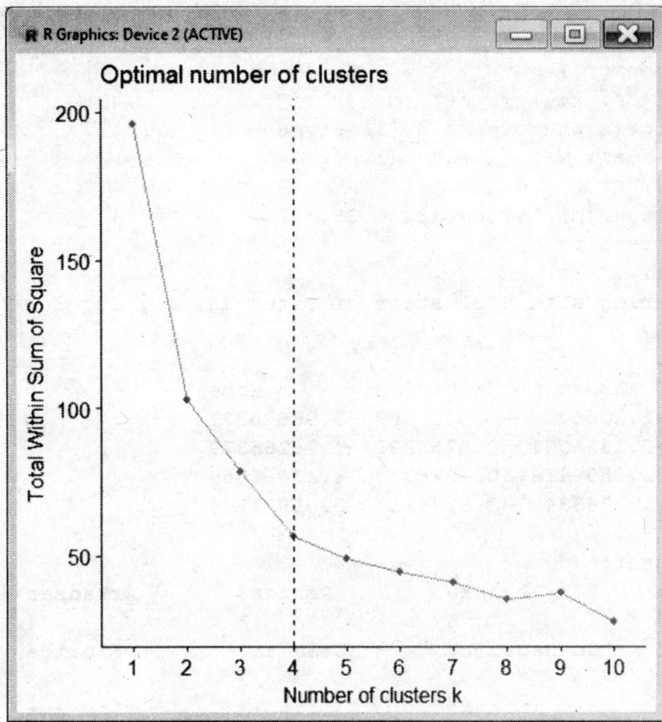

(5) Computing k-means clustering

As k-means clustering algorithm starts with k randomly selected centroids, it's always recommended to use the *set.seed()*function in order to set a seed for *R's random number generator*. The aim is to make reproducible the results, so that the reader of this article will obtain exactly the same results as those shown below.

Enter following code at R-console that shall performs *k-means clustering* with k = 4:

```
# Compute k-means with k = 4
set.seed(123)
km.res <- kmeans(df, 4, nstart = 25)
```

As the final result of k-means clustering result is sensitive to the random starting assignments, we specify nstart = 25. This means that R will try 25 different random starting assignments and then select the best results corresponding to the one with the lowest within cluster variation. The default value of nstart in R is one. But, it's strongly recommended to compute k-means clustering with a large value of nstart such as 25 or 50, in order to have a more stable result.

Enter following code at R-console:

```
# Print the results
print(km.res)
```

After entering data, press "Enter" key to see following visual on programming screen:

```
> library(factoextra)
> fviz_nbclust(df, kmeans, method = "wss") +
+     geom_vline(xintercept = 4, linetype = 2)
> # Compute k-means with k = 4
> set.seed(123)
> km.res <- kmeans(df, 4, nstart = 25)
> # Print the results
> print(km.res)
K-means clustering with 4 clusters of sizes 13, 16, 13, 8

Cluster means:
      Murder    Assault   UrbanPop        Rape
1 -0.9615407 -1.1066010 -0.9301069 -0.96676331
2 -0.4894375 -0.3826001  0.5758298 -0.26165379
3  0.6950701  1.0394414  0.7226370  1.27693964
4  1.4118898  0.8743346 -0.8145211  0.01927104

Clustering vector:
       Alabama         Alaska        Arizona       Arkansas     California
             4              3              3              4              3
      Colorado    Connecticut       Delaware        Florida        Georgia
             3              2              2              3              4
        Hawaii          Idaho       Illinois        Indiana           Iowa
             2              1              3              2              1
        Kansas       Kentucky      Louisiana          Maine       Maryland
             2              1              4              1              3
 Massachusetts       Michigan      Minnesota    Mississippi       Missouri
             2              3              1              4              3
       Montana       Nebraska         Nevada  New Hampshire     New Jersey
             1              1              3              1              2
    New Mexico       New York North Carolina   North Dakota           Ohio
             3              3              4              1              2
      Oklahoma         Oregon   Pennsylvania   Rhode Island South Carolina
             2              2              2              2              4
  South Dakota      Tennessee          Texas           Utah        Vermont
             1              4              3              2              1
      Virginia     Washington  West Virginia      Wisconsin        Wyoming
             2              2              1              1              2

Within cluster sum of squares by cluster:
[1] 11.952463 16.212213 19.922437  8.316061
 (between_SS / total_SS =  71.2 %)

Available components:

[1] "cluster"      "centers"      "totss"        "withinss"     "tot.withinss"
[6] "betweenss"    "size"         "iter"         "ifault"
> |
```

The printed output displays:

- the cluster means or centers: a matrix, which rows are cluster number (1 to 4) and columns are variables
- the clustering vector: A vector of integers (from 1:k) indicating the cluster to which each point is allocated

It's possible to compute the mean of each variables by clusters using the original data: Enter following code at R-console:

```
aggregate(USArrests, by=list(cluster=km.res$cluster), mean)
```

```
> aggregate(USArrests, by=list(cluster=km.res$cluster), mean)
  cluster   Murder   Assault UrbanPop     Rape
1       1  3.60000  78.53846 52.07692 12.17692
2       2  5.65625 138.87500 73.87500 18.78125
3       3 10.81538 257.38462 76.00000 33.19231
4       4 13.93750 243.62500 53.75000 21.41250
> |
```

If you want to add the point classifications to the original data, use this: Enter following code at R-console:

```
dd <- cbind(USArrests, cluster = km.res$cluster)
head(dd)
```

```
> dd <- cbind(USArrests, cluster = km.res$cluster)
> head(dd)
           Murder Assault UrbanPop Rape cluster
Alabama      13.2     236       58 21.2       4
Alaska       10.0     263       48 44.5       3
Arizona       8.1     294       80 31.0       3
Arkansas      8.8     190       50 19.5       4
California    9.0     276       91 40.6       3
Colorado      7.9     204       78 38.7       3
> |
```

(6) Accessing to the results of kmeans() function

kmeans() function returns a list of components, including:

- **cluster**: A vector of integers (from 1:k) indicating the cluster to which each point is allocated
- **centers**: A matrix of cluster centers (cluster means)
- **totss**: The total sum of squares (TSS), i.e "(xi"x¯)2"(xi"x¯)2. TSS measures the total variance in the data.
- **withinss**: Vector of within-cluster sum of squares, one component per cluster
- **tot.withinss**: Total within-cluster sum of squares, i.e. sum(withinss)sum(withinss)

- **betweenss**: The between-cluster sum of squares, i.e. totss"tot.withinsstotss"tot.withinss
- **size**: The number of observations in each cluster

These components can be accessed as follow:

Enter following code at R-console:

```
# Finding Cluster number for each of the observations
km.res$cluster
```

```
R Console
> km.res$cluster
       Alabama         Alaska        Arizona       Arkansas     California
             4              3              3              4              3
      Colorado    Connecticut       Delaware        Florida        Georgia
             3              2              2              3              4
        Hawaii          Idaho       Illinois        Indiana           Iowa
             2              1              3              2              1
        Kansas       Kentucky      Louisiana          Maine       Maryland
             2              1              4              1              3
 Massachusetts       Michigan      Minnesota    Mississippi       Missouri
             2              3              1              4              3
       Montana       Nebraska         Nevada  New Hampshire     New Jersey
             1              1              3              1              2
    New Mexico       New York North Carolina   North Dakota           Ohio
             3              3              4              1              2
      Oklahoma         Oregon   Pennsylvania   Rhode Island South Carolina
             2              2              2              2              4
  South Dakota      Tennessee          Texas           Utah        Vermont
             1              4              3              2              1
      Virginia     Washington  West Virginia      Wisconsin        Wyoming
             2              2              1              1              2
```

```
head(km.res$cluster, 4)
```

```
> head(km.res$cluster, 4)
 Alabama   Alaska  Arizona Arkansas
       4        3        3        4
> |
```

Enter following code at R-console:

```
# Cluster size
km.res$size
```

```
> km.res$size
[1] 13 16 13  8
> |
```

Enter following code at R-console:

```
# Cluster means
km.res$centers
```

```
> km.res$centers
      Murder    Assault   UrbanPop        Rape
1 -0.9615407 -1.1066010 -0.9301069 -0.96676331
2 -0.4894375 -0.3826001  0.5758298 -0.26165379
3  0.6950701  1.0394414  0.7226370  1.27693964
4  1.4118898  0.8743346 -0.8145211  0.01927104
> |
```

(7) Visualizing k-means clusters

It is a good idea to plot the cluster results. These can be used to assess the choice of the number of clusters as well as comparing two different cluster analyses.

Now, we want to visualize the data in a scatter plot with coloring each data point according to its cluster assignment.

The problem is that the data contains more than 2 variables and the question is what variables to choose for the xy scatter plot.

A solution is to reduce the number of dimensions by applying a dimensionality reduction algorithm, such as **Principal Component Analysis (PCA)**, that operates on the four variables and outputs two new variables (that represent the original variables) that you can use to do the plot.

In other words, if we have a multi-dimensional data set, a solution is to perform Principal Component Analysis (PCA) and to plot data points according to the first two principal components coordinates. }

The function fviz_cluster() [factoextra package] can be used to easily visualize k-means clusters. It takes k-means results and the original data as arguments. In the resulting plot, observations are represented by points, using principal components if the number of variables is greater than 2. It's also possible to draw concentration ellipse around each cluster.Enter following code at the R-console:

```
fviz_cluster(km.res, data = df,
         palette = c("#2E9FDF", "#00AFBB", "#E7B800", "#FC4E07"),
         ellipse.type = "euclid", # Concentration ellipse
         star.plot = TRUE, # Add segments from centroids to items
         repel = TRUE, # Avoid label overplotting (slow)
         ggtheme = theme_minimal()
    )
```

After entering data, press "Enter" key to see following visual on programming screen:

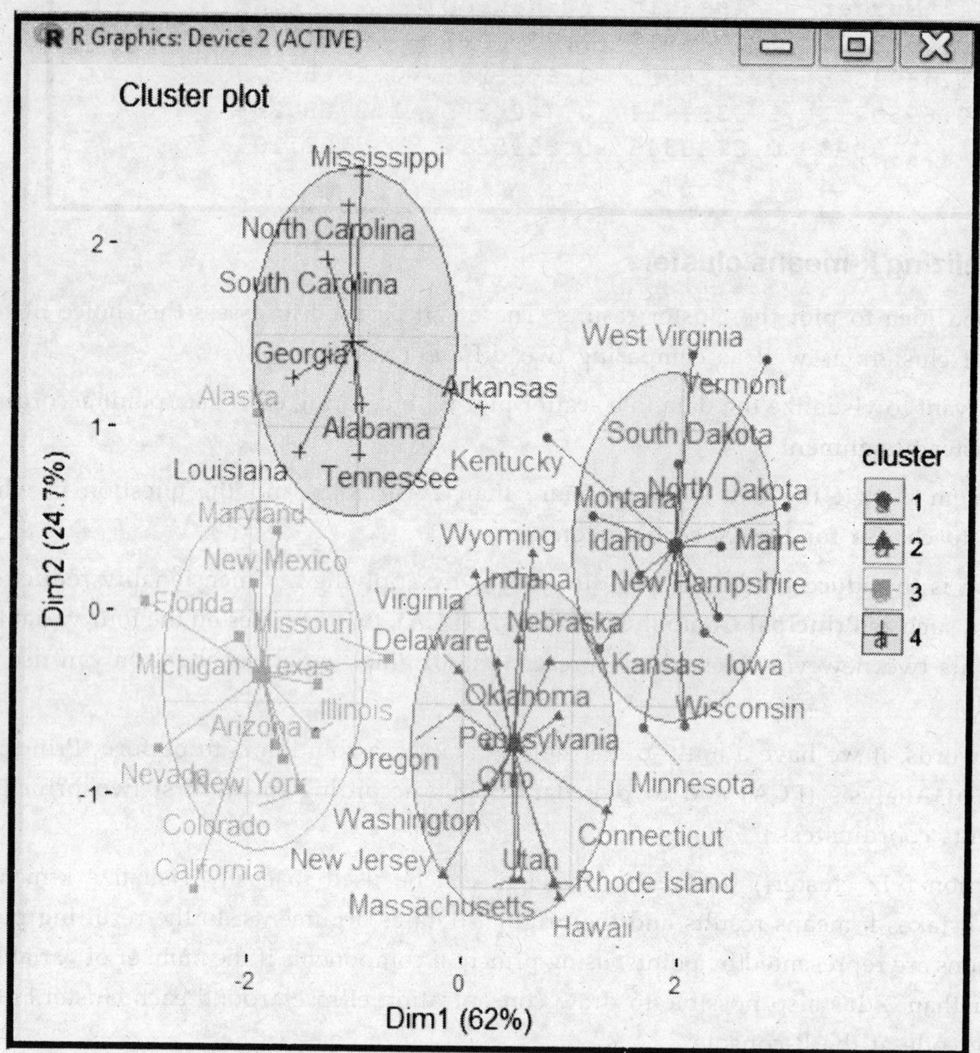

2.10 K-Means Clustering Advantages and Disadvantages

K-means clustering is very simple and fast algorithm. It can efficiently deal with very large data sets. However there are some weaknesses, including:

1. It assumes prior knowledge of the data and requires the analyst to choose the appropriate number of cluster (k) in advance
2. The final results obtained is sensitive to the initial random selection of cluster centers. Why is it a problem? Because, for every different run of the algorithm on the same dataset, you may choose different set of initial centers. This may lead to different clustering results on different runs of the algorithm.

3. It's sensitive to outliers.
4. If you rearrange your data, it's very possible that you'll get a different solution every time you change the ordering of your data.

Possible solutions to these weaknesses, include:

1. Solution to issue 1: Compute k-means for a range of k values, for example by varying k between 2 and 10. Then, choose the best k by comparing the clustering results obtained for the different k values.
2. Solution to issue 2: Compute K-means algorithm several times with different initial cluster centers. The run with the lowest total within-cluster sum of square is selected as the final clustering solution.
3. To avoid distortions caused by excessive outliers, it's possible to use PAM algorithm, which is less sensitive to outliers.

2.11 KERNEL K-MEANS

Kernel k-means clustering method is a non-linear extension of the conventional k-means clustering method (Dhillon et al 2005). Girolami (2002) first proposed the kernel k-means clustering method. It is an iterative method. It first maps the data points from the input space to a higher dimensional feature space through a nonlinear transformation ö(·) and then minimizes the clustering error in that feature space. The distance between a data point and a cluster center in the feature space (i.e., the kernel-induced feature space) can be computed using a kernel function without knowing the explicit form of the transformation (Scholkopf et al 1998). This is, because, the dot product between the images of two data points X and Y in the feature space, which is $\phi(X) \cdot \phi(Y)$, can be computed as a function $K(X, Y)$, where $K : D \times D \rightarrow \bar{R}$ is called **kernel function**. This is often known as the kernel trick and is valid for transformations that satisfies Mercer's conditions (Critianini & Shewe-Taylor 2000)

Kernel k-means uses the 'kernel trick' (i.e. implicitly projecting all data into a non-linear feature space with the use of a kernel) in order to deal with one of the major drawbacks of k-means that is that it cannot capture clusters that are not linearly separable in input space. The algorithm is implemented using the triangle inequality to avoid unnecessary and computational expensive distance calculations. This leads to significant speedup particularly on large data sets with a high number of clusters. With a particular choice of weights this algorithm becomes equivalent to Kernighan-Lin, and the norm-cut graph partitioning algorithms. The function also support input in the form of a kernel matrix or a list of characters for text clustering. The data can be passed to the kkmeans function in a matrix or a data.frame, in addition kkmeans also supports input in the form of a kernel matrix of class kernelMatrix or as a list of character vectors where a string kernel has to be used.

Some standard kernel functions are given below:

- Polynomial kernel of degree p : $K(X,Y) = (X \cdot Y + C)^p$, where p is a positive integer and $c \in R$.
- Gaussian (RBF) kernel: $K(X,Y) = exp\left(-\frac{\| X - Y \|^2}{2a^2}\right)$, where $\sigma \in R$ is called Gaussian kernel parameter.
- Sigmoidal kernel : $K(X,Y) = \tanh(a(X \cdot Y) + b)$, where a, $b \in R$

For two arbitrary data points X_i and X_j, very often, in the iterative process of clustering, $K(X_i, X_j)$ is needed. So, a matrix called kernel matrix $H = (K_{ij}]_{n \times n}$ is found, where the $(i, j)^{th}$ entry is $K_{ij} = K(X_i, Xj)$. Here n is the data set size. The kernel matrix is precomputed and stored. So, the time and space requirements (which is given, in detail, in later sections) are $O(n^2)$. This is the drawback of kernel k-means clustering method and because of which it is not suitable when the data set size is large. Several other drawbacks of the kernel k-means the clustering result on the sed points as well as on the kernel function.

2.11.1 Kernel K-Means Clustering Algorithm

This algorithm applies the same trick as k-means but with one difference that here in the calculation of distance, kernel method is used instead of the Euclidean distance.

Let $D = \{X_1, X_2, \ldots X_n\}$ be the data set of size n. Let k be the number of clusters required and $M^{(0)}$ be the initial seed points Note, $M^{(0)} = \{m_1^{(10)}, m_2^{(0)}, \ldots, m_k^{(0)}\}$ are points in the input space. For each pattern $X \in D$, assign X to the mean $m_i^{(0)}$, such that $m_i^{(0)}$ is at the nearest distance form X in the kenel-induced feature space. Let the resultant intial partition be $\Pi^{(0)}$. The kernel k-means method takes D, k and $P^{(0)}$ as input parameters and produces a partition of the entire data set. Π_D as the output.

The objective function is to minimize the criterion function

$$J = \sum_{j=1}^{k} \sum_{X_i \in C_j} \| \phi(X_i) - \mu_j \|^2, \quad (1)$$

where u_j is the mean of cluster C_j. That is

$$\mu_j = \sum\nolimits_{x_i \in C_j} \frac{\phi(X_i)}{|C_j|} \quad (2)$$

in the induced space.

Distance between two data points (X_i) and $\phi(X_j)$ in the induced space, that is

$$\begin{aligned} \| \phi(X_i) - \phi(X_j) \|^2 & \\ &= \phi^2(X_i) - 2\phi(X_i) \,.\, \phi(X_j) + \phi^2(X_j) \\ &= K(X_i, X_i) - 2K(X_i, Xj) + K(X_j, X_j); \quad (3) \end{aligned}$$

Further, $\| (X_i) - \mu_j \|^2$ can be calculated without knowing the transformafion $\phi(.)$ explicitly as given below:

$$\| \phi(X_i) - \mu_j \|^2$$

$$= \phi^2(X_i) - \sum_{x_j \in C_j} \frac{\phi(X_i)}{|C_j|} ||^2$$

$$= \phi(X_i) \,.\, \phi(X_i) - F(X_i, Xj) + G(C_j), \quad (4)$$

where
$$F(X_i, C_j) = -\frac{2}{|C_j|} \sum_{x_j \in C_j} \phi(X_i).\phi(X_i) \quad (5)$$

and
$$G(C_j) = -\frac{1}{|C_j|} \sum_{X_l \in C_j} \sum_{X_i \in C_j} \phi(X_l) \,.\, \phi(X_s) \quad (6)$$

The iterative method is outlined in the algorithm 1. The time complexity and the sapce complexity of the kernel k-means clustering method are $O(n_2)$.

Algorithm 1. kernel-k-means-clustering-method($\mathcal{D}$, k, $\Pi^{(0)}$).

1. For each cluster C_j, find $|C_j|$ and $G(C_j)$.
2. Compute $F(X_i, C_j)$ for each X_i and for each cluster C_j.
3. Find $||\phi(X_i) - \mu_j||^2$ using equation (4) and assign X_i to its nearest center.
4. Update μ_j, for $j = 1$ to k, using equation (2).
5. Repeat step 1 through step 4 till convergence.
Output:
The final partition $\Pi_{\mathcal{D}} = \{C_1, C_2, \ldots, C_k\}$.

2.11.2 Algorithmic Steps for Kernel k-means Clustering

Let $X = \{a_1, a_2, a_3, ..., a_n\}$ be the set of data points and 'c' be the number of clusters.

1. Randomly initialize 'c' cluster center.
2. Compute the distance of each data point and the cluster center in the transformed space using:

$$D(\{\pi_e\}_{c=1}^{k}) = \sum_{c=1}^{k} \sum_{a_i \in \pi_j} || \phi(a_i) - m_c ||^2, \text{ where } m_e = \frac{\sum_{a_1 \in \pi_e} \phi(a_i)}{|\pi_c|}$$

$$\phi(a_i).\phi(a_i) - \frac{2\sum_{a_1 \in \pi_e} \phi(a_i).\phi(a_j)}{|\pi_c|} + \frac{\sum_{a_1, a_i \in \pi_e} \phi(a_i).\phi(a_j)}{|\pi_c|^2}$$

Where,

c^{th} cluster is denoted by π_c.

'm_c' denotes the mean of the cluster π_c.

'$\Phi(a_i)$' denotes the data point ai in transformed space.

$\Phi(a_i).\ \Phi(a_j) = \exp^{-(||ai\ -\ aj||)aq}$ for qaussian kemel.

$= (c + ai.ai)$d for polynomial kernel.

3. Assig data point to that cluster center whose distance is minimum.
4. Until data points are re-assignd repeat from step 2).

Advantages

1. Algorithm is able to identify the non-linear structures.
2. Algorithm is best suited for real life data set.

Disadvantages

1. Number of cluster centers need to be predefined.
2. Algorithm is complex in nature and time complexity is large.

2.12 KERNEL ALTERNATIVE TO K-MEANS CLUSTERING: PAM

A robust alternative to k-means is PAM, which is based on medoids, the PAM clustering can be computed using the function *pam*() [*cluster* package]. The function *pamk*( ) [fpc package] is a wrapper for PAM that also prints the suggested number of clusters based on optimum average silhouette width.

Enter following program at R console:

```
> # 1. Generating random data
> ###################################
> set.seed(1000)
> N <- 200
>
> #Generate sinusoidal
> make.sinusoidals <- function(m,noise=0.2)
+ {
+   x1 <- c(1:2*m)
+   x2 <- c(1:2*m)
+
+   for (i in 1:m) {
+     x1[i] <- (i/m) * pi
+     x2[i] <- sin(x1[i]) + rnorm(1,0,noise)
+   }
+
+   for (j in 1:m) {
+     x1[m+j] <- (j/m + 1/2) * pi
+     x2[m+j] <- cos(x1[m+j]) + rnorm(1,0,noise)
+   }
+
+   target <- c(rep(+1,m),rep(-1,m))
+
+   return(data.frame(x1,x2,target))
+ }
>
> dataset <- make.sinusoidals (N)
> plot(dataset$x1,dataset$x2,col=as.factor(dataset$target))
>
> |
```

When above snippet is run, it shall produce following graph:

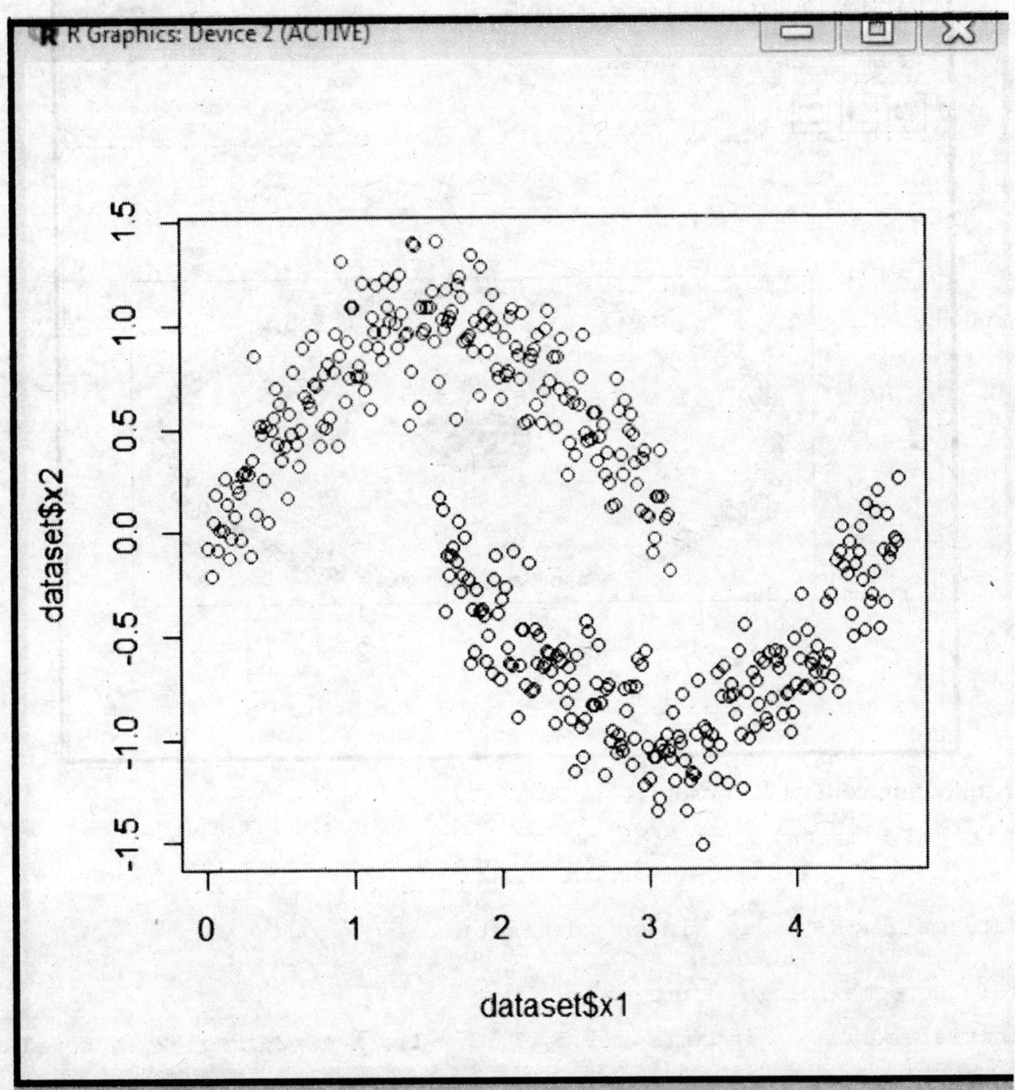

Enter following code at R-console:

```
# Standard K-means, ring
## Run standard k-means
kmeans_obj <- kmeans(ring_dataset, centers=2)

##Plot the clusters
plot(ring_dataset, col=as.factor(kmeans_obj$cluster))
```

When above program is run, it shall give following output:

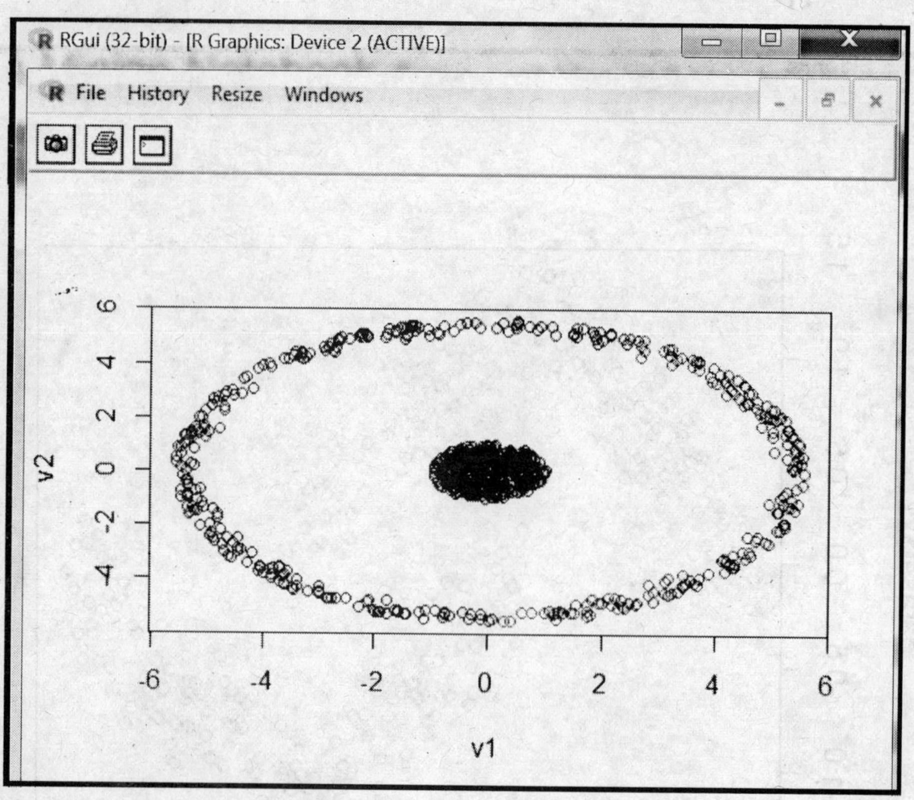

Enter following code at R-console:

```
# Kernel K-means, sinusoid
#Transforming the dataset into a matrix
data_matrix <- as.matrix(new_dataset)

#Giving some initial centers
initial_centers <- matrix(c(1.5, 1, 3, -1), nrow=2, ncol=2, byrow=TRUE)
#Using RBF kernel
kernel_kmeans <- kkmeans(data_matrix, centers=initial_centers,
kernel="rbfdot", alg="kkmeans",  kpar = "automatic")
plot(new_dataset, col = as.factor(kernel_kmeans@.Data))

#Using polynomial kernel
kernel_kmeans <- kkmeans(data_matrix, centers=initial_centers,
kernel="polydot", alg="kkmeans")
plot(new_dataset, col = as.factor(kernel_kmeans@.Data))
```

When above program is run, it shall give following output:

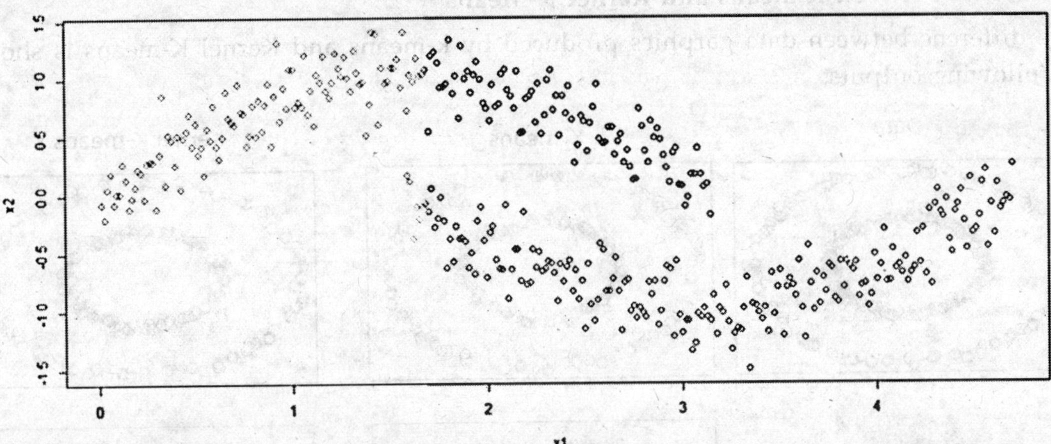

Enter following code:

```
#Using hyperbolic tangent (sigmoid) kernel
 kernel_kmeans <- kkmeans(data_matrix, centers=initial_centers,
kernel="tanhdot", alg="kkmeans")
 plot(new_dataset, col = as.factor(kernel_kmeans@.Data))
```

The above program shall cause the computer to generate following graph:

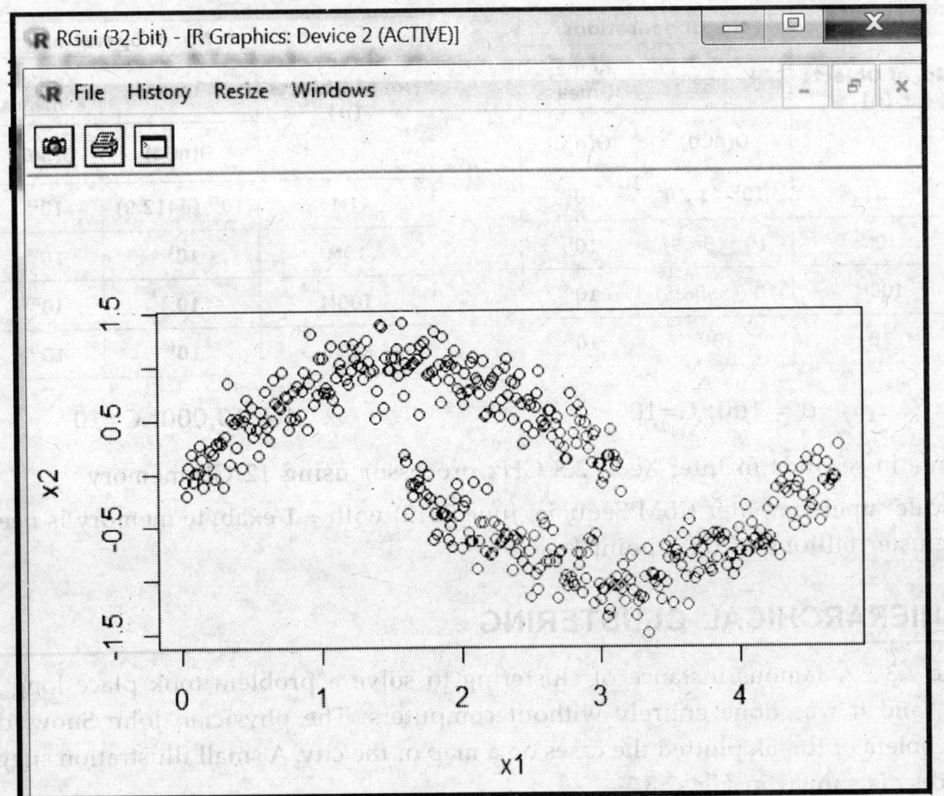

Difference between K-means and Kernel K-Means

The differene between data garphics produced by k-means and Kernel K-means is shown in following outputs:

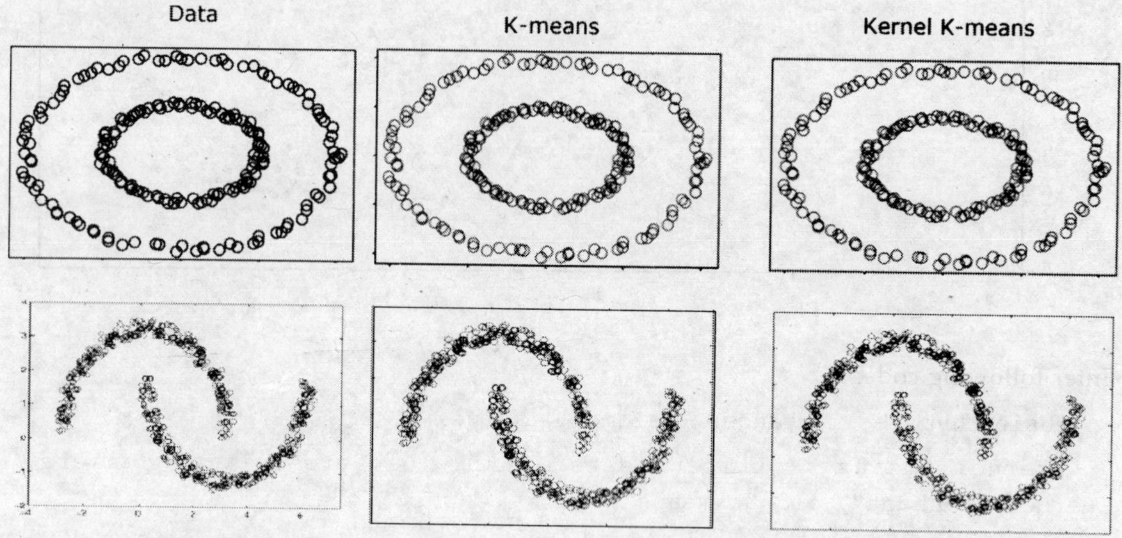

Scalability

No. of Objects (n)	No. of operations	
	K-means	Kernel K-means
	O(nCd)	O(n^2C)
1M	10^{11} (3.2)	10^{15}
10M	10^{12} (34.9)	10^{17}
100M	10^{13}(5508.5)	10^{19}
1B	10^{14}	10^{21}

d = 100; C=10

No. of Objects (n)	No. of operations	
	K-means	Kernel K-means
	O(nCd)	O(n^2C)
1M	10^{13} (6412.9)	10^{16}
10M	10^{14}	10^{18}
100M	10^{15}	10^{20}
1B	10^{16}	10^{22}

d = 10,000; C=10

* Runtime in seconds in Intel Xeon 2.8 GHz processor using 12 GB memory

A petascale supercomputer (IBM Sequoia, June 2012) with ~ 1 exabyte memory is needed to kernel cluster billions of data points!

2.13 HIERARCHICAL CLUSTERING

Example 2.3 : A famous instance of clustering to solve a problem took place long ago in London, and it was done entirely without computers. The physician John Snow, dealing with a Cholera outbreak plotted the cases on a map of the city. A small illustration suggesting the process is shown in Fig. 2.3.

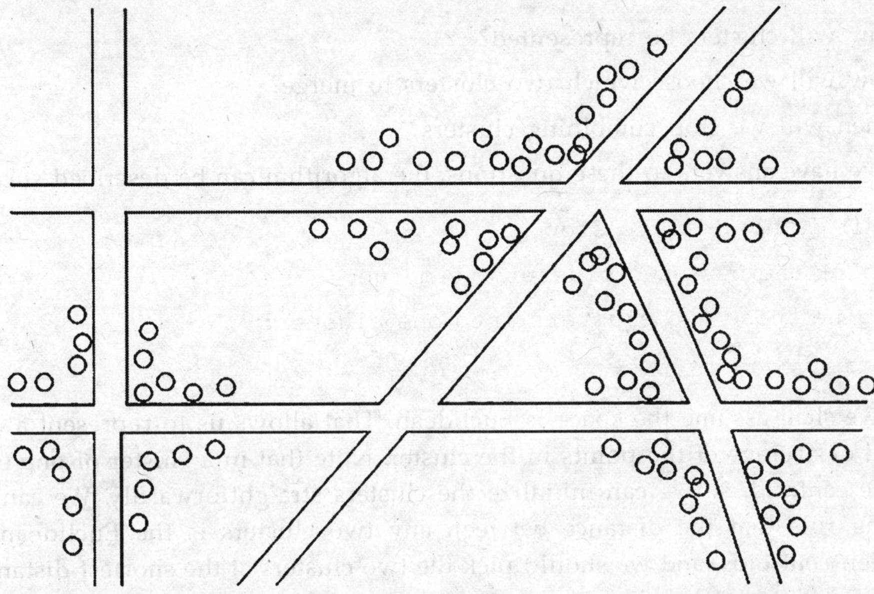

Fig. 2.3: Plotting cholera cases on a map of London

The cases clustered around some of the intersections of roads. These intersections were the locations of wells that had become contaminated; people who lived nearest these wells got sick, while people who lived nearer to wells that had not been contaminated did not get sick. Without the ability to cluster the data, the cause of Cholera would not have been discovered.

We do understand that not all customers are alike and have the same taste. So, this leads to the challenge of marketing the right product to the right customer. An offer or product which might entice a particular customer segment may not be very helpful to other segments. So, you can apply k-means clustering algorithm to segment your entire customer audience into groups with similar traits and preferences based on various metrics (such as their activities, likes and dislikes on social media and their purchase history). Based on these customer segments identified, you can create personalized marketing strategies and bring more business to your organisation.

We begin by considering hierarchical clustering in a Euclidean space. This algorithm can only be used for relatively small datasets, but even so, there are some efficiencies we can make by careful implementation. When the space is non-Euclidean, there are additional problems associated with hierarchical clustering. We therefore consider "clustroids" and the way we can represent a cluster when there is no centroid or average point in a cluster.

2.13.1 Hierarchical Clustering in a Euclidean Space

Any hierarchical clustering algorithm works as follows. We begin with every point in its own cluster. As time goes on, larger clusters will be constructed by combining two smaller clusters, and we have to decide in advance:

(a) How will clusters be represented?

(b) How will we choose which two clusters to merge?

(c) When will we stop combining clusters?

Once we have answers to these questions, the algorithm can be described succinctly as:

```
WHILE it is not time to stop
   DO pick the best two clusters to merge;
   combine those two clusters into one cluster;
END;
```

To begin, we shall assume the space is Euclidean. That allows us to represent a cluster by its centroid or average of the points in the cluster. Note that in a cluster of one point, that point is the centroid, so we can initialize the clusters straightforwardly. We can then use the merging rule that the distance between any two clusters is the Euclidean distance between their centroids, and we should pick the two clusters at the shortest distance. Other ways to define intercluster distance are possible, and we can also pick the best pair of clusters on a basis other than their distance.

Example 2.4: Let us see how the basic hierarchical clustering would work on the data of Fig. 2.2. These points live in a 2-dimensional Euclidean space, and each point is named by its (x, y) coordinates. Initially, each point is in a cluster by itself and is the centroid of that cluster. Among all the pairs of points, there are two pairs that are closest: (10,5) and (11,4) or (11,4) and (12,3). Each is at distance $\sqrt{2}$. Let us break ties arbitrarily and decide to combine (11,4) with (12,3).

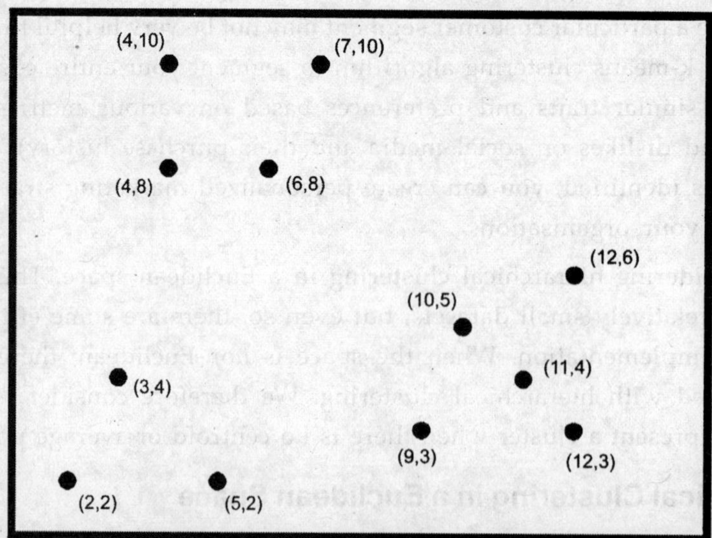

Fig. 2.4: Twelve points to be clustered hierarchically

The result is shown in Fig. 2.5, including the centroid of the new cluster, which is at (11.5, 3.5).

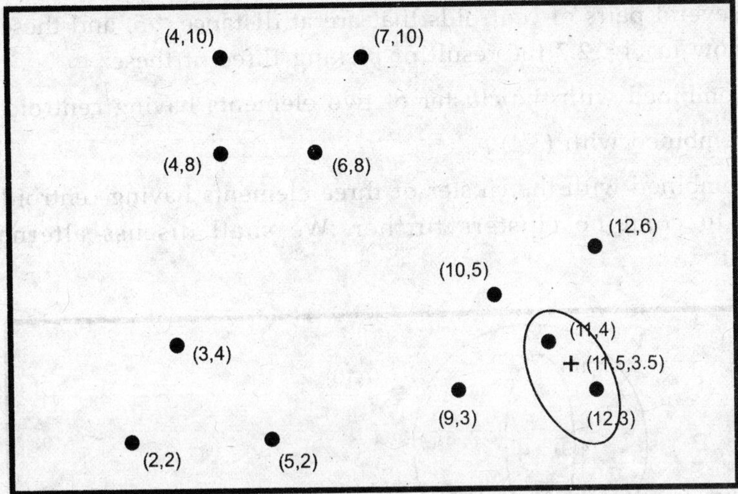

Fig. 2.5: Combining the first two points into a cluster

You might think that (10,5) gets combined with the new cluster next, since it is so close to (11,4). But our distance rule requires us to compare only cluster centroids, and the distance from (10,5) to the centroid of the new cluster is 1.5 " 2, which is slightly greater than 2. Thus, now the two closest clusters are those of the points (4,8) and (4,10). We combine them into one cluster with centroid (4,9).

At this point, the two closest centroids are (10,5) and (11.5, 3.5), so we combine these two clusters. The result is a cluster of three points (10,5), (11,4), and (12,3). The centroid of this cluster is (11,4), which happens to be one of the points of the cluster, but that situation is coincidental. The state of the clusters is shown in Fig. 2.6.

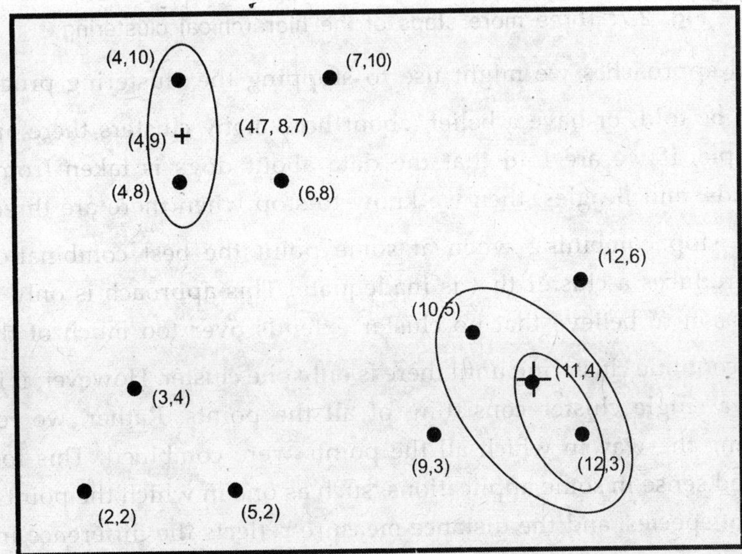

Fig. 2.6: Clustering after two additional steps

Now, there are several pairs of centroids that are at distance " 5, and these are the closest centroids. We show in Fig. 2.7 the result of picking three of these:

1. (6,8) is combined with the cluster of two elements having centroid (4,9).
2. (2,2) is combined with (3,4).
3. (9,3) is combined with the cluster of three elements having centroid (11,4). We can proceed to combine clusters further. We shall discuss alternative stopping rules next.

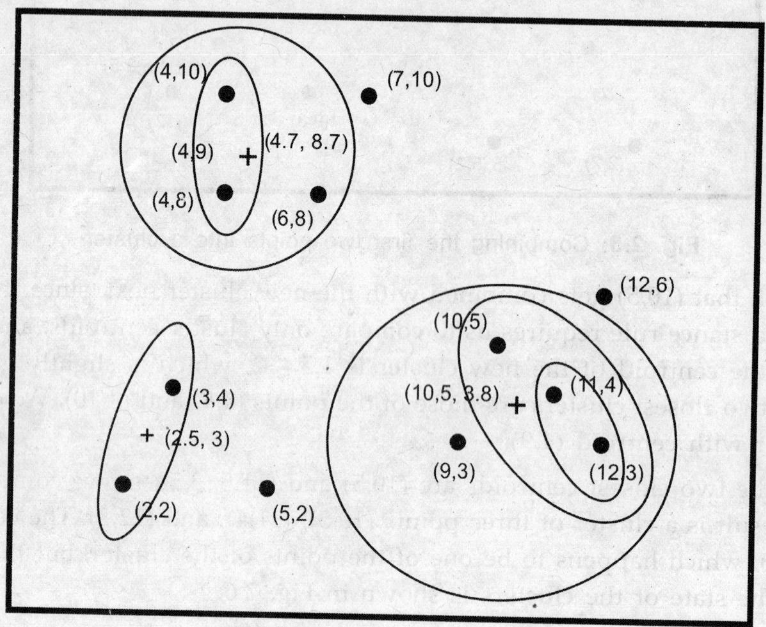

Fig. 2.7: Three more steps of the hierarchical clustering

There are several approaches we might use to stopping the clustering process.

1. We could be told, or have a belief, about how many clusters there are in the data. For example, if we are told that the data about dogs is taken from Chihuahuas, Dachshunds, and Beagles, then we know to stop when there are three clusters left.
2. We could stop combining when at some point the best combination of existing clusters produces a cluster that is inadequate. This approach is only sensible if we have a reason to believe that no cluster extends over too much of the space.
3. We could continue clustering until there is only one cluster. However, it is meaningless to return a single cluster consisting of all the points. Rather, we return the tree representing the way in which all the points were combined. This form of answer makes good sense in some applications, such as one in which the points are genomes of different species, and the distance measure reflects the difference in the genome. 2 Then, the tree represents the evolution of these species, that is, the likely order in which two species branched from a common ancestor.

2.14 DIMENSIONALITY REDUCTION

Real-world data, such as speech signals, digital photographs, or MRI scans, usually has a high dimensionality. In order to handle such real-world data adequately, its dimensionality needs to be reduced.

Dimensionality reduction is the method of transformation of high-dimensional data into a meaningful representation of reduced dimensionality. Ideally, the reduced representation should have a dimensionality that corresponds to the intrinsic dimensionality of the data. The intrinsic dimensionality of data is the minimum number of parameters needed to account for the observed properties of the data . Dimensionality reduction is important in many domains, since it mitigates the curse of dimensionality and other undesired properties of high-dimensional spaces.

Dimension reduction process must ensure that it conveys similar information concisely. These techniques are typically used while solving **machine learning problems** to obtain better features for a classification or regression task.

Let's look at the image shown below. It shows 2 dimensions x1 and x2, which are let us say measurements of several object in cm (x1) and inches (x2). Now, if you were to use both these dimensions in machine learning, they will convey similar information and introduce a lot of noise in system, so you are better of just using one dimension. Here we have converted the dimension of data from 2D (from x1 and x2) to 1D (z1), which has made the data relatively easier to explain.

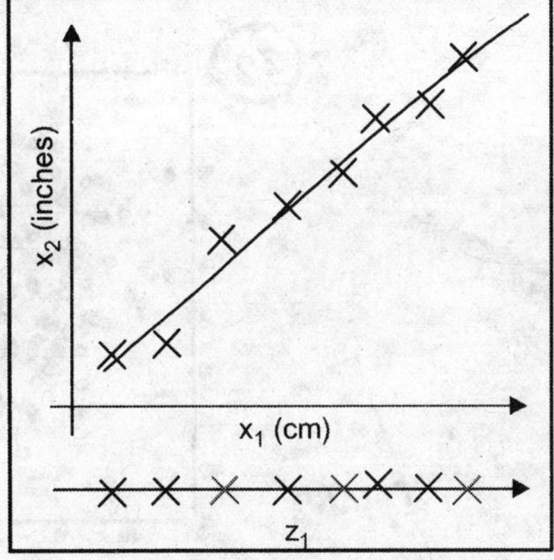

In similar ways, we can reduce n dimensions of data set to k dimensions (k < n) . These k dimensions can be directly identified (filtered) or can be a combination of dimensions (weighted averages of dimensions) or new dimension(s) that represent existing multiple dimensions well.

As per Analytical Vidya Tutorial, one of the most common application of this technique is **Image processing**. You might have come across this Facebook application – "Which Celebrity Do You Look Like?". But, have you ever thought about the algorithm used behind this?

It cab be explained like this: To identify the matched celebrity image, we use pixel data and each pixel is equivalent to one dimension. In every image, there are high number of pixels i.e. high number of dimensions. And every dimension is important here. You can't omit dimensions randomly to make better sense of your overall data set. In such cases, dimension reduction techniques help you to find the significant dimension(s) using various method(s). We'll discuss these methods shortly.

2.14.1 Benefits of Dimension Reduction

Let's look at the benefits of applying Dimension Reduction process:

1. It helps in data compressing and reducing the storage space required
2. It fastens the time required for performing same computations. Less dimensions leads to less computing, also less dimensions can allow usage of algorithms unfit for a large number of dimensions
3. It takes care of multi-collinearity that improves the model performance. It removes redundant features. For example: there is no point in storing a value in two different units (meters and inches).
4. It is helpful in noise removal also and as result of that we can improve the performance of models.
5. Reducing the dimensions of data to 2D or 3D may allow us to plot and visualize it precisely. You can then observe patterns more clearly. Below you can see that, how a 3D data is converted into 2D. First it has identified the 2D plane then represented the points on these two new axis z_1 and z_2.

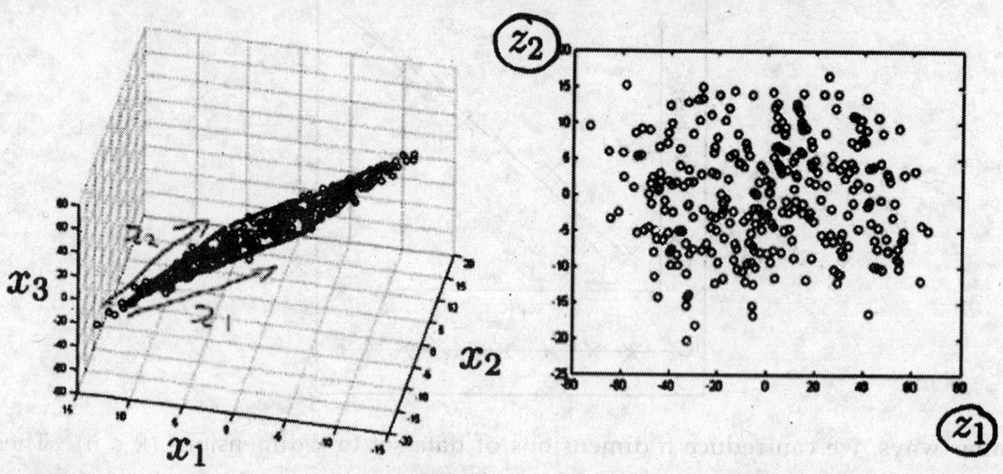

In their article Seven Techniques for Data Dimensionality Reduction by By Rosaria Silipo in KDnuggets Tutorials the following state of the art techniques currently available and accepted in the data analytics landscape are described as below:

(1) **Missing Values Ratio.** Data columns with too many missing values are unlikely to carry much useful information. Thus data columns with number of missing values

greater than a given threshold can be removed. The higher the threshold, the more aggressive the reduction.

(2) Low Variance Filter. Similarly to the previous technique, data columns with little changes in the data carry little information. Thus all data columns with variance lower than a given threshold are removed. A word of caution: variance is range dependent; therefore normalization is required before applying this technique.

(3) High Correlation Filter. Data columns with very similar trends are also likely to carry very similar information. In this case, only one of them will suffice to feed the machine learning model. Here we calculate the correlation coefficient between numerical columns and between nominal columns as the Pearson's Product Moment Coefficient and the Pearson's chi square value respectively. Pairs of columns with correlation coefficient higher than a threshold are reduced to only one. A word of caution: correlation is scale sensitive; therefore column normalization is required for a meaningful correlation comparison.

(4) Random Forests/Ensemble Trees. Decision Tree Ensembles, also referred to as random forests, are useful for feature selection in addition to being effective classifiers. One approach to dimensionality reduction is to generate a large and carefully constructed set of trees against a target attribute and then use each attribute's usage statistics to find the most informative subset of features. Specifically, we can generate a large set (2000) of very shallow trees (2 levels), with each tree being trained on a small fraction of the total number of attributes. If an attribute is often selected as best split, it is most likely an informative feature to retain. A score calculated on the attribute usage statistics in the random forest tells us relative to the other attributes which are the most predictive attributes.

(5) Principal Component Analysis (PCA). Principal Component Analysis (PCA) is a statistical procedure that orthogonally transforms the original n coordinates of a data set into a new set of n coordinates called principal components. As a result of the transformation, the first principal component has the largest possible variance; each succeeding component has the highest possible variance under the constraint that it is orthogonal to (i.e., uncorrelated with) the preceding components. Keeping only the first $m < n$ components reduces the data dimensionality while retaining most of the data information, i.e. the variation in the data. Notice that the PCA transformation is sensitive to the relative scaling of the original variables. Data column ranges need to be normalized before applying PCA. Also notice that the new coordinates (PCs) are not real system-produced variables anymore. Applying PCA to your data set loses its interpretability. If interpretability of the results is important for your analysis, PCA is not the transformation for your project.

(6) Backward Feature Elimination. In this technique, at a given iteration, the selected classification algorithm is trained on n input features. Then we remove one input feature at a time and train the same model on n-1 input features n times. The input feature whose removal has produced the smallest increase in the error rate is removed, leaving us with n-1 input features. The classification is then repeated using n-2 features, and so on. Each iteration k produces a model trained on n-k features and an error rate e(k). Selecting the maximum tolerable error rate, we define the smallest number of features necessary to reach that classification performance with the selected machine learning algorithm.

(7) **Forward Feature Construction.** This is the inverse process to the Backward Feature Elimination. We start with 1 feature only, progressively adding 1 feature at a time, i.e. the feature that produces the highest increase in performance. Both algorithms, Backward Feature Elimination and Forward Feature Construction, are quite time and computationally expensive. They are practically only applicable to a data set with an already relatively low number of input columns.

Dimensionality reduction or dimension reduction is the process of reducing the number of random variables under consideration by obtaining a set of principal variables. It can be divided into feature selection and feature extraction.

(a) Feature Selection

Feature selection approaches try to find a subset of the original variables (also called features or attributes). There are three strategies: the filter strategy (e.g. information gain), the wrapper strategy (e.g. search guided by accuracy), and the embedded strategy (features are selected to add or be removed while building the model based on the prediction errors).

(b) Feature Extraction

Feature extraction transforms the data in the high-dimensional space to a space of fewer dimensions. The data transformation may be linear, as in principal component analysis (PCA), but many nonlinear dimensionality reduction techniques also exist For multidimensional data, tensor representation can be used in dimensionality reduction through multilinear subspace learning

2.15 PRINCIPAL COMPONENT ANALYSIS (PCA)

PCA is a linear Classical Scaling technique for dimensionality reduction, which means that it performs dimensionality reduction by embedding the data into a linear subspace of lower dimensionality. Although there exist various techniques to do so, PCA is by far the most popular (unsupervised) linear technique. PCA constructs a low-dimensional representation of the data that describes as much of the variance in the data as possible. This is done by finding a linear basis of reduced dimensionality for the data, in which the amount of variance in the data is maximal.

The main linear technique for dimensionality reduction, principal component analysis, performs a linear mapping of the data to a lower-dimensional space in such a way that the variance of the data in the low-dimensional representation is maximized. In practice, the covariance (and sometimes the correlation) matrix of the data is constructed and the eigen vectors on this matrix are computed. The eigen vectors that correspond to the largest eigenvalues (the principal components) can now be used to reconstruct a large fraction of the variance of the original data. Moreover, the first few eigen vectors can often be interpreted in terms of the large-scale physical behavior of the system. The original space (with dimension of the number of points) has been reduced (with data loss, but hopefully retaining the most important variance) to the space spanned by a few eigenvectors..

Eigenvalues and eigenvectors feature prominently in the analysis of linear transformations. The prefix eigen- is adopted from the German word eigen for "proper", "characteristic" An eigenvector or characteristic vector of a linear transformation is a non-zero vector that only changes by a scalar factor, when that linear transformation is applied to it. More formally, if *T* is a linear transformation from a vector space *V* over a field *F* into itself and v is a vector in *V* that is not the zero vector, then *v* is an eigenvector of *T* if T(v) is a scalar multiple of *v*. This condition can be written as the equation

$$\mathbf{T(v) = \lambda v,}$$

where ë is a scalar in the field *F*, known as the eigenvalue, characteristic value, or characteristic root associated with the eigenvector *v*.

If the vector space *V* is finite-dimensional, then the linear transformation *T* can be represented as a square matrix *A*, and the vector v by a column vector, rendering the above mapping as a matrix multiplication on the left hand side and a scaling of the column vector on the right hand side in the equation

$$\mathbf{A(v) = \lambda v,}$$

There is a correspondence between n by n square matrices and linear transformations from an n-dimensional vector space to itself. For this reason, it is equivalent to define eigenvalues and eigenvectors using either the language of matrices or the language of linear transformations.

Eigenvalues and eigenvectors of matrices

Eigenvalues and eigenvectors are often introduced to students in the context of linear algebra courses focused on matrices. Furthermore, linear transformations can be represented using matrices, which is especially common in numerical and computational applications.

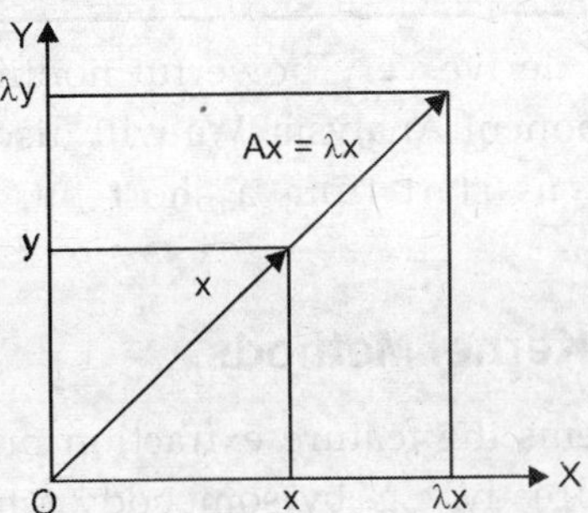

In above figure Matrix *A* acts by stretching the vector x, not changing its direction, so x is an eigenvector of *A*.

Consider n-dimensional vectors that are formed as a list of n scalars, such as the three-dimensional vectors

$$x = \begin{bmatrix} 1 \\ 3 \\ 4 \end{bmatrix} \text{ and } y = \begin{bmatrix} -20 \\ -60 \\ -80 \end{bmatrix}$$

These vectors are said to be scalar multiples of each other, or parallel or collinear, if there is a scalar ë such that

$$x = \lambda y.$$

In this case $\lambda = -1/20.$

Principal component analysis (PCA) is a statistical procedure that uses an orthogonal transformation to convert a set of observations of possibly correlated variables into a set of values of linearly uncorrelated variables called principal components. The number of distinct principal components is equal to the smaller of the number of original variables or the number of observations minus one. This transformation is defined in such a way that the first principal component has the largest possible variance (that is, accounts for as much of the variability in the data as possible), and each succeeding component in turn has the highest variance possible under the constraint that it is orthogonal to the preceding components. The resulting vectors are an uncorrelated orthogonal basis set. PCA is sensitive to the relative scaling of the original variables.

PCA is mostly used as a tool in exploratory data analysis and for making predictive models. It's often used to visualize genetic distance and relatedness between populations. PCA can be done by eigenvalue decomposition of a data covariance (or correlation) matrix or singular value decomposition of a data matrix, usually after mean centering (and normalizing or using Z-scores) the data matrix for each attribute. The results of a PCA are usually discussed in terms of component scores, sometimes called factor scores (the transformed variable values corresponding to a particular data point), and loadings (the weight by which each standardized original variable should be multiplied to get the component score).

2.16 KERNEL PRINCIPAL COMPONENT ANALYSIS (PCA)

In this section effort shal be to derive very powerful nonlinear data transformation which is called Kernel Principal Component Analysis. We will discuss mathematical mathematical ideas behind this method. Let us start from a short introduction to kernel methods of machine learning.

2.16.1 A motivation to use Kernel Methods

In the Machine Learning problems the feature extraction procedure is very often required. Even if features are extracted already, e.g. by somebody who gave you the data, they may be weak for a prediction problem that you need to solve. But those features can be combined and new features can be derived. Let us consider a binary classification problem in $\mathbb{R}^2$ with features x_1 and x_2:

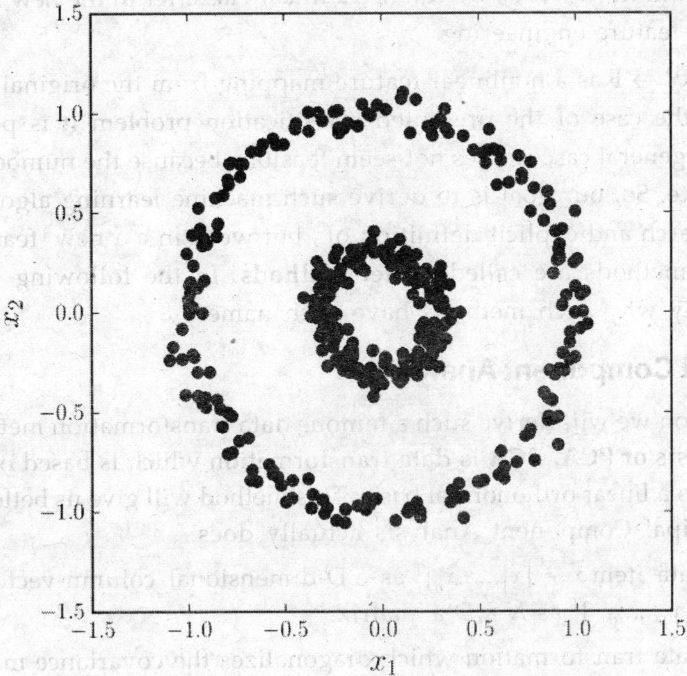

It can be easily seen that the problem is not solvable by any linear classifier such as SVM or logistic regression. Let us try to think, what we can do with this problem. The feature engineering process can be very sophisticated and quite tricky, so in the presented case if we will introduce new feature $x_1^2 + x_2^2$ and extend our space of features we will get the following picture:

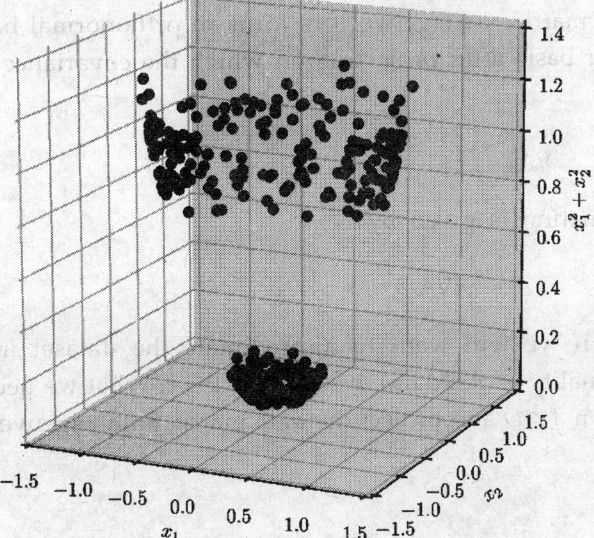

What we can see from it? Yes, it is, we can use a linear classifier in the new space of features. This is a magic of feature engineering.

Let us denote $\varphi : R^D \rightarrow F$ as a nonlinear feature mapping from the original feature space to a new one – . In the case of the presented classification problem it is possible to find a proper , but in the general case it does not seem feasible, because the number of such feature mappings is infinite. So, our goal is to derive such machine learning algorithms which do not require any search and explicit definition of , but work in a a new feature space . Such machine learning methods are called **kernel methods**. In the following sections we will define more strictly why such methods have such name.

2.16.2. Principal Component Analysis

In the present section we will derive such a famous data transformation method as **Principal Component Analysis or PCA. PCA** is data transformation which is based on a projection of covariance matrix to a linear orthonormal basis. This method will give us better understanding what Kernel Principal Component Analysis actually does.

Let us denote a data item $x = [x_1, \ldots x_d]^T$ as a D-dimensional column-vector and a sample of N elements $X = [x_1, \ldots x_N]^T$ as $N \times D$ a matrix.

Let us look for a data transformation which diagonalizes the covariance matrix S of a data sample X. Let us consider, that X is a column-centered matrix, i.e. each column of X has zero mean. It allows us to write an estimate of a covariance matrix as

$$S = \frac{1}{N} X^1 X,$$

Using eigen-decomposition of the matrix $S = VAV^T$, where A is a diagonal matrix having eigenvalues $11 \geq \ldots \geq \lambda_D$ of S on the diagonal and $V_1, \ldots, V_D$ are corresponding eigenvectors stored as columns of V.

Since S is a symmetric matrix, its eigenvectors form an orthonormal basis. It can be easily verified, that the linear basis after projection on which the covariance matrix will become a diagonal is given by

$$VA = \frac{1}{2}$$

and the data transformation is given by

$$Z = XVA - \frac{1}{2},$$

We should note, that if we will want to approximate the dataset in lower dimensions (decrease the dimensionality of the data), we can use PCA. What we need for it is to choose the size of the dimension $l < D$ and project the data matrix onto eigenvectors corresponding to l larges eigenvalues.

Let us look at the picture:

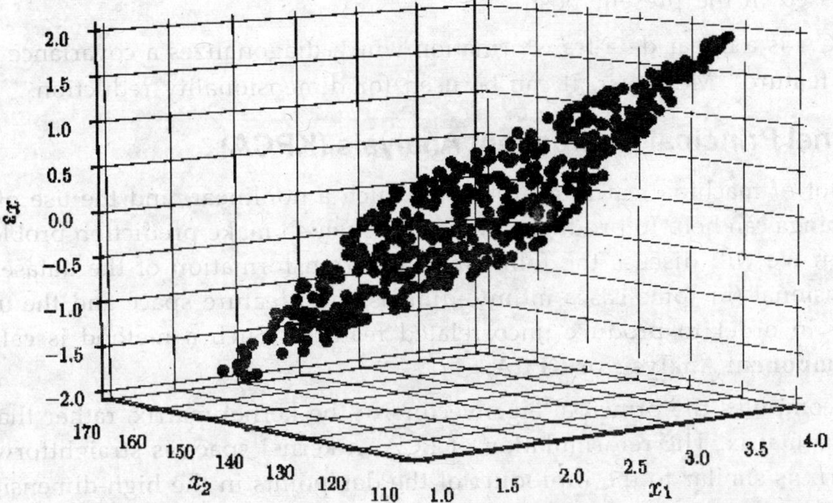

It is clear from the picture, that all the points are located on the plane, which means that the effective dimension of the data actually **equals to 2**. So, we can use PCA and project the data onto two largest eigenvectors of the data. We will get the following picture:

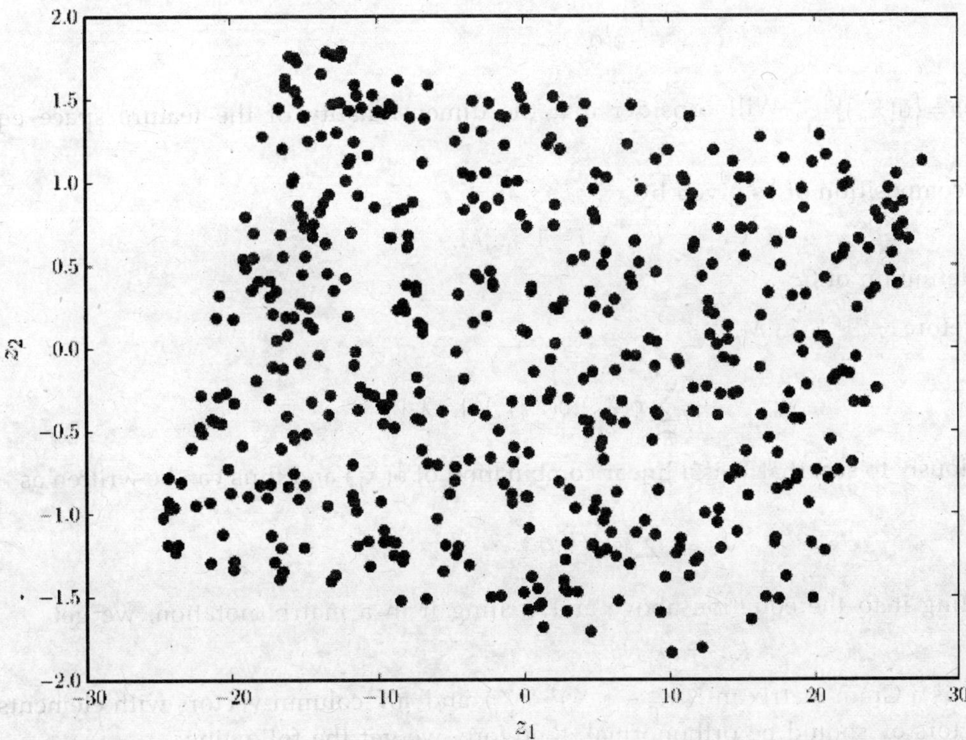

After the use of PCA, we have lost a little bit of variance. There is a couple of useful techniques which allow to chose the optimal number of components for PCA, but they will not be discussed in the present post.

Summary: PCA is a linear data transformation which diagonalizes a covariance matrix, i.e. decorrelates features. Moreover, it can be used for dimensionality reduction.

2.16.3. Kernel Principal Component Analysis (KPCA)

There are a lot of machine learning problems which a nonlinear, and the use of nonlinear feature mappings can help to produce new features which make prediction problems linear. In this section we will discuss the following idea: transformation of the dataset to a new higher-dimensional (in some cases infinite-dimensional) feature space and the use of PCA in that space in order to produce uncorrelated features. Such a method is called **Kernel Principal Component Analysis** or **KPCA.**

Kernel PCA computes the principal eigenvectors of the kernel matrix, rather than those of the covariance matrix. The reformulation of PCA in kernel space is straightforward, since a kernel matrix is similar to the inproduct of the datapoints in the high-dimensional space that is constructed using the kernel function. The application of PCA in the kernel space provides Kernel PCA the property of constructing nonlinear mappings

Let us denote a covariance matrix in a new feature space as C

$$\vartheta: R^D \rightarrow F,$$

$$C = \frac{1}{N}\phi^1\phi$$

where $\Phi = \{\phi(X_n)\}_{n=1}^{N}$, Will consider that the dimensionality of the feature space equals to $M > D$.

Eigendecomposition of is given by

$$Cv_i = l_i v_i, \ \forall\, i = 1, ...M.$$

By the definition of C

and therefore $\forall\, i = 1, ...M.$

$$\frac{1}{N}\sum_{n=1}^{N} \phi(X_n)\{\phi(X_n)^T V_i\} = \lambda_i V_i$$

It is obviously to see, that V_i is a linear combination of $\phi(X_n)$ and thus can be written as

$$Vi = \sum_{n=1}^{N} a_{i_n}\phi(X_n)$$

Substituting it to the equation above and writing it in a matrix notation, we get

$$Ka_i = \lambda_i N a_{i1}$$

where K is a Gram matrix in F, $K_{ij} = \phi(X_i)^T\,\phi(X_j)$ and are column-vectors with elements a_{in}. Eigenvectors of should be orthonormal, therefore, we get the following:

$$N\lambda_i a_i^1 a_i = 1$$

Having eigenvectors of C, we can get the projection of an item x ε R^D on *i*-th eigenvector:

$$c_i(x) = \sum_{n=1}^{N} a_{i_n} \phi(X)^1 \phi(X_n)$$

So far, we have assumed that the mapping φ(.) is known. From the equations above, we can see, that only a thing that we need for the data transformation is the eigendecomposition of a Gram matrix K. Dot products, which are its elements can be defined without any definition of φ(.). The function defining such dot products in some Hilbert space is called kernel. Kernels are satisfied by the Mercer's theorem. There are many different types of kernels, there are several popular:

1. Linear: $k(X_n, X_m) = X_n^1 X_m$;
2. Gaussian: $k(X_m, X_n) = \exp(-\gamma || X_m - X_m ||^2)$;
3. Polynomial: $k(X_m, X_n) = (X_m^1 X_n)^d$

Using a kernel function we can write new equation for a projection of some data item onto *i*-th eigenvector:

$$v_i = \sum_{n=1}^{N} a_{i_n} k(X_1 X_n)$$

So far, we have assumed that the columns of Φ have zero mean. Using

$$\varphi(X) = \varphi(X) - \frac{1}{N}\sum_{n=1}^{N} \varphi(X_n)$$

and substituting it to the equation for , we get

$$Kc = K - 1_N K - K 1_N + 1_N K 1_{N'}$$

where 1_N is a matrix $N \times N$, where each element equals to $\frac{1}{N}$.

Summary: Now we are ready to write the whole sequence of steps to perform KPCA:

1. Calculate K.
2. Calculate K.
3. Find the eigenvectors a_i of K_c corresponding to nonzero eigenvalues λ_ι and normalize them: $a_i = \frac{1}{\sqrt{\lambda_i N}} a_i$.
4. Sort found eigenvectors in the descending order of coresponding eigenvalues.
5. Perform projections onto the given subset of eigenvectors.

The method described above requires to define the number of components, the kernel and its parameters. It should be noted, that the number of nonlinear principal components in the general case is infinite, but since we are computing the eigenvectors of a matrix , at maximum we can calculate nonlinear principal components.

2.17 MATRIX FACTORIZATION

Just as its name suggests, matrix factorization is to, obviously, factorize a matrix, i.e. to find out two (or more) matrices such that when you multiply them you will get back the original matrix.

From an application point of view, matrix factorization can be used to discover latent features underlying the interactions between two different kinds of entities. (Of course, you can consider more than two kinds of entities and you will be dealing with tensor factorization, which would be more complicated.) And one obvious application is to predict ratings in collaborative filtering.

In a recommendation system such as Netflix or MovieLens, there is a group of users and a set of items (movies for the above two systems). Given that each users have rated some items in the system, we would like to predict how the users would rate the items that they have not yet rated, such that we can make recommendations to the users. In this case, all the information we have about the existing ratings can be represented in a matrix. Assume now we have 5 users and 10 items, and ratings are integers ranging from 1 to 5, the matrix may look something like this (a hyphen means that the user has not yet rated the movie):

	D_1	D_2	D_3	D_4
U_1	5	3	-	1
U_2	4	-	-	1
U_3	1	1	-	5
U_4	1	-	-	4
U_5	-	1	5	4

Hence, the task of predicting the missing ratings can be considered as filling in the blanks (the hyphens in the matrix) such that the values would be consistent with the existing ratings in the matrix.

The intuition behind using matrix factorization to solve this problem is that there should be some latent features that determine how a user rates an item. For example, two users would give high ratings to a certain movie if they both like the actors/actresses of the movie, or if the movie is an action movie, which is a genre preferred by both users. Hence, if we can discover these latent features, we should be able to predict a rating with respect to a certain user and a certain item, because the features associated with the user should match with the features associated with the item.

In trying to discover the different features, we also make the assumption that the number of features would be smaller than the number of users and the number of items. It should not be difficult to understand this assumption because clearly it would not be reasonable to assume that each user is associated with a unique feature (although this is not impossible). And anyway if this is the case there would be no point in making recommendations, because each of these users would not be interested in the items rated by other users. Similarly, the same argument applies to the items.

2.17.1 The Mathematics of Matrix Factorization

Having discussed the intuition behind matrix factorization, we can now go on to work on the mathematics. Firstly, we have a set U of users, and a set D of items. Let R of size |U| × |D| be the matrix that contains all the ratings that the users have assigned to the items. Also, we assume that we would like to discover K latent features. Our task, then, is to find two matrics matrices P (a |U| × K matrix) and Q (a |D| × K matrix) such that their product approximates R :

$$R \approx P \times Q^T = R$$

In this way, each row of P would represent the strength of the associations between a user and the features. Similarly, each row of Q would represent the strength of the associations between an item and the features. To get the prediction of a rating of an item d_i by u_i, we can calculate the dot product of the two vectors corresponding to u_i and d_j :

$$\hat{r}_{ij} = p_i^T q_j = \sum_{k=1}^{k} p_{ik} q_{kj}$$

Now, we have to find a way to obtain P and Q. One way to approach this problem is the first intialize the two matrices with some values, calculate how 'different' their product is to M, and then try to minimize this difference iteratively. Such a method is called gradient descent, aiming at finding a local minimum of the difference.

The difference here, usually called the error between the estimated rating and the real rating, can be calculated by the following equation for each user-item pair:

$$e_{ij}^2 = (r_{ij} - \hat{r}_{ij})^2 = (r_{ij} - \sum_{k=1}^{k} p_{ik} q_{kj})^2$$

Here we consider the squared error because the estimated rating can be either higher or lower than the real rating.

To minimize the error, we have to know in which direction we have to modify the values of and . In other words, we need to know the gradient at the current values, and therefore we differentiate the above equation with respect to these two variables separately:

$$\frac{\partial}{\partial p_{ik}} e_{ij}^2 = -2(r_{ij} - \hat{r}_{ij})(q_{jk}) = -2e_{ij} q_{kj}$$

$$\frac{\partial}{\partial q_{ik}} e_{ij}^2 = -2(r_{ij} - \hat{r}_{ij})(p_{jk}) = -2e_{ij} p_{kj}$$

Having obtained the gradient, we can now formulate the update rules for both and :

$$p'_{ik} = p_{ik} + \alpha \frac{\partial}{\partial q_{ik}} e_{ij}^2 = p_{ik} + 2\alpha e_{ij} q_{kj}$$

$$q'_{kj} = q_{kj} + \alpha \frac{\partial}{\partial q_{kj}} e_{ij}^2 = q_{kj} + 2\alpha e_{ij} p_{ik}$$

Here, α is a constant whose value determines the rate of approaching the minimum. Usually we will choose a small value for α, say 0.0002. This is because if we make too large a step towards the minimum we may run into the risk of missing the minimum and end up oscillating around the minimum.

A question might have come to your mind by now: if we find two matrices P and Q such that P × Q approximates R, isn't that our predictions of all the unseen ratings will all be zeros? In fact, we are not really trying to come up with P and Q such that we can reproduce R exactly. Instead, we will only try to minimise the errors of the observed user-item pairs. In other words, if we let T be a set of tuples, each of which is in the form of (u_i, d_h, r_{ji}), such that T contains all the observed user-item pairs together with the associated ratings, we are only trying to minimise every e_{ij} for $(u_i, d_h, r_{ji}) \in$ T. (In other words, T is our set of training data.) As for the rest of the unknowns, we will be able to determine their values once the associations between the users, items and features have been learnt.

Using the above update rules, we can then iteratively perform the operation until the error converges to its minimum. We can check the overall error as calculated using the following equation and determine when we should stop the process.

$$E = \sum_{(u_i,d_j,r_{ij})\in T} e_{ij} = \sum_{(u_i,d_j,r_{ij})\in T} (r_{ij} - \sum_{k=1}^{k} p_{ik}q_{kj})^2$$

2.17.2 Regularization

The above algorithm is a very basic algorithm for factorizing a matrix. There are a lot of methods to make things look more complicated. A common extension to this basic algorithm is to introduce regularization to avoid overfitting. This is done by adding a parameter and modify the squared error as follows:

$$e_{ij}^2 = (r_{ij} - \sum_{k=1}^{k} p_{ik}q_{kj})^2 + \frac{\beta}{2}\sum_{k=1}^{k}(||P||^2 + ||Q||^2)$$

In other words, the new parameter β is used to control the magnitudes of the user-feature and item-feature vectors such that P and Q would give a good approximation of R without having to contain large numbers. In practice, β is set to some values in the range of 0.02. The new update rules for this squared error can be obtained by a procedure similar to the one described above. The new update rules are as follows.

$$p'_{ik} = p_{ik} + \alpha\frac{\partial}{\partial p_{ik}}e_{ij}^2 = p_{ik} + \alpha(2e_{ij}q_{kj} - \beta p_{ik})$$

$$q'_{kj} = q_{kj} + \alpha\frac{\partial}{\partial q_{kj}}e_{ij}^2 = q_{kj} + \alpha(2e_{ij}p_{ik} - \beta q_{kj})$$

MF has several nice properties:

1. It uncovers latent structures in the data, while addressing the data sparseness problem ;
2. It has an elegant probabilistic interpretation ;

3. It can be easily extended with domain specific prior knowledge (e.g., homophily in linked data), thus suitable for various real-world problems;
4. Many optimization methods such as (stochastic) gradient-based methods can be applied to find a good solution

2.18 GENERATIVE MODEL

It's easy to forget just how much you know about the world: you understand that it is made up of 3D environments, objects that move, collide, interact; people who walk, talk, and think; animals who graze, fly, run, or bark; monitors that display information encoded in language about the weather, who won a basketball game, or what happened in 1970.

This tremendous amount of information is out there and to a large extent easily accessible — either in the physical world of atoms or the digital world of bits. The only tricky part is to develop models and algorithms that can analyze and understand this treasure trove of data.

Generative models are one of the most promising approaches towards this goal. To train a generative model we first collect a large amount of data in some domain (e.g., think millions of images, sentences, or sounds, etc.) and then train a model to generate data like it.

A generative model is a model for generating all values for a phenomenon, both those that can be observed in the world and "target" variables that can only be computed from those observed. By contrast, discriminative models provide a model only for the target variable(s), generating them by analyzing the observed variables. In simple terms, discriminative models infer outputs based on inputs, while generative models generate both inputs and outputs, typically given some hidden parameters.

Generative models are used in machine learning for either modeling data directly (i.e., modeling observations drawn from a probability density function), or as an intermediate step to forming a conditional probability density function. Generative models are typically probabilistic, specifying a joint probability distribution over observation and target (label) values. A conditional distribution can be formed from a generative model through Bayes' rule.

2.18.1 Types of Generative Models

Types of generative models are:

- Gaussian mixture model (and other types of mixture model)
- Hidden Markov model
- Probabilistic context-free grammar
- Naive Bayes
- Averaged one-dependence estimators

- Latent Dirichlet allocation
- Restricted Boltzmann machine
- Generative adversarial networks

If the observed data are truly sampled from the generative model, then fitting the parameters of the generative model to maximize the data likelihood is a common method. However, since most statistical models are only approximations to the true distribution, if the model's application is to infer about a subset of variables conditional on known values of others, then it can be argued that the approximation makes more assumptions than are necessary to solve the problem at hand. In such cases, it can be more accurate to model the conditional density functions directly using a discriminative model (see below), although application-specific details will ultimately dictate which approach is most suitable in any particular case.

1. Discriminative models
2. Logistic regression,
3. Support Vector Machines,
4. Maximum Entropy Markov Model,
5. Conditional Random Fields,
6. Neural Networks

2.18.2 Mixture Models

A mixture model is a probabilistic model for representing the presence of subpopulations within an overall population, without requiring that an observed data set should identify the sub-population to which an individual observation belongs. Formally a mixture model corresponds to the mixture distribution that represents the probability distribution of observations in the overall population. However, while problems associated with "mixture distributions" relate to deriving the properties of the overall population from those of the sub-populations, "mixture models" are used to make statistical inferences about the properties of the sub-populations given only observations on the pooled population, without sub-population identity information.

Some ways of implementing mixture models involve steps that attribute postulated sub-population-identities to individual observations (or weights towards such sub-populations), in which case these can be regarded as types of unsupervised learning or clustering procedures. However, not all inference procedures involve such steps.

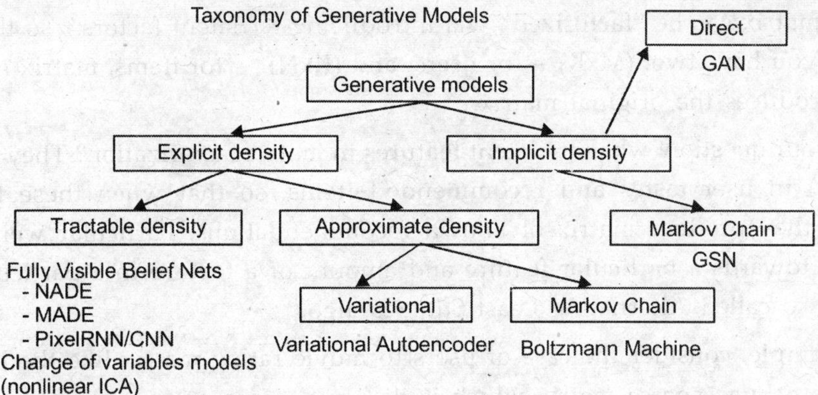

2.18.3 Latent Variable Model

A latent variable model is a statistical model that relates a set of observable variables (so-called manifest variables) to a set of latent variables.

Observable variable or observable quantity (also manifest variables), as opposed to latent variable, is a variable that can be observed and directly measured

Latent variables (from Latin: meaning "lie hidden", as opposed to observable variables), are variables that are not directly observed but are rather inferred (through a mathematical model) from other variables that are observed (directly measured). Mathematical models that aim to explain observed variables in terms of latent variables are called latent variable models. Latent variable models are used in many disciplines, including psychology, demography, economics, engineering, medicine, physics, machine learning/artificial intelligence, bioinformatics, natural language processing, econometrics, management and the social sciences.

At the expense of over-simplication, latent features are 'hidden' features to distinguish them from observed features. Latent features are computed from observed features using matrix factorization. An example would be text document analysis. 'words' extracted from the documents are features. If you factorize the data of words you can find 'topics', where 'topic' is a group of words with semantic relevance. Low-rank matrix factorization maps several rows (observed features) to a smaller set of rows (latent features). To elaborate, the document could have observed features (words) like [sail-boat, schooner, yatch, steamer, cruiser] which would 'factorize' to latent feature (topic) like 'ship' and 'boat'.

[sail-boat, schooner, yatch, steamer, cruiser, ...] -> [ship, boat]

The underlying idea is that latent features are semantically relevant 'aggregates' of observered features. When you have large-scale, high-dimensional, and noisy observered features, it makes sense to build your classifier on latent features.

Suppose you have (MxN) sparse matrix, where M — stands for number of users who gave recommendations, and N is the number of items recommended. The xij element of the matrix is the recommendation given, with some elements missing, i.e. to be predicted.

Then your matrix can be "factorized", via introducing K "latent factors", so that instead of one matrix you have two: (MxK) —for users, and (KxN) — for items, matrix multiplication of which produces the original matrix.

Finally, to your question: what are latent features in matrix factorization? They are unknown features (K) in user tastes and recommended items, so that when these two matrices multiplied, they produce matrix of known recommendations. Particular weights (of user preferences towards a particular feature and amount of a feature in a particular item) are defined via so called Alternating Least Squares algo.

Another example, consider the case of users to movie rating matrix like the Netflix setup. This will be a huge sparse matrix which is difficult to process.

Note that each user will have a specific preference like sci-fi movies or romance movies etc. So, instead of storing all the movie ratings we could store a single latent feature like the movie category which belongs to different Genre's for example: sci-fi or romance, whichever quantifies his taste for each category. These are called Latent Features, which captures the essence of his taste rather than storing the entire movie list.

Of course this will be an approximation, but on the flip-side, you have a very little to store.

This is usually done using matrix decomposition techniques, like SVD which breaks an N*N user to item recommendation matrix to N*1 user preference matrix and 1*N item preference matrix, added Advantage is that instead of storing N2 number we effectively store 2N.

Up to now, we have assumed that when learning a directed or an undirected model, we are given examples of every single variable that we are trying to model.

However, that may not always be the case. Consider for example a probabilistic language model of news articles. A language model p assigns probabilities to sequences of words $x_1, x_2..., x_n$. We can, among other things, sample from p to generate various kinds of sentences. Each article x typically focuses on a specific topic t, e.g. finance, sports, politics. Using this prior knowledge, we may build a more accurate model $p(x \mid t)p(t)$, in which we have introduced an additional, unobserved variable t. This model can be more accurate, because we can now learn a separate $p(x \mid t)$ for each topic, rather than trying to model everything with one $p(x)$.

However, since tt is unobserved, we cannot directly use the learning methods that we have so far. In fact, the unobserved variables make learning much more difficult; in this chapter, we will look at how to use and how to learn models that involve latent variables.

Latent variable models

More formally, a latent variable model (LVM) p is a probability distribution over two sets of variables x, z:

$$p(x, z; \theta)]$$

where the x variables are observed at learning time in a dataset D and the z are never observed.

The model may be either directed or undirected. There exist both discriminative and generative LVMs, although here we will focus on the latter (thekey ideas hold for discriminative models as well).

Example: Gaussian mixture models

Gaussian mixture models (GMMs) are a latent variable model that is also one of the most widely used models in machine learning.

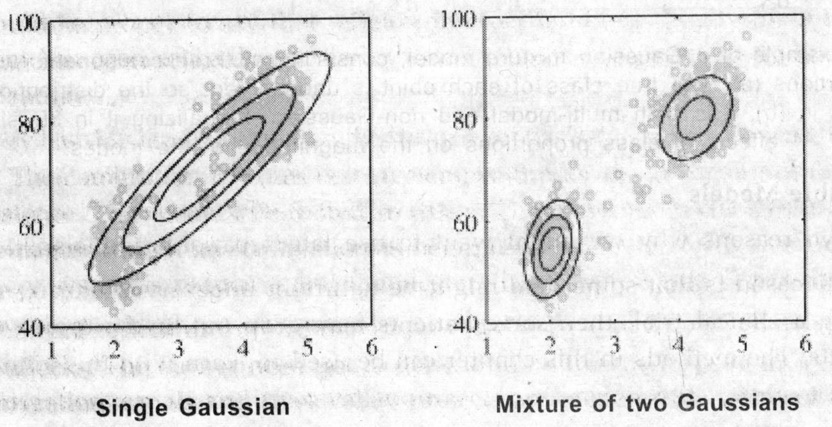

Fig. 2.8: Example of a dataset that is best fit with a mixture of two Gaussians. Mixture models allow us to model clusters in the dataset.

In a GMM, each data point is a tuple (x_i, z_i) with $x_i \in R^d$ and $z_i \in 1,2,....,K$ (zi is discrete). The joint p is a directed model

$$p(x, z) = p(x|z)\, p(z),$$

where $p(z = k) = \pi_k$ for some vector of class probalilities $\pi \in \Delta_{k-1}$ and

$$p(x|\, z = k) = N(x; \mu_k, \Sigma_k)$$

is a multivariate Gaussian with mean and variance μ_k, Σ_k.

This model postulate that our observed data is comprised of K clusters with proportions specified $\pi_1,....,\pi_k$; the distribution within each cluster is a Gaussian, We can see that $p(x)$ is a mixture by explicitly writing out this probability:

$$p(x) = \sum_{k=1}^{K} p(x\,|\,z=k)p(z=k) = \sum_{k=1}^{K} \pi_k N(x;\, \mu_k, \Sigma_k)$$

To generate a new data point, we sample a cluster k and then sampl Gaussian $N\,(x;\, \mu_k, \Sigma_k)$.

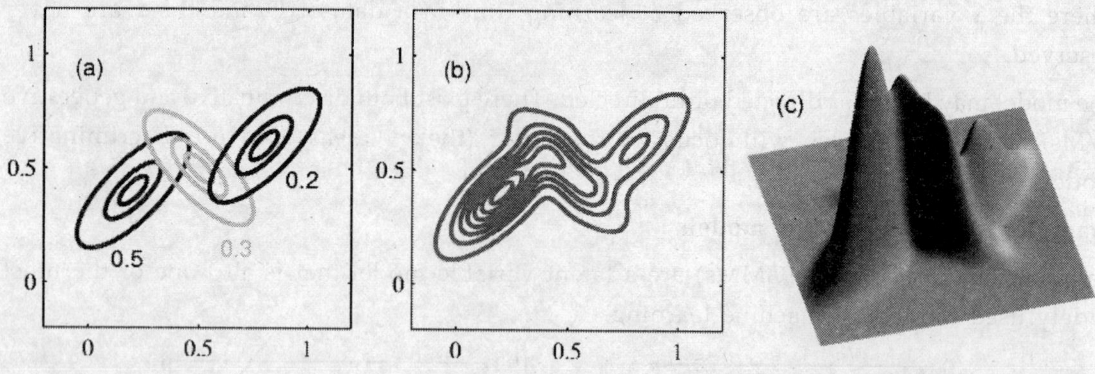

Fig. 2.9 : Example of a Gaussian mixture model, consisting of three components with different class proportions (a). The true class of each point is unobserved, so the distribution over \$x\$ looks like in (b); it is both multi-modal and non-Gaussian. Visualizing it in 3D shows the effects of class proportions on the magnitudes of the modes.

Latent Variable Models

There are two reasons why we might want to use latent variable models.

The simplest reason is that some data might be naturally unobserved. For example, if we are modeling a clinical trial, then some patients may drop out, and we won't have their measurements. The methods in this chapter can be used to learn with this kind of missing data.

However, the most important reason for studying LVMs is that they enable us to leverage our prior knowledge when defining a model. Our topic modeling example from the introduction illustrates this. We know that our set of news articles is actually a mixture of KK distinct distributions (one for each topic); LVMs allow us to design a model that captures this.

LVMs can also be viewed as increasing the expressive power of our model. In the case of GMMs, the distribution that we can model using a mixture of Gaussian components is much more expressive than what we could have modeled using a single component.

One advantage of using latent variables is that they can serve to reduce the dimensionality of data. A large number of observable variables can be aggregated in a model to represent an underlying concept, making it easier to understand the data.

A hidden Markov model can be considered a generalization of a mixture model where the hidden variables (or latent variables), which control the mixture component to be selected for each observation, are related through a Markov process rather than independent of each other.

References

1. L.O. jimenez and D.A. Landgrebe. Supervised classification in high dimensional space geometrical, statistical and asympotical properties of multivariate data. IEEE Transaction and systems, Man and Cybernetics, 28(1): 39-54. 1997.

2. Article seven techniques for data dimensionality reduction by Rosaria Silipo in KD nuggets tutorials. doi:10.1126/science.290.5500.2323. PMID 11125150.
3. Hastie, T., Tibshirani, R., Friedman, J., Hastie, T., Friedman, J., & Tibshirani, R. (2009). *The elements of statistical learning* (Vol. 2, No. 1). New York.
4. Pudil, P.; Novovièová, J. (1998). "Novel Methods for Feature Subset Selection with Respect to Problem Knowledge". In Liu, Huan; Motoda, Hiroshi. Feature Extraction, Construction and Selection. p. 101. doi:10.1007/978-1-4615-5725-8_7. ISBN 978-1-4613-7622-4.
5. Samet, H. (2006) Foundations of Multidimensional and Metric Data Structures. Morgan Kaufmann. ISBN 0-12-369446-9
6. C. Ding, X. He, H. Zha, H.D. Simon, Adaptive Dimension Reduction for Clustering High Dimensional Data, Proceedings of International Conference on Data Mining, 2002
7. Lu, Haiping; Plataniotis, K.N.; Venetsanopoulos, A.N. (2011). "A Survey of Multilinear Subspace Learning for Tensor Data" (PDF). Pattern Recognition. 44 (7): 1540–1551. doi:10.1016/j.patcog.2011.01.004

Unit 3

EVALUATING MACHINE LEARNING ALGORITHMS AND MODEL SELECTION

Learning Objectives and Outcome

After reading the contents of this unit, the reader shall be learn:

- Evaluating Machine Learning algorithms and Model Selection
- Introduction to Statistical Learning Theory,
- Ensemble Methods (Boosting, Bagging, Random Forests) and how to evaluate them through Python Programming.

3.1 MACHINE LEARNING ALGORITHMS

It is a process or collection of rules or set to complete a task. It is one of the primary concept in, or building blocks of, computer science: the basis of the design of elegant and efficient code, data processing and preparation, and software engineering.

In data science there are mainly three algorithms are used:

1. Data preparation, munging, and process algorithms
2. Optimization algorithms for parameter estimation which includes Stochastic Gradient Descent, Least Squares, Newton's Method
3. Machine learning algorithms

Once you have defined your problem and prepared your data you need to apply machine learning algorithms to the data in order to solve your problem. You can spend a lot of time choosing, running and tuning algorithms. You want to make sure you are using your time effectively to get closer to your goal.

3.2 DESIGNING MACHINE LEARNING ALGORITHMS

The following are the ingradients of designprocedure:

1. Test Harnessing
2. Performance Measure

3. Test and Train Datasets
4. Cross Validation

1. Test Harnessing

You need to define a test harness. The test harness is the data you will train and test an algorithm against and the performance measure you will use to assess its performance. It is important to define your test harness well so that you can focus on evaluating different algorithms and thinking deeply about the problem.

The goal of the test harness is to be able to quickly and consistently test algorithms against a fair representation of the problem being solved. The outcome of testing multiple algorithms against the harness will be an estimation of how a variety of algorithms perform on the problem against a chosen performance measure. You will know which algorithms might be worth tuning on the problem and which should not be considered further.

The results will also give you an indication of how learnable the problem is. If a variety of different learning algorithms university perform poorly on the problem, it may be an indication of a lack of structure available to algorithms to learn. This may be because there actually is a lack of learnable structure in the selected data or it may be an opportunity to try different transforms to expose the structure to the learning algorithms.

2. Performance Measure

The performance measure is the way you want to evaluate a solution to the problem. It is the measurement you will make of the predictions made by a trained model on the test dataset.

Performance measures are typically specialized to the class of problem you are working with, for example classification, regression, and clustering. Many standard performance measures will give you a score that is meaningful to your problem domain. For example, classification accuracy for classification (total correct correction divided by the total predictions made multiple by 100 to turn it into a percentage).

You may also want a more detailed breakdown of performance, for example, you may want to know about the false positives on a spam classification problem because good email will be marked as spam and cannot be read.

There are many standard performance measures to choose from. You rarely have to devise a new performance measure yourself as you can generally find or adapt one that best captures the requirements of the problem being solved. Look to similar problems you uncovered and at the performance measures used to see if any can be adopted.

3. Testing and Training Datasets

From the transformed data, you will need to select a test set and a training set. An algorithm will be trained on the training dataset and will be evaluated against the test set. This may be as simple as selecting a random split of data (66% for training, 34% for testing) or may involve more complicated sampling methods.

A trained model is not exposed to the test dataset during training and any predictions made on that dataset are designed to be indicative of the performance of the model in general. As such you want to make sure the selection of your datasets are representative of the problem you are solving.

4. Cross Validation

A more sophisticated approach than using a test and train dataset is to use the entire transformed dataset to train and test a given algorithm. A method you could use in your test harness that does this is called cross validation.

It first involves separating the dataset into a number of equally sized groups of instances (called folds). The model is then trained on all folds exception one that was left out and the prepared model is tested on that left out fold. The process is repeated so that each fold get's an opportunity at being left out and acting as the test dataset. Finally, the performance measures are averaged across all folds to estimate the capability of the algorithm on the problem.

For example, a 3-fold cross validation would involve training and testing a model 3 times:

- #1: Train on folds 1 + 2, test on fold 3
- #2: Train on folds 1 + 3, test on fold 2
- #3: Train on folds 2 + 3, test on fold 1

The number of folds can vary based on the size of your dataset, but common numbers are 3, 5, 7 and 10 folds. The goal is to have a good balance between the size and representation of data in your train and test sets.

When you're just getting started, stick with a simple split of train and test data (such as 66%/34%) and move onto cross validation once you have more confidence.

3.2.1 Testing Algorithms

When starting with a problem and having defined a test harness you are happy with, it is time to spot check a variety of machine learning algorithms. Spot checking is useful because it allows you to very quickly see if there is any learnable structures in the data and estimate which algorithms may be effective on the problem.

Spot checking also helps you work out any issues in your test harness and make sure the chosen performance measure is appropriate.

The best first algorithm to spot check is a **random**. Plug in a random number generator to generate predictions in the appropriate range. This should be the worst "algorithm result" you achieve and will be the measure by which all improvements can be assessed.

Select 5-10 standard algorithms that are appropriate for your problem and run them through your test harness. By standard algorithms, I mean popular methods no special configurations. Appropriate for your problem means that the algorithms can handle regression if you have a regression problem.

Choose methods from the groupings of algorithms we have already reviewed. I like to include a diverse mix and have 10-20 different algorithms drawn from a diverse range of algorithm types. Depending on the library I am using, I may spot check up to a 50+ popular methods to flush out promising methods quickly.

If you want to run a lot of methods, you may have to revisit data preparation and reduce the size of your selected dataset. This may reduce your confidence in the results, so test with various data set sizes. You may like to use a smaller size dataset for algorithm spot checking and a fuller dataset for algorithm tuning.

3.3 CLASSIFICATION METRICS

Classification problems are perhaps the most common type of machine learning problem and as such there are a myriad of metrics that can be used to evaluate predictions for these problems.

In this section we will review how to use the following metrics:

1. Classification Accuracy.
2. Logarithmic Loss.
3. Area Under ROC Curve.
4. Confusion Matrix.
5. Classification Report.

3.3.1 Classification Accuracy

Classification accuracy is the number of correct predictions made as a ratio of all predictions made.

This is the most common evaluation metric for classification problems, it is also the most misused. It is really only suitable when there are an equal number of observations in each class (which is rarely the case) and that all predictions and prediction errors are equally important, which is often not the case.

Below is an example of calculating classification accuracy.

```
import pandas
from sklearn import model_selection
from sklearn.linear_model import LogisticRegression
url = "https://archive.ics.uci.edu/ml/machine-learning-databases/pima-indians-diabetes/pima-indians-c
names = ['preg', 'plas', 'pres', 'skin', 'test', 'mass', 'pedi', 'age', 'class']
dataframe = pandas.read_csv(url, names=names)
array = dataframe.values
X = array[:,0:8]
Y = array[:,8]
seed = 7
kfold = model_selection.KFold(n_splits=10, random_state=seed)
model = LogisticRegression()
scoring = 'accuracy'
results = model_selection.cross_val_score(model, X, Y, cv=kfold, scoring=scoring)
print("Accuracy: %.3f (%.3f)") % (results.mean(), results.std())
```

You can see that the ratio is reported. This can be converted into a percentage by multiplying the value by 100, giving an accuracy score of approximately 77% accurate.

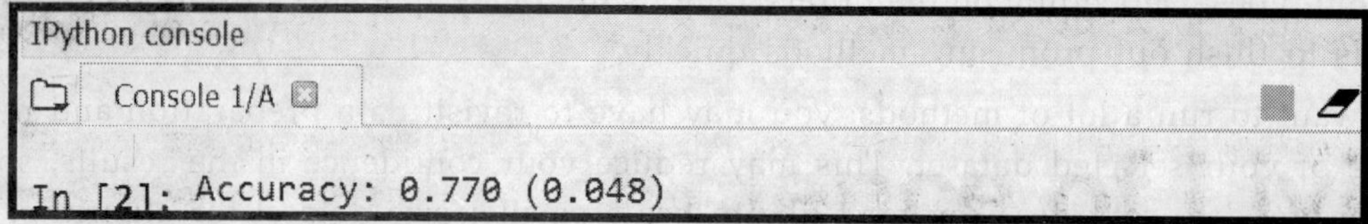

3.3.2 Logarithmic Loss

Logarithmic loss (or logloss) is a performance metric for evaluating the predictions of probabilities of membership to a given class.

The scalar probability between 0 and 1 can be seen as a measure of confidence for a prediction by an algorithm. Predictions that are correct or incorrect are rewarded or punished proportionally to the confidence of the prediction.

```
import pandas
from sklearn import model_selection
from sklearn.linear_model import LogisticRegression
url = "https://archive.ics.uci.edu/ml/machine-learning-databases/pima-indians-diabetes/pima-indians-diabetes.data"
names = ['preg', 'plas', 'pres', 'skin', 'test', 'mass', 'pedi', 'age', 'class']
dataframe = pandas.read_csv(url, names=names)
array = dataframe.values
X = array[:,0:8]
Y = array[:,8]
seed = 7
kfold = model_selection.KFold(n_splits=10, random_state=seed)
model = LogisticRegression()
scoring = 'neg_log_loss'
results = model_selection.cross_val_score(model, X, Y, cv=kfold, scoring=scoring)
print("Logloss: %.3f (%.3f)") % (results.mean(), results.std())
```

After running above code you will get following result:

Smaller logloss is better with 0 representing a perfect logloss. As mentioned above, the measure is inverted to be ascending when using the *cross_val_score()* function.

3.3.3 Area Under ROC Curve

Area under ROC Curve (or AUC for short) is a performance metric for binary classification problems.

The AUC represents a model's ability to discriminate between positive and negative classes. An area of 1.0 represents a model that made all predictions perfectly. An area of 0.5 represents a model as good as random.

ROC can be broken down into sensitivity and specificity. A binary classification problem is really a trade-off between sensitivity and specificity.

- Sensitivity is the true positive rate also called the recall. It is the number instances from the positive (first) class that actually predicted correctly.
- Specificity is also called the true negative rate. Is the number of instances from the negative class (second) class that were actually predicted correctly.

```
import pandas
from sklearn import model_selection
from sklearn.linear_model import LogisticRegression
url = "https://archive.ics.uci.edu/ml/machine-learning-databases/pima-indians-diabetes/pima-indians-diabetes.data"
names = ['preg', 'plas', 'pres', 'skin', 'test', 'mass', 'pedi', 'age', 'class']
dataframe = pandas.read_csv(url, names=names)
array = dataframe.values
X = array[:,0:8]
Y = array[:,8]
seed = 7
kfold = model_selection.KFold(n_splits=10, random_state=seed)
model = LogisticRegression()
scoring= 'roc_auc'
results = model_selection.cross_val_score(model, X, Y, cv=kfold, scoring=scoring)
print("AUC: %.3f (%.3f)") % (results.mean(), results.std())
```

You can see the the AUC is relatively close to 1 and greater than 0.5, suggesting some skill in the predictions.

```
IPython console
Console 1/A
AUC: 0.824 (0.041)
```

3.3.4 Confusion Matrix

The confusion matrix is a handy presentation of the accuracy of a model with two or more classes.

The table presents predictions on the x-axis and accuracy outcomes on the y-axis. The cells of the table are the number of predictions made by a machine learning algorithm.

For example, a machine learning algorithm can predict 0 or 1 and each prediction may actually have been a 0 or 1. Predictions for 0 that were actually 0 appear in the cell for prediction=0 and actual=0, whereas predictions for 0 that were actually 1 appear in the cell for prediction = 0 and actual=1. And so on.

Below is an example of calculating a confusion matrix for a set of prediction by a model on a test set.

```
# Cross Validation Classification Confusion Matrix
import pandas
from sklearn import model_selection
from sklearn.linear_model import LogisticRegression
from sklearn.metrics import confusion_matrix
url = "https://archive.ics.uci.edu/ml/machine-learning-databases/pima-indians-diabetes/pima-indians-diabetes.data"
names = ['preg', 'plas', 'pres', 'skin', 'test', 'mass', 'pedi', 'age', 'class']
dataframe = pandas.read_csv(url, names=names)
array = dataframe.values
X = array[:,0:8]
Y = array[:,8]
test_size = 0.33
seed = 7
X_train, X_test, Y_train, Y_test = model_selection.train_test_split(X, Y, test_size=test_size, random_state=seed)
model = LogisticRegression()
model.fit(X_train, Y_train)
predicted = model.predict(X_test)
matrix = confusion_matrix(Y_test, predicted)
print(matrix)
```

Although the array is printed without headings, you can see that the majority of the predictions fall on the diagonal line of the matrix (which are correct predictions).

```
[[141  21]
 [ 41  51]]
```

3.3.5 Classification Report

Scikit-learn does provide a convenience report when working on classification problems to give you a quick idea of the accuracy of a model using a number of measures.

The *classification_report()* function displays the precision, recall, f1-score and support for each class.

The example below demonstrates the report on the binary classification problem.

```
# Cross Validation Classification Report
import pandas
from sklearn import model_selection
from sklearn.linear_model import LogisticRegression
from sklearn.metrics import classification_report
url = "https://archive.ics.uci.edu/ml/machine-learning-databases/pima-indians-diabetes/pima-indians-diabetes.data"
names = ['preg', 'plas', 'pres', 'skin', 'test', 'mass', 'pedi', 'age', 'class']
dataframe = pandas.read_csv(url, names=names)
array = dataframe.values
X = array[:,0:8]
Y = array[:,8]
test_size = 0.33
seed = 7
X_train, X_test, Y_train, Y_test = model_selection.train_test_split(X, Y, test_size=test_size, random_state=seed)
model = LogisticRegression()
model.fit(X_train, Y_train)
predicted = model.predict(X_test)
report = classification_report(Y_test, predicted)
print(report)
```

You can see good prediction and recall for the algorithm.

```
IPython console
Console 1/A

             precision    recall  f1-score   support

        0.0       0.77      0.87      0.82       162
        1.0       0.71      0.55      0.62        92

avg / total       0.75      0.76      0.75       254
```

3.4 REGRESSION METRICS

The following three are the most common metrics for evaluating predictions on regression machine learning problems:

1. Mean Absolute Error.
2. Mean Squared Error.
3. R^2.

3.4.1 Mean Absolute Error

The Mean Absolute Error (or MAE) is the sum of the absolute differences between predictions and actual values. It gives an idea of how wrong the predictions were. The measure gives an idea of the magnitude of the error, but no idea of the direction (e.g. over or under predicting). The example below demonstrates calculating mean absolute error on the Boston house price dataset.

```
# Cross Validation Regression MAE
import pandas
from sklearn import model_selection
from sklearn.linear_model import Linear
Regressionurl = “https://archive.ics.uci.edu/ml/machine-learning-
databases/housing/housing.data”
names = ['CRIM', 'ZN', 'INDUS', 'CHAS', 'NOX', 'RM', 'AGE', 'DIS',
'RAD', 'TAX', 'PTRATIO', 'B', 'LSTAT', 'MEDV']
dataframe = pandas.read_csv(url, delim_whitespace=True, names=names)
array = dataframe.values
X = array[:,0:13]
Y = array[:,13]
seed = 7
kfold = model_selection.KFold(n_splits=10, random_state=seed)
model = LinearRegression()
scoring = 'neg_mean_absolute_error'r
esults = model_selection.cross_val_score(model, X, Y, cv=kfold, scoring=scoring)
print(“MAE: %.3f (%.3f)”) % (results.mean(), results.std())
```

A value of 0 indicates no error or perfect predictions. Like logloss, this metric is inverted by the *cross_val_score()* function.

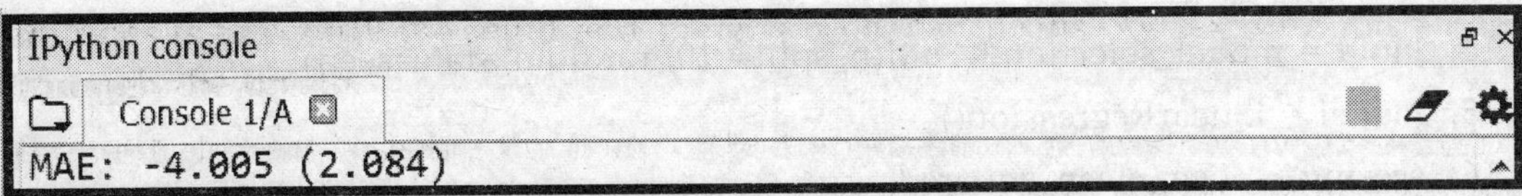

3.4.2 Mean Squared Error (MSE)

MSE is much like the mean absolute error in that it provides a gross idea of the magnitude of error. It is a measure of difference between two continuous variables. Assume *X* and *Y* are variables of paired observations that express the same phenomenon. Examples of *Y* versus *X* include comparisons of predicted versus observed, subsequent time versus initial time, and one technique of measurement versus an alternative technique of measurement. Consider a scatter plot of n points, where point i has coordinates (x_i, y_i)... Mean Absolute Error (MAE) is the average vertical distance between each point and the *Y*=*X* line, which is also known as the One-to-One line. MAE is also the average horizontal distance between each point and the *Y*=*X* line.

The Mean Absolute Error is given by:

$$\text{MAE} = \frac{\sum_{i=1}^{n} |y_i - x_i|}{n} = \frac{\sum_{i=1}^{n} |e_i|}{n} \text{ [1]}$$

Taking the square root of the mean squared error converts the units back to the original units of the output variable and can be meaningful for description and presentation. This is called the Root Mean Squared Error (or RMSE).

$$\text{ME} = \frac{\sum_{i=1}^{n} y_i - x_i}{n}$$

The example below provides a demonstration of calculating mean squared error.

```
# Cross Validation Regression MSE
import pandas
from sklearn import model_selection
from sklearn.linear_model import LinearRegression
url = "https://archive.ics.uci.edu/ml/machine-learning-
databases/housing/housing.data"
names = ['CRIM', 'ZN', 'INDUS', 'CHAS', 'NOX', 'RM', 'AGE', 'DIS',
'RAD', 'TAX', 'PTRATIO', 'B', 'LSTAT', 'MEDV']
dataframe = pandas.read_csv(url, delim_whitespace=True, names=names)
array = dataframe.values
X = array[:,0:13]
```

```
Y = array[:,13]
seed = 7
kfold = model_selection.KFold(n_splits=10, random_state=seed)
model = LinearRegression()
scoring = 'neg_mean_squared_error'
results = model_selection.cross_val_score(model, X, Y, cv=kfold,
scoring=scoring)
print("MSE: %.3f (%.3f)") % (results.mean(), results.std())
```

This metric too is inverted so that the results are increasing. Remember to take the absolute value before taking the square root if you are interested in calculating the RMSE.

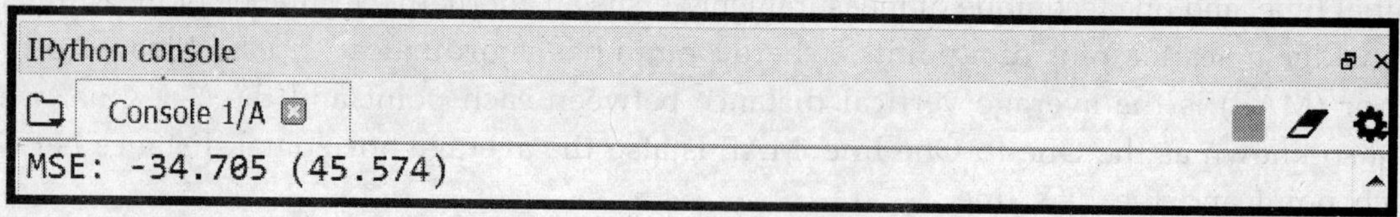

3.4.3 R^2 Metric

The R^2 (or R Squared) metric provides an indication of the goodness of fit of a set of predictions to the actual values. In statistical literature, this measure is called the coefficient of determination.

This is a value between 0 and 1 for no-fit and perfect fit respectively.

The example below provides a demonstration of calculating the mean R^2 for a set of predictions.

```
# Cross Validation Regression R^2
import pandas
from sklearn import model_selection
from sklearn.linear_model import LinearRegression
url = "https://archive.ics.uci.edu/ml/machine-learning-
databases/housing/housing.data"
names = ['CRIM', 'ZN', 'INDUS', 'CHAS', 'NOX', 'RM', 'AGE', 'DIS',
'RAD', 'TAX', 'PTRATIO', 'B', 'LSTAT', 'MEDV']
dataframe = pandas.read_csv(url, delim_whitespace=True, names=names)
array = dataframe.values
X = array[:,0:13]
Y = array[:,13]
seed = 7
kfold = model_selection.KFold(n_splits=10, random_state=seed)
```

```
15. model = LinearRegression()
16. scoring = 'r2'
    results = model_selection.cross_val_score(model, X, Y, cv=kfold,
    scoring=scoring)
    print("R^2: %.3f (%.3f)") % (results.mean(), results.std())
```

You can see that the predictions have a poor fit to the actual values with a value close to zero and less than 0.5.

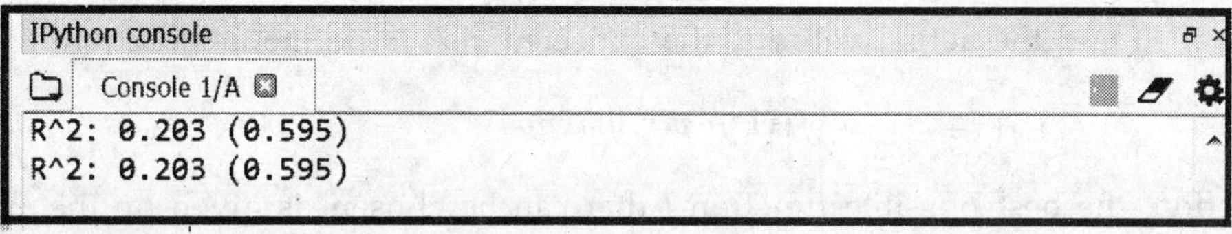

3.5 STATISTICAL LEARNING THEORY

The goals of learning are understanding and prediction. Learning falls into many categories, including supervised learning, unsupervised learning, online learning, and reinforcement learning. From the perspective of statistical learning theory, supervised learning is best understood. Supervised learning involves learning from a training set of data. Every point in the training is an input-output pair, where the input maps to an output. The learning problem consists of inferring the function that maps between the input and the output, such that the learned function can be used to predict output from future input.

Depending on the type of output, supervised learning problems are either problems of regression or problems of classification. If the output takes a continuous range of values, it is a regression problem. Using Ohm's Law as an example, a regression could be performed with voltage as input and current as output. The regression would find the functional relationship between voltage and current to be $\frac{1}{R}$, such that

$$I = \frac{1}{R}V$$

Classification problems are those for which the output will be an element from a discrete set of labels. Classification is very common for machine learning applications. In facial recognition, for instance, a picture of a person's face would be the input, and the output label would be that person's name. The input would be represented by a large multidimensional vector whose elements represent pixels in the picture.

After learning a function based on the training set data, that function is validated on a test set of data, data that did not appear in the training set.

Formal description

Take X to be the vector space of all prossible outputs. Statistical learning theory takes the spective that there is some unknown probability distribution over the product space

$Z - X \times Y$, i.e. there exists some unknown $p(z) - p(\bar{x}, y)$. The training set is mode up of n samples from this probability distribution and is notated

$$S = \{(\vec{x}_1, y_i), ...(\vec{x}_n, y_n)\} = \{\vec{z}_1, ..., \vec{z}_n)$$

Every $\bar{x}$ is an input vector from the traning data, y_i is the output that corresponds to it.

In this formalism the inference problem consists of finding a function $f : X \rightarrow Y$ such that $f(\bar{x}) \approx y$. Let H be a space of function $f : X \rightarrow Y$ called the hypothesis space. The hypothesis space is the space of functions the algorithm will search through. Let V $(f(\bar{x}), y)$ between the predicted value $f(\bar{x})$ and the actual value y. the expected risk is defined to be

$$I|f| = \int_{x \times y} V(f(\vec{x}), y), p(\vec{x}, y) d\vec{x}\, dy$$

The target function, the best possible function f that can be chosen, is given by the f that satisfies

$$I[f] = \inf_{h \in H} I[h]$$

Because the probability distribution $p(x, y)$ is inknown

is unknown, a proxy measure for the expected risk must be used. This measure is based on the on the training set, a sample from this unknown probability distribution. It is called the empirical risk

$$I_S[f] = \frac{1}{N} \sum_{i=t}^{n} V(f(\vec{x}_i), y_i)$$

A learning algorithm that chooses the function f_s that minimizes the empirical risk is called empirical risk minimization.

Loss functions

The choice of loss function is a defermining factor on the function fs that will be chosen by the learning algorithm. The loss function also affects the convrgence rate for an algontim. it is important for the loss functon to be converx (3)

Diifferent loss functions are used depending on whether the problem is one of classifiction.

Regression

The most common loss function for regression is the square loss function (also know as the L2-norm). This familiar loss function is used in ordinary least squares regression. The form is:

$$V(f)(\bar{x}), y) = (y - f(\bar{x}))^2$$

The absolute value loss (also knows as the L1-norm) is also sometimes used:

$$V(f)(\bar{x}), y) = |y - f(\bar{x})|$$

Classification

In some sense the 0-1 indicator function is the most natural loss function for classification. It takes the value 0 if the predicted output is the same as the actual output, and it takes the value 1 if the predicted output is different from the actual output. For binary classification with Y = {–1, 1}, this is:

$$V(f(\vec{x}), y) = \theta(y f(\vec{x}))$$

where θ is the Heaviside step function.

Regularization

In machine learning problems, a major problem that arises is that of overfitting. Because learning is a prediction problem, the goal is not to find a function that most closely fits the (previously observed) data, but to find one that will most accurately predict output from future input. Empirical risk minimization runs this risk of overfitting: finding a function that matches the data exactly but does not predict future output well.

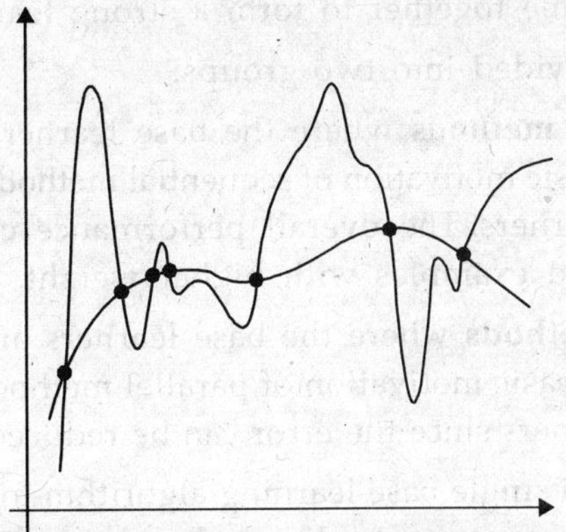

Fig. 3.1: Overfitting in Lerned Function

Fig. 3.1 represents an example of overfitting in machine learning. The red dots represent training set data. The green line represents the true functional relationship, while the blue line shows the learned function, which has fallen victim to overfitting.

Overfitting is symptomatic of unstable solutions; a small perturbation in the training set data would cause a large variation in the learned function. It can be shown that if the stability for the solution can be guaranteed, generalization and consistency are guaranteed as well. Regularization can solve the overfitting problem and give the problem stability.

Regularization can be accomplished by restricting the hypothesis space $\mathcal{H}$. A common example would be restricting $\mathcal{H}$ to linear functions: this can be seen as a reduction to the standard problem of linear regression. $\mathcal{H}$ could also be restricted to polynomial of degree p exponentials, or bounded functions on L1. Restriction of the hypothesis space avoids overfitting because the form of the potential functions are limited, and so does not allow for the choice of a function that gives empirical risk arbitrarily close to zero.

One example of regularization is Tikhonov regularization. This consists of minimizing

$$\frac{1}{N}\sum_{i=1}^{n} V(f(\vec{x}_i, y_i)) + \gamma \| f \|_H^2$$

where γ is a fixed and positive parameter, the regularization parameter. Tikhonov regularization ensures existence, uniqueness, and stability of the solution.

3.6 ENSEMBLE METHODS

Ensemble methods are meta-algorithms that combine several machine learning techniques into one predictive model in order to

1. decrease variance(bagging),
2. bias (boosting), or
3. improve predictions (stacking).

Ensemble methods, combines several decision trees to produce better predictive performance than utilizing a single decision tree. The main principle behind the ensemble model is that a group of weak learners come together to form a strong learner.

Ensemble methods can be divided into two groups:

1. **Sequential ensemble methods** where the base learners are generated sequentially (e.g. AdaBoost).The basic motivation of sequential methods is to exploit the dependence between the base learners. The overall performance can be boosted by weighing previously mislabelled examples with higher weight.
2. **Parallel ensemble methods** where the base learners are generated in parallel (e.g. Random Forest). The basic motivation of parallel methods is to exploit independence between the base learners since the error can be reduced dramatically by averaging.

Most ensemble methods use a single base learning algorithm to produce homogeneous base learners, i.e. learners of the same type, leading to homogeneous ensembles.

There are also some methods that use heterogeneous learners, i.e. learners of different types, leading to heterogeneous ensembles. In order for ensemble methods to be more accurate than any of its individual members, the base learners have to be as accurate as possible and as diverse as possible.

3.6.1 Bias and Variance

The error emerging from any model can be broken down into three components mathematically. Following are these component:

$$Err(x) = (E|\hat{f}(x)| - f(x)^2 + E\left[\hat{f}(x) - E|\hat{f}(x)|\right]^2 + \alpha_e^2$$

$$Err(x) = \textbf{Bias}^2 + \textbf{Variance} + \textbf{Irreducible Error}$$

Why is this important in the current context? To understand what really goes behind an ensemble model, we need to first understand what causes error in the model. We will briefly introduce you to these errors and give an insight to each ensemble learner in this regards.

Bias error is useful to quantify how much on an average are the predicted values different from the actual value. A high bias error means we have a under-performing model which keeps on missing important trends.

The error due to bias is taken as the difference between the expected (or average) prediction of our model and the correct value which we are trying to predict. Of course you only have one model so talking about expected or average prediction values might seem a little strange. However, imagine you could repeat the whole model building process more than once: each time you gather new data and run a new analysis creating a new model. Due to randomness in the underlying data sets, the resulting models will have a range of predictions. Bias measures how far off in general these models' predictions are from the correct value.

The error due to variance is taken as the variability of a model prediction for a given data point. Again, imagine you can repeat the entire model building process multiple times. The variance is how much the predictions for a given point vary between different realizations of the model.

Variance on the other side quantifies how are the prediction made on same observation different from each other. A high variance model will over-fit on your training population and perform badly on any observation beyond training. Following diagram will give you more clarity (Assume that red spot is the real value and blue dots are predictions) :

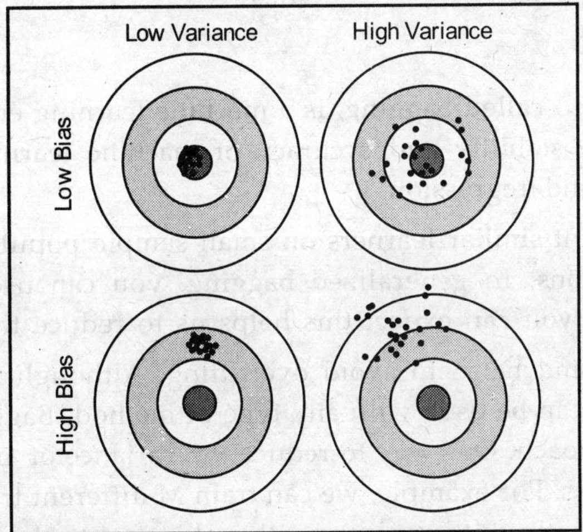

Fig. 3.2: Variance and Bias depicted (Credit: Scott Fortman)

Normally, as you increase the complexity of your model, you will see a reduction in error due to lower bias in the model. However, this only happens till a particular point. As you continue to make your model more complex, you end up over-fitting your model and hence your model will start suffering from high variance.

A champion model should maintain a balance between these two types of errors. This is known as the **trade-off management** of bias-variance errors. Ensemble learning is one way to execute this trade off analysis.

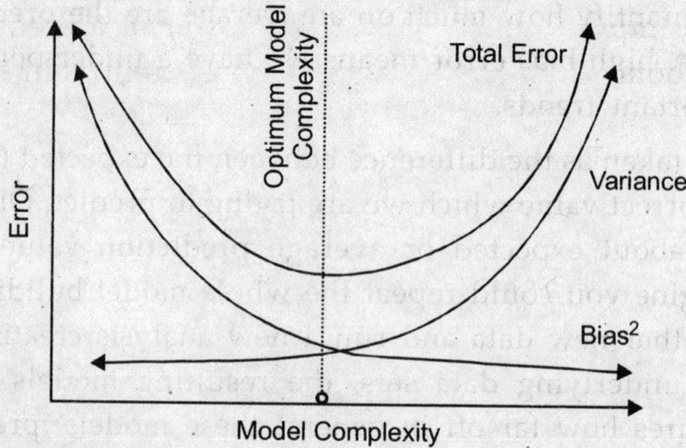

3.6.2 Basic Ensemble Methods

The three most popular methods for combining the predictions from different models are:

- **Bagging**. Building multiple models (typically of the same type) from different subsamples of the training dataset.
- **Boosting**. Building multiple models (typically of the same type) each of which learns to fix the prediction errors of a prior model in the chain.
- **Stacking**. Building multiple models (typically of differing types) and supervisor model that learns how to best combine the predictions of the primary models.

3.6.3 Bagging

Bootstrap aggregating, also called bagging, is a machine learning ensemble meta-algorithm designed to improve the stability and accuracy of machine learning algorithms used in statistical classification and regression.

Bagging tries to implement similar learners on small sample populations and then takes a mean of all the predictions. In generalized bagging, you can use different learners on different population. As you can expect this helps us to reduce the variance error.

It also reduces variance and helps to avoid overfitting. Although it is usually applied to decision tree methods, it can be used with any type of method. Bagging is a special case of the model averaging approach. One way to reduce the variance of an estimate is to average together multiple estimates. For example, we can train M different trees on different subsets of the data (chosen randomly with replacement) and compute the ensemble:

$$f(x) = 1/M \sum_{m=1}^{m} f_m(x)$$

Bagging uses bootstrap sampling to obtain the data subsets for training the base learners. For aggregating the outputs of base learners, bagging uses voting for classification and averaging for regression.

Bootstrapping is a process of selecting samples from original sample (or population) and using these samples for estimating various statistics or model accuracy. Bagging (Bootstrap aggregating) was proposed by Leo Breiman in 1994 for improving classification accuracy.

Bagging is a relatively simple way to increase the power of a predictive statistical model by taking multiple random samples(with replacement) from your training data set, and using each of these samples to construct a separate model and separate predictions for your test set. These predictions are then averaged to create a, hopefully more accurate, final prediction value.

One can quickly intuit that this technique will be more useful when the predictors are more unstable. In other words, if the random samples that you draw from your training set are very different, they will generally lead to very different sets of predictions. This greater variability will lead to a stronger final result. When the samples are extremely similar, all of the predictions derived from the samples will likewise be extremely similar, making bagging a bit superfluous.

Taking smaller samples from your training set will induce greater instability, but taking samples that are too small will result in useless models. Generally, some fraction of your training set between 1/50th and 1/2 will be useful for bagging purposes(of course, this greatly depends on how many observations are in your training set). The smaller your bagging samples, the more samples you will need to collect and the more models you will need to generate to create more stability in the final predictors.

Bootstrapping Sampling Example

N = {23,45,55,47,34,88,95,27,87,78,26,19,10,3,4,17} – Original sample with 16 elements

Bootstrap sample 1: {10, 78, 87, 55, 26, 88, 10}

Bootstrap sample 2: {55, 78, 45, 78, 55, 23, 23}

Bootstrap sample 3: {88, 27, 10, 27, 34, 34, 23}

Why do we create bootstrap samples? Bootstrap samples are created to estimate and validate models for improved accuracy, reduced variance and bias, and improved stability of a model.

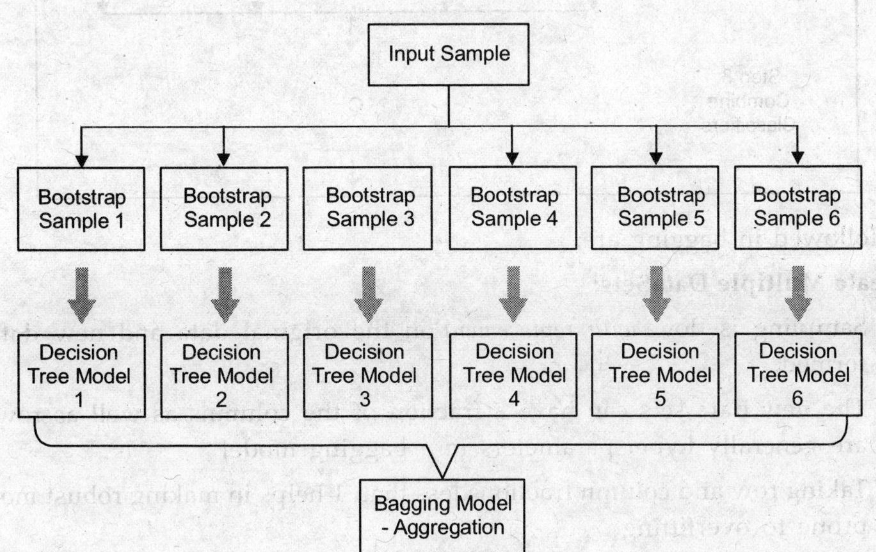

Once bootstrap samples are created, model classifier is used for training or building a model and then selecting model based on popularity votes. In classification model, a label with maximum votes will assigned to the observations. Average value is used in case of a regression model.

Bagging is an ensembling process – where a model is trained on each of the bootstrap samples and the final model is an aggregated models of the all sample models. For a numeric target variable/regression problems the predicted outcome is an average of all the models and in the classification problems, the predicted class is defined based on plurality.

Bagging is short for bootstrap aggregation, so named because it takes a number of samples from the dataset, with each sample set being regarded as a bootstrap sample. The results of these bootstrap samples are then aggregated.

Bagging is a technique used to reduce the variance of our predictions by combining the result of multiple classifiers modeled on different sub-samples of the same data set. The following figure will make it clearer:

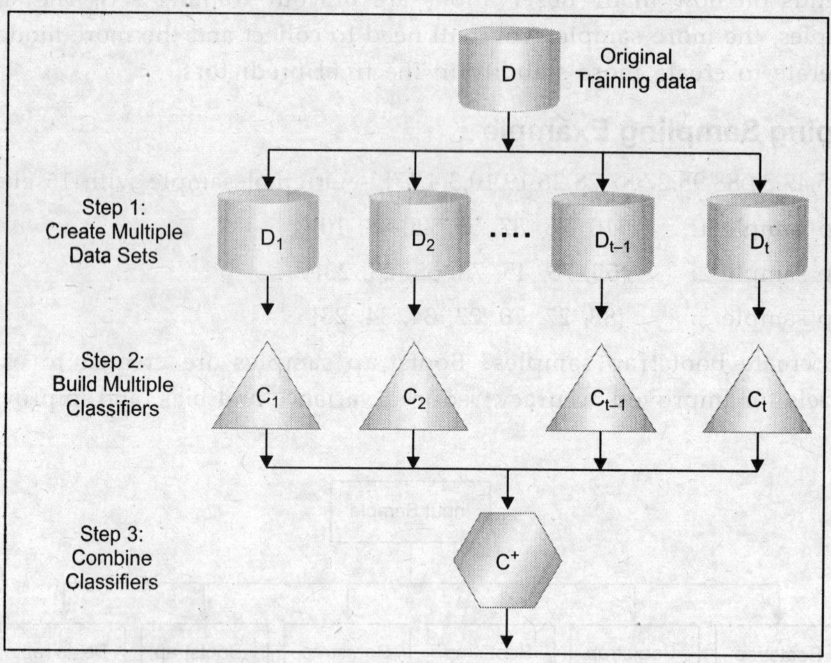

The steps followed in bagging are:

1. **Create Multiple DataSets**:
   - o Sampling is done *with replacement* on the original data and new datasets are formed.
   - o The new data sets can have a fraction of the columns as well as rows, which are generally hyper-parameters in a bagging model
   - o Taking row and column fractions less than 1 helps in making robust models, less prone to overfitting

2. **Build Multiple Classifiers:**
   - o Classifiers are built on each data set.
   - o Generally the same classifier is modeled on each data set and predictions are made.
3. **Combine Classifiers:**
   - o The predictions of all the classifiers are combined using a mean, median or mode value depending on the problem at hand.
   - o The combined values are generally more robust than a single model.

Note that, here the number of models built is not a hyper-parameters. Higher number of models are always better or may give similar performance than lower numbers. It can be theoretically shown that the variance of the combined predictions are reduced to 1/n (n: number of classifiers) of the original variance, under some assumptions.

There are various implementations of bagging models. Random forest is one of them and we'll discuss it next.

Characteristics of Bagging

1. Operates via equal weighting of models
2. Settles on result using majority voting
3. Employs multiple instances of same classifier for one dataset
4. Builds models of smaller datasets by sampling with replacement
5. Works best when classifier is unstable (decision trees, for example), as this instability creates models of differing accuracy and results to draw majority from
6. Bagging can hurt stable model by introducing artificial variability from which to draw inaccurate conclusions

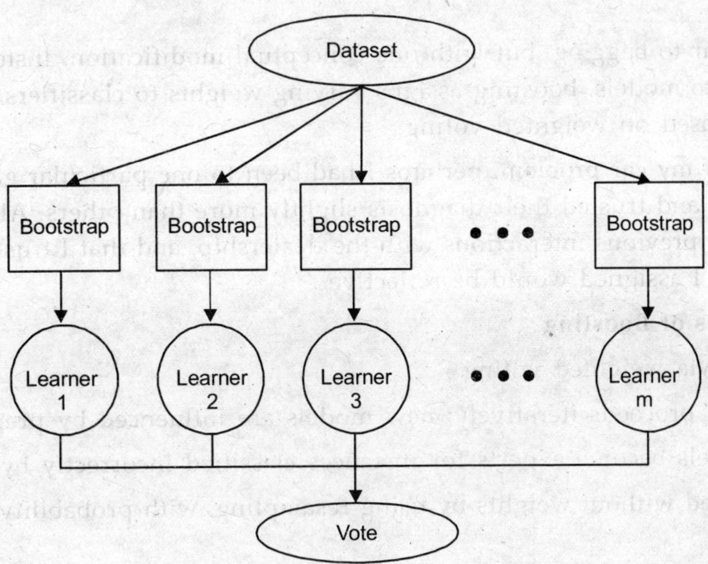

3.6.4 Boosting

'Boosting' refers to a family of algorithms which converts weak learner to strong learners.

Boosting is an iterative technique which adjust the weight of an observation based on the last classification. If an observation was classified incorrectly, it tries to increase the weight of this observation and vice versa. Boosting in general decreases the bias error and builds strong predictive models. However, they may sometimes over fit on the training data.

To convert weak learner to strong learner, we'll combine the prediction of each weak learner using methods like:

- Using average/weighted average
- Considering prediction has higher vote

For example: Above, we have defined 5 weak learners. Out of these 5, 3 are voted as 'SPAM' and 2 are voted as 'Not a SPAM'. In this case, by default, we'll consider an email as SPAM because we have higher(3) vote for 'SPAM'.

Boosting is a machine learning ensemble meta-algorithm for primarily reducing bias, and also variance in supervised learning, and a family of machine learning algorithms that convert weak learners to strong ones.A weak learner is defined to be a classifier that is only slightly correlated with the true classification (it can label examples better than random guessing). In contrast, a strong learner is a classifier that is arbitrarily well-correlated with the true classification.

The main variation between many boosting algorithms is their method of weighting training data points and hypotheses. AdaBoost is very popular and perhaps the most significant historically as it was the first algorithm that could adapt to the weak learners. However, there are many more recent algorithms such as LPBoost, TotalBoost, BrownBoost, xgboost, MadaBoost, LogitBoost, and others. Many boosting algorithms fit into the AnyBoost framework, which shows that boosting performs gradient descent in function space using a convex cost function.

Boosting is similar to bagging, but with one conceptual modification. Instead of assigning equal weighting to models, boosting assigns varying weights to classifiers, and derives its ultimate result based on weighted voting.

Thinking again of my car problem, perhaps I had been to one particular garage numerous times in the past, and trusted their diagnosis slightly more than others. Also suppose that I was not a fan of previous interactions with the dealership, and that I trusted their insight less. The weights I assigned would be reflective.

Characteristics of Boosting

1. Operates via weighted voting
2. Algorithm proceeds iteratively; new models are influenced by previous ones
3. New models become experts for instances classified incorrectly by earlier models
4. Can be used without weights by using resampling, with probability determined by weights

5. Works well if classifiers are not too complex
6. Also works well with weak learners
7. AdaBoost (Adaptive Boosting) is a popular boosting algorithm
8. LogitBoost (derived from AdaBoost) is another, which uses additive logistic regression, and handles multi-class problems

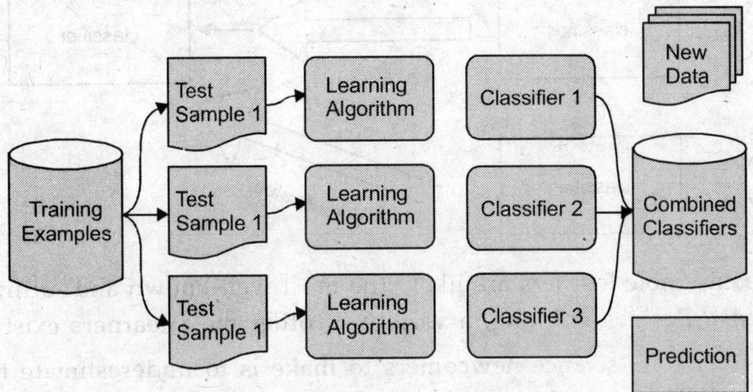

Stacking

Stacking is a bit different from the previous 2 techniques as it trains multiple single classifiers, as opposed to various incarnations of the same learner. While bagging and boosting would use numerous models built using various instances of the same classification algorithm (eg. decision tree), stacking builds its models using different classification algorithms (perhaps decision trees, logistic regression, an ANNs, or some other combination).

A combiner algorithm is then trained to make ultimate predictions using the predictions of other algorithms. This combiner can be any ensemble technique, but logistic regression is often found to be an adequate and simple algorithm to perform this combining. Along with classification, stacking can also be employed in unsupervised learning tasks such as density estimation.

Stacking

- Trains multiple learners (as opposed to bagging/boosting which train a single learner)
- Each learner uses a subset of data
- A "combiner" is trained on a validation segment
- Stacking uses a meta learner (as opposed to bagging/boosting which use voting schemes)
- Difficult to analyze theoretically ("black magic")
- Level-1 → meta learner
- Level-0 → base classifiers
- Can also be used for numeric prediction (regression)
- The best algorithms to use for base models are smooth, global learners

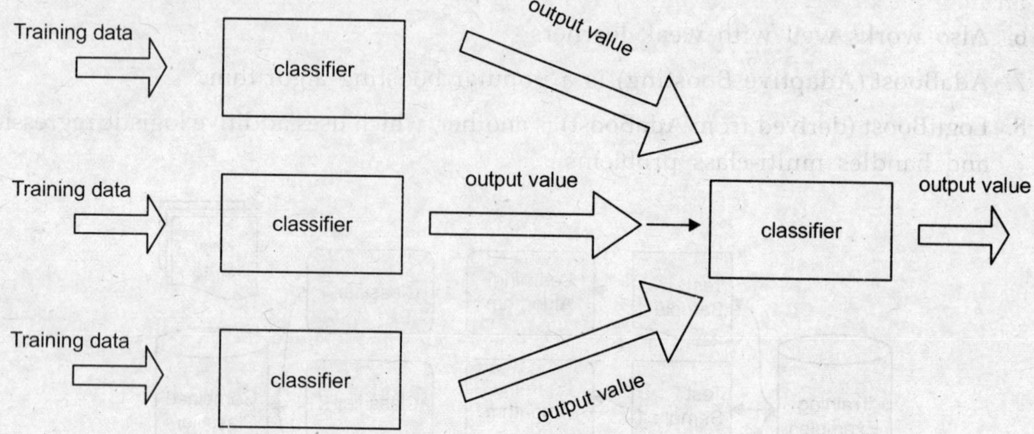

While the above ensemble learners are likely the most well-known and -utilized, numerous other options exist. Besides stacking, a variety of other meta learners exist as well.

An easy mistake for data science newcomers to make is to underestimate the complexity of the algorithm landscape, thinking that a decision tree is a decision tree, a neural network is a neural network, etc. Besides overlooking the fact that there is significant difference between various specific implementations of algorithm families (look at the vast amount of research being done in neural networks over the past few years for explicit evidence), the idea that various algorithms can be used in tandem (via ensemble or intervening meta-learners) to accomplish greater accuracy in a given task, or even to tackle tasks which, alone, would not be solvable, does not even register. Any form of recent "artificial intelligence" you can think of takes this approach. But that's a different conversation completely.

Comparison of Bagging and Boosting Ensemble Methods

	Bagging	Boosting	Stacking
Partitioning of the data into subsets	Random	Giving mis-classified samples higher preference	Various
Goal to achieve	Minimize variance	Increase predictive force	Both
Methods where this is used	Random subspace	Gradient descent	Blending
Function to combine single models	(Weighted) average	Weighted majority vote	Logistic regression

How does it work?

Now we know that, boosting combines weak learner a.k.a. base learner to form a strong rule. An immediate question which should pop in your mind is, *'How boosting identify weak rules?'*

To find weak rule, we apply base learning (ML) algorithms with a different distribution. Each time base learning algorithm is applied, it generates a new weak prediction rule. This is an iterative process. After many iterations, the boosting algorithm combines these weak rules into a single strong prediction rule.

Here's another question which might haunt you, *'How do we choose different distribution for each round?'*

For choosing the right distribution, here are the following steps:

Step 1: The base learner takes all the distributions and assign equal weight or attention to each observation.

Step 2: If there is any prediction error caused by first base learning algorithm, then we pay higher attention to observations having prediction error. Then, we apply the next base learning algorithm.

Step 3: Iterate Step 2 till the limit of base learning algorithm is reached or higher accuracy is achieved.

Finally, it combines the outputs from weak learner and creates a strong learner which eventually improves the prediction power of the model. Boosting pays higher focus on examples which are mis-classiûed or have higher errors by preceding weak rules.

There are many boosting algorithms which impart additional boost to model's accuracy. In this tutorial, we'll learn about the two most commonly used algorithms i.e. Gradient Boosting (GBM) and XGboost.

Stacking is a similar to boosting: you also apply several models to your original data. The difference here is, however, that you don't have just an empirical formula for your weight function, rather you introduce a meta-level and use another model/approach to estimate the input together with outputs of every model to estimate the weights or, in other words, to determine what models perform well and what badly given these input data

3.7 WHAT IS RANDOM FOREST

Random Forest is an extension over bagging. It takes one extra step where in addition to taking the random subset of data, it also takes the random selection of features rather than using all features to grow trees. When you have many random trees. It's called Random Forest.

Let's look at the steps taken to implement Random forest:

1. Suppose there are N observations and M features in training data set. First, a sample from training data set is taken randomly with replacement.
2. A subset of M features are selected randomly and whichever feature gives the best split is used to split the node iteratively.
3. The tree is grown to the largest.
4. Above steps are repeated and prediction is given based on the aggregation of predictions from n number of trees.

Random Forest is considered to be a *panacea* of all data science problems. On a funny note, when you can't think of any algorithm (irrespective of situation), use random forest!

Random Forest is a versatile machine learning method capable of performing both *regression* and *classification* tasks. It also undertakes dimensional reduction methods, treats missing values, outlier values and other essential steps of data exploration, and does a fairly good job. It is a type of ensemble learning method, where a group of weak models combine to form a powerful model.

In Random Forest, we grow multiple trees as opposed to a single tree in CART model. To classify a new object based on attributes, each tree gives a classification and we say the tree "votes" for that class. The forest chooses the classification having the most votes (over all the trees in the forest) and in case of regression, it takes the average of outputs by different trees.

It works in the following manner. Each tree is planted & grown as follows:

1. Assume number of cases in the training set is N. Then, sample of these N cases is taken at random but *with replacement*. This sample will be the training set for growing the tree.
2. If there are M input variables, a number m<M is specified such that at each node, m variables are selected at random out of the M. The best split on these m is used to split the node. The value of m is held constant while we grow the forest.
3. Each tree is grown to the largest extent possible and there is no pruning.
4. Predict new data by aggregating the predictions of the ntree trees (i.e., majority votes for classification, average for regression).

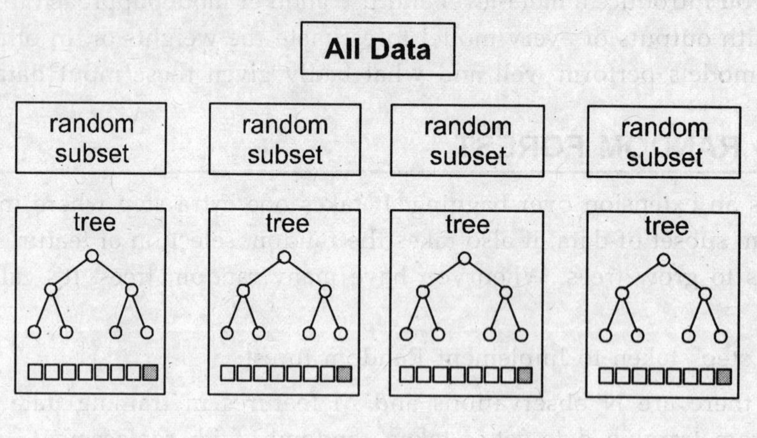

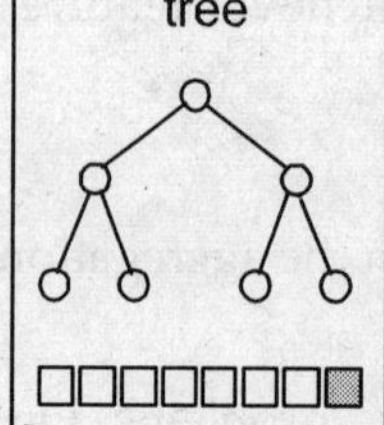

At each node:
choose some ball subset of variables at random
find a variable (and a value for that variable)
which optimizes the split

In the random forest approach, a large number of decision trees are created. Every observation is fed into every decision tree. The most common outcome for each observation is used as the final output. A new observation is fed into all the trees and taking a majority vote for each classification model.

An error estimate is made for the cases which were not used while building the tree. That is called an **OOB (Out-of-bag)** error estimate which is mentioned as a percentage.

The R package **"randomForest"** is used to create random forests.

Install R Package

Use the below command in R console to install the package. You also have to install the dependent packages if any.

```
install.packages("randomForest)
```

The package "randomForest" has the function **randomForest()** which is used to create and analyze random forests.

Syntax

The basic syntax for creating a random forest in R is "

```
randomForest(formula, data)
```

Following is the description of the parameters used "

- **formula** is a formula describing the predictor and response variables.
- **data** is the name of the data set used.

Input Data

We will use the R in-built data set named readingSkills to create a decision tree. It describes the score of someone's readingSkills if we know the variables "age","shoesize","score" and whether the person is a native speaker.

```
Here is the sample data.
# Load the party package. It will automatically load other required packages.
library(party)

# Print some records from data set readingSkills.
print(head(readingSkills))
```

When we execute the above code, it produces the following result and chart –

```
R Console
  nativeSpeaker age shoeSize    score
1           yes   5 24.83189 32.29385
2           yes   6 25.95238 36.63105
3            no  11 30.42170 49.60593
4           yes   7 28.66450 40.28456
5           yes  11 31.88207 55.46085
6           yes  10 30.07843 52.83124
> |
```

Example 3.3

We will use the **randomForest()** function to create the decision tree and see it's graph.

```
# Loadind the party package. It will automatically load other required
packages.
library(party)
library(randomForest)
# This will create the forest.
output.forest <- randomForest(nativeSpeaker ~ age + shoeSize + score,
        data = readingSkills)
# View the forest results.
print(output.forest)
# Importance of each predictor.
print(importance(fit, type = 2))
plot(output.forest)
```

When we execute the above code, it produces the following result–

```
randomForest 4.6-12
Type rfNews() to see new features/changes/bug fixes.
>
> # This will create the forest.
> output.forest <- randomForest(nativeSpeaker ~ age + shoeSize + score,
+         data = readingSkills)
>
> # View the forest results.
> print(output.forest)

Call:
 randomForest(formula = nativeSpeaker ~ age + shoeSize + score, data = readingSkills)
               Type of random forest: classification
                     Number of trees: 500
No. of variables tried at each split: 1

        OOB estimate of  error rate: 1.5%
Confusion matrix:
    no yes class.error
no  99   1        0.01
yes  2  98        0.02
>
> # Importance of each predictor.
> print(importance(fit, type = 3))
plot(output.forest)
|
```

From the random forest plotr shown above we can conclude that the shoesize and score are the important factors deciding if someone is a native speaker or not. Also the model has only 1% error which means we can predict with 99% accuracy.

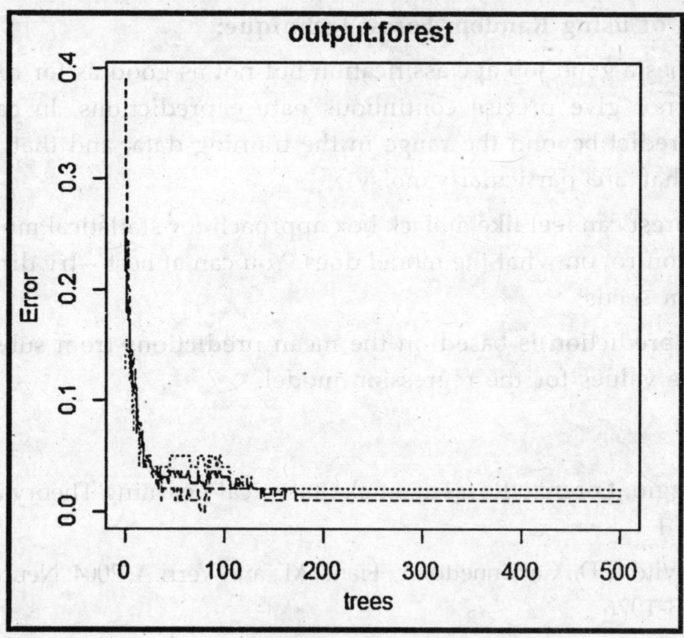

Advantages of using Random Forest technique

1. This algorithm can solve both type of problems i.e. classification and regression and does a decent estimation at both fronts.
2. One of benefits of Random forest which excites me most is, the power of handle large data set with higher dimensionality. It can handle thousands of input variables and identify most significant variables so it is considered as one of the dimensionality reduction methods. Further, the model outputs **Importance of variable,** which can be a very handy feature (on some random data set).
3. It has an effective method for estimating missing data and maintains accuracy when a large proportion of the data are missing.
4. It has methods for balancing errors in data sets where classes are imbalanced.
5. The capabilities of the above can be extended to unlabeled data, leading to unsupervised clustering, data views and outlier detection.
6. Random Forest involves sampling of the input data with replacement called as bootstrap sampling. Here one third of the data is not used for training and can be used to testing. These are called the **out of bag** samples. Error estimated on these out of bag samples is known as *out of bag error*. Study of error estimates by Out of bag, gives evidence to show that the out-of-bag estimate is as accurate as using a test set of the same size as the training set. Therefore, using the out-of-bag error estimate removes the need for a set aside test set.
7. Handles higher dimensionality data very well.
8. Handles missing values and maintains accuracy for missing data.

Disadvantages of using Random Forest technique:

1. It surely does a good job at classification but not as good as for regression problem as it does not give precise continuous nature predictions. In case of regression, it doesn't predict beyond the range in the training data, and that they may over-fit data sets that are particularly noisy.
2. Random Forest can feel like a black box approach for statistical modelers – you have very little control on what the model does. You can at best – try different parameters and random seeds!
3. Since final prediction is based on the mean predictions from subset trees, it won't give precise values for the regression model.

References

1. Tomaso Poggio, Lorenzo Rosasco, et al. Statistical Learning Theory and Applications, 2012, Class 1
2. Rosasco, L., Vito, E.D., Caponnetto, A., Fiana, M., and Verri A. 2004. Neural computation Vol 16, pp 1063-1076
3. Vapnik, V.N. and Chervonenkis, A.Y. 1971. On the uniform convergence of relative frequencies of events to their probabilities. Theory of Probability and its Applications Vol. 16, pp 264-280.
4. Mukherjee, S., Niyogi, P. Poggio, T., and Rifkin, R. 2006. Learning theory: stability is sufficient for generalization and necessary and sufficient for consistency of empirical risk minimization. Advances in Computational Mathematics. Vol 25, pp 161-193.

Unit 4

Sparse Modelling and Estimation

Learning Objectives and Outcome

At the end of this unit the reader shall be able to learn:

- Sparse Modelling and Estimation,
- Modelling Sequence/Time-Series Data, Deep
- Learning and Feature Representation Learning

4.1 SPARSE MODELLING AND ESTIMATION

A *sparse matrix or sparse array* is a matrix in which most of the elements are zero. By contrast, if most of the elements are nonzero, then the matrix is considered dense. The number of zero-valued elements divided by the total number of elements (*e.g.*, $m \times n$ for an $m \times n$ matrix) is called the sparsity of the matrix (which is equal to 1 minus the density of the matrix).

$$\begin{pmatrix} 11 & 22 & 0 & 0 & 0 & 0 & 0 \\ 0 & 33 & 44 & 0 & 0 & 0 & 0 \\ 0 & 0 & 55 & 66 & 77 & 0 & 0 \\ 0 & 0 & 0 & 0 & 0 & 88 & 0 \\ 0 & 0 & 0 & 0 & 0 & 0 & 99 \end{pmatrix}$$

The above sparse matrix contains only 9 non-zero elements, with 26 zero elements. Its sparsity is 74%, and its density is 26%.

4.2 TIME SERIES

Time series is a series of data points in which each data point is associated with a timestamp. A simple example is the price of a stock in the stock market at different points of time on a given day. Another example is the amount of rainfall in a region at different months of the year. R language uses many functions to create, manipulate and plot the time series data. The data for the time series is stored in an R object called **time-series object**. It is also a R data object like a vector or data frame.

The time series object is created by using the **ts()** function.

Syntax

The basic syntax for **ts()** function in time series analysis is "

```
timeseries.object.name <-  ts(data, start, end, frequency)
```

Following is the description of the parameters used "

- **data** is a vector or matrix containing the values used in the time series.
- **start** specifies the start time for the first observation in time series.
- **end** specifies the end time for the last observation in time series.
- **frequency** specifies the number of observations per unit time.

Except the parameter "data" all other parameters are optional.

Example 4.1

Consider the annual rainfall details at a place starting from January 2017. We create an R time series object for a period of 12 months and plot it.

```
------------------------------------------------------------
# Assuming the raifall data points in form of a R vector.
rainfall1 <- c(800,1180,870,1340,635,920,690,990,780,985,880,1070)
# Converting the data  to form a matrix.
combined.rainfall <-  matrix(c(rainfall1),nrow = 12)
# Convert it to a time series object starting from Jan. 2017.
rainfall.timeseries <- ts(combined.rainfall,start = c(2017,1),frequency = 12)
# Print the timeseries data.
print(rainfall.timeseries)
# Give the chart file a name.
png(file = "rainfall_combined0.png")
# Plot a graph of the time series.
plot(rainfall.timeseries, main = "Multiple Time Series")
# Save the file.
dev.off()
------------------------------------------------------------
```

When we execute the above code, it produces the following result and chart–

R Console

```
> # Assuming the raifall data points in form of a R vector.
> rainfall1 <- c(800,1180,870,1340,635,920,690,990,780,985,880,1070)
>
> # Converting the data  to form a matrix.
> combined.rainfall <-  matrix(c(rainfall1),nrow = 12)
>
> # Convert it to a time series object starting from Jan. 2017.
> rainfall.timeseries <- ts(combined.rainfall,start = c(2017,1),frequency = 12)
>
> # Print the timeseries data.
> print(rainfall.timeseries)
      Jan  Feb  Mar  Apr  May  Jun  Jul  Aug  Sep  Oct  Nov  Dec
2017  800 1180  870 1340  635  920  690  990  780  985  880 1070
>
> # Give the chart file a name.
> png(file = "rainfall_combined0.png")
>
> # Plot a graph of the time series.
> plot(rainfall.timeseries, main = "Multiple Time Series")
>
> # Save the file.
> dev.off()
png
  2
> |
```

The output graph file shall be diverted to your computer in documents folder.

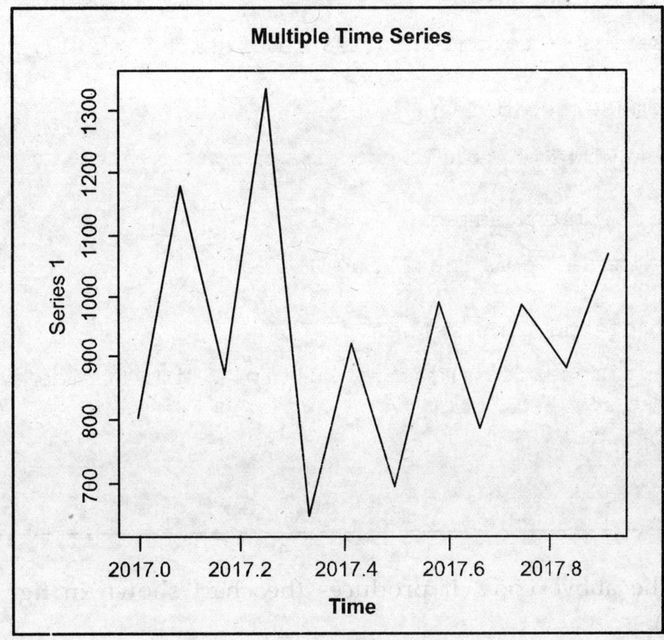

Fig. 4.1: The Time series chart

4.1.1 Different Time Intervals

The value of the **frequency** parameter in the ts() function decides the time intervals at which the data points are measured. A value of 12 indicates that the time series is for 12 months. Other values and its meaning is as below."

- **frequency** = **12** pegs the data points for every month of a year.
- **frequency** = **4** pegs the data points for every quarter of a year.
- **frequency** = **6** pegs the data points for every 10 minutes of an hour.
- **frequency** = **24*6** pegs the data points for every 10 minutes of a day.

4.1.2 Multiple Time Series

We can plot multiple time series in one chart by combining both the series into a matrix.

```
---------------------------------------------------------------
# Assuming the raifall data points in form of a R vector.
rainfall1 <- c(800,1180,870,1340,635,920,690,990,780,985,880,1070)
rainfall2 <-
      c(655,1310,1320,1180,560,824,825,1265,800,1100,1107,1207)

# Converting the data  to form a matrix.
combined.rainfall <-  matrix(c(rainfall1,rainfall2),nrow = 12)

# Convert it to a time series object starting from Jan. 2017.
rainfall.timeseries <- ts(combined.rainfall,start = c(2017,1),frequency = 12)

# Print the timeseries data.
print(rainfall.timeseries)

# Give the chart file a name.
png(file = "rainfall_combined1.png")

# Plot a graph of the time series.
plot(rainfall.timeseries, main = "Multiple Time Series")

# Save the file.
dev.off()
---------------------------------------------------------------
```

When we execute the above code, it produces the chart shown in fig. 4.2(a) and Curve shown in Fig. 4.2(b)

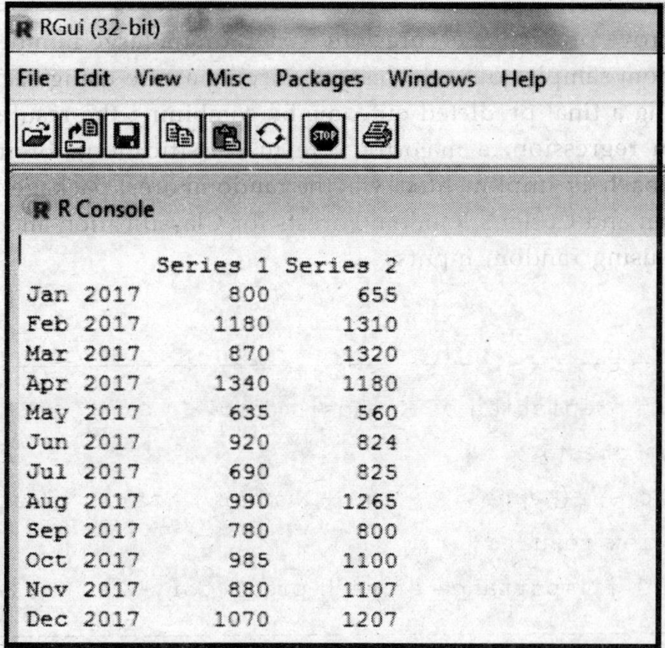

RGui (32-bit)

File Edit View Misc Packages Windows Help

R Console

	Series 1	Series 2
Jan 2017	800	655
Feb 2017	1180	1310
Mar 2017	870	1320
Apr 2017	1340	1180
May 2017	635	560
Jun 2017	920	824
Jul 2017	690	825
Aug 2017	990	1265
Sep 2017	780	800
Oct 2017	985	1100
Nov 2017	880	1107
Dec 2017	1070	1207

Fig. 4.2(a): The Multiple Time series chart

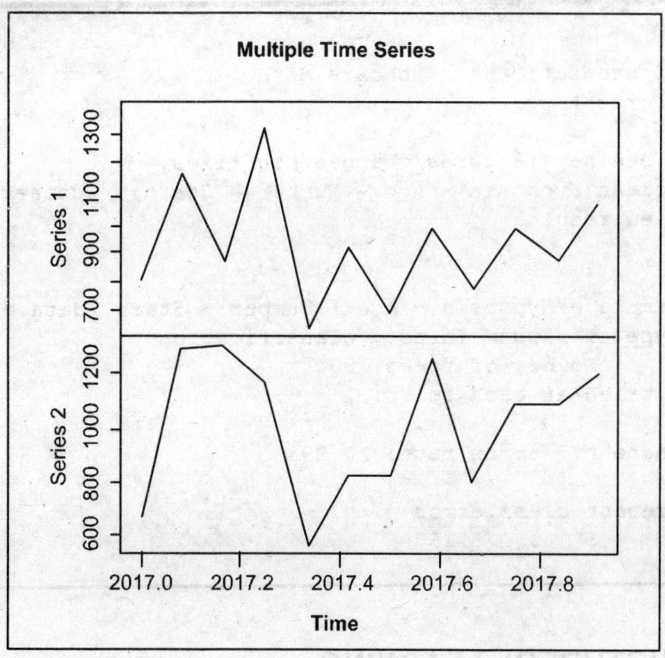

Fig. 4.2(b): The Multiple Time series curves

4.3 RANDOM FORESTS

Random forests improve predictive accuracy by generating a large number of bootstrapped trees (based on random samples of variables), classifying a case using each tree in this new "forest", and deciding a final predicted outcome by combining the results across all of the trees (an average in regression, a majority vote in classification). Breiman and Cutler's random forest approach is implimented via the randomForest package. randomForest is envisaged by Breiman and Cutler's Random Forests for Classification and Regression based on a forest of trees using random inputs.

Here is an example.

```
# Random Forest prediction of Kyphosis data
library(randomForest)
fit <- randomForest(Kyphosis ~ Age + Number + Start,   data=kyphosis)
print(fit) # view results
importance(fit) # importance of each predictor
```

When we execute the above code, it produces the following results:

```
R Console
> # Random Forest prediction of Kyphosis data
> library(randomForest)
randomForest 4.6-12
Type rfNews() to see new features/changes/bug fixes.
> fit <- randomForest(Kyphosis ~ Age + Number + Start,   data=kyphosis)
> print(fit) # view results

Call:
 randomForest(formula = Kyphosis ~ Age + Number + Start, data = kyphosis)
               Type of random forest: classification
                     Number of trees: 500
No. of variables tried at each split: 1

        OOB estimate of  error rate: 20.99%
Confusion matrix:
        absent present class.error
absent      59       5   0.0781250
```

4.4 DEEP (STRUCTURED) LEARNING

Machine-learning technology powers many aspects of modern society: from web searches to content filtering on social networks to recommendations on e-commerce websites, and it is increasingly present in consumer products such as cameras and smart phones. Machine-learning systems are used to identify objects in images, transcribe speech into text, match news items, posts or products with users' interests, and select relevant results of search.Increasingly, these applications make use of a class of techniques called deep learning.

Deep learning (also known as *deep structured learning*, hierarchical learning or deep machine learning) is a branch of machine learning based on a set of algorithms that attempt to model high level abstractions in data. In a simple case, you could have two sets of neurons: ones that receive an input signal and ones that send an output signal. When the input layer receives an input it passes on a modified version of the input to the next layer. In a deep network, there are many layers between the input and output (and the layers are not made of neurons but it can help to think of it that way), allowing the algorithm to use multiple processing layers, composed of multiple linear and non-linear transformations.

Deep Learning has revolutionized the machine learning recently with some of the great works being done in this field. These methods have dramatically improved the state-of-the-art in speech recognition, visual object recognition, object detection and many other domains such as drug discovery and genomics. But, the ancient term "Deep Learning" was first introduced to Machine Learning by Dechter (1986) and to Artificial Neural Networks (NNs) by Aizenberg et al (2000) It was further popularized by the development of Convolutional Networks Architecture by Alex Krizhevsky named 'AlexNet' that won the competition of ImageNet in 2012 by defeating all the image processing methods and creating a way for deep learning architectures to be used in Image Processing.

4.4.1 Deep Learning Architecture

1. **Generative deep architectures**, which are intended to characterize the high-order correlation properties of the observed or visible data for pattern analysis or synthesis purposes, and/or characterize the joint statistical distributions of the visible data and their associated classes. In the latter case, the use of Bayes rule can turn this type of architecture into a discriminative one.
2. **Discriminative deep architectures**, which are intended to directly provide discriminative power for pattern classification, often by characterizing the posterior distributions of classes conditioned on the visible data; and **Hybrid deep architectures**, where the goal is discrimination but is assisted (often in a significant way) with the outcomes of generative architectures via better optimization or/and regularization, or discriminative criteria are used to learn the parameters in any of the deep generative models in category 1) above.

4.4.2 Types of Deep Learning Architectures

Despite the complex categorization of the deep learning architectures, the one's that are in practice are:

1. **Deep feed-forward networks,**
2. **Convolution networks** and
3. **Recurrent Networks.**

Deep learning is although a relatively new term, it has existed prior to the dramatic uptick in online searches of late. Enjoying a surge in research and industry, due mainly to its incredible successes in a number of different areas, deep learning is the process of applying deep neural network technologies - that is, neural network architectures with multiple hidden layers - to solve problems. Deep learning is a process, like data mining, which employs deep neural network architectures, which are particular types of machine learning algorithms.

So, with that, let's have a look at some deep learning related terminology, with a focus on concise, no-nonsense definitions.

Deep Learning is a subfield of machine learning concerned with algorithms inspired by the structure and function of the brain called artificial neural networks.

4.5 NEURAL NETWORK

A Neural Network consists of an interconnected group of nodes called **neurons**. The input feature variables from the data are passed to these neurons as a *multi-variable linear combination,* where the values multiplied by each feature variable are known as weights. A non-linearity is then applied to this linear combination which gives the neural network the ability to model complex *non-linear* relationships. A neural network can have multiple layers where the output of one layer is passed to the next one in the same way. At the output, there is generally no non-linearity applied. Neural Networks are trained using Stochastic Gradient Descent (SGD) and the backpropagation algorithm. Stochastic gradient descent is a popular algorithm for training a wide range of models in machine learning, including (linear) support vector machines, logistic regression and graphical models. When combined with the backpropagation algorithm, it is the de facto standard algorithm for training artificial neural networks.

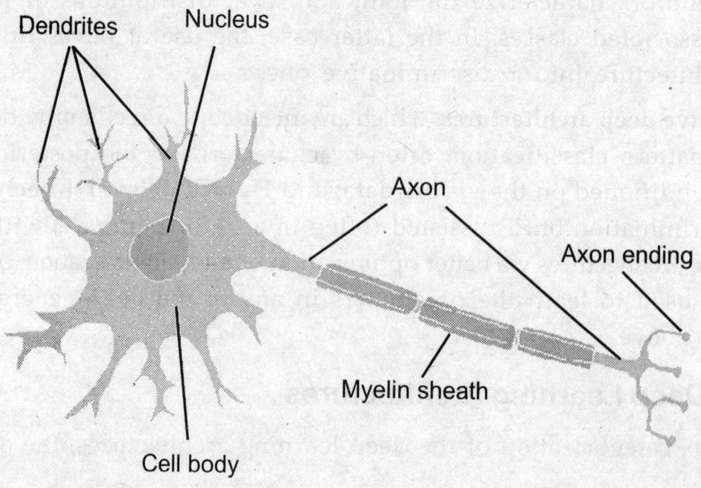

Fig. 4.3: Anatomy of a neuron of human mind

Pros:

- Since neural networks can have many layers (and thus parameters) with non-linearities, they are very effective at modelling highly complex non-linear relationships.
- We generally don't have to worry about the structure of the data at neural networks are very flexible in learning almost any kind of feature variable relationships.
- Research has consistently shown that simply giving the network more training data, whether totally new or from augmenting the original data set, benefits network performance.

Cons:

- Because of the complexity of these models, they're not easy to interpret and understand.
- They can be quite challenging and computationally intensive to train, requiring careful hyper-parameter tuning and setting of the learning rate schedule.
- They require a lot of data to achieve high performance and are generally outperformed by other ML algorithms in "small data" cases.

4.5.1 Deep Feed Forward Networks

Deep feed-forward networks, also often called **feed-forward neural networks**, or **multilayer perceptrons (MLPs)**, are the quintessential deep learning models.

The goal of a feed-forward network is to approximate some function *f"*. For example, for a classifier, *y* = *f" (x)* maps an input x to a category *y*. A feed-forward network defines a mapping *y* = *f(x;è)* and learns the value of the parameters *è* that result in the best function approximation.

In simple terms, the network can be defined as input, hidden and output nodes with data coming in from input nodes, processing is done in hidden nodes and then the output is produced through output nodes. The information flows through the function being evaluated from x, through the intermediate computations used to define f, and finally to the output y. There are no feedback connections in which outputs of the model are fed back into itself and hence the models is called as feed-forward network. The model is shown in Figure 4.4·

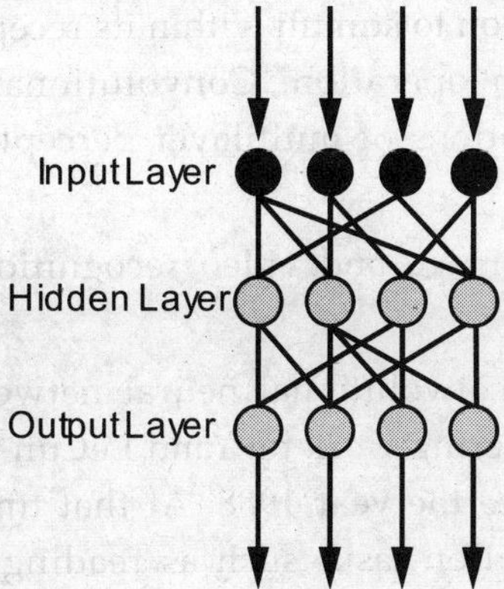

Fig. 4.4: Feed-forward neural network

4.5.2 Convolution Neural Networks

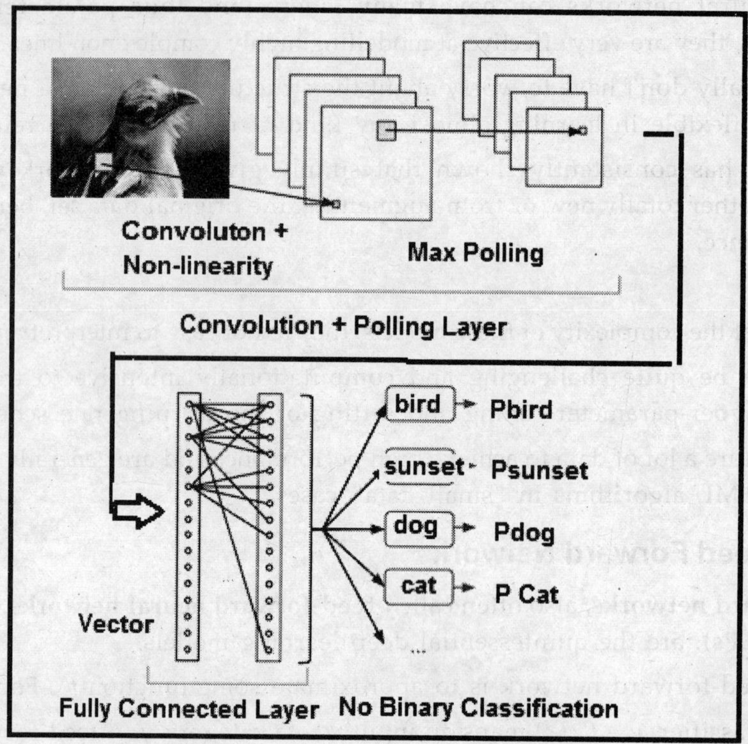

Fig. 4.5: Convolution Neural Networks

In machine learning, a **convolutional neural network** (CNN, or ConvNet) is a type of feed-forward artificial neural network in which the connectivity pattern between its neurons is inspired by the organization of the animal visual cortex.

Individual cortical neurons respond to stimuli in a restricted region of space known as the **receptive field**. The receptive fields of different neurons partially overlap such that they tile the visual field.

The response of an individual neuron to stimuli within its receptive field can be approximated mathematically by a convolution operation. Convolutional networks were inspired by biological processes and are variations of multilayer perceptrons designed to use minimal amounts of preprocessing.

They have wide applications in image and video recognition, recommender systems and natural language processing.

LeNet was one of the very first convolutional neural networks which helped propel the field of Deep Learning. This pioneering work by Yann LeCun was named LeNet5 after many previous successful iterations since the year 1988. At that time the LeNet architecture was used mainly for character recognition tasks such as reading zip codes, digits, etc.

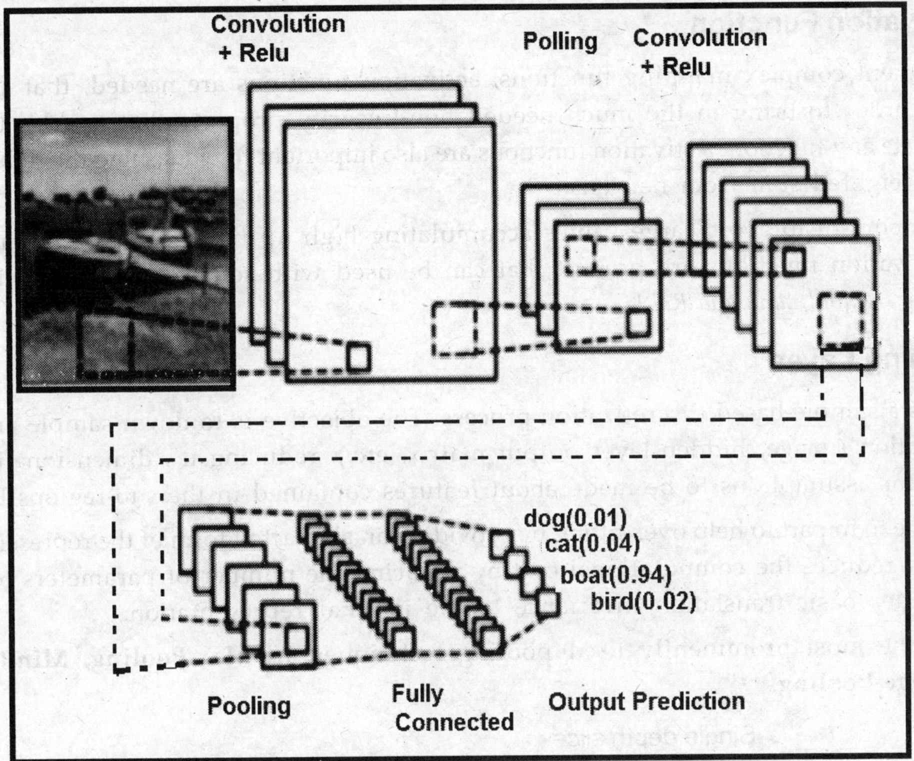

Fig. 4.6: A simple convolutional neural network model

There are four main components in a ConvNet shown in Figure 4.6:

1. Convolutional Layer
2. Activation Function
3. Pooling Layer
4. Fully Connected Layer

(1) Convolutional layer

Convolutional Layer is based on the term 'Convolution', which is a mathematical operation performed on two variables ($f*g$) to produce a third variable. It is similar to cross-correlation. The input to a convolutional layer is a $m \times m \times r$ image where m is the height and width of the image and r is the number of channels, e.g. an RGB image has $r = 3$. The convolutional layer will have k filters (or kernels) of size $n \times n \times q$ where n is smaller than the dimension of the image and q can either be the same as the number of channels r or smaller and may vary for each kernel. The size of the filters gives rise to the locally connected structure which are each convolved with the image to produce k feature maps of size $m - n + 1.8$.

(2) Activation Function

To implement complex mapping functions, activation functions are needed, that are non-linear in order to bring in the much needed non-linearity property that enables them to approximate any function. Activation functions are also important for squashing the unbounded linearly weighted sum from neurons.

This is important to avoid large values accumulating high up the processing hierarchy. A lot of activation functions are present that can be used with some of the primarily used ones being *sigmoid, tanh and ReLU*.

(3) Pooling Layer

Pooling is a sample-based discretization process. The objective is to down-sample an input representation (image, hidden-layer output matrix, etc.), reducing it's dimensionality and allowing for assumptions to be made about features contained in the sub-regions binned. This is done to in part to help over-fitting by providing an abstracted form of the representation. As well, it reduces the computational cost by reducing the number of parameters to learn and provides basic translation invariance to the internal representation.

Some of the most prominently used pooling techniques are **Max-Pooling, MinPooling** and **Average-Pooling**.

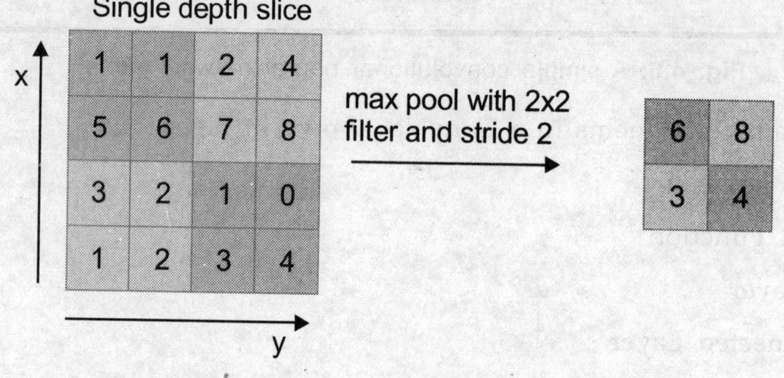

Fig. 4.7: Example of Max-Pooling of 2*2 filters

(4) Fully Connected Layer

The term "Fully Connected" implies that every neuron in the previous layer is connected to every neuron on the next layer. The Fully Connected layer is a traditional Multi Layer Perceptron that uses a softmax activation function or any other similar function in the output layer.

4.5.3 Recurrent Neural Networks

In a traditional neural network we assume that all inputs (and outputs) are independent of each other. But for many tasks that's a very bad idea. If you want to predict the next word in a sentence you better know which words came before it. RNNs are called recurrent because they perform the same task for every element of a sequence, with the output being depended on the previous computations. Another way to think about RNNs is that they have a "memory" which captures information about what has been calculated so far.

A RNN has loops in them that allow information to be carried across neurons while reading in input. In the figure, x_t is some input, A is a part of the RNN and h_t is the output. Essentially you can feed in words from the sentence or even characters from a string as x_t and through the RNN it will come up with a h_t.s. Some of the types of RNNs are LSTM, Bidirectional RNNs, GRUs and more.

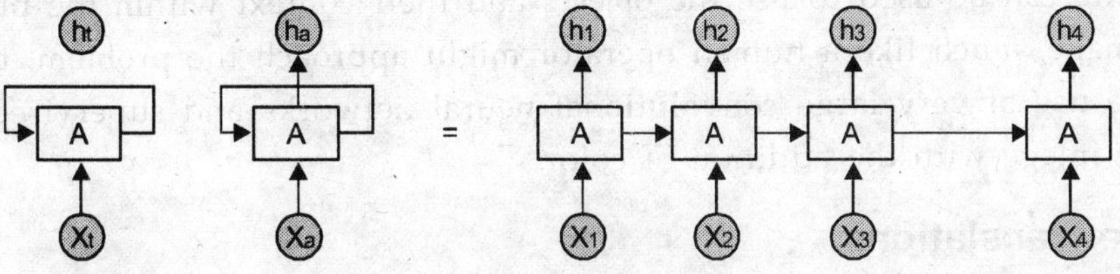

An unrolled RNN

Fig. 4.8: Model of a RNN

RNNs can be used in NLP, Machine Translations, Language Modeling, Computer vision, Video Analysis, Image generation, Image captioning, and so on due to the fact that any number of inputs and outputs can be fixed in a RNN making it one to one — many to many model possible. Some of the possible architectures are shown in figure with possible explanation of the models.

Each rectangle is a vector and arrows repesent functions (e.g. matrix multiply). Input vectors are in red, output vectors are in ble and green vectors hold the RNN's satage (more in this soon). From left to right: (1) vanilla mode of processing with out RNN from fixed-sized input to fixed-sized output (e.g. image classification). (2) Sequence output (e.g. image captioning takes an image and outputs a sentence of words) (3) Sequence input (e.g. sentiment analysis where a given sentence is classified as expressing positive or negative sentiment). (4) Sequence input and sequence output (e.g. Machine Translation: an RNN reads a where we wish to label each frame of the video). Notice that in every case are no pre-specified constraints on the lenghts sequences because the recurrent transformation (green) in fixed and can be applied as many times as we like.

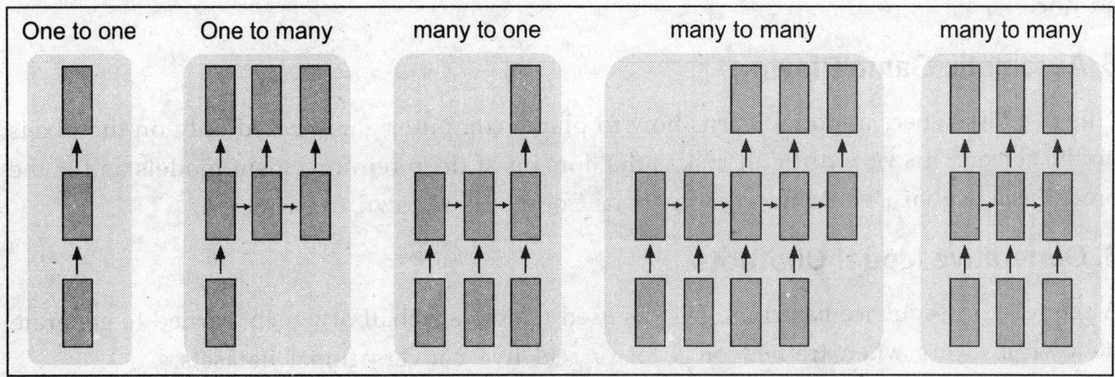

Fig. 4.9: RNN depicting operations over sequence of vectors

4.6 APPLICATIONS OF DEEP LEARNING METHODS

There has been a lot of research going on in the field of Deep Learning and a lot of unique questions are solved using deep learning models. Some of the best applications of deep learning are:

1. Colorization of Black and White Images

Deep learning can be used to use the objects and their context within the photograph to color the image, much like a human operator might approach the problem. the approach involves the use of very large convolutional neural networks and supervised layers that recreate the image with the addition of color.

2. Machine Translations

Text translation can be performed without any pre-processing of the sequence, allowing the algorithm to learn the dependencies between words and their mapping to a new language. Stacked networks of large LSTM recurrent neural networks are used to perform this translation.

3. Object Classification and Detection in Photographs

This task requires the classification of objects within a photograph as one of a set of previously known objects. State-of-the-art results have been achieved on benchmark examples of this problem using very large convolutional neural networks. A breakthrough in this problem by Alex Krizhevsky et al. results on the ImageNet classification problem called AlexNet.

4. Automatic Handwriting Generation

This is a task where given a corpus of handwriting examples, generate new handwriting for a given word or phrase. The handwriting is provided as a sequence of coordinates used by a pen when the handwriting samples were created. From this corpus the relationship between the pen movement and the letters is learned and new examples can be generated ad hoc.

5. Automatic Game Playing

This is a task where a model learns how to play a computer game based only on the pixels on the screen.This very difficult task is the domain of deep reinforcement models and is the breakthrough that DeepMind (now part of Google) is renown for achieving.

6. Generative Model Chatbots

A sequence to sequence based model was used to create a chatbot which learned to generate it's own answers when trained on a lot of real live conversational datasets.

4.7 FEATURE REPRESENTATION LEARNING

An ***algorithm*** is a systematic way of repeatedly applying mathematical operations to a representation in order to achieve some computational goal. Asking what algorithms a representation supports, therefore, is a matter of asking what mathematical operations can be meaningfully applied to it.

The performance of machine learning methods is heavily dependent on the choice of data representation (or **features**) on which they are applied. For that reason, much of the actual effort in deploying machine learning algorithms goes into the design of pre-processing pipelines and data transformations that result in a representation of the data that can support effective machine learning. Such feature engineering is important but labor-intensive and highlights the weakness of current learning algorithms: their inability to extract and organize the *discriminative information* from the data. **Feature engineering** is a way to take advantage of human ingenuity and prior knowledge to compensate for that weakness. In order to expand the scope and ease of applicability of machine learning, it would be highly desirable to make learning algorithms less dependent on feature engineering, so that novel applications could be constructed faster, and more importantly, to make progress towards **Artificial Intelligence** (AI). An AI must fundamentally understand the world around us, and it is argued that this can only be achieved if it can learn to identify and disentangle the underlying explanatory factors hidden in the observed milieu of low-level sensory data (collected by automation instruments).

There are also a wide variety of representation learning algorithms built around mathematical operations other than the ones given above:

1. **Greater/less than**. TrueSkill is a model of people's performance in multiplayer games which represents each player with a scalar, and whoever has a larger value is expected to win.
2. **L_p distance**. There is a variant of MDS which uses general L_p distance rather than Euclidean distance.
3. **Hamming distance**. Semantic hashing is a technique in image retrieval which tries to represent images in terms of binary representations where the Hamming distance reflects the semantic dissimilarity between the images. The idea is that we can use the binary representation as a "hash key" and find semantically similar images by flipping random bits and finding the corresponding hash table entries.
4. **Projection onto an axis**. We might want the individual coordinates of a representation to represent something meaningful. As Shepard discusses, MDS with L1 distance often results in such a representation. Another MDS-based technique he describes is INDSCAL, which tries to model multiple subjects' similarity judgments with MDS in a single coordinate system, but where the individual axes can be rescaled for each subject.
5. **Matrix multiplication**. Paccanaro and Hinton proposed a model called linear relational embedding, where entities are represented by vectors and relations between them are represented by matrices. Matrix multiplication corresponds to function

composition: if we compose "father of" and "father of," we get the relation "paternal grandfather of."

Roger Shepard's classic 1980 paper, "Multidimensional scaling, tree fitting, and clustering," highlights a variety of different representation learning methods. The paper is written from a cognitive science perspective, where the algorithms are used to model human similarity judgments and reaction time data, with the goal of understanding what our internal mental representations might be like. But the same kinds of models are widely used today, albeit in a more modern form, in statistics and machine learning.

Feature learning or representation learning is a set of techniques that allows a system to automatically discover the representations needed for feature detection or classification from raw data. This replaces manual feature engineering and allows a machine to both learn the features and use them to perform a specific task.

4.7.1 Broad Categories of Feature Representation Learning

Feature learning can be either :

1. Supervised or
2. Unsupervised.

In supervised feature learning, features are learned using labelled input data. Examples include supervised neural networks, multilayer perceptron and (supervised) dictionary learning.

In unsupervised feature learning, features are learned with unlabeled input data. Examples include dictionary learning, independent component analysis, auto-encoders, matrix factorization and various forms of clustering.

4.7.2 Supervised Feature Learning

Supervised feature learning is learning features from labelled data. The data label allows the system to compute an error term, the degree to which the system fails to produce the label, which can then be used as feedback to correct the learning process (*reduce/minimize the error*). Approaches include:

(1) Supervised dictionary learning

Dictionary learning develops a set (dictionary) of representative elements from the input data such that each data point can be represented as a weighted sum of the representative elements. The dictionary elements and the weights may be found by minimizing the average representation error (over the input data), together with L1 regularization on the weights to enable sparsity (i.e., the representation of each data point has only a few nonzero weights).

Supervised dictionary learning exploits both the structure underlying the input data and the labels for optimizing the dictionary elements. For example, a supervised dictionary learning technique applied dictionary learning on classification problems by jointly optimizing the dictionary elements, weights for representing data points, and parameters of the classifier based on the input data. In particular, a minimization problem is formulated, where the objective function consists of the classification error, the representation error, an L1 regularization on the representing weights for each data point (to enable sparse representation of data), and an L2 regularization on the parameters of the classifier.

(2) Neural Networks

Neural networks are a family of learning algorithms that use a "network" consisting of multiple layers of inter-connected nodes. It is inspired by the animal nervous system, where the nodes are viewed as neurons and edges are viewed as synapses. Each edge has an associated weight, and the network defines computational rules for passing input data from the network's input layer to the output layer. A network function associated with a neural network characterizes the relationship between input and output layers, which is parameterized by the weights. With appropriately defined network functions, various learning tasks can be performed by minimizing a cost function over the network function (weights).

Multilayer neural networks can be used to perform feature learning, since they learn a representation of their input at the hidden layer(s) which is subsequently used for classification or regression at the output layer.

4.7.3 Unsupervised Feature Learning

Unsupervised feature learning is learning features from unlabeled data. The goal of unsupervised feature learning is often to discover low-dimensional features that captures some structure underlying the high-dimensional input data. When the feature learning is performed in an unsupervised way, it enables a form of semisupervised learning where features learned from an unlabeled dataset are then employed to improve performance in a supervised setting with labeled data. Several approaches are introduced in the following.

Consider some of the most widely used unsupervised learning techniques and the sorts of representations they produce:

1. **Clustering maps data** points to a discrete set (say, the integers) where the only meaningful operation is equality.
2. **Nonlinear dimensionality reduction algorithms** (e.g. multidimensional scaling, Isomap) map data points to a low-dimensional space where Euclidean distance is meaningful.
3. **Linear dimensionality reduction algorithms** like PCA and factor analysis map data points to a low-dimensional space where Euclidean distance, linear combination, and dot products are all meaningful.

This list doesn't tell the whole story: there are a lot of variants on each of these categories, and there are more nuances in terms of precisely which operations are meaningful. For instance, in some versions of MDS, only the rank order of the Euclidean distances is meaningful. Still, it gives a useful coarse description of each of these categories.

(1) K-means clustering

K-means clustering is an approach for vector quantization. In particular, given a set of n vectors, k-means clustering groups them into k clusters (i.e., subsets) in such a way that each vector belongs to the cluster with the closest mean. The problem is computationally NP-hard, although suboptimal greedy algorithms have been developed.

K-means clustering can be used to group an unlabeled set of inputs into k clusters, and then use the centroids of these clusters to produce features. These features can be produced in several ways. The simplest is to add k binary features to each sample, where each feature j has value one iff the jth centroid learned by k-means is the closest to the sample under consideration. It is also possible to use the distances to the clusters as features, perhaps after transforming them through a radial basis function (a technique that has been used to train RBF networks. Coates and Ng note that certain variants of k-means behave similarly to sparse coding algorithms.

In a comparative evaluation of unsupervised feature learning methods, Coates, Lee and Ng found that k-means clustering with an appropriate transformation outperforms the more recently invented auto-encoders and RBMs on an image classification task. K-means also improves performance in the domain of NLP, specifically for named-entity recognition; there, it competes with Brown clustering, as well as with distributed word representations (also known as neural word embeddings).

(2) Principal Component Analysis (PCA)

PCA is often used for dimension reduction. Given an unlabeled set of n input data vectors, PCA generates p (which is much smaller than the dimension of the input data) right singular vectors corresponding to the p largest singular values of the data matrix, where the kth row of the data matrix is the kth input data vector shifted by the sample mean of the input (i.e., subtracting the sample mean from the data vector). Equivalently, these singular vectors are the eigenvectors corresponding to the p largest eigenvalues of the sample covariance matrix of the input vectors. These p singular vectors are the feature vectors learned from the input data, and they represent directions along which the data has the largest variations.

PCA is a linear feature learning approach since the p singular vectors are linear functions of the data matrix. The singular vectors can be generated via a simple algorithm with p iterations. In the ith iteration, the projection of the data matrix on the $(i-1)^{th}$ eigenvector is subtracted, and the ith singular vector is found as the right singular vector corresponding to the largest singular of the residual data matrix.

PCA has several limitations. First, it assumes that the directions with large variance are of most interest, which may not be the case. PCA only relies on orthogonal transformations of the original data, and it exploits only the first- and second-order moments of the data, which may not well characterize the data distribution. Furthermore, PCA can effectively reduce dimension only when the input data vectors are correlated (which results in a few dominant eigenvalues).

(3) Local Linear Embedding (LLE)

LLE is a nonlinear learning approach for generating low-dimensional neighbour-preserving representations from (unlabeled) high-dimension input. The approach was proposed by Roweis and Saul (2000). The general idea of LLE is to reconstruct the original high-dimensional data using lower-dimensional points while maintaining some geometric properties of the neighbourhoods in the original data set.

LLE consists of two major steps. The first step is for *"neighbor-preserving"*, where each input data point Xi is reconstructed as a weighted sum of K nearest neighbor data points, and the optimal weights are found by minimizing the average squared reconstruction error (i.e., difference between an input point and its reconstruction) under the constraint that the weights associated with each point sum up to one. The second step is for *"dimension reduction,"* by looking for vectors in a lower-dimensional space that minimizes the representation error using the optimized weights in the first step. Note that in the first step, the weights are optimized with fixed data, which can be solved as a least squares problem. In the second step, lower-dimensional points are optimized with fixed weights, which can be solved via sparse eigenvalue decomposition.

The reconstruction weights obtained in the first step capture the "intrinsic geometric properties" of a neighborhood in the input data. It is assumed that original data lie on a smooth lower-dimensional manifold, and the "intrinsic geometric properties" captured by the weights of the original data are also expected to be on the manifold. This is why the same weights are used in the second step of LLE. Compared with PCA, LLE is more powerful in exploiting the underlying data structure.

(4) Independent Component Analysis

ICA is a technique for forming a data representation using a weighted sum of independent non-Gaussian components. The assumption of non-Gaussian is imposed since the weights cannot be uniquely determined when all the components follow Gaussian distribution.

(5) Unsupervised Dictionary Learning

Unsupervised dictionary learning does not utilize data labels and exploits the structure underlying the data for optimizing dictionary elements. An example of unsupervised dictionary learning is sparse coding, which aims to learn basis functions (dictionary elements) for data representation from unlabeled input data. Sparse coding can be applied to learn overcomplete dictionaries, where the number of dictionary elements is larger than the dimension of the input data. Aharon et al. proposed algorithm K-SVD for learning a dictionary of elements that enables sparse representation.

(6) Multilayer/deep architectures

The hierarchical architecture of the biological neural system inspires deep learning architectures for feature learning by stacking multiple layers of learning nodes. These architectures are often designed based on the assumption of distributed representation: observed data is generated by the interactions of many different factors on multiple levels. In a deep learning architecture, the output of each intermediate layer can be viewed as a representation of the original input data. Each level uses the representation produced by previous level as input, and produces new representations as output, which is then fed to higher levels. The input at the bottom layer is raw data, and the output of the final layer is the final low-dimensional feature or representation.

(7) Restricted Boltzmann Machines (RBMs)

RBMs are often used as a building block for multilayer learning architectures. An RBM can be represented by an undirected bipartite graph consisting of a group of binary hidden variables, a group of visible variables, and edges connecting the hidden and visible nodes. It is a special case of the more general Boltzmann machines with the constraint of no intra-node connections. Each edge in an RBM is associated with a weight. The weights together with the connections define an energy function, based on which a joint distribution of visible and hidden nodes can be devised. Based on the topology of the RBM, the hidden variables are independent, conditioned on the visible (hidden) variables.Such conditional independence facilitates computations.

An RBM can be viewed as a single layer architecture for unsupervised feature learning. In particular, the visible variables correspond to input data, and the hidden variables correspond to feature detectors. The weights can be trained by maximizing the probability of visible variables using Hinton's *Contrastive Divergence* (CD) algorithm.

In general training RBM by solving the maximization problem tends to result in non-sparse representations. Sparse RBM[was proposed to enable sparse representations. The idea is to add a regularization term in the objective function of data likelihood, which penalizes the deviation of the expected hidden variables from a small constant.

(8) Auto-encoder

An autoencoder consisting of an encoder and a decoder is a paradigm for deep learning architectures. An example is provided by Hinton and Salakhutdinov where the encoder uses raw data (e.g., image) as input and produces feature or representation as output and the decoder uses the extracted feature from the encoder as input and reconstructs the original input raw data as output. The encoder and decoder are constructed by stacking multiple layers of RBMs. The parameters involved in the architecture were originally trained in a greedy layer-by-layer manner: after one layer of feature detectors is learned, they are fed up as visible variables for training the corresponding RBM. Current approaches typically apply end-to-end training with stochastic gradient descent methods. Training can be repeated until some stopping criteria are satisfied.

One of the most exciting threads of representation learning in recent years has been learning feature representations which could be fed into standard machine learning (usually supervised learning) algorithms. Depending on the intended learning algorithm, the representation has to support some set of operations. For instance,

For nonparametric regression/classification methods like nearest neighbors or an SVM with an RBF kernel, we want Euclidean distance to be meaningful.

1. For linear classifiers, we want dot products to be meaningful.
2. For decision trees or L1 regularization, we want projection onto an axis to be meaningful.

For instance, PCA is often used as a preprocessing step in linear regression or kernel SVMs, because it produces a low-dimensional representation in which Euclidean distance and dot products are likely to be more semantically meaningful than the same operations in the original space. However, it would probably not be a good preprocessing step for decision trees or L1 regularization, since the axes themselves (other than possibly the first few) don't have any special meaning. The issues have become somewhat blurred with the advent of deep learning, since we can argue endlessly about which parts of the representation are semantically meaningful. Still, I think these issues at least implicitly guide the research in the area.

The question of which operations and algorithms are supported is, of course, only one aspect of the representation learning problem. We also want representations which where both the mapping and the inverse mapping can be computed efficiently, which can be learned in a data efficient way, and so on.

References

1. Ian Goodfellow, Yoshua Bengio, and Aaron Courville (2016). Deep Learning. MIT Press. Online
2. Deng, L.; Yu, D. (2014)."Deep Learning: Methods and Applications"(PDF).Foundations and Trends in Signal Processing.7(3–4): 1–199.doi:10.1561/2000000039.
3. Bengio, Yoshua (2009)."Learning Deep Architectures for AI"(PDF).Foundations and Trends in Machine Learning.2(1): 1–127.doi:10.1561/2200000006.
4. Bengio, Y.; Courville, A.; Vincent, P. (2013). "Representation Learning: A Review and New Perspectives".IEEE Transactions on Pattern Analysis and Machine Intelligence.35 (8):17981828.arXiv:1206.5538.doi:10.1109/tpami.2013.50.
5. Schmidhuber, J. (2015). "Deep Learning in Neural Networks: An Overview". Neural Networks. 61:85117.arXiv:1404.7828.doi:10.1016/j.neun et.2014.09.003.
6. Bengio, Yoshua; LeCun, Yann; Hinton, Geoffrey (2015). "Deep Learning".Nature.521: 436–444.doi:10.1038/nature14539.PMID26017442.
7. Deep Machine Learning – A New Frontier in Artificial Intelligence Research– a survey paper by Itamar Arel, Derek C. Rose, and Thomas P. Karnowski. IEEE Computational Intelligence Magazine, 2013
8. Schmidhuber,Jürgen(2015)."DeepLearning".Scholarpedia.10(11):32832.d oi:10.4249/scholarpedia.32832.
9. Carlos E. Perez."A Pattern Language for Deep Learning".

10. Matusugu, Masakazu; Katsuhiko Mori; Yusuke Mitari; Yuji Kaneda (2003). "Subject independent facial expression recognition with robust face detection using a convolutional neural network"(PDF). Neural Networks. (5): 555–559. doi:10.1016/ S0893–6080(03)00115–1.
11. LeNet-5, convolutional neural networks
12. Collobert, Ronan; Weston, Jason (2008–01–01). "A Unified Architecture for Natural Language Processing: Deep Neural Networks with Multitask Learning".Proceedings of the 25th International Conference on Machine Learning. ICML '08. New York, NY, USA: ACM: 160–167.doi:10.1145/1390156.1390177. ISBN 978–1–60558–205–4.
13. CNN
14. RECURRENT NEURAL NETWORKS TUTORIAL, PART 1 – INTRODUCTION TO RNNS
15. Sutskever, Ilya, Oriol Vinyals, and Quoc V. Le. "Sequence to Sequence Learning with Neural Networks." arXiv preprint arXiv:1409.3215 (2014).
16. Application Deep Learning
17. Mnih, Volodymyr, et al. "Playing atari with deep reinforcement learning." arXiv preprint arXiv:1312.5602 (2013).
29. Generative Model Chatbots
18. Ralf Herbrich, Tom Minka, and Thore Graepel, TrueSkill(TM): A Bayesian Skill Rating System, in Advances in Neural Information Processing Systems 20, MIT Press, January 2007
19. Roger Shepard. "Multidimensional scaling, tree-fitting, and clustering." Science, 1980.
20. Ruslan Salakhutdinov and Geoffrey Hinton. "Semantic Hashing." SIGIR Workshop on Information Retrieval and Applications of Graphical Models, 2007.
21. Nathan Srebro; Jason D. M. Rennie; Tommi S. Jaakkola (2004). Maximum-Margin Matrix Factorization. NIPS.
22. Daniel Jurafsky; James H. Martin (2009). Speech and Language Processing. Pearson Education International. pp. 145–146.
23. Mairal, Julien; Bach, Francis; Ponce, Jean; Sapiro, Guillermo; Zisserman, Andrew (2009). "Supervised Dictionary Learning". Advances in Neural Information Processing Systems.
24. Joseph Turian; Lev Ratinov; Yoshua Bengio (2010). Word representations: a simple and general method for semi-supervised learning (PDF). Proceedings of the 48th Annual Meeting of the Association for Computational Linguistics.
25. Schwenker, Friedhelm; Kestler, Hans A.; Palm, Günther (2001). "Three learning phases for radial-basis-function networks". Neural Networks. 14: 439–458. CiteSeerX 10.1.1.109.312/ . doi:10.1016/s0893-6080(01)00027-2.

26. Coates, Adam; Ng, Andrew Y. (2012). "Learning feature representations with k-means". In G. Montavon, G. B. Orr and K.-R. Müller. Neural Networks: Tricks of the Trade. Springer.
27. Roweis, Sam T; Saul, Lawrence K (2000). "Nonlinear Dimensionality Reduction by Locally Linear Embedding". Science, New Series. 290 (5500): 2323–2326. doi:10.1126/science.290.5500.2323. JSTOR 3081722. PMID 11125150.
28. Saul, Lawrence K; Roweis, Sam T (2000). "An Introduction to Locally Linear Embedding".
29. Hinton, G. E.; Salakhutdinov, R. R. (2006). "Reducing the Dimensionality of Data with Neural Networks" (PDF). Science. 313 (5786): 504–507. doi:10.1126/science.1127647. PMID 16873662.

Unit 5

Scalable Machine Learning (Online and Distributed Learning)

Learning Objectives and Outcome

At the end of this unit the reader shall be able to learn:

- Semi-supervised Learning,
- Active Learning,
- Inference in Graphical Models,
- Introduction to Bayesian Learning and Inference

5.1 MACHINE LEARNING: ALGORITHMS TYPES REVISITED AND MODIFIED

Machine learning is about designing algorithms that allow a computer to learn. Learning is not necessarily involves consciousness but learning is a matter of finding statistical regularities or other patterns in the data. Thus, many machine learning algorithms will barely resemble how human might approach a learning task. However, learning algorithms can give insight into the relative difficulty of learning in different environments.

Machine learning algorithms are organized into taxonomy, based on the desired outcome of the algorithm. Common algorithm types include:

- **Supervised learning** — where the algorithm generates a function that maps inputs to desired outputs. One standard formulation of the supervised learning task is the classification problem: the learner is required to learn (to approximate the behaviour of) a function which maps a vector into one of several classes by looking at several input-output examples of the function.
- **Unsupervised learning** — which models a set of inputs: labelled examples are not available.
- **Semi-supervised learning** — which combines both labelled and unlabeled examples to generate an appropriate function or classifier.

- **Reinforcement learning** – where the algorithm learns a policy of how to act given an observation of the world. Every action has some impact in the environment, and the environment provides feedback that guides the learning algorithm.
- **Transduction** – similar to supervised learning, but does not explicitly construct a function: instead, tries to predict new outputs based on training inputs, training outputs, and new inputs.
- **Learning to learn** – where the algorithm learns its own inductive bias based on previous experience. The performance and computational analysis of machine learning algorithms is a branch of statistics known as computational learning theory.

Machine learning is about designing algorithms that allow a computer to learn. Learning is not necessarily involves consciousness but learning is a matter of finding statistical regularities or other patterns in the data. Thus, many machine learning algorithms will barely resemble how human might approach a learning task. However, learning algorithms can give insight into the relative difficulty of learning in different environments.

Semi-supervised learning algorithms are trained on a combination of labeled and unlabeled data. This is useful for a few reasons. First, the process of labeling massive amounts of data for supervised learning is often prohibitively time-consuming and expensive. What's more, too much labeling can impose human biases on the model. That means including lots of unlabeled data during the training process actually tends to improve the accuracy of the final model while reducing the time and cost spent building it.

For that reason, semi-supervised learning is a win-win for use cases like webpage classification, speech recognition, or even for genetic sequencing. In all of these cases, data scientists can access large volumes of unlabeled data, but the process of actually assigning supervision information to all of it would be an insurmountable task.

The biggest difference between supervised and unsupervised machine learning is this: Supervised machine learning algorithms are trained on datasets that include labels added by a machine learning engineer or data scientist that guide the algorithm to understand which features are important to the problem at hand. Unsupervised machine learning algorithms, on the other hand, are trained on unlabeled data and must determine feature importance on their own based on inherent patterns in the data. (If the ideas of training algorithms or quantifying feature importance seem completely foreign, be sure to check out our executive's guide to predictive modeling!)

As you may have guessed, semi-supervised learning algorithms are trained on a combination of labelled and unlabeled data. This is useful for a few reasons. First, the process of labeling massive amounts of data for supervised learning is often prohibitively time-consuming and expensive. What's more, too much labelling can impose human biases on the model. That means including lots of unlabeled data during the training process actually tends to improve the accuracy of the final model while reducing the time and cost spent building it.

For that reason, semi-supervised learning is a win-win for use cases like webpage classification, speech recognition, or even for genetic sequencing. In all of these cases, data scientists can access large volumes of unlabeled data, but the process of actually assigning supervision information to all of it would be an insurmountable task.

Using classification as an example, let's compare how these three approaches work in practice:

Supervised classification: The algorithm learns to assign labels to types of webpages based on the labels that were inputted by a human during the training process.

Unsupervised clustering: The algorithm looks at inherent similarities between webpages to place them into groups.

Semi-supervised classification: Labeled data is used to help identify that there are specific groups of webpage types present in the data and what they might be. The algorithm is then trained on unlabeled data to define the boundaries of those webpage types and may even identify new types of webpages that were unspecified in the existing human-inputted labels.

The structure and volume of the data at hand should always inform the data modeling approach you take, no matter the use case. That's why critically evaluating your data and resources is an integral part of an efficient data science workflow.

5.2 SEMI-SUPERVISED MACHINE LEARNING

Learning In order to understand the nature of semi-supervised learning, it will be useful first to take a look at supervised and unsupervised learning.

Traditionally, there have been two fundamentally different types of tasks in machine learning. Supervised and Unsupervised, but semi-supervised learning is an idea in between these two Processes.

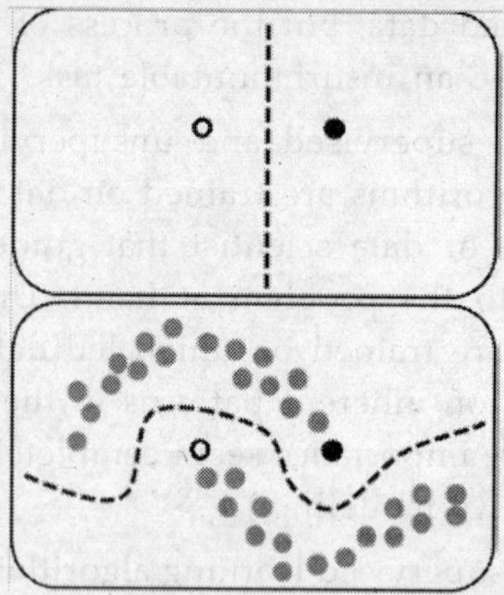

An example of the influence of unlabeled data in semi-supervised learning. The top panel shows a decision boundary we might adopt after seeing only one positive label (white circle) and one negative label (black circle) example. The bottom panel shows a decision boundary we might adopt if, in addition to the two labeled examples, we were given a collection of unlabeled data (gray circles). This could be viewed as performing clustering and then labeling the clusters with the labeled data, pushing the decision boundary away from high-density regions, or learning an underlying one-dimensional manifold where the data reside.

In order to understand the nature of semi-supervised learning, it will be useful first to take a look at unsupervised and supervised learning.

5.2.1 Unsupervised Learning

The first one is unsupervised learning Let X = (x_1,....., x_n) be a set of n examples (or points), where x_1 E x For all $i \in$ [n] : = {1,...., n}. Typically it is assumed that the points are drawn i.i.d. (independently and identically distributed) from a common distribution on X. It is often convenient to define the ($n \times d$)-matrix X = $\left(y_i^T\right)_{i \in [n]}^T$ that contains the data points as its rows. The goal of unsupervised learning is to find intersting structure in the data X. It has been argued that the problem of unsupervised learning is fundamentally that of estimating a density which is likely to have generated X. However, there are also weaker forms of unsupervised learning, such as quantile estimation, clustering, outlier detection, and dimensionality reduction.

5.2.2 Supervised Learning

The second task is supervised learning. The goal is to learn a mapping from x to y given a traning set made of pars (x_i, y_i). Here, the $y_i \in y$ are called the labels or targets of the examples x_i. If the labels are numbers. $y = \left(y_i^T\right)_{i \in [n]}^T$ denotes the column vector of labels. Again, a standard requierement is that the pairs (x_i, y_i) are sampled i.e.d. from some distribution which here ranges over $x \times y$. The task is well defined, since a mapping can be evaluated through its prodictive performance on test examples. When $y = R$ or $y = R^d$ (or more generally, when the labels are continuous), the task is called regression, Most of this book will focus on classification (there is some work on regression in chapter 23). i.e., the case where y takes values in a finite set (discrete labels).

There are two families of supervised learning algorithms:

1. Generative for supervised learning
2. Discriminative algorithms

5.2.3 Generative for Supervised Learning

Generative algorithms try to model the class-conditional density $p(x \mid y)$ by some unsupervised learning procedure. A predictive density can then be infereed by applying Bayes theorem:

$$p(x|y) = \frac{p(x \mid y)p(y)}{\int_y p(x \mid y\} p(y) dy}$$

In fact, $p(x \mid y)\ p(y) = p(x, y)$ is the joint density of the data, from which pairs ($x_i \mid y_i$) could be generated.

5.2.4 Discriminative Algorithms

Discruminative algorithms do not try to estimate how the x_i have been generated, but instead concentrate on estimating $p(y|x)$. Some discriminative methods even limit themselves to modeling whether $p(y|x)$ is greater than or less than 0.5; an example of this is the support vector machine (SVM). It has been argued that discriminative models are more directly aligned with the goal of supervised learning and therefore tend to be more efficient in practice.

5.3 SEMI-SUPERVISED LEARNING

5.3.1 Standard Setting of SSL

Semi-supervised learning (SSL) is halfway between supervised and unsupervised learning. In addition to unableled data, the algorithm is provided with some super vision information – but not necessarily for all examples. Often, this infomation will be the targets associated with some of the examples. In this case, the data set $X = (x_i)_{i \in [n]}$ can be divided into two parts: the points $X_i := (x_1, \ldots. x_l)$, for which labels $Y_i := (y_1, \ldots. y_l)$ are provided, and the points $X_u := (x_i + 1, \ldots., x_i + u)$, the labels of which are not known. This is 'standard' semi-supevised learning as investingated in this book; mostchapters will refer to his setting.

5.3.2 SSL with Constraints

Other forms of partial supervision are possible. For example, there may be consraints such as 'these pooints have (or do not have) the same target (cf. abu-Mostafa, 1995. The different setting corresponds to a different view of semi-supervised learning: In chapter 5, SSL is seen as unspervised learning guided by constraints. In contrast, most other approaches see SSL as supervised learing with additional information on the distribution of the examples x. The latter interpretation seems to be more in line with most applications, where the goal is the same as in supervsed learning; to predict a target value for a given x_i. However, this view does not readily apply if the number and nature of the classes are not known in advance but have to be inferred from the data. In constrast. SSL as unsupervised learning with constraints may still remain applicable in such situations.

5.3.3 Transductive and Inductive Learning

A problem related to SSL was introduced by Vapnik already several decades ago: so-called transductive learning. In this setting, one is given a (labeled) training set and an (unlabeled) test set. The idea of transduction is to perform predictions only for the test points. This is in contrast to inductive learning, where the goal is to output a prediction function which is defined on theentire space x. Many methods described in this book will be transductive; in particular, this is rather natural for inference based on graph representations of the data.

5.4 WHEN CAN SEMI-SUPERVISED LEARNING WORK?

A natural question arises: is semi-supervised learning meaningful? More precisely: in comparison with a supervised algorithm that uses only labeled data, can one hope to have a more accurate prediction by taking into account the unlabeled points? As per Olivier Chapelle,Bernhard Schölkopf, and Alexander Zien the editor trio, in principle the answer is "yes." However, there is an important prerequisite: that the distribution of examples, which the unlabeled data will help elucidate, be relevant for the classification problem.

In a more mathematical formulation, one could say that the knowledge on $p(x)$ that one gains through the unlabeled data has to carry information that is useful in the inference of $p(y \mid x)$. If this is not the case, semi-supervised learning will not yield an improvement over supervised learning. It might even happen that using the unlabeled data degrades the prediction accuracy by misguiding the inference; One should thus not be too surprised that for semi-supervised learning to work, certain assumptions will have to hold. In this context, note that plain supervised learning also has to rely on assumptions.

One of the most popular such assumptions can be formulated as follows:

(1) Continuity Assumption

Continuity Assumption: Points which are close to each other are more likely to share a label.

This is also generally assumed in supervised learning and yields a preference for geometrically simple decision boundaries. In the case of semi-supervised learning, the smoothness assumption additionally yields a preference for decision boundaries in low-density regions, so that there are fewer points close to each other but in different classes.

(2) The Semi-Supervised Smoothness Assumption

While in the supervised case according to our prior beliefs the output varies smoothly with the distance, we now also take into account the density of the inputs. The assumption is that the label function is smoother in high-density regions than in low-density regions:

Semi-supervised smoothness assumption: If two points x_1, x_2 in a high-density regionare close, then so should be the corresponding outputs y_1, y_2.

Note that by transitivity, this assumption implies that if two points are linked by a path of high density (e.g., if they belong to the same cluster), then their outputs are likely to be close. If, on the other hand, they are separated by a low-density region, then their outputs need not be close.

Note that the semi-supervised smoothness assumption applies to both regression and classification. In the next section, we will show that in the case of classification, it reduces to assumptions commonly used in SSL. At present, it is less clear how useful the assumption is for regression problems.

(3) The Cluster Assumption

Suppose we knew that the points of each class tended to form a cluster. Then the unlabeled data could aid in finding the boundary of each cluster more accurately: one could run a clustering algorithm and use the labeled points to assign a class to each cluster. That is in fact one of the earliest forms of semi-supervised learning. The underlying, now classical, assumption may be stated as follows:

> Cluster Assumption: If points are in the same cluster, they are likely to be of the same class.

This assumption may be considered reasonable on the basis of the sheer existence of classes: if there is a densely populated continuum of objects, it may seem unlikely that they were ever distinguished into different classes.

Note that the cluster assumption does not imply that each class forms a single, compact cluster: it only means that, usually, we do not observe objects of two distinct classes in the same cluster. The cluster assumption can easily be seen as a special case of the above-proposed semi-supervised smoothness assumption, considering that clusters are frequently defined as being sets of points that can be connected by short curves which traverse only high-density regions.

(4) The Manifold Assumption

A different but related assumption that forms the basis of several semi-supervised learning methods is the manifold assumption:

> Manifold assumption: The (high-dimensional) data lie (roughly) on a low-dimensional manifold.

How can this be useful? A well-known problem of many statistical methods and learning algorithms is the so-called curse of dimensionality. It is related to the fact that volume grows exponentially with the number of dimensions, and an exponentially growing number of examples is required for statistical tasks such as the reliable estimation of densities. This is a problem that directly affects generative approaches that are based on density estimates in input space. A related problem of high dimensions, which may be more severe for discriminative methods, is that pair-wise distances tend to become more similar, and thus less expressive. If the data happen to lie on a low-dimensional manifold, however, then the learning algorithm can essentially operate in a space of corresponding dimension, thus avoiding the curse of dimensionality.

As above, one can argue that algorithms working with manifolds may be seen as approximately implementing the semi-supervised smoothness assumption: such algorithms use the metric of the manifold for computing geodesic distances. If we view the manifold as an approximation of the high-density regions, then it becomes clear that in this case, the semi-supervised smoothness assumption reduces to the standard smoothness assumption of supervised learning, applied on the manifold.

Note that if the manifold is embedded into the high-dimensional input space in a curved fashion (i.e., it is not just a subspace), geodesic distances differ from those in the input space. By ensuring more accurate density estimates and more appropriate distances, the manifold assumption may be useful for classification as well as for regression.

The manifold assumption is practical when high-dimensional data are being generated by some process that may be hard to model directly, but which only has a few degrees of freedom. For instance, human voice is controlled by a few vocal folds, and images of various facial expressions are controlled by a few muscles. We would like in these cases to use distances and smoothness in the natural space of the generating problem, rather than in the space of all possible acoustic waves or images respectively.

(5) Transduction

As mentioned before, some algorithms naturally operate in a transductive setting. According to the philosophy put forward by Vapnik, high-dimensional estimation problems should attempt to follow the following principle:

Vapnik's principle: When trying to solve some problem, one should not solve a more difficult problem as an intermediate step.

Consider as an example supervised learning, where predictions of labels y corresponding to some objects x are desired. Generative models estimate the density of x as an intermediate step, while discriminative methods directly estimate the labels.

In a similar way, if label predictions are only required for a given test set, transduction can be argued to be more direct than induction: while an inductive method infers a functions $f: X \to y$ on the entire space X, and afterward returns the evaluations f(xi) at the test points, transduction consists of directly estimating the finite set of test labels, i.e., a function $f: X \to y$ only defined on the test set. Note that transductiion (as defined in this book) is not the same as SSL: some semi-supervised algorithms are transductive, but others are inductives.

Now suppose we are given a transductive algorithm which produces a solution superior to an inductive algorithm trained on the same labelled data (but discarding the unlabeled data). Then the performance difference might be due to one of the following two points (or a combination thereof): 1. transduction follows Vapnik's principle more closely than induction does, or 2. The transductive algorithm takes advantage of the unlabeled data in a way similar to semi-supervised learning algorithms. There is ample evidence for improvements being due to the second of these points. We are presently not aware of empirical results that selectively support the first point.

5.5 SEMI-SUPERVISED LEARNING IN PRACTICE

Semi-supervised learning is a fast developing field in machine learning that combines supervised learning, which is based on labeled data, with unsupervised learning, in which underlying structures are discovered based on unlabeled data (Zhu, 2005). The idea is that the distribution of unlabeled data adds relevant information to a supervised learning algorithm and hence, positively influences the ability to assign labels to data points (Chapelle et al., 2009). Semi-supervised learning will be most useful whenever there are far more unlabeled data than labelled. This is likely to occur if obtaining data points is cheap, but obtaining the labels costs a lot of time, effort, or money. This is the case in many application areas of machine learning, for example: In speech recognition, it costs almost nothing to record huge amounts of speech, but labeling it requires some human to listen to it and type a transcript. Billions of webpages are directly available for automated processing, but to classify them reliably, humans have to read them. Protein sequences are nowadays acquired at industrial speed (by genome sequencing, computational gene finding, and automatic translation), but to resolve a three dimensional (3D) structure or to determine the functions of a single protein may require years of scientific work. Since unlabeled data carry less information than labelled data, they are required in large amounts in order to increase prediction accuracy significantly. This implies the need for fast and efficient SSL algorithms.Image classification is one of the important tasks in the field of computer vision. This task is highly relevant for various applications like autonomous driving, service robotics, remote sensing and medical diagnosis. Most of the latest image classification methods like Deep Residual Networks require a large collection of manually labelled images to perform well. Collecting labelled samples can be difficult and very expensive for specific real-world applications.

One way to tackle this challenge is by leveraging information from unlabeled data in an unsupervised or semi-supervised manner. Although image classification in a completely unsupervised manner is not yet practical for complex distributions like natural images, recent methods based on neural networks have shown promising results for semi-supervised learning. In semi-supervised learning methods, we can make use of unlabeled data for training - typically a small amount of labelled data with a large amount of unlabeled data. Semi-supervised methods make use of unlabeled data to better capture the shape of underlying data distribution and generalize better to new samples. In fields like medical science and robotics, it is much easier to obtain unlabeled data as compared to obtaining labelled data. For example, in robotics, a mobile robot can autonomously interact with the environment and collect unlabeled data in abundance without any human supervision. Therefore, semi-supervised learning is very well suited to fields like robotics.

Online learning is a related task which is highly relevant for robotics. For example in service robotics, every time a new mobile robot is set up in a new environment, it needs to adapt to the environment and learn the objects in that environment for an interactive application. The traditional way is to annotate all the objects manually to recognize and interact with them. Additionally, the variety of objects also changes dynamically in any given environment. To reduce these expenses, we can deploy a robot with a semi-supervised learning approach. The robot's learning model can be initially trained with only a few labeled instance of the objects, and then the robot can adapt its model to increase the classification performance over time by collecting more unlabeled data. In this work, we also show how this semi-supervised learning method may be used for online learning on real-world data. Since our real-world data is similar to the data captured by the robots, this method can be readily applied to robotics.

Some applications of semi-supervised classification can be highly relevant for the society, for example, cancer tumor detection in magnetic resonance spectroscopic images. Since we all know that cancer is a fatal disease and more than 10 million people are diagnosed with cancer every year worldwide, it is one of the main challenges that our society faces. Detection of a cancer tumor in early stages can help in curing it before it becomes fatal. In oncology, medical diagnosis of cancer involves differentiating between tumor types and grades. The classifi-cation requires the availability of accurate diagnosis of past cases such that they can be used as training samples. Such labelled data is scarce in most areas of medical science while unlabeled data can be acquired in abundance without keeping the identity of the person undisclosed.

Therefore, semi-supervised recognition can be a sensible choice for such applications. In our opinion, semi-supervised classification methods can have a positive societal impact. They can help us learn a model for applications where supervision is scarce, and anonymity of the data is the foremost priority. One of the major ethical challenge in most of the computer vision applications is the privacy of the individual's private image data. But this work majorly concerns about the common household objects, thus it poses weaker challenges to privacy breach of an individual. The method discussed in this work makes the application of object recognition to different fields relatively easier as we need lesser labeled images to accomplish the same task. This method can also be used for ecological sustainability by applying this method for better planning of land and forest usage. This method can help us classify different species and landmarks using aerial images. Similarly, such methods can also be applied for applications in spatial informatics, which in general lack labelled data. In conclustion, sustainable usage of technologies based on semi-supervised learning can help to improve the performance of systems in various such areas which are crucial for social and ecological preservation.

5.6 ACTIVE (MACHINE) LEARNING

Active learning is a special case of semi-supervised machine learning in which a learning algorithm is able to interactively query the user (or some other information source) to obtain the desired outputs at new data points. it is sometimes also called optimal experimental design, in case of statistics literature.

There are situations in which unlabeled data is abundant but manually labelling is expensive. In such a scenario, learning algorithms can actively query the user/teacher for labels. This type of iterative supervised learning is called active learning. Since the learner chooses the examples, the number of examples to learn a concept can often be much lower than the number required in normal supervised learning. With this approach, there is a risk that the algorithm be overwhelmed by uninformative examples.

Recent developments are dedicated to multi-label active learning, hybrid active learning and active learning in a single-pass (on-line) context, combining concepts from the field of Machine Learning (e.g., conflict and ignorance) with adaptive, incremental learning policies in the field of Online machine learning.

Let T be the total set of all data under consideration. For example, in a protein engineering problem, T would include all proteins that are known to have a certain interesting activity and all additional proteins that one might want to test for that activity.

During each iteration, i, T is broken up into three subsets

1. $T_{K,i}$: Data points where the label is known.
2. $T_{U,i}$: Data points where the label is unknown.
3. $T_{C,i}$: A subset of TU,i that is chosen to be labeled.

Most of the current research in a active learning involves the best method to choose the data points for $T_{C,i}$.

5.6.1 Query strategies

Algorithms for determining which data points should be labeled can be organized into a number of different categories:

Uncertainty sampling: label those points for which the current model is least certain as to what the correct output should be:

1. **Query by committee**: a variety of models are trained on the current labeled data, and vote on the output for unlabeled data; label those points for which the "committee" disagrees the most
2. **Expected model change**: label those points that would most change the current model
3. **Expected error reduction**: label those points that would most reduce the model's generalization error Variance reduction: label those points that would minimize output variance, which is one of the components of error,
4. **Balance exploration and exploitation:** the choice of examples to label is seen as a dilemma between the exploration and the exploitation over the data space representation. This strategy manages this compromise by modelling the active learning problem as a contextual bandit problem. For example, Bouneffouf et al. propose a sequential algorithm named Active Thompson Sampling (ATS), which, in each round, assigns a sampling distribution on the pool, samples one point from this distribution, and queries the oracle for this sample point label.
5. Exponentiated Gradient Exploration for Active Learning:

   A wide variety of algorithms have been studied that fall into these categories.

5.7 GRAPHICAL MODEL

Graphical model refers to a graph to represent relationships among a set of variables. By a set of nodes (vertices) and edges, we design these models to connect those nodes.

Define a graph G by the following equation:

$$G = (V, E)$$

Here:

V is a finite set of vertices or nodes

$E \subseteq V \times V$ is a finite set of edges, links, or arcs

A graphical model encodes conditional independence assumptions between variables. It represents random variables as nodes or vertices. Conditional independence assumptions as missing arcs.

Some other real-life examples of graphical models are:

1. Road maps – Represent crossings and streets by nodes and edges.
2. Electrical circuits – Represent Electronic components and edges by nodes and edges.
3. Computer networks – Represent computers and connections by nodes and edges.
4. World Wide Web – Represent web pages and links by nodes and edges.
5. Flowcharts – Represent boxes and arrows by nodes and edges.

Graphical models are a unifying framework for describing the statistical relationships between large collections of random variables. Given a graphical model, the most fundamental (and yet highly non-trivial) task is compute the marginal distribution of one or a few such variables. This task is usually referred to as 'inference'.

5.7.1 Types of Graphical Models

There are 2 main types of graphical models:

1. Undirected graphical models (Markow Random Fields (MRFs)
2. Directed or Bayesian Networks

Both families encompass the properties of factorization and independences. They differ in the set of independences they can encode and the factorization of the distribution that they induce.

5.7.2 Undirected Graphical Models

An undirected graph is one in which edges have no orientation. The edge (a, b) is identical to the edge (b, a), i.e., they are not ordered pairs, but sets $\{u, v\}$ (or 2-multi sets) of vertices. The largest number of edges in an undirected graph without a self-loop is $n(n - 1)/2$.

A graph G is indirect if "A, B" V: (A, B) "E ⇒ (B, A)" E

Identify the two ordered pairs (A, B) and (B, A) and represent by only one undirected edge. Undirected graphical models are also called Markov networks.

A Markov random field, also known as a Markov network, is a model over an undirected graph.

These models are useful in modeling a variety of phenomena. Where one cannot ascribe a directionality to the interaction between variables. The undirected models also offer a different and often simpler perspective on directed models. Both in terms of the independence structure and the inference task.

MRF is an undirected conditional independence graph of a probability distribution. PD along with the family of non-negative functions M of the factorization created by the graph.

Suppose that G = (V, E)

Here, vertex set **V = {0,1,2,3,4,5,6} and edge set**

E = {(0,2), (0,4), (0,5), (1,0), (2,1), (2,5), (3,1), (3,6), (4,0), (4,5),(6,3),(6,5)}

5.7.3 Undirected Graph Terminology

Let us see few terminologies related to undirected graph:

(a) **Adjacent Node** – A node B ∈ V is adjacent to a node A ∈ V or a neighbor of A. If and only if (that is, if and only if) there is an edge between them: (A, B) ∈ E. Two nodes are adjacent if they share a common edge in which case the common edge is to join the two vertices. The two endpoints of an edge are also said to be next to each other.

(b) **Set of neighbors** – The **set** of all neighbors of A is neighbors (A) = {B ∈ V | (A,B) ∈ E}. The set neighbors(A) is sometimes also called the **boundary** of A

(c) **Degree of node** – The **degree** of the node A (number of incident edges) is deg(A) = | neighbors (A) |. The degree of a node is the number of edges that connect to it, where an edge that connects to the node at both ends (a loop). Count the edge twice. Degree, especially that of a vertex, is usually a measure of immediate adjacency.

(d) **Closure of node** – The boundary of A together with A is the closure of A: closure(A) = neighbors(A) ∪ {A}

(e) **Connected nodes** – Two distinct nodes A, B ∈ V are called **connected** in G if and only if there exists a sequence C1, . ., Ck, $k \geq 2$, of distinct nodes, called a path, with C1 = A, Ck = B, and ∀ i, 1 ≤ i < k : (C_i, C_i + 1) ∈ E

(f) **Tree** – An undirected graph is singly connected or a **tree** if and connect only if any pair of distinct nodes is by exactly one path. A tree is a connected graph with no cycles. Connect end 2 vertices by exactly 1 simple path.

(g) **Subgraph** – A subgraph is a subset of a graph's edges (and associated vertices) that forms a graph. An undirected graph GX = (X, EX) is called a subgraph of G (induced by X). If and only if X ∈ V and EX = (X × X) ∩ E, that is if it contains a subset of the nodes in G and all corresponding edges

(h) **Complete graph** – The complete graph Kn of order n is a simple graph with n vertices in which every vertex is next to every other. An undirected graph G = (V, E) is complete if and only if its set of edges is complete, that is, if and only if all possible edges are present, or if and only if: E = V × V – {(A, A) | A ∈ V}

(i) **Clique** – A clique in a graph is a set of pairwise adjacent vertices. Since any subgraph induced by a clique is a complete subgraph, the two terms and their notations are usually used interchangeably. A complete subgraph is called a clique. A **clique** is **maximal** if and only if it is not a subgraph of a larger clique, that is, a clique having more nodes

5.7.4 Directed Graphical Models

A directed graph or digraph is an ordered pair $D = (V, A)$ with

1. Va set whose elements are called vertices or nodes, and
2. Aa set of ordered pairs of vertices, called arcs, directed edges, or arrows.

Consider an edge (A, B) and direct it from A towards B.

Directed graphical models are also called Bayesian networks or Bayes nets (BN).

A Bayesian network is a directed conditional independence graph of a probability distribution. It is along with the family of conditional probabilities of the factorization brought by the graph

A Bayesian network, Bayes network, belief network, Bayes(ian) model is a probabilistic graphical model. It represents a set of random variables and their conditional dependencies via a **directed acyclic graph (DAG).** For example, it could represent the probabilistic relationships between diseases and symptoms. Given symptoms, the network can use to compute the probabilities of the presence of various diseases.

Suppose, vertex set V = {0,1,2,3,4,5,6} and edge set E = {(0,2), (0,4), (0,5), (1,0), (2,1), (2,5), (3,1), (3,6), (4,0), (4,5), (6,3), (6,5)}.

A directed graph can be created from it.

5.7.5 Directed Graph Terminology

Let us see few terms related to the directed graph:

(a) Parent and child note – Given an edge, the node that the edge points from is called the parent and the node that the edge points to is called the child. A node B $\in$ V is called a parent **of** a node A $\in$ V. A is called the **child** of B, if and only if there is a directed edge from B to A, that is, if and only if (B, A) $\in$ E.

B is called **adjacent** to A, if and only if it is either a parent or a child of A. Denotes the set of all parents of parent of a node A :

parents **(A) = {B $\in$ V | (B, A) $\in$ E}**

Denote the set of its children:

children **(A) = {B $\in$ V | (A, B) $\in$ E}**

(b) D-connected nodes – Two nodes A, B $\in$ V are called **d-connected** in G, if and only if there is a sequence C1, ., Ck, k $\geq$ 2, of distinct nodes, called a directed path, with C1 = A, Ck = B, and $\forall$ i, 1 $\leq$ i< k : (Ci, Ci + 1) $\in$ E.

x and y are d-connected if there is an unblocked path between them.

For Example:

$$x \rightarrow r \rightarrow s \rightarrow t \leftarrow u \leftarrow v \rightarrow y$$

Directed Graphs terminologies – D-Connected Nodes

This graph contains one collider, at t. Unblock the path x-r-s-t, hence x and t are d-connected. So is also the path t-u-v-y, hence t and y are d-connected, as well as the pairs u andy, t and *v*, *t*, and *u*, *x* and *s* etc.... Yet, *x* and *y* are not d-connected; there is no way of tracing a path from *x* to *y* without traversing the collider at *t*.

(c) **Connected nodes** – Two nodes A, B Î V are called **connected** in G, if and only if there is a sequence C1, . ., Ck, k $\geq$ 2, of distinct nodes, called a path, with C1 = A, Ck = B, and $\forall$ i, 1 $\leq i < k$: (C*i*, C*i* + 1) $\in$ E v (C*i* + 1, C*i*) $\in$ E

(d) **Polytree** – A directed acyclic graph is called singly connected or a polytree if and only if each pair of distinct nodes is connected by exactly one path.

(e) **Tree** – A directed acyclic graph is called a (directed) tree if and only if:

It is a polytree and exactly one node (the root node) has no parents.

5.7.6 Conditional Independence in Graphs

In this, each vertex or node represents an attribute to describe the domain in the study. Each edge represents a direct dependence between two attributes.

A graphical model extracts conditional independence relationships between variables from their parametric forms.

In principle, all parts depend on each other. Knowing where the head is put constraints on where the feet.

can be. Suppose you want to know if the left foot's position depends on the torso position given you know the position of the left leg. **Conditional independences** in the graph state that it does not.

Define conditional independence as :

$$X \perp\!\!\!\perp Y \mid V \Leftrightarrow p(X \mid Y, V) = P(X \mid V)$$

Graphical Models

Or

$$X\ \Pi\ \gamma \mid \Delta \Leftrightarrow b(X \mid \Delta) = b(\lambda \mid \Delta)$$

Graphical Models

Here, $(\cdot \perp\!\!\!\perp \cdot \mid \cdot)$ depicts a three-place relation.

Some real-life examples of conditional independence are as follows:

- Speeding fine $\perp\!\!\!\perp$ type of car | speed
- Lung cancer $\perp\!\!\!\perp$ yellow teeth | smoker

5.7.7 Conditional Independence and Separation in Graphs

Associate conditional independence with separation in graphs. Here, 'separation' depends on whether the graph is undirected or directed:

(1) Undirected Graph

1. G = (V, E) Here, X, Y, and Z are three disjoint subsets of nodes.

2. If all paths from a node in X to a node in Y contain a node in Z, then Z **u-separates** X and Y in G, written as < X | Z | Y > G.
3. A path that contains a node in Z is called blocked (by Z), otherwise, it is called active
4. Thus, separation means that all paths get a block.

(2) Directed Graph

1. G = (V, E) X, Y, and Z are three disjoint subsets of nodes.
2. X and Y are d-connected if there is an unblocked path between them.
3. X and Y are d-connected and conditioned on a set Z of nodes if there is a collider-tree path between X and Y that traverses no member of Z. If there is no such collider-tree path, then X and Y are d-separated by Z. In other words, Z blocks the every path between X and Y.
4. A path satisfying the above conditions is called active, otherwise, we can say blocked (by Z). Thus, separation means that all paths are blocked.
5. Z **d-separates** X and Y in G, written < X | Z | Y > G, if there is no path from a node in X to a node in Y along which the following two conditions hold:
6. Every node with converging edges (from its predecessor and its successor on the path) either is in Z or has a descendant in Z
7. Every other node is not in Z.

5.7.8 Decomposition or Factorization in Graphs

Conditional independences in graphs is only a path to find a decomposition of a distribution. To determine it for a given distribution is the same as determining the terms that need in a decomposition of the distribution.

Finding a minimal conditional independence graph is like finding the best decomposition.

In this part, we are going to learn about:

1. Decomposition or factorization wrt undirected graphs
2. Decomposition or factorization wrt directed graphs

5.7.9 Decomposition and Undirected Graphs

- A probability distribution over a set U of attributes is called It can also call factorizable with respect to an undirected graph G = (U, E) and write it as a product of non-negative functions on the maximal cliques of G.
- M is a family of subsets of attributes, such that the sub graphs of G induced by the sets M ∈ M are the maximal cliques of G.
- Then, the functions öM: φM → IR + 0, M ∈ M:

$$\forall a_1 \in dom(A_1) : .... \forall a_S \in dom(A_1) :$$

$$pu(\bigwedge_{A_i \in u} A_i = a_1) = \prod_{M \in a} \Phi_M(\bigwedge_{A_i \in u} A_i = a_1)$$

Decomposition and Undirected Graphs – Graphical Models

- A possibility distribution U over U is called decomposable with respect to an undirected graph G = (U, E). If is written as the least of the marginal possibility distributions on the maximal cliques of G, that is, if:

$$\forall a_1 \in dom(A_1) : .... \forall a_S \in dom(A_n) :$$

$$\pi u(\underset{A_i \in u}{\wedge} A_i = a_i) = \underset{M \in m}{\min} \pi_M(\underset{A_i \in u}{\wedge} A_i = a_1)$$

5.7.10 Decomposition and Undirected Graphs

The figure represents a decomposition/factorization into four terms for an undirected graph: These 4 terms correspond to 4 maximal cliques induced by the four sets $\{A_1, A_2, A_3\}$, $\{A_3, A_5, A_6\}$, $\{A_2, A_4\}$ and $\{A_4, A_6\}$.

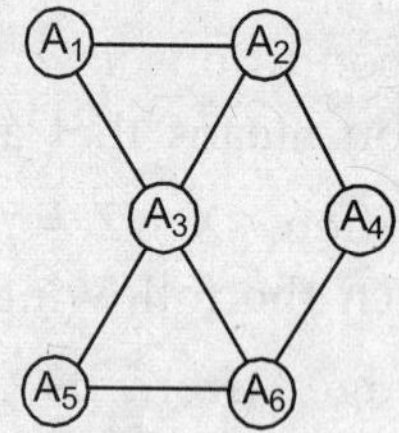

Decomposition Undirected Graphs

5.7.11 Decomposition and Directed Graphs

A probability distribution pu over a set U of attributes is called It can also call factorizable with respect to a directed acyclic graph G = (U, E). If it is written as a product of the conditional probabilities of the attributes given their parent in G, if:

$$^{\forall}a_i^{\in dom}(A_i) : .... ^{\forall}a_i^{\in dom}(A_n) :$$

$$p^u(\underset{A_i^{\in U}}{\wedge} A_i = a_1) \underset{A_i^{\in U}}{\Pi} P(A_i = a_i \mid \underset{A_i^{\in Uporabc}(A_i)}{\wedge} A_i = a_1)$$

Graphical Model – Product of the Conditional Probabilities

- A possibility distribution ðU over U is called decomposable with respect to a directed acyclic graph G = (U, E). If it is written as the least of conditional probabilities of the attributes given their parent in G, if:

$$^{\forall}a_i^{\in dom}(A_i) : .... ^{\forall}a_i^{\in dom}(A_n) :$$

$$\pi^U(\underset{A_i^{\in U}}{\wedge} A_i = a_1) \underset{A_i^{\in U}}{\min} \Pi(A_i = a_i \mid \underset{A_i^{\in Uporabc}(A_i)}{\wedge} A_i = a_1)$$

Graphical Model – Least of Conditional Probabilities

- The figure represents a decomposition/factorization into four terms for a directed graph:

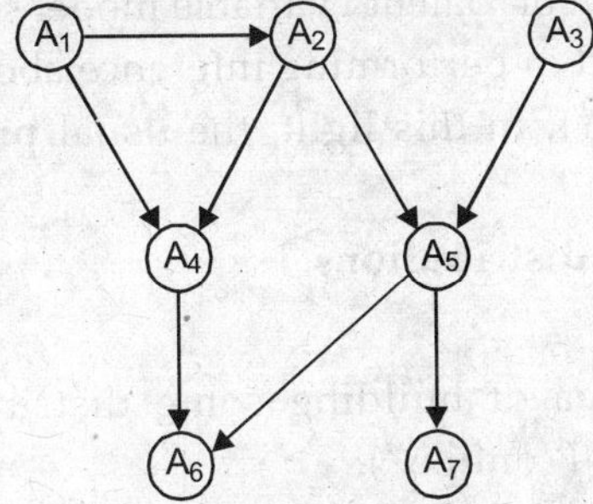

Graphical Model – Decomposition and Directed Graphs

5.8 INFERENCE ON GRAPHICAL MODELS

Over here we consider the problem of computing (usually estimating) some marginals of a probability density p that factorizes according to a Graphical Model G = (V,E). A case that is often considered is the Markov Random Field (MRF) with pairwise interaction with

$$p(x) x \prod_{i \in V} \psi_i(x_i) \prod_{(i,j) \in f} \psi_{ij}(x_i, x_j) \qquad (1)$$

where øi and øij are non-negative functions (we will usually make the assumption that they are strictly positive) known as the *node potential* and *edge potential* These potential functions need not be proportional to distribution functions as long as the product (1) is.

In the next few points we review some of the standard graphs and corresponding usual inference problems which all amount to computing (approximations of) marginal distributions.

5.8.1 Some standard undirected graphs

(1) Hidden Markov Model

The HMMs correspond to densities factorizing as follows:

$$p(x_{1:T}, y_{1:T}) \alpha \mu_1(x_1) \prod_{i=1}^{T} p(y_i \mid x_i) \prod_{i=1}^{T-1} p(x_{i+1} \mid x_i) \qquad (2)$$

the ubiquitous corresponding graph is illustrated below.

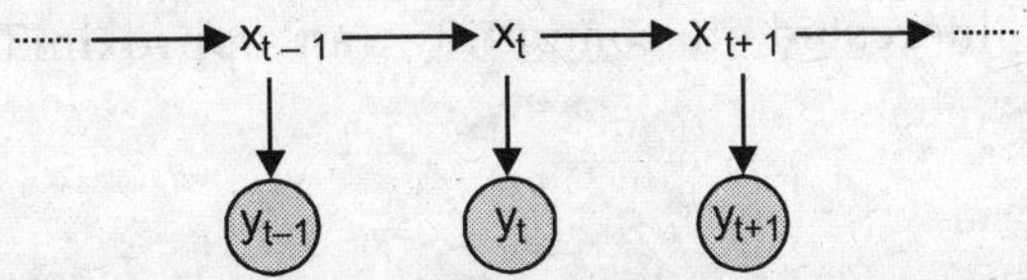

Illustration of the structure of a Hidden Markov Model.

The yy-nodes are shaded to indicate that they are observed. The arrows give an idea of progression through time and are routinely represented although it is not necessary to invoke the Directed Acyclic Graph (DAG) formalism here.

This type of model appears often in signal processing (e.g., tracking algorithms) or wherever we might have a simple notion of a sequential process (e.g., bioinformatics, weather forecasting, dynamical systems, dots).

This model is known as a "hidden" or "latent" variable model since the random variables Xt are not observed and one is interested in performing inference about them using the observations of dependent random variables Yt. In this light, the usual problems one is concerned with when using HMMs are:

- determining the **filtering distributions**:
  $\{p(x_t \mid y_{1:T})\}_{t=1:T}$
  corresponding to the idea of building some distributional representation of the hidden variable *on the fly* ("online").
- determining the **smoothing distributions**:
  $\{p(x_t \mid y_{1:T})\}_{t=1:T}$
  corresponding to the idea of building some distributional representation of the hidden variable *a posteriori* i.e., after the whole process has been observed.

(2) Star Graph

The "star graph" looks at densities factorizing as follows:

$$p(\theta, y...., yK) \alpha\, \mu(\theta) \prod_{i=1}^{K} p(y_i \mid \theta) \qquad (3)$$

with the corresponding graph below.

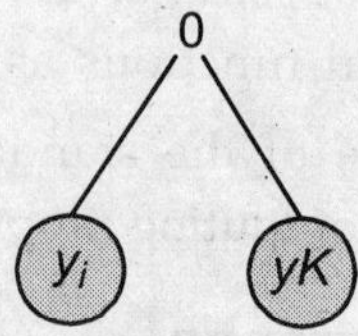

Illustration of the "star graph". The "master node" θ can for example be the parameters of a regression model whilst the *yi* can correspond to batches of iid data.

This is a standard model for distributed computations where the full dataset is scattered across Kk nodes (servers). In that framework, we typically work with:

- some prior μ(θ) on the parameters of interest,
- a model with corresponding likelihood $p(yk \mid \theta)$ of a batch of data given the parameters and we are then interested in computing (an approximation of) the posterior $p(\theta\text{ly } y_1...\text{K})$.

(3) Ising model

The Ising Model is the archetypal example of a pairwise MRF coming from statistical physics. The graph is simply a grid with each node being connected with its four neighbors. An extension of this model is the **Potts** model.

Illustration of the Ising Model. Each node is connected to its neighbors, the edge can represent some notion of similarity.

This graph has been used widely in imaging for denoising or segmentation tasks. The nodes then represent pixel values and the links can then represent some similarity enforcing potential with, for example, the idea that is is likely that neighboring pixels have similar values or belong to the same image segment.

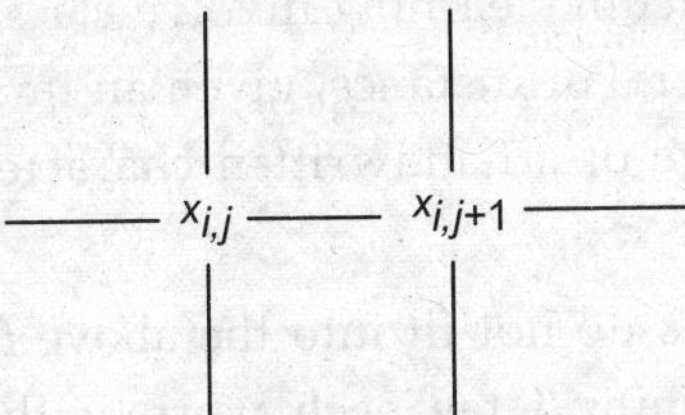

5.8.2 Inference On Graphs

We can consider two categories of MRFs: **trees** and **loopy graphs**. In the previous section, the HMM and the star graph both correspond to trees and the Ising model is obviously loopy.

Belief propagation

A popular algorithm for inference on graphs is the belief propagation (BP) algorithm. For a tree graph, one can show that the following set of equations will *exactly lead* to quantities (the *beliefs*) proportional to the marginals:

Belief propagation equations:

(pre-messages) $$M_{ts}(x_t) = \psi_t(x_t) \prod_{u \in T_i / s} m_{ut}(x_i), \quad (4)$$

(messsages) $$B_{ts}(x_t) = \int_{x_1} \psi_{ts}(x_{t1}, x_s) M_{ts}(x_i), \quad (5)$$

(beliefs) $$B_s(x_s) = m_{ts}(x_s) M_{st}(x_s). \quad (6)$$

where Γ_t denotes theset of nodes connected to t (neighbors).

A solution to these equations on a tree will verify Bs(xs)∝p(xs).

On a loopy graph, one can still apply the BP algorithm but iteratively and it will still lead to very good results in a wide range of case although the guarantee of converging to something proportional to the marginals does not hold anymore.

In these notes we will be mostly concerned by continuous state spaces. In that case there is essentially only one situation where one can compute the marginals exactly: the Gaussian tree (i.e., a tree with gaussian potentials). In other situations, one has to resort to general approximations such as:

- **Nonparametric BP** (NBP): where one propagates a mixture of Gaussians across the graph, the corresponding BP equations can then be solved analytically **Stochastic Message-Passing** (SOSMP): where one represents the messages as some combination of orthogonal functions **Particle BP** (PBP): where one propagates a set of particles across the graph, the corresponding BP equations are then computed in a Monte-Carlo fashion or more ad-hoc variants.

5.9 PROBABILISTIC GRAPHICAL MODELS (PGM)

A lot of common problems in machine learning involve classification of isolated data points that are independent of each other. For instance, given an image, predict whether it contains a cat or a dog, or given an image of a handwritten character, predict which digit out of 0 through 9 it is.

It turns out that a lot of problems do not fit into the above framework. For example, given a sentence, "I like machine learning," tag each word with its part-of-speech (a noun, a pronoun, a verb, an adjective, etc.). As even this simple example demonstrates, this task cannot be solved by treating each word independently – "learning" could be a noun or a verb depending on its context. This task is important for a lot of more complex tasks on text, such as translating from one language to another, text to speech, etc.

It is not obvious how you would use a standard classification model to handle these problems. A powerful framework which can be used to learn such models with dependency is **probabilistic graphical models (PGM).** Much of this is based ontutorial by the data scientist, Prasoon Goyal.

Before talking about how to apply a probabilistic graphical model to a machine learning problem, we need to understand the PGM framework. Formally, a probabilistic graphical model (or graphical model for short) consists of a graph structure. Each node of the graph is associated with a random variable, and the edges in the graph are used to encode relations between the random variables.

Depending on whether the graph is directed or undirected, we can classify graphical modes into two categories – Bayesian networks and Markov networks.

5.9.1 Bayesian Networks: Directed Graphical Models

A canonical example of Bayesian networks is the so-called "student network," which looks like this:

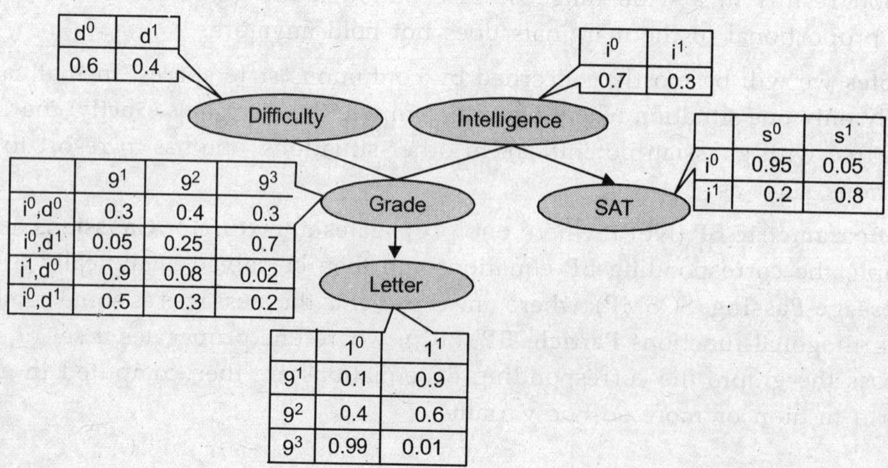

The Student / Network Example

This graph describes a setting for a student enrolled in a university class. There are 5 random variables in the graph:

1. Difficulty (of the class): Takes values 0 (low difficulty) and 1 (high difficulty)
2. Intelligence (of the student): Takes values 0 (not intelligent) and 1 (intelligent)
3. Grade (the student gets in the class): Takes values 1 (good grade), 2 (average grade), and 3 (bad grade)
4. SAT (student's score in the SAT exam): Takes values 0 (low score) and 1 (high score)
5. Letter (quality of recommendation letter the student gets from the professor after completing the course): Takes values 0 (not a good letter) and 1 (a good letter)

The edges in the graph encode dependencies in the graph.

- The "Grade" of the student depends on the "Difficulty" of the class and the "Intelligence" of the student.
- The "Grade," in turn, determines whether the student gets a good letter of recommendation from the professor.
- Also, the "Intelligence" of the student influences their "SAT" score, in addition to influencing the "Grade."

Note that the direction of arrows tells us about cause-effect relationships — "Intelligence" affects the "SAT" score, but the "SAT" score does not influence the "Intelligence."

Finally, let's look at the tables associated with each of the nodes. Formally, these are called conditional probability distributions (CPDs).

5.9.1.1 Ñonditional Probability Distributions (CPD)

The *CPDs for "Difficulty" and "Intelligence"* are fairly simple, because these variables do not depend on any of the other variables. The tables basically encode the probabilities of these variables, taking 0 or 1 as values. As you might have noticed, the values in each of the tables must sum to 1.

Next, let's look at the *CPD for "SAT."* Each row corresponds to the values that its parent ("Intelligence") can take, and each column corresponds to the values that "SAT" can take. Each cell has the conditional probability p(SAT=s | Intelligence=i), that is, given that the value of "Intelligence" is i, what is the probability of the value of "SAT" being s.

For instance, we can see that p(SAT=s^1 | Intelligence = i^1) is 0.8, that is, if the intelligence of the student is high, then the probability of the SAT score being high as well is 0.8. On the other hand, p(SAT=s^0 | Intelligence = i^1), which encodes the fact that if the intelligence of the student is high, then the probability of the SAT score being low is 0.2.

Note that the sum of values in each row is 1. That makes sense because given that Intelligence=i^1, the SAT score can be either sp or s^1, so the two probabilities must add up to 1. Similarly, the CPD for "Letter" encodes the conditional probabilities p(Letter=l | Grade=g). Because "Grade" can take three values, we have three rows in this table.

The *CPD for "Grade"* is easy to understand with the above knowledge. Because it has two parents, the conditional probabilities will be of the form p(Grade=g | Difficulty=d, SAT=s), that is, what is the probability of "Grade" being g, given that the value of "Difficulty" is d and that of "SAT" is s. Each row now corresponds to a *pair* of values of "Difficulty" and "Intelligence." Again, the row values add up to 1.

An essential requirement for Bayesian networks is that the graph must be a Directed Acyclic Graph (DAG).

5.9.2 Markov Networks: Undirected Graphical Models

Here's a simple example of a Markov network:

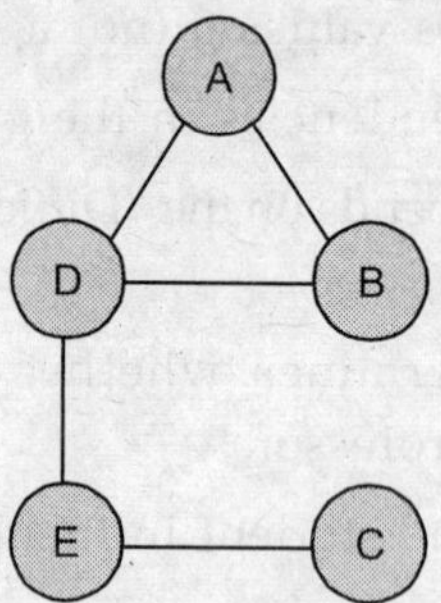

In the interest of brevity, we will look at this abstract graph, where nodes A, B, etc. do not directly correspond to real-world quantities, as above. Again, the edges represent the interaction between variables. We see that while A and B directly influence each other, A and C do not. Note that Markov networks do not need to be acyclic, as was the case with Bayesian networks.

(1) Potential Functions

Just as we had CPDs for Bayesian networks, we have tables to incorporate relations between nodes in Markov networks. However, there are two crucial differences between these tables and CPDs.

First, the values do not need to sum to one, that is, the table does not define a probability distribution. It only tells us that configurations with higher values are more likely. Second, there is no conditioning. It is proportional to the joint distribution of all the variables involved, as opposed to conditional distributions in CPDs.

A	B	C	ϕ(A, B, C)
0	0	0	10
0	0	1	1
0	1	0	1
0	1	1	10
1	0	0	1
1	0	1	10
1	1	0	10
1	1	1	1

The resulting tables are called "factors" or "potential functions," and denoted using the Greek symbol. So, for example, we can use the following potential function to capture the relation between three variables A, B, and C, where C is the "soft" XOR of A and B, that is, C is likely to be 1 if A and B are different, and C is likely to be 0 if A and B are identical:

In general, you will have a potential function defined for each maximal clique in the graph.

The graph structure and the tables succinctly capture the joint probability distribution over the random variables.

A question you may have at this point is, why do we need directed as well as undirected graphs? The reason is that for some problems, it is more natural to represent them as directed graphs, such as the student network above, where it is easy to describe the causal relationship between variables — the intelligence of the student affects the SAT score, but the SAT score does not affect the intelligence of the student (although it may tell us about the intelligence of the student).

For other kinds of problems, say, images, you may want to represent each pixel as a node, and we know that neighboring pixels affect each other, but there is no cause-effect relationship between the pixels; instead, the interaction is symmetric. So, we use undirected graphical models in such cases.

(2) The Problem Understanding and Setting

We've been discussing graphs and random variables and tables so far, and you may be thinking what the point of all this is? What are we actually trying to do? Where is machine learning in all this — *data, training, prediction*, etc.? This section will address these questions.

Let's go back to the student network. Suppose we have the graph structure with us, which we can create from our knowledge of the world (referred to as "domain knowledge" in machine learning). But we don't have CPD tables, only their sizes. We do have some data though — for ten different classes in a university, we have a measure of their difficulty.

Also, we have data about each student in each of the courses — their intelligence, what their SAT score was, what grade they got, and whether they got a good letter from the professor. From this data, we can estimate the parameters of the CPDs. For instance, the data might show that students with high intelligence often get good SAT scores, and we might be able to learn from it that p(SAT=s1 | Intelligence = i1)is high. This is the learning phase. We will soon see how we do this parameter estimation in Bayesian and Markov networks.

Now, for a new data point, you will observe *some* of the variables, but not all. For example, in the graph below, you know about the difficulty of a course and a student's SAT score, and you want to estimate the probability of the student getting a good grade. (By now, you already have values in the tables from the learning phase.)

While we don't have a CPD that gives us that information directly, we can see that a high SAT score from the student would suggest that the student is likely intelligent, and consequently, the probability of a good grade is high if the difficulty of the course is low, as shown using the red arrows in the above image. We may also want to estimate the probability of multiple variables simultaneously, like what is the probability of the student getting a good grade and a good letter?

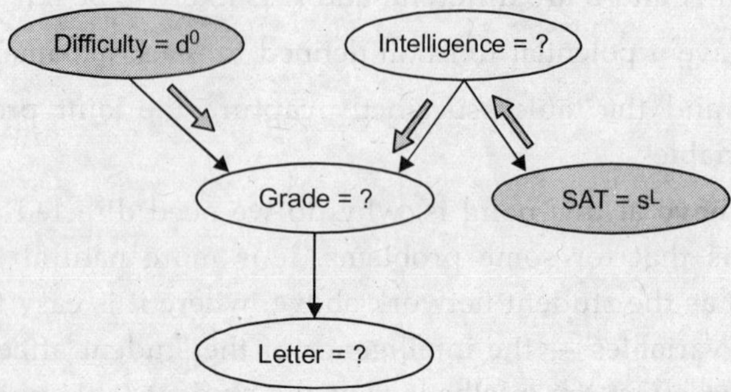

The variables with known values are called "observed variables," while those whose values are unobserved are called "hidden variables" or "latent variables." Conventionally, observed variables are denoted using grey nodes, while latent variables are denoted using white nodes, as in the above image. We may be interested in finding the values of some or all of the latent variables.

Answering these questions is analogous to prediction in other areas of machine learning — in graphical models, this process is called "inference."

While we used Bayesian networks to describe the terminology above, it applies as is to Markov networks as well. Before we get into the algorithms for learning and inference, let's formalize the idea that we just looked at — given the value of some node, which other nodes can we get information about?

(3) Conditional Independences

The graph structures that we've been talking about so far actually capture important information about the variables. Specifically, they define a set of conditional independences between the variables, that is, statements of the form — "If A is observed, then B is independent of C." Let's look at some examples.

In the student network, let's say you know that a student had a high SAT score. What can you say about her grade? As we saw earlier, a high SAT score suggests that the student is intelligent, and therefore, you would expect a good grade. What if the student has a low SAT score? In this case, you would not expect a good grade.

Now, let's say that you also know that the student is intelligent, in addition to her SAT score. If the SAT score was high, then you would expect a good grade. What if the SAT score was low? *You would still expect a good grade* because you know that the student is intelligent, and you would assume that she just didn't perform well enough on the SAT. Therefore, knowing the SAT score doesn't tell us anything if we see the intelligence of the student. To put this as a conditional independence statement, we would say —"If Intelligence is observed, then SAT and Grade are independent."

We got this conditional independence information from the way these nodes were connected in the graph. If they were connected differently, we would get different conditional independence information.

Let's see this with another example.

Let's say you know that the student is intelligent. What can you say about the difficulty of the course? Nothing, right? Now, what if I tell you that the student got a bad grade on the course? This would suggest that the course was hard because we know that an intelligent student got a bad grade. Therefore we can write our conditional independence statement as follows — "If Grade is unobserved, then Intelligence and Difficulty are independent."

Because these statements capture an *independence* between two nodes subject to a *condition*, they are called *conditional independences*. Note that the two examples have opposite semantics — in the first one, the independence holds if the connecting node is *observed*; in the second one, the independence holds if the connecting node is *unobserved*. This difference is because of the way the nodes are connected, that is, the directions of arrows.

We will not go into all possible cases in the interest of brevity, but it is straightforward to come up with these using intuition as above.

In Markov networks, we can use a similar intuition, but because there are no directional edges (arrows), the conditional independence statements are relatively simple — if there is no path between nodes A and B such that all nodes on the path are unobserved, then A and B are independent. Said differently, if there is at least one path from A to B where all intermediate nodes are unobserved, then A and B are *not* independent.

We will look at the details of how parameter estimation and inference are done in the second part of this blog post. For now, let's look at an application of Bayesian networks, where we can use the idea of conditional independence we just learned.

5.9.3 Application: Monty Hall Problem

You must have seen some version of this in a TV game show:

The host shows you three closed doors, with a car behind one of the doors and something invaluable behind the others. You get to pick a door. Then, the host opens one of the remaining doors, and shows that it does not contain the car. Now, you have an option to switch the door, from the one you picked initially to the one that the host left unopened. Do you switch?

Intuitively, it appears that the host did not divulge any information. It turns out that this intuition is not entirely correct. Let's use the new tool in our arsenal — graphical models — to understand this.

Let's start by defining some variables:

- D : The door with the car.
- F : Your first choice.
- H : The door opened by the host.
- I : Is F = D?

D, F, and H take values 1, 2, or 3 and I takes values 0 or 1. D and I are unobserved, while F is observed. Until the host opens one of the doors, H is unobserved. Therefore, we get the following Bayesian network for our problem:

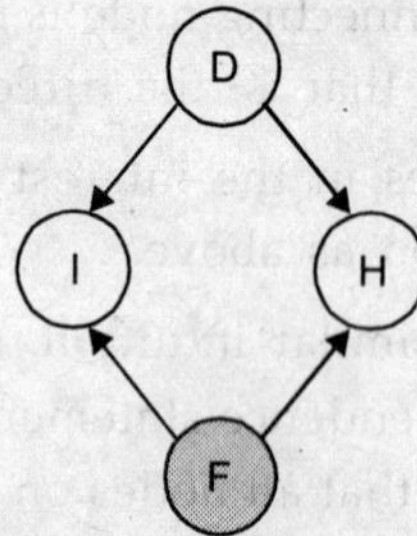

Note the directions of arrows —D and F are independent, I clearly depends on D and F, and the door picked by the host H also depends on D and F. So far, you don't know anything about D. (This is similar to the structure in the student network, where knowing the intelligence of the student does not tell you anything about the difficulty of the course.)

Now, the host picks a door H and opens it. So, H is now observed.

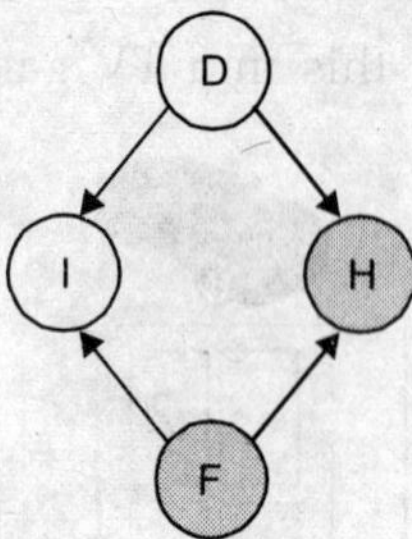

Observing H does not tell us anything about I, that is, whether we have picked the right door. That is what our intuition tells us. However, it does tell us *something* about D! (Again, drawing analogy with the student network, if you know that the student is intelligent, and the grade is low, it tells you something about the difficulty of the course.)

Let's see this using numbers. The CPD tables for the variables are as follows (This is when no variables have been observed.).

p(D)

1	2	3
1/3	1/3	1/3

p(F)

1	2	3
1/3	1/3	1/3

p(I | D, F)

	0	1
D=1, F=1	0	1
D=1, F=2	1	0
D=1, F=3	1	0
D=2, F=1	1	0
D=2, F=2	0	1
D=2, F=3	1	0
D=3, F=1	1	0
D=3, F=2	1	0
D=3, F=3	0	1

p(H | D, F)

	1	2	3
D=1, F=1	0	1/2	1/2
D=1, F=2	0	0	1
D=1, F=3	0	1	0
D=2, F=1	0	0	1
D=2, F=2	1/2	0	1/2
D=2, F=3	1	0	0
D=3, F=1	0	1	0
D=3, F=2	1	0	0
D=3, F=3	1/2	1/2	0

The tables for D and F are straightforward — the door with the car could be any door with equal probability, and we pick one of the doors with equal probability. The table for I simply says that I=1 when D and F are identical, and I=0 when D and F are different. The table for H says that if D and F are equal, then the host picks one door from the other two with equal probability, while if D and F are different, then the host picks the third door. Now, let's assume that we have picked a door, that is, F is now observed, say F=1. What are the conditional probabilities of I and D, given F?

$$p(I|F=1 = \frac{p(I,F=1)}{p(F=1)} = \frac{\Sigma_D p(I\mid F=1,D)p(D)}{p(F=1)}$$

$$p(D|F=1 = \frac{p(D,F=1)}{p(F=1)} = \frac{p(D)p(F=1)}{p(F=1)}$$

Using these equations, we get the following probabilities:

p(I | F=1)

0	1
2/3	1/3

p(D | F=1)

1	2	3
1/3	1/3	1/3

These numbers make sense — so far, the probability that we have picked the correct door is S! and the car could still be behind any door with equal probability.

Now, the host opens one of the doors other than F, so we observe H. Assume H=2. Let's compute the new conditional probabilities of I and D given both F and H.

$$p(D|F=1,\ H=2) = \frac{p(D,F=1,H=2)}{p(F=1,H=2)} = \frac{p(D)p(F=1)p(H=2\mid D,F=1)}{\sum_D p(D)p(F=1)p(H=2\mid D,F=1)}$$

$$p(I|F=1,\ H=2) = \frac{p(I,F=1,H=2)}{p(F=1,H=2)} = \frac{\sum_D p(I\mid D,F=1)p(D)p(F=1)p(H=2\mid D,F=1)}{\sum_D p(D)p(F=1)p(H=2\mid D,F=1)}$$

Using the above equations, we get the following probabilities:

p(I | F=1, H=2)

0	1
2/3	1/3

p(D | F=1, H=2)

1	2	3
1/3	0	2/3

Therefore, we don't know anything additional about I — our first choice is correct still with probability $\frac{1}{3}$, and this is what our intuition tells us. However, we now know that the car is behind door 3 with probability $\frac{2}{3}$, instead of $\frac{1}{3}$.

So, if we switch, we get the car with probability T!; if we don't, we get the car with probability $\frac{1}{3}$.

We could have gotten the same answer without using graphical models too, but graphical models give us a framework that scales well to larger problems.

References

1. *Settles, Burr (2010),* "Active Learning Literature Survey" *(PDF), Computer Sciences Technical Report 1648. University of Wisconsin–Madison,* retrieved 2014-11-18
2. *Rubens, Neil;* Elahi, *Mehdi; Sugiyama, Masashi; Kaplan, Dain (2016).* "Active Learning in Recommender Systems". *In Ricci, Francesco; Rokach, Lior; Shapira, Bracha.* Recommender Systems Handbook *(2 ed.). Springer US.* doi:10.1007/978-1-4899-7637-6. ISBN 978-1-4899-7637-6.
3. *Das, Shubhomoy; Wong, Weng-Keen; Dietterich, Thomas; Fern, Alan; Emmott, Andrew (2016). "Incorporating Expert Feedback into Active Anomaly Discovery". In Bonchi, Francesco; Domingo-Ferrer, Josep; Baeza-Yates, Ricardo; Zhou, Zhi-Hua; Wu, Xindong.* IEEE 16th International Conference on Data Mining. *IEEE.* doi:10.1109/ICDM.2016.0102.
4. *Olsson, Fredrik.* "A literature survey of active machine learning in the context of natural language processing".
5. Yang B, Sun J T, Wang T J, et al.(2009), "Effective Multi-Label Active Learning for Text Classification". Proceedings of the 15th ACM SIGKDD international conference on Knowledge discovery and data mining. ACM, 2009: 917-926.
6. E. Lughofer (2012), Hybrid Active Learning (HAL) for Reducing the Annotation Efforts of Operators in Classification Systems. Pattern Recognition, vol. 45 (2), pp. 884-896, 2012.
7. E. Lughofer (2012), Single-Pass Active Learning with Conflict and Ignorance.Evolving Systems, vol. 3 (4), pp. 251-271, 2012.
8. Bouneffouf et al. (2014), Contextual Bandit for Active Learning: Active Thompson Sampling. Neural Information Processing - 21st International Conference, ICONIP 2014.
9. Bouneffouf et al. (2016), Exponentiated Gradient Exploration for Active Learning. Computers, vol. 5 (1), 2016, pp. 1-12.

Unit 6

RECENT TRENDS MACHINE LEARNING

Learning Objectives and Outcome

At the end of this unit the reader shall be able to learn

- Internet of Things (IoT)
- Recent trends in various learning techniques of machine learning and classification methods for IoT applications.
- Various models for IoT applications.

6.1 INTERNET OF THINGS

The Internet is a massive network of networks, It is a massive combination of billions of computers and other connected devices located worldwide and connected via *cables and wireless signals*. This enormous network represents *personal, business, educational and government devices* that *include large mainframes, desktop computers, smartphones, smart home gadgets, personal tablets, laptops and other devices*. It connects millions of computers together globally, forming a network in which any computer can communicate with any other computer as long as they are both connected to the Internet.

The Internet of Things (IoT), also called the **Internet of Everything** or the **Industrial Internet**, (according to me it should be called "**Digital Internetwork of Smart Objects**) is a new technology paradigm envisioned as a global network of machines and devices capable of interacting with each other. The IoT is recognized as one of the most important areas of future technology and is gaining vast attention from a wide range of industries. IoT, the term first introduced by Kevin Ashton in 1998, is a future of Internet and ubiquitous computing. This technological revolution represents the future of connectivity and reachability. In IoT, 'things' refer to any smart object on face of the Earth, whether it is a communicating device or a non-communicating dumb object.

IoT is the network of physical devices, vehicles, home appliances and other items embedded with electronics, software, sensors, actuators, and connectivity which enables these objects to connect and exchange data. Each thing is uniquely identifiable through its embedded computing system but is able to inter-operate within the existing Internet infrastructure.

The Web of Things (WoT) is a term used to describe approaches, software architectural styles and programming patterns that allow real-world objects to be part of the World Wide Web. Similarly to what the Web (Application Layer) is to the Internet (Network Layer), the Web of Things provides an Application Layer that simplifies the creation of Internet of Things applications

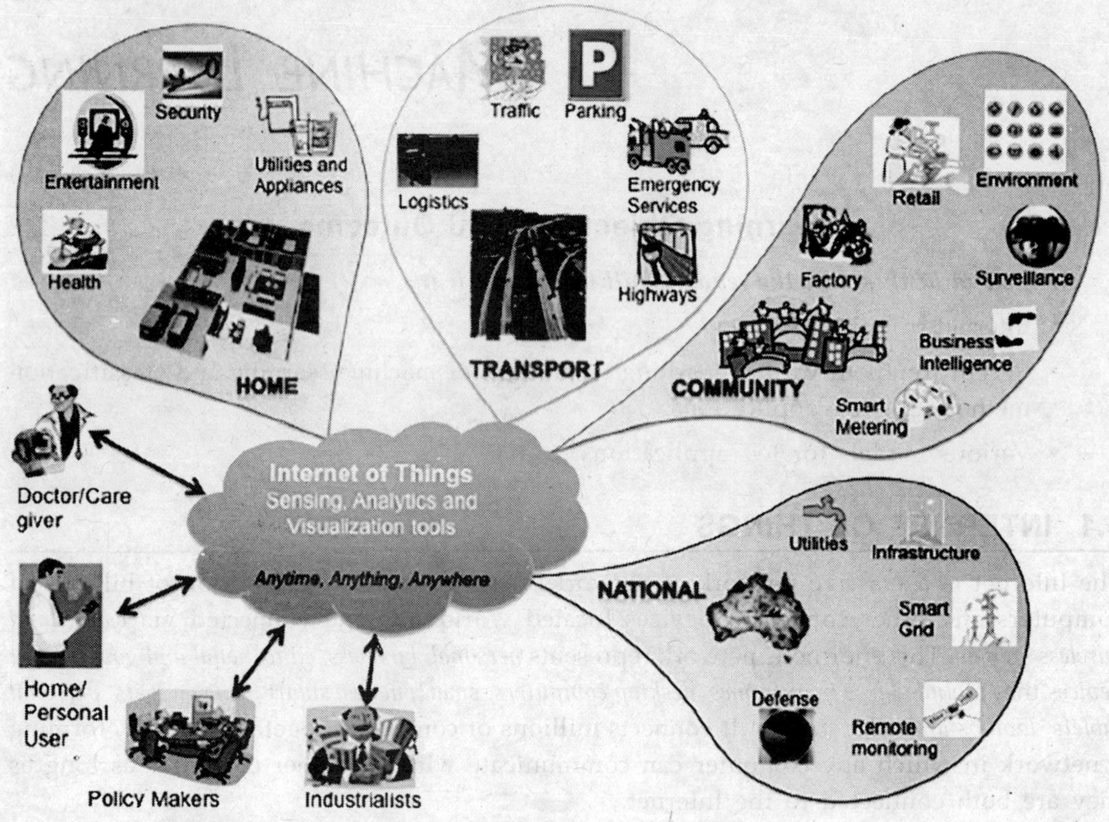

Fig. 6.1: Internet of Things Schematic showing the end users and application areas based on data

The figure of online capable devices increased 31% from 2016 to 8.4 billion in 2017. Experts estimate that the IoT will consist of about 30 billion objects by 2020. It is also estimated that the global market value of IoT will reach $7.1 trillion by 2020.

The IoT allows objects to be sensed or controlled remotely across existing network infrastructure, creating opportunities for more direct integration of the physical world into computer-based systems, and resulting in improved efficiency, accuracy and economic benefit in addition to reduced human intervention. When IoT is augmented with sensors and actuators, the technology becomes an instance of the more general class of cyber-physical systems, which also encompasses technologies such as smart grids, virtual power plants, smart homes, intelligent transportation and smart cities.

IoT can be divided into 3 categories, based on usage and clients base:

- Consumer IoT includes the connected devices such as smart cars, phones, watches, laptops, connected appliances, and entertainment systems.
- Commercial IoT includes things like inventory controls, device trackers, and connected medical devices.
- Industrial IoT covers such things as connected electric meters, waste water systems, flow gauges, pipeline monitors, manufacturing robots, and other types of connected industrial devices and systems.

"Things", in the IoT sense, can refer to a wide variety of devices such as heart monitoring implants, biochip transponders on farm animals, cameras streaming live feeds of wild animals in coastal waters, automobiles with built-in sensors, DNA analysis devices for environmental/ food/pathogen monitoring, or field operation devices that assist firefighters in search and rescue operations. Legal scholars suggest regarding "things" as an "inextricable mixture of hardware, software, data and service". We will first learn how many types of network are in vogue currently and what rae different types of facilities to get connected to internet.

Common types of area *networks* are:

1. LAN - Local Area Network.
2. WAN - Wide Area Network.
3. WLAN - Wireless Local Area Network.
4. MAN - Metropolitan Area Network.
5. SAN - Storage Area Network, System Area Network, Server Area Network, or sometimes Small Area Network.

Different types of Internet facilities

1. Dial-Up (Analog 56K).
2. DSL. DSL stands for Digital Subscriber Line. ...
3. Cable. Cable provides an internet connection through a cable modem and operates over cable TV lines. ...
4. Wireless. Wireless, or Wi-Fi (or Wi-max), as the name suggests, does not use telephone lines or cables to connect to the internet. ...
5. Satellite. ...
6. Cellular Mobile transreceivers.

6.2 INTERNET WEB ACCESS

Internet access is the ability of individuals and organizations to connect to the Internet using computer terminals, computers, and other devices; and to access services such as email and the World Wide Web. Various technologies, at a wide range of speeds have been used by Internet service providers (ISPs) to provide this service.

Broadband Internet access, often shortened to just broadband, is simply defined as "Internet access that is always on, and faster than the traditional dial-up access and so covers a wide range of technologies. Broadband connections are typically made using a computer's built in Ethernet networking capabilities, or by using a NIC expansion card.

Most broadband services provide a continuous "always on" connection; there is no dial-in process required, and it does not interfere with voice use of phone lines. Broadband provides improved access to Internet services such as:

1. Faster world wide web browsing
2. Faster downloading of documents, photographs, videos, and other large files
3. Telephony, radio, television, and videoconferencing
4. Virtual private networks and remote system administration
5. Online gaming, especially massively multiplayer online role-playing games which are interaction-intensive

The Web is ideally is a way of accessing information over the medium of the Internet. A collection of pages, of information connected to each other around the globe. Each page can be a combination of text, pictures, audio clips, video clips, animations, and other essentials. You have to access the internet to view the World Wide Web and any of the web pages or other content it contains. The web is the information-sharing portion of the internet. It is the broad name for the HTML pages that are served on the internet. The Web also utilizes browsers, such as Internet Explorer or Firefox, to access Web documents called Web pages that are linked to each other via hyperlinks.

Simply put The Internet, linking your computer to other computers around the world, is a way of transporting content. The Web is software that lets you use that content…or contribute your own. The Web, running on the mostly invisible Internet, is what you see and click on in your computer's browser.

The web is a large portion of the internet but it isn't all of it. It is Just The One Part that lives "on top of" of the Internet. The two terms should not be confused.

6.3 EMERGENCE OF INTERNET OF THINGS

The term ''Internet-of-Things'' is used as an umbrella keyword for covering various aspects related to the extension of the Internet and the Web into the physical realm, by means of the widespread deployment of spatially distributed devices with embedded identification, sensing and/or actuation capabilities. Internet-of-Things envisions a future in which digital and physical entities can be linked, by means of appropriate information and communication technologies, to enable a whole new class of applications and services.

Nowadays(2018), two billions people around the world use the Internet for browsing the Web, sending and receiving emails, accessing multimedia content and services, playing games, using social networking applications and many other tasks. While more and more people will gain access to such a global information and communication infrastructure, another big leap forward is coming, related to the use of the Internet as a global platform for letting machines and smart objects communicate, dialogue, compute and coordinate.

It is predictable that, within the next decade, the Internet will exist as a seamless fabric of classic networks and networked objects. Content and services will be all around us, always available, paving the way to new applications, enabling new ways of working; new ways of interacting; new ways of entertainment; new ways of living.

The Internet-of-Things is emerging as one of the major trends shaping the development of technologies in the ICT sector at large. The shift from an Internet used for interconnecting end-user devices to an Internet used for interconnecting physical objects that communicate with each other and/or with humans in order to offer a given service encompasses the need to rethink anew some of the conventional approaches customarily used in networking, computing and service provisioning/management.

From a conceptual standpoint, the IoT builds on three pillars, related to the ability of smart objects to:

(1) be identifiable (anything identifies itself),

(2) communicate (anything communicates) and

(3) interact (anything interacts) – either among themselves, building networks of interconnected objects, or with end-users or other entities in the network.

Developing technologies and solutions for enabling such a vision is the main challenge ahead of us the Internet of Things demands:

(1) a shared understanding of the situation of its users and their appliances,

(2) software architectures and pervasive communication networks to process and convey the contextual information to where it is relevant, and

(3) the analytics tools in the Internet of Things that aim for autonomous and smart behavior. With these three fundamental grounds in place, smart connectivity and context-aware computation can be accomplished.

A radical evolution of the current Internet into a Network of interconnected objects that not only harvests information from the environment (sensing) and interacts with the physical world (actuation/command/control), but also uses existing Internet standards to provide services for information transfer, analytics, applications and communications. Fuelled by the prevalence of devices enabled by open wireless technology such as Bluetooth, Radio Frequency Identification (RFID), Wi-Fi and telephonic data services as well as embedded sensor and actuator nodes,

IoT has stepped out of its infancy and is on the verge of transforming the current static Internet into a fully integrated Future Internet. Internet revolution led to the interconnection between people at an unprecedented scale and pace.

Table 6.1 shows projected evolution in the area of foundational IoT technologies: network, software and algorithms, hardware, and data processing.

The network is the backbone of the IoT. It refers to uniquely identifiable objects (things) and their virtual representations in an Internet-like structure. Network technology is moving to unobtrusive wirefree communication technology that allows deviceto-device applications to be deployed more flexibly.

Network technology is evolving toward a contextaware autonomous network.

Table 6.1 Projected Evolution in the Area of Foundational Iot Technologies

	Before 2010	2010–2015	2015–2020	Beyond 2020
Network	• Sensor networks	• Self-aware and self-organizing networks • Sensor network location transparency • Delay-tolerant networks • Storage networks and power networks • Hybrid networking technologies	• Network context awareness	• Network cognition • Self-learning, self-repairing networks
Software and Algorithms	• Relational database integration • IoT-oriented RDBMS • Event-based platforms • Sensor middleware • Sensor networks middleware • Proximity/ Localization algorithms	• Large-scale, open semantic software modules • Composable algorithms • Next generation IoT-based social software • Next generation IoT-based enterprise applications	• Goal-oriented software • Distributed intelligence, problem solving • Things-to-Things collaboration environments	• User-oriented software • The invisible IoT • Easy-to-deploy IoT software • Things-to-Humans collaboration • IoT 4 All
Hardware	• RFID tags and some sensors • Sensors built into mobile devices • NFC in mobile phones • Smaller and cheaper MEMs technology	• Multiprotocol, multistandards readers • More sensors and actuators • Secure, low-cost tags (e.g., Silent Tags)	• Smart sensors (biochemical) • More sensors and actuators (tiny sensors)	• Nanotechnology and new materials
Data Processing	• Serial data processing • Parallel data processing • Quality of services	• Energy, frequency spectrum-aware data processing • Data processing context adaptable	• Context-aware data processing and data responses	• Cognitive processing and optimization

Source: Adapted from Sundmaeker, Guillemin, Friess, and Woelffle´ (2010, p. 74)

6.4 TECHNOLOGY ROADMAP: INTERNET OF THINGS

The IoT's major significant trend in recent years is the explosive growth of devices connected and controlled by the internet. The wide range of applications for IoT technology mean that the specifics can be very different from one device to the next but there are basic characteristics shared by most.

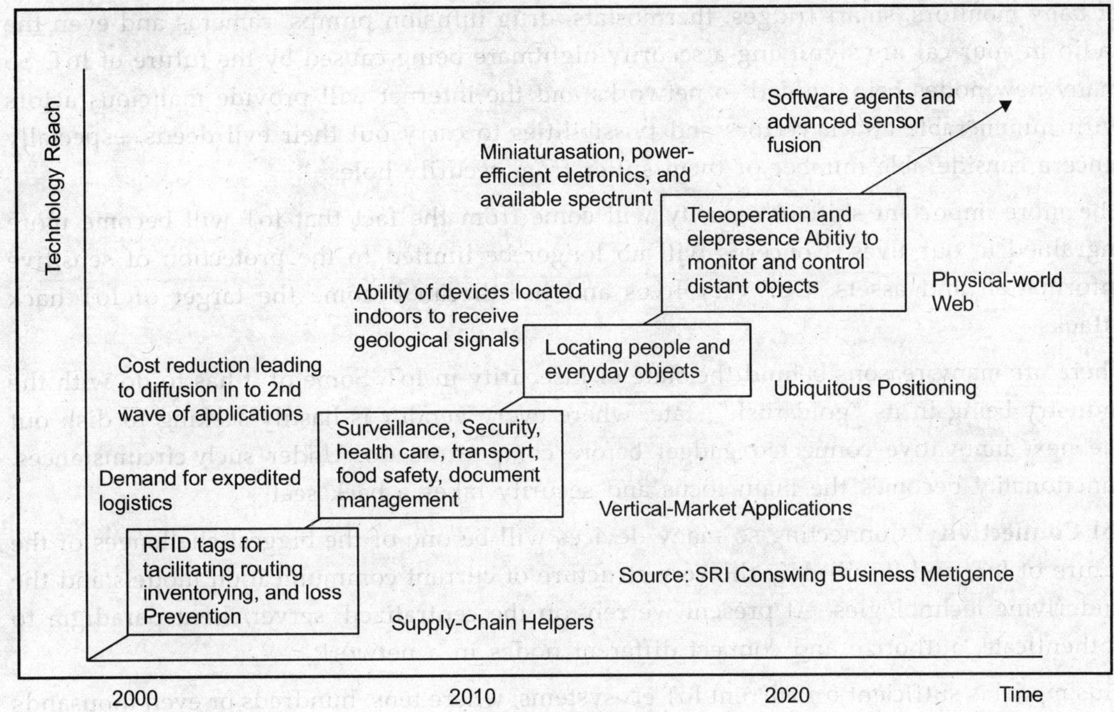

Fig. 6.2: Technology Road Map

6.5 CHALLANGES FOR IOT TO BECOME POPULAR

For the IoT industry to thrive there are three categories of challenges to overcome and this is true for any new trend in technology not only IoT: (1) technology, (2) business and (3) society.

6.5.1 Technology

This part is covering all technologies needed to make IoT systems function smoothly as a standalone solution or part of existing systems and that's not an easy mission, there are many technological challenges, including Security, Connectivity, Compatibility & Longevity, Standards and Intelligent Analysis & Actions.

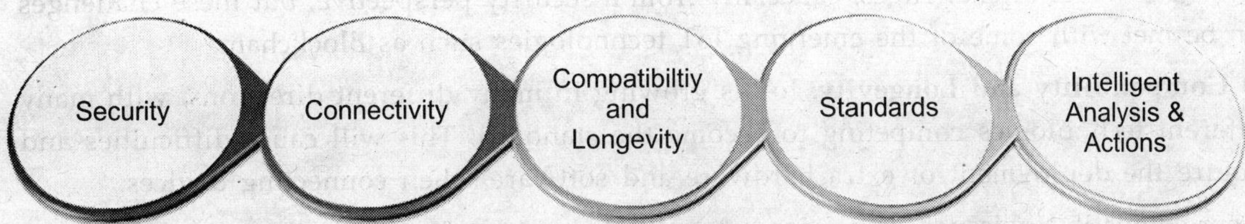

Fig. 6.3: Technological Challenges

(a) Security : IoT has already turned into a serious security concern that has drawn the

of baby monitors, smart fridges, thermostats, drug infusion pumps, cameras and even the radio in your car are signifying a security nightmare being caused by the future of IoT. So many new nodes being added to networks and the internet will provide malicious actors with innumerable attack vectors and possibilities to carry out their evil deeds, especially since a considerable number of them suffer from security holes.

The more important shift in security will come from the fact that IoT will become more ingrained in our lives. Concerns will no longer be limited to the protection of sensitive information and assets. Our very lives and health can become the target of IoT hack attacks.

There are many reasons behind the state of insecurity in IoT. Some of it has to do with the industry being in its "gold rush" state, where every vendor is hastily seeking to dish out the next innovative connected gadget before competitors do. Under such circumstances, functionality becomes the main focus and security takes a back seat.

(b) Connectivity: Connecting so many devices will be one of the biggest challenges of the future of IoT, and it will defy the very structure of current communication models and the underlying technologies. At present we rely on the centralized, server/client paradigm to authenticate, authorize and connect different nodes in a network.

This model is sufficient for current IoT ecosystems, where tens, hundreds or even thousands of devices are involved. But when networks grow to join billions and hundreds of billions of devices, centralized systems will turn into a bottleneck. Such systems will require huge investments and spending in maintaining cloud servers that can handle such large amounts of information exchange, and entire systems can go down if the server becomes unavailable.

The future of IoT will very much have to depend on decentralizing IoT networks. Part of it can become possible by moving some of the tasks to the edge, such as using fog computing models where smart devices such as IoT hubs take charge of mission-critical operations and cloud servers take on data gathering and analytical responsibilities.

Other solutions involve the use of peer-to-peer communications, where devices identify and authenticate each other directly and exchange information without the involvement of a broker. Networks will be created in meshes with no single point of failure. This model will have its own set of challenges, especially from a security perspective, but these challenges can be met with some of the emerging IoT technologies such as Blockchain.

(c) Compatibility and Longevity: IoT is growing in many different directions, with many different technologies competing to become the standard. This will cause difficulties and require the deployment of extra hardware and software when connecting devices.

Other compatibility issues stem from non-unified cloud services, lack of standardized M2M protocols and diversities in firmware and operating systems among IoT devices.

Some of these technologies will eventually become obsolete in the next few years, effectively rendering the devices implementing them useless. This is especially important, since in contrast to generic computing devices which have a lifespan of a few years, IoT appliances (such as smart fridges or TVs) tend to remain in service for much longer, and should be able to function even if their manufacturer goes out of service.

(d) Standards: Technology standards which include network protocols, communication protocols, and data-aggregation standards, are the sum of all activities of handling, processing and storing the data collected from the sensors. This aggregation increases the value of data by increasing, the scale, scope, and frequency of data available for analysis.

Challenges facing the adoptions of standards within IoT

1. **Standard for handling unstructured data**: Structured data are stored in relational databases and queried through SQL for example. Unstructured data are stored in different types of NoSQL databases without a standard querying approach.
2. **Technical skills to leverage newer aggregation tools:** Companies that are keen on leveraging big-data tools often face a shortage of talent to plan, execute, and maintain systems.
3. **Intelligent Analysis & Actions**: The last stage in IoT implementation is extracting insights from data for analysis, where analysis is driven by cognitive technologies and the accompanying models that facilitate the use of cognitive technologies.

Factors driving adoption intelligent analytics within the IoT

1. Artificial intelligence models can be improved with large data sets that are more readily available than ever before, thanks to the lower storage.
2. **Growth in crowd sourcing and open- source analytics software:** Cloud-based crowdsourcing services are leading to new algorithms and improvements in existing ones at an unprecedented rate.
3. **Real-time data processing and analysis:** Analytics tools such as complex event processing (CEP) enable processing and analysis of data on a real-time or a near real-time basis, driving timely decision making and action.

Challenges facing the adoptions of intelligent analytics within IoT

1. **Inaccurate analysis due to flaws in the data and/or model:** A lack of data or presence of outliers may lead to false positives or false negatives, thus exposing various algorithmic limitations.
2. **Legacy systems' ability to analyze unstructured data**: Legacy systems are well suited to handle structured data; unfortunately, most IoT/business interactions generate unstructured data.
3. **Legacy systems' ability to manage real- time data:** Traditional analytics software generally works on batch-oriented processing, wherein all the data are loaded in a batch and then analyzed.

(e) Intelligent Analysis and Actions : The second phase of this stage is intelligent actions which can be expressed as M2M and M2H interfaces for example with all the advancement in UI and UX technologies.

Factors driving adoption of intelligent actions within the IoT

1. Lower machine prices
2. Improved machine functionality
3. Machines "influencing" human actions through behavioral-science rationale
4. Deep Learning tools

Challenges facing the adoption of intelligent actions within IoT

1. Machines' actions in unpredictable situations
2. Information security and privacy
3. Machine interoperability
4. Mean-reverting human behaviors
5. Slow adoption of new technologies

6.6 COMPUTING FRAMEWORK

Another important part of IoT is *computing frameworks* for processing data, the most famous of which are fog and cloud computing. IoT applications use both frameworks depending on application and process location. In some applications, data should be processed upon generation, while in other applications, it is not necessary to process data immediately. The instant processing of data and the network architecture that supports it is known as fog computing. Collectively, they are applied for edge computing .

6.6.1 Ubiquitous Computing

Ubiquitous Computing (or "ubicomp") is a concept in software engineering and computer science where computing is made to appear anytime and everywhere. In contrast to desktop computing, ubiquitous computing can occur using any device, in any location, and in any format. A user interacts with the computer, which can exist in many different forms, including laptop computers, tablets and terminals in everyday objects such as a refrigerator or a pair of glasses. The underlying technologies to support ubiquitous computing include Internet, advanced middleware, operating system, mobile code, sensors, microprocessors, new I/O and user interfaces, networks, mobile protocols, location and positioning, and new materials.

6.6.2 Ambient Intelligence

Ambient intelligence (AmI) refers to electronic environments that are sensitive and responsive to the presence of people. Ambient intelligence is a vision on the future of consumer electronics, telecommunications and computing Ambient intelligence and autonomous control are not part of the original concept of the Internet of things. Ambient intelligence and autonomous control do not necessarily require Internet structures, either. However, there is a shift in research to integrate the concepts of the Internet of Things and autonomous control, with initial outcomes towards this direction considering objects as the driving force for autonomous

IoT. Most of the works related to intelligent IoT exploit the capabilities of cloud computing to perform the analytics and return the outcome to the IoT devices if needed. However, the attempts are going on to bring some level of intelligence and machine learning at the resource-constrained devices, edge and fog computing nodes.

In the future, the Internet of Things may be a non-deterministic and open network in which auto-organized or intelligent entities (Web services, SOA components) and virtual objects (avatars) will be interoperable and able to act independently (pursuing their own objectives or shared ones) depending on the context, circumstances or environments. Autonomous behavior through the collection and reasoning of context information as well as the object's ability to detect changes in the environment (faults affecting sensors) and introduce suitable mitigation measures constitutes a major research trend, clearly needed to provide credibility to the IoT technology. Modern IoT products and solutions in the marketplace use a variety of different technologies to support such context-aware automation but more sophisticated forms of intelligence are requested to permit sensor units to be deployed in real environments.

The ambient intelligence paradigm builds upon pervasive computing, ubiquitous computing, profiling, context awareness, and human-centric computer interaction design, of which, is characterized by systems and technologies that are:

1. **Embedded**: many networked devices are integrated into the environment
2. **Context aware:** these devices can recognize you and your situational context
3. **Personalized**: they can be tailored to your needs
4. **Adaptive:** they can change in response to you
5. **Anticipatory:** they can anticipate your desires without conscious mediation.

A typical context of ambient intelligence environment is home, but may also be extended to work spaces (offices, co-working), public spaces (based on technologies such as smart street lights), and hospital environments.

(1) Fog Computing

Here, the architecture of fog computing is applied to migrate information from the data centers task to the edge of the servers. This architecture is built based on the edge servers.

The Internet of Things (IoT) is generating an unprecedented volume and variety of data. But by the time the data makes its way to the cloud for analysis, the opportunity to act on it might be gone. Fog is a new model for analyzing and acting on IoT data. It is called either *edge computing or Fog computing:*

(1) Analyzes the most time-sensitive data at the network edge, close to where it is generated instead of sending vast amounts of IoT data to the cloud.

(2) Acts on IoT data in milliseconds, based on policy.

(3) Sends selected data to the cloud for historical analysis and longer-term storage.

The fog extends the cloud to be closer to the things that produce and act on IoT data. These devices, called fog nodes, can be deployed anywhere with a network connection: on a factory floor, on top of a power pole, alongside a railway track, in a vehicle, or on an oil rig. Any device with computing, storage, and network connectivity can be a fog node. Examples include industrial controllers, switches, routers, embedded servers, and video surveillance cameras.

When to Consider Fog Computing

(1) Data is collected at the extreme edge: vehicles, ships, factory floors, roadways, railways, etc.

(2) Thousands or millions of things across a large geographic area are generating data.

(3) It is necessary to analyze and act on the data in less than a second.

Fog computing provides limited computing, storage, and network services, also providing logical intelligence and filtering of data for data centers. This architecture has been and is being implemented in vital areas like eHealth and military applications.

(2) Edge Computing

In this architecture, processing is run at a distance from the core, toward the edge of the network. This type of processing enables data to be initially processed at the edge devices. Devices at the edge may not be connected to the network in a continuous manner, so they need a copy of master data/reference data for offline processing. Edge devices have different features such as

(1) enhancing security,

(2) filtering and cleaning of the data, and

(3) storing local data for local use.

(3) Cloud Computing

Cloud computing, the recent trend in IT, takes computing from desktop to the whole World Wide Web and yet, the user doesn't need to worry about maintenance and managing all the resources. The user data is kept in safe custody of remote servers on payment basis. User has to bear only the cost of usage of service(s), which is called, pay-as-you-use, in cloud computing terms.

With this cloud computing, a smart phone can become a large data center. Cloud computing is extended form of distributed computing, parallel computing, and grid computing. Cloud computing provides four categories of services, namely:

Software as a Service (SaaS) refers to application working over the Internet which is available for the user on pay-as-you-go basis. User does not need to store, install, and maintain the application. Instead, only Internet connectivity is required to access the service that has been rented out by the SaaS service provider on the cloud. ***SaaS is*** where a distributed software model is presented. In this model, all the practical software will be hosted from a service provider, and practical software can be accessible to the users through the Internet.

Platform as a Service (PaaS) is providing a platform to build applications and services, with all the toolkits and resources required to do so.

Networks as a Service (NaaS) provides virtual network(s) to the users. User can have as many numbers of networks as required, with desired segmentation and policy enforcement. With NaaS, user can also have heterogeneous networks, for example, IPv4 and IPv6 segments working in co-existence or separately.

Infrastructure as a Service (IaaS) where the company purchases all the equipment like hardware, servers, and networks and gets computation and storage services on rental basis. Instead of purchasing expensive machines, servers, and storage devices, even for small tasks, user can outsource this task to the IaaS service provider. With storage in IaaS, not only the data is stored by the IaaS service, but also, it makes the data universally accessible over the Internet.

Mobile Backend as a Service (MBaaS): also known as a Backend as a Service (BaaS), provides the web and mobile application with a path in order to connect the application to the backend cloud storage. MBaaS provides features like user management, push notification and integrates with the social network services. This cloud service benefits from application programming interface (API) and software development kits (SDK).

We are moving towards web3, the ubiquitous computing web. Since 2011, number of connected devices has already exceeded the number of people on Earth. Already, connected devices have reached 9 billion and are expected to grow more rapidly and reach 24 billion by 2020.

This architecture has high latency and high load balancing, indicating that this architecture is not sufficient enough for processing IoT data because most processing should run at high speeds. The volume of this data is high, and Big Data processing will increase the CPU usage of the cloud servers. There are different types of cloud computing:

(4) Big Data Cloud Computing

Handling the volume, variety, and velocity of IoT data requires a new computing model. The main requirements are to:

(1) **Minimize latency**: Milliseconds matter when you are trying to prevent manufacturing line shutdowns or restore electrical service. Analyzing data close to the device that collected the data can make the difference between averting disaster and a cascading system failure.

Analyzing data close to the device that collected the data can make the difference between averting disaster and a cascading system failure.

(2) **Conserve network bandwidth**: Offshore oilrigs generate 500 GB of data weekly. Commercial jets generate 10 TB for every 30 minutes of flight. It is not practical to transport vast amounts of data from thousands or hundreds of thousands of edge devices to the cloud. Nor is it necessary, because many critical analyses do not require cloud-scale processing and storage.

(3) **Address security concerns**: IoT data needs to be protected both in transit and at rest. This requires monitoring and automated response across the entire attack continuum: before, during, and after.

(4) **Operate reliably**: IoT data is increasingly used for decisions affecting citizen safety and critical infrastructure. The integrity and availability of the infrastructure and data cannot be in question.

(5) Collect and secure data across a wide geographic area with different environmental conditions: IoT devices can be distributed over hundreds or more square miles. Devices deployed in harsh environments such as roadways, railways, utility field substations, and vehicles might need to be ruggedized. That is not the case for devices in controlled, indoor environments.

(6) Move data to the best place for processing: Which place is best depends partly on how quickly a decision is needed. Extremely time-sensitive decisions should be made closer to the things producing and acting on the data. In contrast, big data analytics on historical data needs the computing and storage resources of the cloud.

Traditional cloud computing architectures do not meet all of these requirements. The prevailing approach—moving all data from the network edge to the data center for processing—adds latency. Traffic from thousands of devices soon outstrips bandwidth capacity. Industry regulations and privacy concerns prohibit offsite storage of certain types of data. In addition, cloud servers communicate only with IP, not the countless other protocols used by IoT devices

(5) Distributed Computing

This architecture is designed for processing high volume data. In IoT applications, because the sensors generate data on a repeated manner, Big Data challenges are encountered[30,33]. To overcome this phenomenon, a distributed computing is designed to divide data into packets, and assign each packet to different computers for processing. This distributed computing has different frameworks like Hadoop and Spark. When migrating from cloud to fog and distributed computing, the following occur:

1. a decrease in network loading,
2. an increase in data processing speed,
3. a reduction in CPU usage,
4. a reduction in energy consumption, and
5. higher data volume processing.

Because the Smart City is one of the primary applications of IoT.

6.7. ESSENTIAL IOT TECHNOLOGIES

Five IoT technologies are widely used for the deployment of successful IoT-based products and services:

1. Radio frequency identification (RFID);
2. Wireless sensor networks (WSN);
3. Middleware;

4. Cloud computing; and
5. IoT application software
   (a) **WSN hardware** - Typically a node (WSN core hardware) contains sensor interfaces, processing units, transceiver units and power supply. Almost always, they comprise of multiple A/D converters for sensor interfacing and more modern sensor nodes have the ability to communicate using one frequency band making them more versatile.
   (b) **WSN communication stack** - The nodes are expected to be deployed in an adhoc manner for most applications.

Designing an appropriate topology, routing and MAC layer is critical for scalability and longevity of the deployed network. Nodes in a WSN need to communicate among themselves to transmit data in single or multi-hop to a base station. Node drop outs, and consequent degraded network lifetimes, are frequent. The communication stack at the sink node should be able to interact with the outside world through the Internet to act as a gateway to the WSN subnet and the Internet

6.8 THE ARCHITECTURE OF IOT

The architecture of IoT is usually considered to be 3-layer, with *Perception layer, Network layer, and Application layer*, but some add two more layers: *Middleware layer and Business layer.*

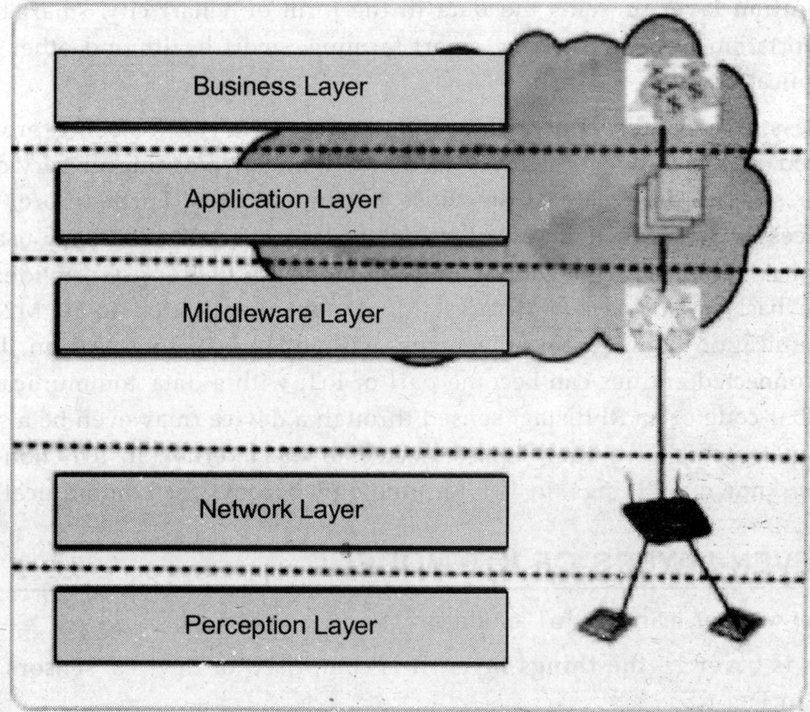

Fig. 6.4: Layers in Iot Architecture

This five layer architecture is described in figure 6.4.

(1) **Perception Layer** It is the lowest layer in the IoT architecture. As the name suggests, its purpose is to perceive the data from environment. All the data collection and data sensing part is done on this layer. Sensors, bar code labels, RFID tags, GPS, camera, lie in this layer. Identifying object/thing and gathering data is the main purpose of this layer. Network layer collects the data perceived by the Perception layer.

(2) **Network layer** is like the Network and Transport layer of OSI model. It collects the data from the lower layer and sends to the Internet. Network layer may only include a gateway, having one interface connected to the sensor network and another to the Internet. In some scenarios, it may include network management center or information processing center.

(3) **Middleware** layer receives data from Network layer. Its purpose is service management and storage of data. It also performs information processing and takes decisions automatically based on results. It then passes the output to the next, Application layer. Application layer performs the final presentation of data. Application layer receives information from the Middleware layer and provides global management of the application presenting that information, based on the information processed by Middleware layer. Depending upon the type of devices and their purpose in Perception layer and then on the way they have been processed by the Middleware layer, according to the needs of user,

(4) **Application layer** presents the data in the form of: smart city, smart home, smart transportation, vehicle tracking, smart farming, smart health and other many kinds of applications.

(5) **Business layer** is all about making money from the service being provided. Data received at the application layer is molded into a meaningful service and then further services are created from those existing services. Furthermore, information is processed to make it knowledge and further efficient means of usage make it wisdom, which can earn a good amount of money to the service provider. IoT works on the basis of *Machine-to-Machine* (M2M), but not limited to it. M2M refers to communication between two machines, without human intervention. In IoT, even non- connected entities can become part of IoT, with a data communicating device, like a bar-code or an RFID tag, sensed through a device (may even be a smart phone sensing it), which eventually is connected to the Internet. In IoT, non- intelligent objects, known as 'things' in IoT terminology, become the communicating nodes.

6.9 THE SEVEN LAYERS OF IOT MODEL

This is another way of learning IoT model.

At the bottom is Layer 1 - **the things layer**. It is comprised of devices, sensors, controllers etc as shown in Fig. 6.5.

Layer 2 is **Connectivity/Edge computing layer** - This layer defines the various communication protocols and networks used for connectity and edge computing.

Layer 3 is **Global infrastructure layer**. This layer is typically implemented in cloud infrastructures.

Layer 4 and Layer 5 are related to **Data ingestion and data analysis**. This includes bigdata, cleansing, streaming and storage of data. Then layer 5 relates to data reporting, mining, machine learning etc.

Application layer 6 comprise of the custom applications that is actually making use of the things data.

As a 7th layer, there could also be **People and Process layer**. This includes people, businesses, collaboration and decision making based on the information derived from IoT computing.

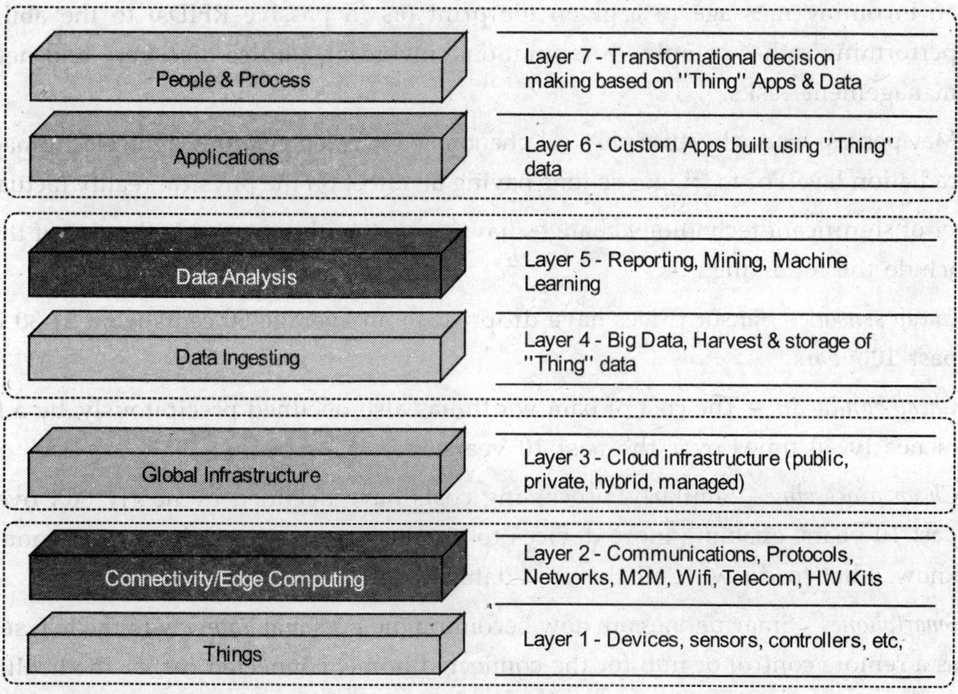

Fig. 6.5: The Seven Layers of Iot Model

6.10 MACINE LEARNING ALGORITHM FOR IOT

With respect to the challenges posed by Big Data, it is necessary to divert to a new concept termed *Smart Data*, which means: "realizing productivity, efficiency, and effectiveness gains by using semantics to transform raw data into Smart Data". A more recent definition of this concept is: "Smart Data provides value from harnessing the challenges posed by volume, velocity, variety, and veracity of Big Data, and in turn providing actionable information and improving decision making." At last, Smart Data can be a good representative for IoT data.

6.10.1 Smart Objects (or Things)

We define smart objects (or things) as entities that:

1. Have a physical embodiment and a set of associated physical features (e.g., size, shape, etc.).
2. Have a minimal set of communication functionalities, such as the ability to be discovered and to accept incoming messages and reply to them.
3. Possess a unique identifier.
4. Are associated to at least one name and one address. The name is a human-readable description of the object and can be used for reasoning purposes. The address is amachine-readable string that can be used to communicate to the object.
5. Possess some basic computing capabilities. This can range from the ability to match an incoming message to a given footprint (as in passive RFIDs) to the ability of performing rather complex computations, including service discovery and network management tasks.
6. May possess means to sense physical phenomena (e.g.,temperature, light, electromagnetic radiation level) or to trigger actions having an effect on the physical reality (actuators).

A number of significant technology changes have come together to enable the rise of the IoT. These include the following:

- *Cheap sensors* – Sensor prices have dropped to an average 60 cents from $1.30 in the past 10 years.
- *Cheap bandwidth* – The cost of bandwidth has also declined precipitously, by a factor of nearly 40 times over the past 10 years.
- *Cheap processing* – Similarly, processing costs have declined by nearly 60X over the past 10 years, enabling more devices to be not just connected, but smart enough to know what to do with all the new data they are generating or receiving.
- *Smartphones* – Smartphones are now becoming the personal gateway to the IoT, serving as a remote control or hub for the connected home, connected car, or the health and fitness devices consumers are increasingly starting to wear.
- *Ubiquitous wireless coverage* – With Wi-Fi coverage now ubiquitous, wireless connectivity is available for free or at a very low cost, given Wi-Fi utilizes unlicensed spectrum and thus does not require monthly access fees to a carrier.
- *Big data* – As the IoT will by definition generate voluminous amounts of unstructured data, the availability of big data analytics is a key enabler.
- *IPv6* – Most networking equipment now supports IPv6, the newest version of the Internet Protocol (IP) standard that is intended to replace IPv4. IPv4 supports 32-bit addresses, which translates to about 4.3 billion addresses – a number that has

become largely exhausted by all the connected devices globally. In contrast, IPv6 can support 128-bit addresses, translating to approximately 3.4 x 1038 addresses – an almost limitless number that can amply handle all conceivable IoT devices.

To have a deeper insight into IoT smart data, patterns must be extracted and the generated data interpreted. Cognitive algorithms will undertake interpretation and matching, much as the human mind would do. Cognitive IoT systems will learn from the data previously generated and will improve when performing repeated tasks. Cognitive computing as as a prosthetic for human cognition by analyzing massive amounts of data and being able to respond to questions humans might have when making certain decisions. Cognitive Iot plays an important role in enabling the extraction of meaningful patterns form the IoT smart data generated .Table 6.2 describes the place of data processing of various use cases of smart cities.

Table 6.2 Place of data processing of various use cases of smart cities.

Smart City Use Cases	Type of Data	Where Data Processed
Smart Traffic	Sttream/Massive Data	Edge
Smart Health	Stream/Massive Data	Edge/Cloud
Smart Environment	Stream/Massive Data	Cloud
Smart Weather Prediction	Stream Data	Edge
Smart Citizen	Stream Data	Cloud
Smart Agriculture	Stream Data	Edge/Cloud
Smart Home	Massive/Historical Data	Cloud
Smart Air Controlling	Massive/Historical Data	Cloud
Smart Public Place Monitoring	Historical Data	Cloud
Smart Human Activity Control	Stream/Historical Data	Edge/Cloud

6.11 INTERNET OF THINGS COMMUNICATION PROTOCOLS

IoT includes four main components:

1. Sensors,
2. Processing networks,
3. Analyzing data, and
4. Monitoring the system.

In IoT, communication protocols can be divided into three major components:

(1) ***Device to Device (D2D)***: this type of communication enables communication between nearby mobile phones. This is the next generation of cellular networks.

(2) ***Device to Server (D2S)***: in this type of communication devices, all the data is sent to the servers, which can be close or far from the devices. This type of communication mostly is applied in cloud processing.

(3) ***Server to Server (S2S)***: in this type of communication, servers transmit data between each other.

This type of communication mostly is applied in cellular networks.

Processing and preparing data for these communications is a critical challenge. To respond to this challenge, different kinds of data processing, such as analytics at the edge, stream analysis, and IoT analysis at the database, must be applied. The decision to apply any one of the mentioned processes depends on the particular application and its needs. Fog and cloud processing are two analytical methods adopted in processing and preparing data before transferring to the other things. The whole task of IoT is summarized as follows: first, sensors and IoT devices collect the information from the environment. Next, knowledge should be extracted from the raw data. Then, the data will be ready for transfer to other objects, devices, or servers through the Internet.

6.12 THE IOT ARCHITECTURAL REFERENCE MODEL

The first major contribution of the IoT Architectural Reference Model (IoT ARM) is the IoT Reference Model itself.

An ARM processor is one of a family of CPUs based on the RISC (reduced instruction set computer) architecture developed by Advanced RISC Machines (ARM). ARM processors are extensively used in consumer electronic devices such as smartphones, tablets, multimedia players and other mobile devices, such as wearables. Because of their reduced instruction set, they require fewer transistors, which enables a smaller die size for the integrated circuitry (IC). The ARM processor's smaller size, reduced complexity and lower power consumption makes them suitable for increasingly miniaturized devices.Besides models, the IoT Reference Model provides the concepts and definitions on which IoT architectures can be built. The primary and thus the key model is the IoT Domain Model, which describes all the concepts that are relevant in the Internet of Things.

6.12.1 IoT Domain Model

All other models and the IoT Reference Architecture are based on the concepts introduced in the IoT Domain Model. While certain models, such as the IoT Communication Model and the IoT Trust, Security, and Privacy Model might be less critical in certain application scenarios, the IoT Domain Model is mandatory for all usages of the IoT ARM.The IoT Reference Model aims at establishing a common grounding and a common language for IoT architectures and IoT systems. It consists of the sub-models shown in Fig. 6.6, which is furher expalined in text below.

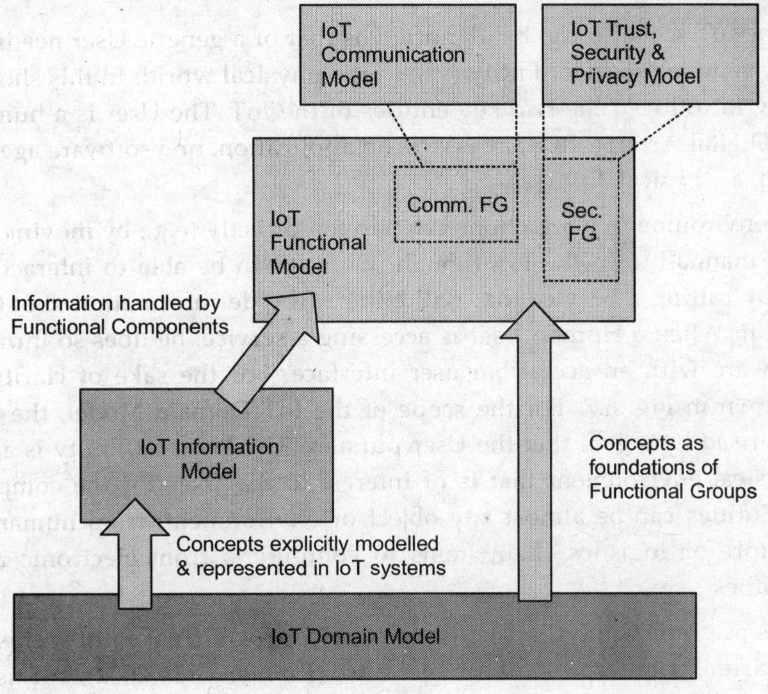

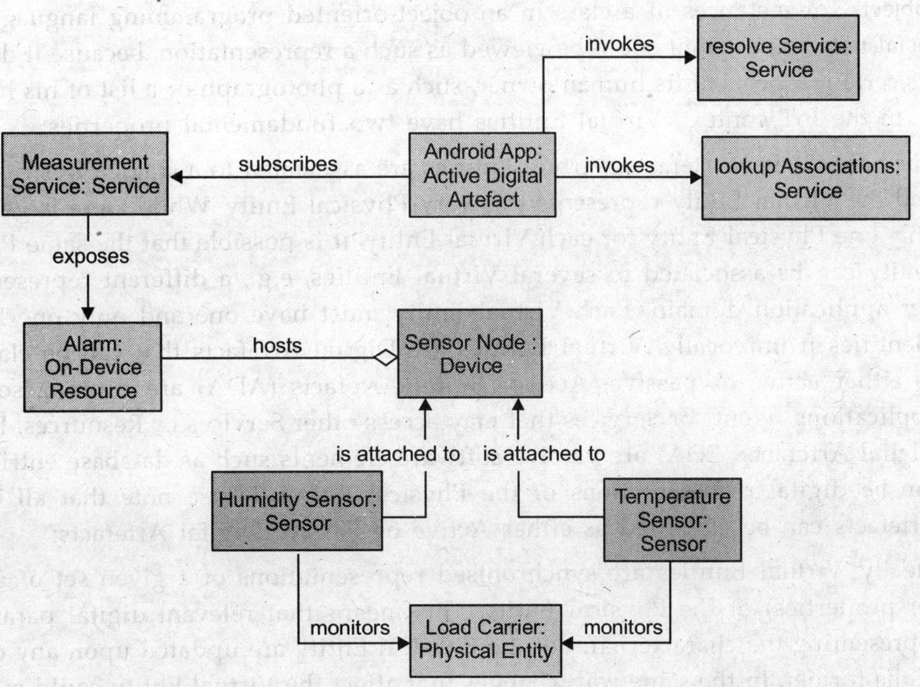

Fig. 6.6: Example, instantiated IoT Domain Model for the Red Thread Example

6.12.1.1 The Concepts of the IoT Domain Model

The most generic IoT scenario can be identified as that of a generic User needing to interact with a (possibly remote) Physical Entity (PE) in the physical world. In this short description we have already introduced the two key entities of the IoT. The User is a human person or some kind of a Digital Artefact (e.g., a Service, an application, or a software agent) that needs to interact with a Physical Entity.

In the physical environment, interactions can happen directly (e.g., by moving a pallet from location X to Y manually). In the IoT though, we want to be able to interact indirectly or mediated, i.e., by calling a Service that will either provide information about the Physical Entity or act on it. When a Human User is accessing a service, he does so through a service client, i.e., software with an accessible user interface. For the sake of clarity, the service client is not shown in Fig. 6.7. For the scope of the IoT Domain Model, the interaction is usually characterised by a goal that the User pursues. The Physical Entity is an identifiable part of the physical environment that is of interest to the User for the completion of her goal. Physical Entities can be almost any object or environment; from humans or animals to cars; from store or logistics chain items to computers; from electronic appliances to jewellery or clothes.

Physical Entities are represented in the digital world by a Virtual Entity. This term is also referred to as "virtual counterpart" in the literature (Ro¨mer et al. 2002), but using the same root term "entity" in both concepts clearer shows the relationship of these concepts. There are many kinds of digital representations of Physical Entities: 3D models, avatars, database entries, objects (or instances of a class in an object-oriented programming language), and even a social-network account could be viewed as such a representation, because it digitally represents certain aspects of its human owner, such as a photograph or a list of his hobbies. However, in the IoT context, Virtual Entities have two fundamental properties:

- They are Digital Artefacts. Virtual Entities are associated to a single Physical Entity and the Virtual Entity represents this very Physical Entity. While there is generally only one Physical Entity for each Virtual Entity, it is possible that the same Physical Entity can be associated to several Virtual Entities, e.g., a different representation per application domain. Each Virtual Entity must have one and only one ID that identifies it univocally. Virtual Entities are Digital Artefacts that can be classified as either active or passive. Active Digital Artefacts (ADA) are running software applications, agents or Services that may access other Services or Resources. Passive Digital Artefacts (PDA) are passive software elements such as database entries that can be digital representations of the Physical Entity. Please note that all Digital Artefacts can be classified as either Active or Passive Digital Artefacts;
- Ideally, Virtual Entities are synchronised representations of a given set of aspects (or properties) of the Physical Entity. This means that relevant digital parameters representing the characteristics of the Physical Entity are updated upon any change of the former. In the same way, changes that affect the Virtual Entity could manifest themselves in the Physical Entity. For instance, manually locking a door might

result in changing the state of the door in home automation software, and correspondingly, setting the door to "locked" in the software might result in triggering an electric lock in the physical world.

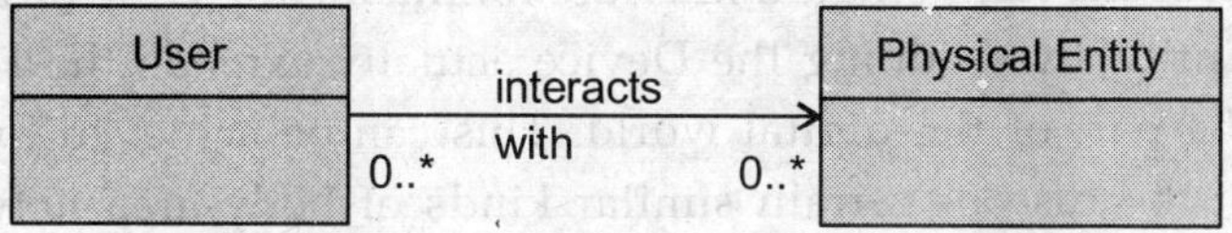

Fig. 6.7: Basic abstraction of an IoT interaction

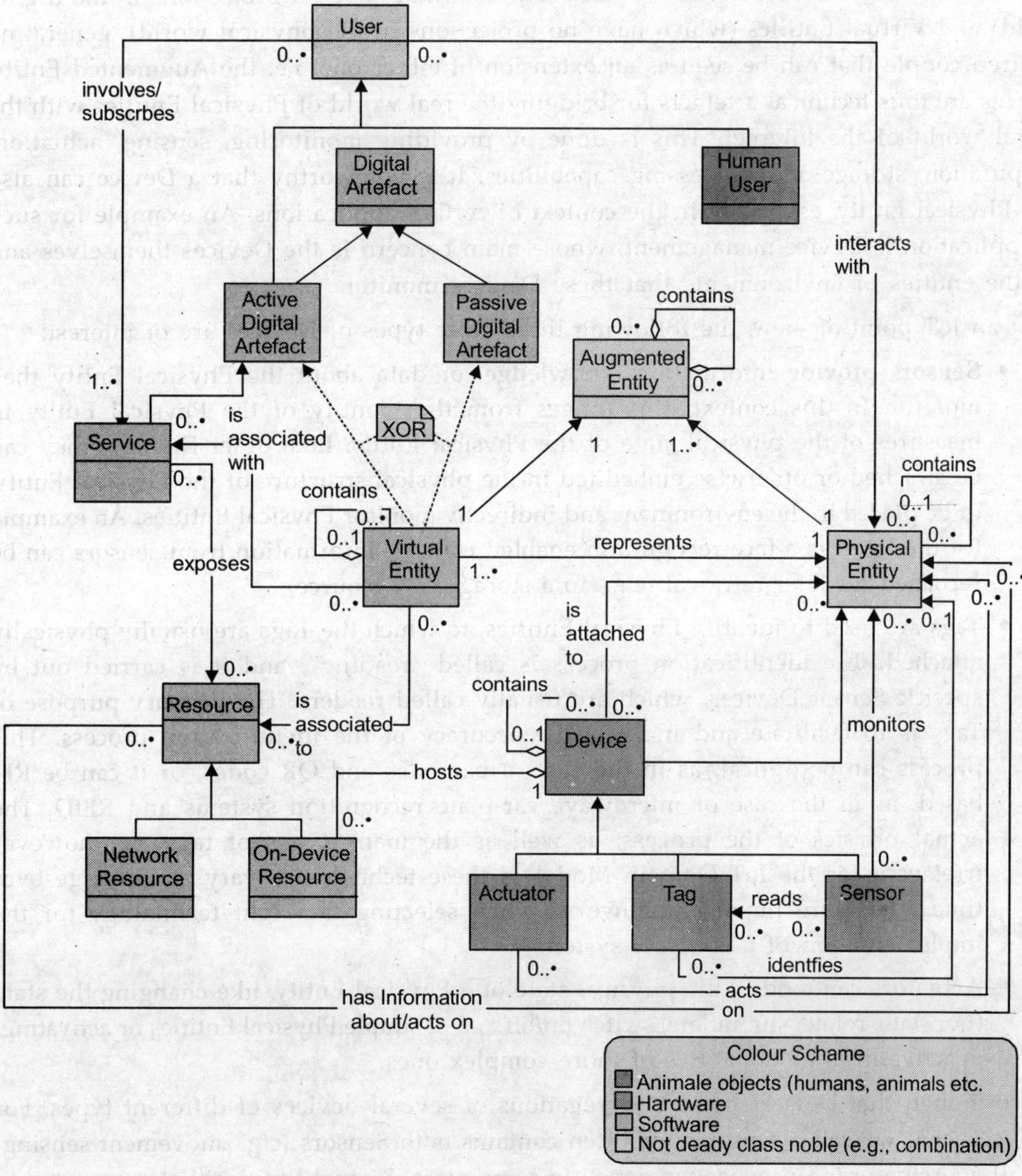

Colour Schame
Animale objects (humans, animals etc.
Hardware
Software
Not deady class noble (e.g., combination)

Fig. 6.8: UML representation of the IoT Domain Model

The relation between *Virtual Entity* and *Physical Entity* is usually achieved by embedding into, by attaching to, or by simply placing in close vicinity of the Physical Entity, one or more ICT Devices that provide the technological interface for interacting with, or gaining information about the Physical Entity. By so doing the Device actually extends the Physical Entity and allows the latter to be part of the digital world. This can be achieved by using Devices of the same class, as in the case of certain similar kinds of body-area network nodes, or by using Devices of different classes, as in the case of an RFID tag and reader. A Device thus mediates the interactions between Physical Entities (that have no projections in the digital world) and Virtual Entities (which have no projections in the physical world), generating a paired couple that can be seen as an extension of either one, i.e. the Augmented Entity. Devices are thus technical artefacts for bridging the real world of Physical Entities with the digital world of the Internet. This is done by providing monitoring, sensing, actuation, computation, storage and processing capabilities. It is noteworthy that a Device can also be a Physical Entity, especially in the context of certain applications. An example for such an application is Device management, whose main concern is the Devices themselves and not the entities or environments that these Devices monitor.

From an IoT point of view, the following three basic types of Devices are of interest:

- **Sensors** provide information, knowledge, or data about the Physical Entity they monitor. In this context, this ranges from the identity of the Physical Entity to measures of the physical state of the Physical Entity. Like other Devices, they can be attached or otherwise embedded in the physical structure of the Physical Entity, or be placed in the environment and indirectly monitor Physical Entities. An example for the latter is a face-recognition enabled camera. Information from sensors can be recorded for later retrieval (e.g., in a storage of Resource);
- **Tags** are used to identify Physical Entities, to which the Tags are usually physically attached. The identification process is called "reading", and it is carried out by specific Sensor Devices, which are usually called readers. The primary purpose of Tags is to facilitate and increase the accuracy of the identification process. This process can be optical, as in the case of barcodes and QR codes, or it can be RF-based, as in the case of microwave car-plate recognition systems and RFID. The actual physics of the process, as well as the many types of tags, are however irrelevant for the IoT Domain Model as these technologies vary and change over time. These are important however when selecting the right technology for the implementation of a concrete system;
- **Actuators** can modify the physical state of a Physical Entity, like changing the state (translate, rotate, stir, inflate, switch on/off,. . .) of simple Physical Entities or activating/deactivating functionalities of more complex ones.

Notice though that Devices can be aggregations of several devices of different types. For instance, what we call a sensor node often contains both Sensors (e.g., movement sensing) as well as Actuators (e.g., wheel engines). In some cases, Virtual Entities that are related to large Physical Entities might need to rely on several, possibly heterogeneous, Resources and

Devices in order to provide a meaningful representation of the Physical Entity, c.f. in our Red Thread example, the values of several temperature Sensors are aggregated to determine the temperature of the truck.

Resources are software components that provide data from or are used in the actuation on Physical Entities. Resources typically have native interfaces. There is a distinction between On-Device Resources and Network Resources. As the name suggests, On-Device Resources are hosted on Devices, viz. software that is deployed locally on the Device that is associated with the Physical Entity. They include executable code for accessing, processing, and storing Sensor information, as well as code for controlling Actuators. On the other hand, Network Resources are Resources available somewhere in the network, e.g., back-end or cloud-based databases. A Virtual Entity can also be associated with Resources that enable interaction with the Physical Entity that the Virtual Entity represents.

6.12.1.2 Services

Services are a widely used concept in today's IT systems. According to MacKenzie et al. 2006, "Services are the mechanism by which needs and capabilities are brought together". This definition is very broad, and the Service concept in the IoT Domain Model is covering this broad definition – but Services are restricted to technical Services implemented in software (in contrast to general, non-technical services that e.g. a lawyer or a consultant provides). As such, Services provide the link between the IoT aspects of a system and other, non-IoT specific parts of an information system, like e.g. various enterprise systems; IoT-related Services and non-IoT Services can be orchestrated together in order to form a complete system.

IoT Services provide well-defined and standardised interfaces, hiding the complexity of accessing a variety of heterogeneous Resources. The interaction with a Physical Entity can be accomplished via one or more Services associated with the corresponding Virtual Entity. This association becomes important in the process of look-up and discovery. An IoT Service can thus be defined as a type of Service enabling interactions with the real world. According to Martý´n 2012, IoT Services can be classified according by their level of abstraction:

- **Resource-level** Services expose the functionality, usually of a Device, by accessing its hosted Resources. These kinds of Services refer to a single Resource. In addition to exposing the Resource's functionality, they deal with quality aspects, such as dependability, security (e.g., access control), resilience (e.g., availability) and performance (e.g., scalability, timeliness). Resources can also be Network Resources, i.e. the Resources do not necessarily reside on a Device in the sense of the IoT Domain Model (normal computers are not regarded as IoT Devices by the IoT Domain Model), but can also be hosted somewhere else. The concrete location of where the Network Resource is situated is commonly abstracted away by the Service;
- **Virtual Entity-level Services** provide access to information at a Virtual Entitylevel. They can be Services associated to a single Virtual Entity that give access to attributes for reading attribute information or for updating attributes in order to trigger associations. An alternative is to provide a common Virtual Entitylevel Service with

an interface for accessing attributes of different Virtual Entities, as, for instance, the NGSI Context Interface (NGSI 2010) provides for getting attribute information of the Virtual Entities;

- **Integrated Services** are the result of a Service composition of Resource-level or Virtual Entity-level Services as well as any combinations of both Service abstractions.

6.12.1.4 Identification of Physical Entities

In order to track and monitor Physical Entities, they have to be identified. There are basically two ways for how this can be done, as is very well described in (Furness 2009): Using either natural-feature identification (classified as "primary identification") or using some type of Tags or labels (classified as "secondary identification") that are attached to the Physical Entity.

Both means of identification are covered in the IoT Domain Model. Tags are modelled as Devices that explicitly identify a Physical Entity. Natural-feature identification can be modelled, for example, by using a camera – a kind of Sensor – that monitors the Physical Entity and an additional Resource that does the natural feature extraction (i.e. a dedicated software component). The result of the natural feature extraction can be used as search term for looking up the corresponding Virtual Entity.

RFID Tags are a prominent example in IoT. As they come with their own electronic circuitry it seems quite natural to classify RFID Tags as Devices in terms of the IoT Domain Model. The case is less clear-cut regarding the classification of a barcode label, however. As pointed out elsewhere (Haller 2010), classifying a barcode label as a Device seems a little far-fetched; regarding it as a "natural feature" of the Physical Entity it is attached to, seems to be more appropriate. However, as with many modelling questions, this is a matter of taste – the IoT Domain Model is not prescribing which variant to use.

6.12.1.5 Context and Location

As the IoT pertains to the physical world, the characteristics of the physical world play an important role. All elements of the physical world are situated within a certain context, and location is an essential aspect of this context. All concepts in the IoT Domain Model that refer to elements of the physical world, i.e., Physical Entities, Devices, and Human Users inherently have a location. This location may or may not be known within the IoT system

6.12.2 Information Model

The IoT Information Model defines the structure (e.g. relations, attributes, services) of all the information for Virtual Entities on a conceptual level. The IoT Information Model details the modelling of a Virtual Entity. The Virtual Entity (VirtualEntity) has attributes with a name (resp. Attribute and AttributeName) and a type (AttributeType) and one or more values (Value) to which meta-information (MetaData) can be associated. Important meta-information is, e.g., at what time a value was measured (i.e. time stamp), the location where a measurement took place, or the quality of the measurement.

Metadata can itself contain additional metadata, e.g. the unit in which the metadata is measured. The association (Association) between a Virtual Entity and a Service is detailed in the sense that is pertains to a certain Attribute of the Virtual Entity. The serviceType can be set either to INFORMATION, if the Service provides the attribute value to be read or to ACTUATION, if the Service allows the Attribute value to be set, as resulting of a corresponding change in the physical world.

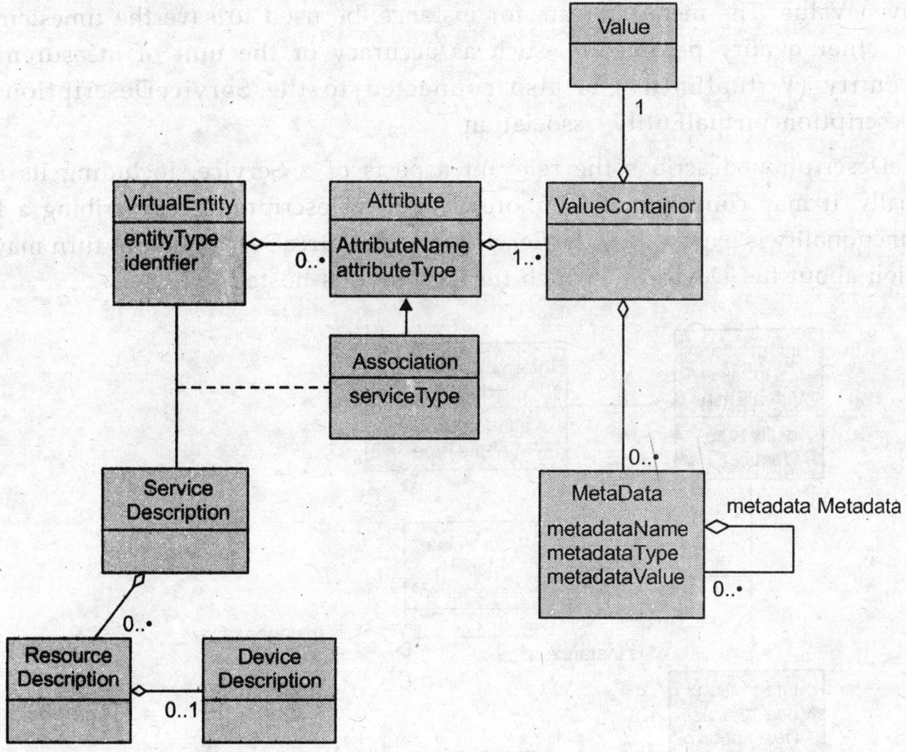

Fig. 6.9: IoT Information Model

6.12.2.1 IoT Information Model

The diagram in Fig. 6.9 shows the structure of the information that is handled and processed in an IoT System. The main aspects are represented by the elements VirtualEntity, ServiceDescription and Association. A Virtual Entity models a Physical Entity and ServiceDescription describes a Service that serves information about the Physical Entity itself or the environment. Through an Association, the connection between an Attribute of a Virtual Entity and the ServiceDescription is modelled, e.g. the Service acts as a "get" function for an Attribute value. Every Virtual Entity needs to have a unique identifier (identifier) or entity type (entityType), defining the type of the Virtual Entity representation, e.g. a human, a car or a temperature sensor. Furthermore, a Virtual Entity can have zero to many different attributes (Attribute class in Fig. 6.9).

The entityType of the VirtualEntity class may refer to concepts in an ontology that defines what attributes a Virtual Entity of this type has (see, for instance, [Group, W3C OWL]). Each Attribute has a name (attributeName), a type (attributeType), and one to many values

(ValueContainer). The attributeType specifies the semantic type of an attribute, for example, that the value represents temperature. It can reference an ontologyconcepts, e.g., qu:temperature taken from "Quantity Kinds and Units"-ontology (Lefort 2005). This way, one can for instance, model an attribute, e.g. a list of values, which itself has several values. Each ValueContainer groups one Value and zero to many metadata information units belonging to the given Value. The metadata can, for instance, be used to save the timestamp of the Value, or other quality parameters, such as accuracy or the unit of measurement. The Virtual Entity (VirtualEntity) is also connected to the ServiceDescription via the ServiceDescription-VirtualEntity association.

A ServiceDescription describes the relevant aspects of a Service, including its interface. Additionally, it may contain one (or more) ResourceDescription(s) describing a Resource whose functionality is exposed by the Service. The ResourceDescription in turn may contain information about the Device on which the Resource is hosted.

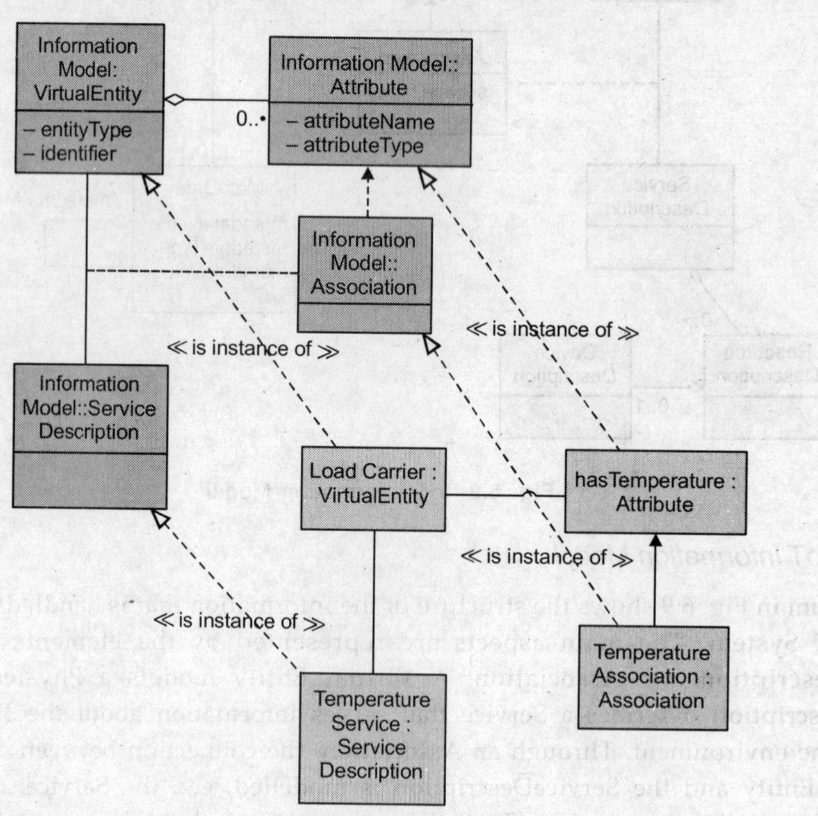

Fig. 6.10: Illustrating example for IoT Information Model

6.12.2.2 Relation of Information Model to Domain Model

The IoT Information Model models all the concepts of the Domain Model that are to be explicitly represented and manipulated in the digital world. Additionally, the IoT Information Model models relations between these concepts. The IoT Information Model is a meta-model that provides a structure for the information being handled by IoT Systems. This structure provides the basis for all aspects of the system that deal with the representation, gathering, processing, storage and retrieval of information and as such is used as a basis for defining the functional interfaces of the IoT system.

Figure 6.11 shows the relation between the Domain Model concepts and the IoT Information Model elements. The main Domain Model concepts that are explicitly represented in an IoT system are the Virtual Entity and the service. The latter also comprises aspects of the Resource and the Device. As the Virtual Entity is the representation of the Physical Entity in the digital world, there is no other representation of the Physical Entity in the IoT Information Model.

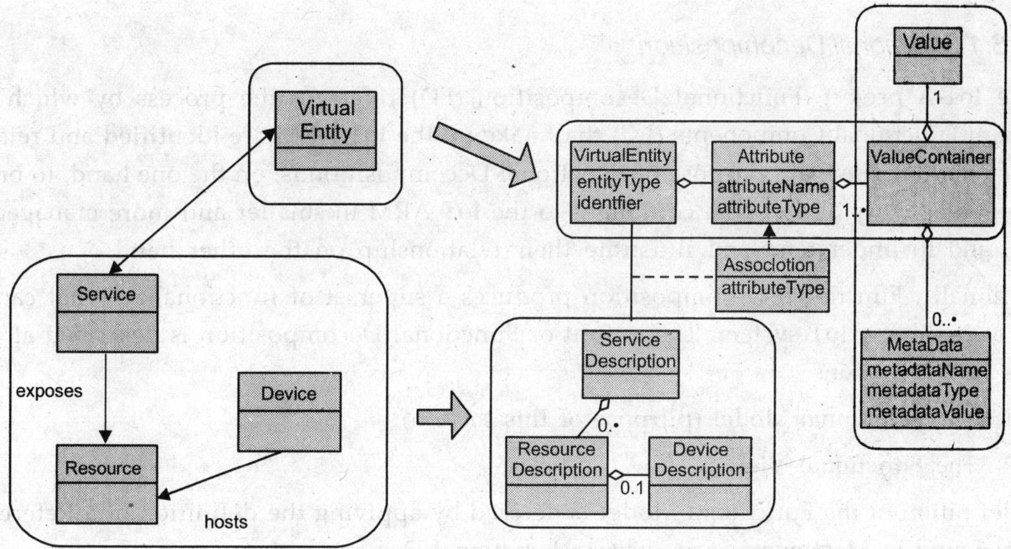

Fig. 6.11: Relation between the core concepts of the IoT Domain Model and IoT InformationModel

6.12.2.3 Other Information-Related Models in IoT-

A Throughout IoT-A several other information- related models exist. Most of them are defined in the technical work packages WP2, WP3, WP4 and WP5.

- **Entity Model:** The Entity Model specifies which attributes and features of real word objects are represented by the virtual counterpart, i.e. the Virtual Entity of the respective Physical Entity. For every attribute specified in the entity model, services can be found that are able to either provide information about the attribute (sensing) or manipulate it, leading to an effect in the real world (actuating).
- **Resource Model:** The Resource Model contains the information that is essential to identify Resources by a unique identifier and to classify Resources by their type, like sensor, actuator, processor or tag. Furthermore the model specifies the geographic location of the Resource, the Device the Resource is hosted on (if so) as well as the IoT Services the Resource is exposed through.

- **Service description model**: Services provide access to Resources and are used to access information or to control Physical Entities. An IoT Service accesses IoT Resources in order to provide information about attributes of entities or manipulates them leading to an effect in the real world. A Service Description describes a Service, using for instance a service description language such as USDL.
- **Event Model**: Event models are quite essential in today's IoT architectures, e.g. in the EPCglobal Information Services. Normally events are used to track dynamic changes in a (software) system, showing who or what has triggered it and when, where and why the change occurred.

6.12.3 Functional Model

6.12.3.1 Functional Decomposition

In the IoT-A project, Functional Decomposition (FD) refers to the process by which the different Functional Components (FC) that make up the IoT ARM are identified and related to one another. The main purpose of Functional Decomposition is, on the one hand, to break up the complexity of a system compliant to the IoT ARM in smaller and more manageable parts, and to understand and illustrate their relationship on the other hand.

Additionally, Functional Decomposition produces a superset of functionalities that can be used to build any IoT system. The output of Functional Decomposition is described at two levels of abstraction:

1. The Functional Model (purpose of this section);
2. The Functional View

The definition of the Functional Model is derived by applying the definition of a Reference Model found in MacKenzie et al. 2006 to Functional Decomposition:

"The Functional Model is an abstract framework for understanding the main Functionality Groups (FG) and their interactions. This framework defines the common semantics of the main functionalities and will be used for the development of IoT-A compliant Functional Views."

The definition contains the following concepts that need to be explained in more detail:

- **Abstract:** The Functional Model is not directly tied to a certain technology, application domain, or implementation. It does not explain what the different Functional Components are that make up a certain Functionality Group;
- **Functionality Groups and their interactions:** The Functional Model contains both the Functionality Groups and the interaction between those parts. A list of the Functionality Groups alone would not be enough to make up the Functional Model. Both the Functionality Groups and their interaction are mandatory;
- **Functional View:** The Functional View describes the system's runtime Functional Components, including the components' responsibilities, their default functions,

their interfaces, and their primary interactions. The Functional View is derived from the Functional Model on the one hand and from the Unified Requirements on the other hand. Note that various Functional Views could be derived from the Functional Model.

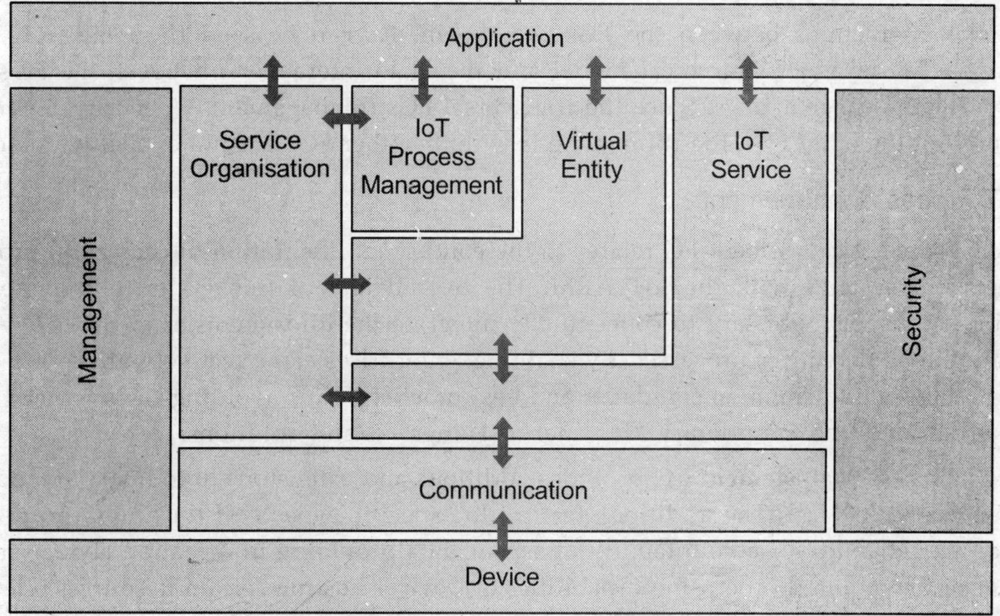

Fig. 6.12: Functional Model

6.12.3.2 Functional Model Diagram

The Functional Model diagram is depicted in Fig. 6.12 and was derived as follows:

- From the main abstractions identified in the Domain Model (Virtual Entities, Devices, Resources and Users) the "Application", "Virtual Entity", "IoT Service" and "Device" FGs are derived;
- With regards to the plethora of communication technologies that the IoT ARM needs to support, the need for a "Communication" FG is identified;
- Requirements expressed by stakeholders regarding the possibility to build services and applications on top of the IoT are covered by the "IoT Process Management" and "Service Organisation" FGs;
- To address consistently the concern expressed about IoT Trust, Security and Privacy, the need for a "Security" transversal FG is identified;
- Finally, the "Management" transversal FG is required for the management of and/or interaction between the functionality groups.

The Functional Model contains seven longitudinal Functionality Groups complemented by two transversal Functionality Groups (*Management and Security*). These transversal groups provide functionalities that are required by each of the longitudinal groups. The policies governing the transversal groups will not only be applied to the groups themselves, but do also pertain to the longitudinal groups.

As an example: for a security policy to be effective, it must ensure that there is no functionality provided by a component that would circumvent the policy and provide unauthorised access.

Next, the interactions between the FGs are shown. As can be seen from Fig. 6.12, the Functional Model is a hierarchical model and the main interactions between the FG's are depicted with orange arrows. Since the transversal FGs (Management & Security) interface with most of the other FGs, their interactions with the other FG's are not explicitly depicted.

(1) IoT Process Management

The IoT Process Management FG relates to the conceptual integration of (business) process management systems with the IoT ARM. The overall aim of this FG is to provide the functional concepts necessary to conceptually integrate the idiosyncrasies of the IoT world into traditional (business) processes. By so doing, enterprises can effectively utilise IoT sub-systems adhering to common standards and best practices, thus avoiding the overhead and costs of isolated and proprietary "Intranet-of-Things" island solutions.

The IoT Process Management FG provides additions and extensions to industry standards, for instance BPMN 2.0. The additions feature IoT-specific aspects of (business) processes, such as the reliability or accountability of sensor data providing information about Virtual Entities or the required processing capabilities of Devices hosting certain Resources relevant for the real world. Applications that interact with the IoT Process Management FG via IoT-augmented process models can effectively be shielded from IoT-specific details of lower layers of the functional model, which greatly reduces integration costs and thus contributes to an increased adoption of IoT-A based IoT systems (Meyer et al. 2011).

The IoT Process Management FG is conceptually closely related to the Service Organisation FG and acts as a proxy to applications that integrate an IoT-A-compliant IoT system. Naturally, the IoT Process Management FG has a dependency on the Service Organisation FG, as a central concept in the execution of (business) processes is the finding, binding, and invoking of Services that are used for each process step. The IoT Process Management FG therefore relies on Service Organisation to map the abstract process definitions to more concrete Service invocations.

Applications can utilise the tools and interfaces defined for the IoT Process Management FG in order to stay on the (abstract) conceptual level of a (business) process, while, at the same time, making use of IoT-related functionality without the necessity of dealing with the complexities of IoT Services. In this respect, the IoT Process Management FG provides conceptual interfaces to the IoT ARM, that are alternatives to the more concrete Virtual Entity FG and Service Organisation FG interfaces.

(2) Service Organisation

The Service Organisation FG is a central Functionality Group that acts as a communication hub between several other Functionality Groups. Since the primary concept of communication within the IoT ARM is the notion of the Service, the Service Organisation FG is used for composing and orchestrating Services of different levels of abstraction. Within the IoT Reference Architecture, it effectively links the Service requests from high level FGs such as the IoT Process Management FG, or even external applications, to basic services that expose Resources (such as services hosted on a WSN gateway), and enables the association of entities with these services by utilising the Virtual Entity FG, so that a translation of high-level requests dealing with properties of entities (e.g., "give me please the temperature in the room 123") down to the concrete IoT services (e.g., "sensor service XYZ") can be realised. In order to allow for querying Virtual Entities or IoT Services that are associated with these entities, the Service Organisation FG is responsible for resolving and orchestrating IoT Services and also deal with the composition and choreography of Services.

Service Composition is a central concept within the architecture, since IoT Services are very frequently capable of rather limited functionality due to the constraints in computing power and battery life that are typical for WS&ANs or embedded Devices comprising the IoT. Service Composition then helps combining multiple of such basic Services in order to answer requests at a higher level of Service abstraction (e.g. the combination of a humidity sensing Service and a temperature Service could serve as input for an air-conditioning). Service Choreography is a concept that supports brokerage of Services so that Services can subscribe to other Services available in the system.

(3) Virtual Entity and IoT Service

The Virtual Entity and IoT Service FGs include functions that relate to interactions on the Virtual-Entity and IoT-Service abstraction levels, respectively.

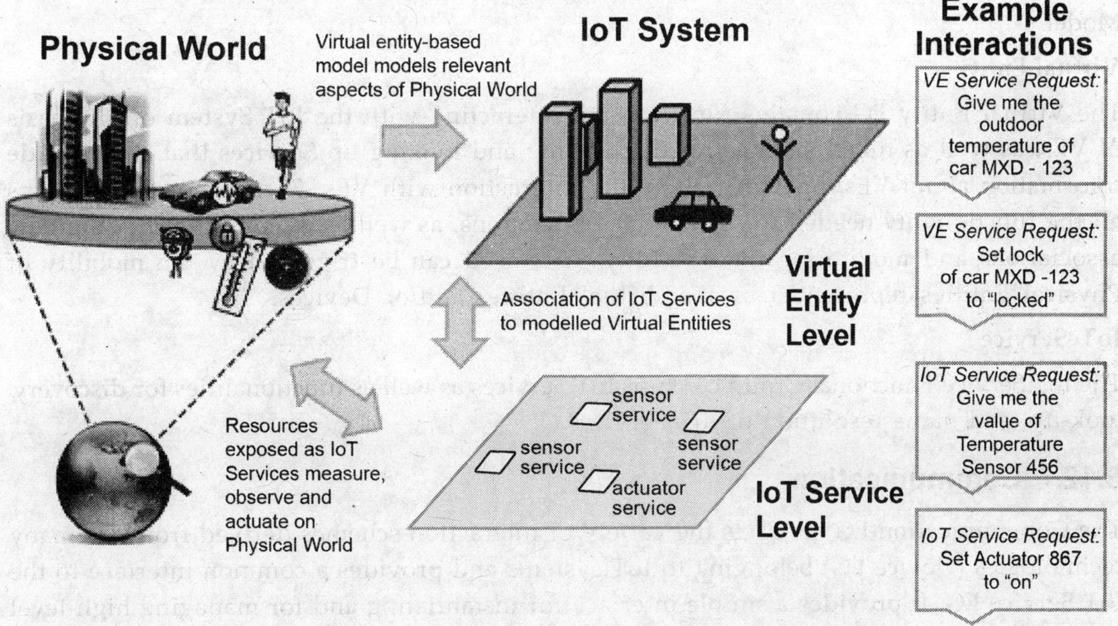

Fig. 6.13: IoT-Service and Virtual-Entity abstraction levels

Figure 6.13 shows the abstraction levels and how they are related. On the left side of this figure, the physical world is depicted. In the physical world, there are a number of Sensors and Actuators that capture and facilitate the change of certain aspects of the physical world. The Resources associated to the Sensors and Actuators are exposed as IoT Services on the IoT Service level. Example interactions between applications and the IoT system on this abstraction level are "Give me the value of Sensor 456" or "Set Actuator 867 to On". Applications can only interact with these Services in a meaningful way, if they already know the semantics of the values, e.g. if Sensor 456 returns the value 20, the application has to be programmed or configured in such a way that it knows that this is the outdoor temperature of the car of interest, e.g. Car MXD – 123. So, on this level no semantics is encoded in the information itself, nor does the IoT system have this information, it has to be a-priori shared between the Sensor and the application.

Whereas interaction on the IoT Service level is useful for a certain set of applications that are programmed or configured for a specific environment, there is another set of applications that wants to opportunistically use suitable Services in a possibly changing environment. For these types of applications, and especially the Human Users of such applications, the Virtual Entity level models higher-level aspects of the physical world, and these aspects can be used for discovering Services. Examples for interactions between applications and the IoT system on this abstraction level are "Give me the outdoor temperature of Car MXD – 123" or "Set lock of Car MXD – 123 to locked". To support the interactions on the Virtual Entity level, the relation between IoT Services and Virtual Entities needs to be modelled, which is done in form of associations. For example, the association will contain the information that the outdoor temperature of Car MXD – 123 is provided by Sensor 456. Associations between Virtual Entities and IoT Services are modelled in the Information Model.

Virtual Entity

The Virtual Entity FG contains functions for interacting with the IoT System on the basis of VEs, as well as functionalities for discovering and looking up Services that can provide information about VEs, or which allow the interaction with VEs. Furthermore, it contains all the functionality needed for managing associations, as well as dynamically finding new associations and monitoring their validity. This need can be triggered by the mobility of Physical Entities represented by the Virtual Entities and/or Devices.

IoT Service

The IoT Service Functional Group contains IoT Services as well as functionalities for discovery, look-up, and name resolution of IoT Services.

6.12.4 Communication

The Communication FG abstracts the variety of interaction schemes derived from the many technologies (Device FG) belonging to IoT systems and provides a common interface to the IoT Service FG. It provides a simple interface for instantiating and for managing high-level information flow. In particular, the following aspects are taken into account: starting from the top layers of the ISO/OSI model it considers data representation, end to end path information, addressing issues (i.e. Locator/ID split), network management and device specific features. The Communication FG can be customised according to the different requirements defined in the Unified Requirements list and, in particular, those related to communication specified within WP3. For instance, integrity and security can be enforced exploiting many different signature and encryption schemes at various ISO/OSI layers; reliability is achieved either by means of link layer.

6.12.5 Management Functional Group

The Management FG combines all functionalities that are needed to govern an IoT system. The need for management can be traced back to at least four high-level system goals (Pras 1995):

1. Cost reduction;
2. Attending unexpected usage issues;
3. Fault handling; and
4. Flexibility.

Cost reduction: In order to control the cost of a system, it is designed for a maximum amount of users and/or use cases. "A way for the designer to deal with the requirements of multiple groups of users is to abstract from the differences in [the] requirements and [to] parameterise the design" (Pras 1995). Upon commissioning or start-up of the system, these parameters will be initialised by the Management FG.

Attending unexpected events: The IoT system is based on an incomplete model of reality – as literally all systems are. For example, even for the same type of user, unforeseen activity patterns in the physical world and thus unforeseen usage may arise may arise. For instance, errors are introduced into the system through explicit, erroneous management directives (Harrisburg, Chernobyl). Another example is that Devices can suddenly just die. The latter is most likely to become prevalent in the IoT, since the cost margins for IoT equipment and thus their reliability can be much lower than that for traditional telecommunications equipment (back-bone routers, etc.). The management FG can provide strategies and actions for the mitigation of impacts from unforeseen situations. Such impacts can be link failure, queue overload, etc. In order to better adapt to new situations, it is of course paramount that the Management FG has a good overview of the system state. To that end the management system provides supports collection.

Fault handling: This goal addresses the unpredictability of the future behaviour of the system itself. This is of special interest in complex IoT systems and also in IoT systems in which, for instance, the devices in an IoT system do not provide a model for their behaviour. The measures implied by this goal are:

1. Prediction of potential failures;
2. Detection of existing failures;
3. Reduction of the effects of failures;
4. Repair

system components with previous and/or expected behaviour.

Flexibility: The design of a system is based on use-case requirements. However, these use-case requirements are not static. Instead of designing a new system every time the requirements change, some flexibility should be built into the system. Due to this flexibility, the Management FG of the IoT system will be able to react to changes in the user requirements. This can take place during boot up, commissioning or also at run time.

All of the above goals rely on shared common functionality and repositories, as, for instance, a state repository. Other functionalities are:

- Management of the membership and accompanying information of a given entity to the IoT system. Such entity may be a Functional Component (FC), a Virtual Entity, an IoT Service, an application, a Device. The information considered may cover ownership, administrative domain, capabilities, rules, and rights;
- Retrieval of the list of members pertaining to a given property such as the ownership/administrative domain;

  Finally, some more examples for the above goals are provided:

- Enforcing rules attached to the usage of a certain entity e.g.
- Attending unexpected events: A service needs temperature measurements every microsecond, but the rule file for the associated device says: maximum measurement frequency of this device is 100 Hz. The rule file also might say: no continuous operation of said device for more than 1 h (due to energy constraints);
- Fault handling: A service wants to run a business process that would consume all IoT services and the VE lookup for more than a day. An example for this is a query for the geo-location of all temperature Sensors on planet Earth. The rule file may contain instructions about how many resources can be consumed by an application;
- Cost reduction: Logging entity usage by a user for further processing (e.g. billing).

  Besides the above, "traditional" goals of management, the Management FG also needs to address needs that arise when IoT systems can actuate and/or if the they are embedded in critical infrastructure. Examples for such situations are

- Bringing the entire system to an emergency stop, for instance a train;
- Turning the entire system into a sleep/energy-saving mode in order to relax to load on a failing Smart Grid

6.12.6 Security Functionality Group (Security FG)

Security FG is responsible for ensuring the security and privacy of IoT-A-compliant systems. It is in charge of handling the initial registration of a client to the system in a secure manner. This ensures that only legitimate clients may access services provided by the IoT infrastructure. The Security FG is also in charge of protecting private parameters of users. This is achieved by providing anonymity (ensuring that the user's identity remains confidential when she/he/it accesses a Resource or a service) and "unlink-ability" (ensuring that the user may make multiple uses of Resources or services without an attacker being able to establish links between those uses). This privacy support relies on fine-tuned identity management, which is able to assign various pseudorandom identifiers to a single user.

The Security FG also ensures that legitimate interaction occurs between peers that are statically authorised to interact with each other, or that are trusted by each other. This is achieved through the use of dedicated authorisation functions or through the reliance on a trust – and-reputation model, which is able to identify trustworthy peers in a privacy-capable and highly mutable architecture. Finally, the Security FG enables secure communications between peers by managing the establishment of integrity and confidentiality features between two entities lacking initial knowledge of each other.

6.12.7 Communication Model

The IoT Communication Model aims at defining the main communication paradigms for connecting elements, as defined in the IoT Domain Model. We provide a reference set of communication rules to build interoperable stacks, together with insights about the main interactions among the elements of the IoT Domain Model. We propose a Communication Model that leverages on the ISO OSI 7-layer model for networks and aims at highlighting those peculiar aspects inherent to the interoperation among different stacks, which we will call in what follows, interoperability features. Further, the application of communication schemes, such as application layer gateways, transparent proxy, network virtualization, etc., to different IoT network types is discussed. The IoT Communication Model can be used to model how the monitoring Sensors of the truck can seamlessly interact with Ted's phone and how it can communicate with the store enterprise system.

The IoT Communication Model has multiple usages. For instance, it can guide the definition of the Communication Functional Components from which the Communication Functional Group is composed of. Finally, it can be used to derive the Communication best practices, as depicted in the Fig. 6.14.

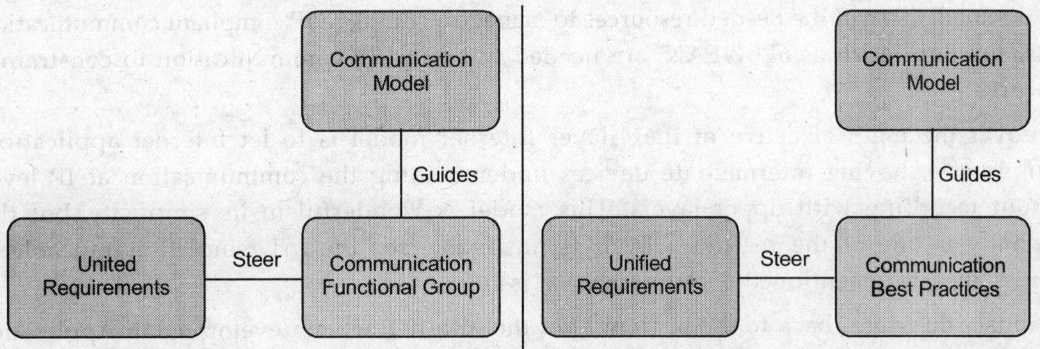

Fig. 6.14: IoT Communication Model usages: (left) using the CM together with the Unified Requirements to define the Communication FG; (right) deriving Communication Best Practices thanks to the CM and the Unified Requirements

6.12.7.1 Communication Interoperability Aspects

The model we are going to propose in this section takes its roots from the ISO/OSI (ISO 1994) stack, the US Department of Defense 4 layer model (DoD4) (Darpa 1970) and, the Internet stack, but it puts its focus on IoT specific features and issues. All the previous models have a great value, going beyond any discussion, but simply they have not been conceived with the IoT issues and features in mind. In Fig. 6.15 we can see the Internet and the DoD4 stacks. It is evident how they map onto each other, thus in what follows we will address the 4 layers Internet model only.

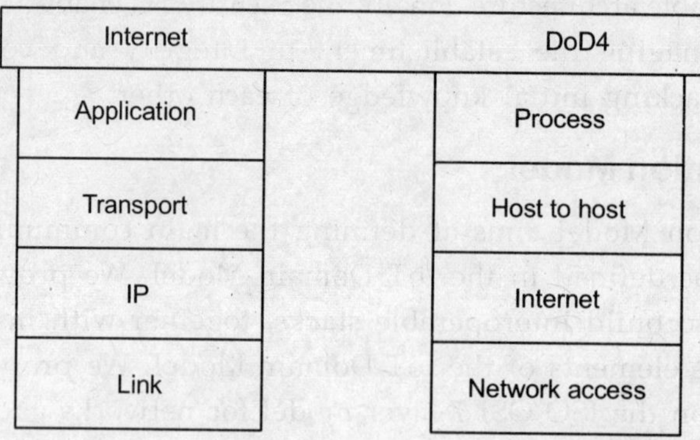

Fig. 6.15: Four layers Internet stack (left) and DoD4 stack

The 4-layer Internet stack abstracts from the underlying Physical Layer; in fact its lowest layer is represented by the Link Layer. This choice is indeed the right one for the Internet, as the Link Layer is not visible from the Application Layer, and the same can be applied to fully homogeneous networks, since applications can be totally agnostic of the underlined common physical technology. However, the Physical Layer rises to a great importance when talking about the IoT; in fact the IoT is characterized by a high heterogeneity of hardware and technologies and the necessity of making different system interoperable. Moreover, this is a clear statement on the fact that IP is conceived in order to be implemented on top of any hardware networking technologies, while in the IoT there exist technologies that do not dispose of the needed resources to manage a complete IP compliant communication. Thus, solutions such as 6LoWPAN, are needed to extend IP communication to constrained networks.

Moreover the main objective of the 4-layer Internet model is to let Internet applications communicate, having intermediate devices understanding the communication at IP level, without meddling with upper layers. This model is wonderful in its simplicity, but this simplicity is one of the reasons why it is unsuitable for the IoT, since it is not able to address the aforementioned interoperability issues.

Obviously this dates back to the beginning of the Internet, when developing an Application Protocol for each application was best practice. While in principle that is a reasonable approach, even in the current Internet we can perceive how it is misleading. We are not here to discuss pros and cons of developing an Application Protocol for each application but we have just to notice this is not a common practice anymore, with the majority of applications leveraging on HTTP or even on more specific HTTP constructs like REST protocols. So nowadays it is crucial to have a distinction between *Applications and the Application Protocols*. Another major issue of the 4 layers Internet model arises from the lack of expression for the so called security layers, the two major examples being SSL (IETF 2011)/TLS (IETF 2008) and IPsec (IETF 1998).

The main reference point for communication system developers is the ISO/OSI stack, and, although its validity as an implementation guideline is out of question, it fails to depict the overall complexity of IoT systems as it is meant to represent single technology stacks. After the considerations on the model discussed so far we felt necessary a different approach for highlighting the peculiar features of IoT communication, which are not directly evident using the ISO/OSI model alone.

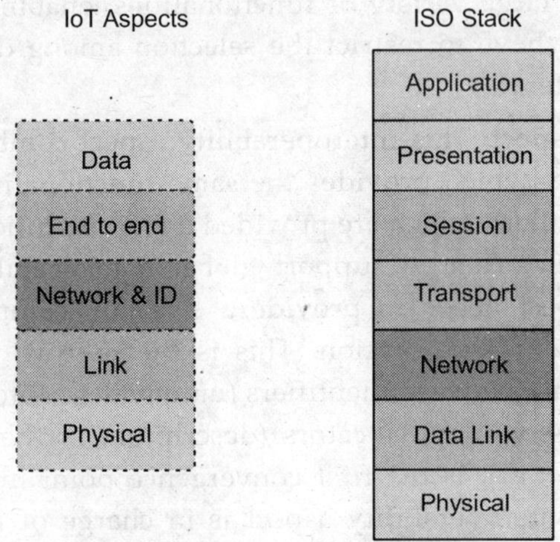

Fig. 6.16: The interoperability aspects of the IoT Communication Model (left) compared to the ISO/OSI communication stack (right): dashed lines have been used for the IoT aspects to make them graphically different from stack layers

The model, as depicted in Fig. 6.16 on the left-hand side, stresses the relevance of the wide range of interoperability aspects that characterise IoT systems. In fact, instead of focusing on a specific realisation of the communication stack, the IoT Communication Model provides a transversal approach from which one or more communication stacks can be derived: in fact a single interoperability aspect can be used to describe the interactions of stacks belonging to different communicating systems. Once a system is modelled according to the IoT Communication Model it is easy to derive a set of ISO/OSI interoperable stacks in order to provide the needed interoperability features.

Below, the different interoperability aspects are described:

- **Physical aspect:** This interoperability aspect concerns the physical characteristics of the communication technologies used in the system. It is similar to the OSI Physical Layer. This is necessary in order to neither exclude any available technology, and to prevent emerging solutions from being integrated into the Reference Model. This aspect does not force the adoption of any specific technology, but it uses the adopted technologies as a base to model the remaining of the system. In fact, as per the recurring example the Mote Runner Node can communicate using some low-power radio transceiver such as ZigBee, while the AndroidApp can be hosted in an IoT-Phone connected to the Internet either via WiFi or 3G cellular networks

- **Link aspect:** In order to address the heterogeneousness of networking technologies represented in the IoT field, the Link aspect requires special attention. In fact, most networks implement similar, but customised communication schemes and security solutions. In order for IoT systems to achieve full interoperability, as well as the support of heterogeneous technologies and a comprehensive security framework, this layer must support solution diversity. At the same time, it needs to provide upper layers with standardised capabilities and interfaces. Therefore, this layer needs to abstract a large variety of functionalities, enabling direct communication. IoT systems do not have to restrict the selection among data link layers, but must enable their coexistence;
- **Network and ID aspect:** This interoperability aspect combines two communication aspects: networking, which provides the same functionalities as the correspondent OSI layer; and identifiers, which are provided using resolution functionalities between locators and IDs. In order to support global manageability, interoperability, and scalability, this aspect needs to provide a common communication paradigm for every possible networking solution. This is the narrow waist for the Internet of Things. The difference between identifiers (unique descriptors of the Digital Artefact; either active or passive), and locators (descriptors of the position of a given IoT element in the network), is the first convergence point in the IoT Communication Model. Thus, this interoperability aspect is in charge of making any two systems addressable from one another notwithstanding the particular technologies they are adopting. In the case of our recurring example the AndroidApp must be able to receive alarms generated by the alarm Service, which in turns, must receive information from the Mote Runner Device: in order for this to be possible the system must ensure that the correct identifiers are supported by all the communicating technologies or can be resolved via appropriate methods;
- **End-to-end aspect:** this aspect takes care of reliability, transport issues, translation functionalities, proxies/gateways support and parameter configuration when the communication crosses different networking environments. By providing additional interoperability aspects on top of those of the Network and ID aspect, this aspect provides the final component for achieving a global M2M communication model. Connections are also part of the end-to-end scope. Also, Application Layer aspects are taken care of here. Moreover Application Protocols in the IoT tend to embed confirmation messages, and congestion control techniques require being more complex than what is achievable in the Transport Layer in the legacy models. With reference to the recurring example, this aspect will take care of modelling the overall communication between the Alarm Service and the Mote Runner Node and between the AndroidApp and the Alarm Service;

- **Data aspect:** the topmost aspect of the IoT Communication Model is related to data definitions and transfers. While the Information Model provides a highlevel description for data of IoT systems, the purpose of this aspect is to model data exchange between any two actors in the IoT. Data exchanged in IoT can adopt many different representations, ranging from raw data to complex structures where meta-information is added to provide context specific links. Finally, to make this possible, the data aspect needs to model the following characteristics (Rossi 2013):
  (1) capability of providing structured attributes for data description;
  (2) capability of being translated (possibly by compression/decompression) the one to each other, e.g. CoAP is translatable to HTTP by decompression or XML is translatable to EXI by compression, IPv4 is translatable to IPv6 by mapping;
  (3) constrained device support. For instance, in the recurring example, the raw data produced by the Mote Runner Sensors shall be converted into machinereadable formats in order for the Alarm Service to be able to interpret and use them.

6.13 TAXONOMY OF MACHINE LEARNING ALGORITHMS

Machine learning is a sub field of computer science, a type of *Artificial Intelligence*, (AI), that provides machines with the ability to learn without explicit programming. Machine learning evolved from pattern recognition and Computational Learning Theory. There, some essential concepts of machine learning are discussed as well as, the frequently applied machine learning algorithms for smart data analysis.

A learning algorithm takes a set of samples as an input named a *training set*. In general, there exist three main categories of learning: *supervised*, *unsupervised*, and *reinforcement*. In an informal sense, in supervised learning, the training set consists of samples of input vectors together with their corresponding appropriate target vectors, also known as *labels*.

In unsupervised learning, no labels are required for the training set. Reinforcement learning deals with the problem of learning the appropriate action or sequence of actions to be taken for a given situation in order to maximize payoff. Focus is on *supervised and unsupervised learning* since they have been and are being widely applied in IoT smart data analysis. The objective of supervised learning is to learn how to predict the appropriate output vector for a given input vector. Applications where the target label is a finite number of discrete categories are known as *classification* tasks. Cases where the target label is composed of one or more continuous variables are known as *regression*.

Defining the objective of unsupervised learning is difficult. One of the major objectives is to identify the sensible clusters of similar samples within the input data, known as *clustering*. Moreover, the objective may be the discovery of a useful internal representation for the input data by *preprocessing* the original input variable in order to transfer it into a new variable space. This preprocessing stage can significantly improve the result of the subsequent machine learning algorithm and is named *feature extraction*. The frequently applied machine learning algorithms for smart data analysis are tabulated in Table 6.3.

Table 6.3. Overview of Frequently Used Machine Learning Algorithms for Smart Data Analysis.

Mechine learning algorithm	Data processing tasks	Mechine learning algorithm	Data processing tasks
K-Nearest Neighbors	Classification	Bagging	Classification/Regression
Naive Bayes	Classification	K-Means	Classification
Support Vector Machine	Classification	Density-Based Spatial Clustaring of Applications with Noise	Classification
Linear Regression	Regression		
Support Vector Regression	Regression	Principal commonent Analysis	Feature extraction
Classification and Regression Trees	Classification/ Regression	Canonical Correlation Analysis	Feature extraction
Random Forests	Classification/Regression	Feed Forward Nearal Network	Regression/Classification/ Clustering/Feature extraction
Begging	Classification/Regression		
One-class Support Vector Machines	Anomaly detection		

$$p(t=e \mid x_i K) = \frac{1}{K}\sum_{i \in N_{i(x)}} \mathbf{1}(t_i = e),$$

$$y = \arg\max_c p(t=c \mid x_i K) \tag{1}$$

i.e. the input vector x will be labeled by the mode of its neighbors' labels One limitation of KNN is that it requires storing the entire training set, which makes KNN unable to scale large data sets. In Ref, authours have addressed thisissue by constructing atree-based searchwith some one-off computation. Moreover,there existsan online version of KNN calcification. It is worth noting that KNN can also be used for regression task.

6.12.2 Naive Bayes

Given a new, unseen data point (input vector) z = (z1,.....,zM), naive Bayes classifiers, which are a family of probabilistic classifiers. Classify z based on applying Bayes' theorem with the "naive" assumption of independence between the features (attributes) of z given theclass variable t. By applying the Bayes/theorem we have

$$p(t = c \mid z_1,\ldots,z_M) = \frac{p(z_1,\ldots z_M \mid t=c)p(t=c)}{p(z_1,\ldots z_M)} \tag{2}$$

and by applying the naive independence assumption and some simplifications we have

$$p(t = c \mid z_1,\ldots,z_M) \propto p(t=c)\prod_j^M p(z_j \mid t=c) \tag{3}$$

Therefore, the form of the classification task is

$$\mathbf{y} = \mathbf{arg}\ \underset{c}{max} p(t=c)\prod_{j}^{M} p(z_j \mid t=c) \tag{4}$$

where y denotes the predicted class label for z. The different naive bayes classifiers use different approaches and distributions to estimate $p(t = c)$ and $p(z_j \mid t = c)$.

Naive Bayes classifiers require a small number of data points to be trained, can deal with high-dimensionl data points, and are fast and highly scalable, Moreover, they are a popular model for applications such as spam filtering text categorization and automatic medical diagnosis.

6.12.6 Support machine

The classical Support Vector Machines (SVMs) are non-probabilistic, binary classifiers that aim at finding the dividing hyperplane wich separates both classes of the training set with the maximum margin. Then, the predicted label of a new, unseen data point, is determined based on which side of the hyperplane if falls. First, we discuss the linear SVM that finds a hyperplane, which is a linear function of the input variable. To formulate the problem, we denote the normal vector to the hyperplane by w and the parameter for controlling the offset of the hyperplane from the origin along its normal vector by b. Moreover, in order to ensure that SVMs can deal with outliers in the data, we introduce variable e_i, that is, a *slack variable,* for every training point x_i that gives the distance of how far this training point violates the margin in the units of $|w|$. This binary linear classification task in described using a constrained optimization problem of the form

$$\begin{aligned} &\underset{w.b.\xi}{\mathbf{min}\, imize}\, f(w,b,\xi) \qquad \frac{1}{2} w^T w + C \sum\nolimits_{i=1}^{n} \xi_i \\ &\text{subject to } y_i\ (w^T x_i + b) - 1 + \zeta_i \geq 0 = 1, \ldots, n, \\ &\qquad\qquad\qquad\qquad\qquad \zeta_i \geq 0 = 1, \ldots, n, \end{aligned} \tag{5}$$

where parameter C > 0 determines how heavily a violation is punished. It should be noted that although here we used L_1 norm for the penalty term $\sum\nolimits_{i=1}^{n} \xi_i$ there exist other penalty terms such as L_2 norm which should be chosen with respect to the needs of the application. Moreover, parameter C is a hyperparameter which can be chosed via cross-validation or bayesian optimization. To solve the constrained optimization problem of equation (5), there are various techniques such as quadratic programming optimization, sequential minimal optimization, and P-pack SVM. One important property of SVMs is that the resulting classifier only uses a few training points, which are called support vectors, to classify a new data point. In addition to performing linear classification, SVMs can perform a non-linear classification which finds a hyperplane that is a non-linear function fo the input variable. To do so, we implicity map an input varible into high-dimenstonal feature spaces, a process which is called kernel trick. In addition to performing binary classification. SVMs can perform multiclass classification. There are various ways to do so, such sa One-vs-all (OVA) SVM, All-vs-all(AVA) SVM, Structured SVM, and the Weston and Watkins version.

SVMs are among the best off-theshelf, supervised learning models that are capable of effectively dealing with high-dimensional data sets and are efficient regarding memory usage due to the employment of support vectors for prediction. One significant drawback of this model is that it does not directly provide probablity estimates. When given a solved SVM model, its parameters are difficult to interpret. SVMsare of use in many real-world applications such as hand-written character recognition, image classification, and protein classification.

6.14 RESEARCH TRENDS AND OPEN ISSUES

Data analysis have a significant contribution to IoT; therefore to applied a full potential of analysis to extract new insights from data, IoT must overcome some major problems. These problems can be categorized in three different types.

6.14.1 Iot Data Characteristics

Because the data are the basis of extracting knowledge, it is vital to have high quality information. This condition can affect the accuracy of knowledge extraction in a direct manner. Since IoT produces high volume, fast velocity, and varieties of data, preserving the data quality is a hard and challenging task. Although many solutions have been and are being introduced to solve these problems, none of them can handle all aspects of data characteristics in an accurate manner because of the distributed nature of Big Data management solutions and real-time processing platforms. The abstraction of IoT data is low, that is, the data that comes from different resources in IoT are mostly of raw data and not sufficient enough for analysis. A wide variety of solutions are proposed, while most of them need further improvements. For instance, semantic technologies tend to enhance the abstraction of IoT data through annotation algorithms, while they need more efforts to overcome its velocity and volume.

6.14.2 Iot Applications

IoT applications have different categories according to their unique attributions and features. Certain issues should be proposed in running data analysis in IoT applications in an accurate manner. First, the privacy of the collected data is very critical, since data collection process can include personal or critical business data, which is inevitable to solve the privacy issues. Second, according to the vast number of resources and simple-designed hardware in IoT, it is vital to consider security parameters like network security, data encryption, etc. Otherwise, by ignoring the security in design and implementation, an infected network of IoT devices can cause a crisis.

6.14.3 Iot Data Analytics Algorithms

According to the smart data characteristics, analytic algorithms should be able to handle Big Data, that is, IoT needs algorithms that can analyze the data which comes from a variety of sources in real time. Many attempts are made to address this issue. For example, deep learning algorithms, evolutionized form of neural networks can reach to a high accuracy rate if they have enough data and time. Deep learning algorithms can be easily influenced by the smart noisy data, furthermore, neural network based algorithms lack interpretation, this is, data scientists can not understand the reasons for the model results. In the same manner, semi-supervised algorithms which model the small amount of labelled data with a large amount of unlabeled data can assist IoT data analytics as well.

6.14.4 Conclusions

IoT consists of a vast number of devices with varieties that are connected to each other and transmit huge amounts of data. The Smart City is one of the most important applications of IoT and provides different services in domains like energy, mobility, and urban planning. These services can be enhanced and optimized by analyzing the smart data collected from these areas. In order to extract knowledge from collected data, many data analytic algorithms can be applied. Choosing a proper algorithm for specific IoT and Smart City application is an important issue. In this article, many IoT data analytic studies are reviewed to address this issue. Here three facts should be considered in applying data analytic algorithms to smart data. The first fact is that different applications in IoT and smart cities have their characteristics as the number of devices and types of the data that they generate; the second fact is that the generated data have specific features that should be realized. The third fact is that the taxonomy of the algorithms is another important point in applying data analysis to smart data. The findings in this article make the choice of proper algorithm for a particular problem easy. The analytic algorithms are of eight categories, described in detail. This is followed by reviewing application specifics of Smart City use cases. The data characteristics and quality of smart data are described in detail. In the discussion section, how the data characteristics and application specifics can lead to choosing a proper data analytic algorithms is reviewed. In the future trend section the recent issues and the future path for research in the field of smart data analytics are discussed

References

1. Miao Wu et. al., "Research on the architecture of Internet of things", in the proceedings of 3rd International Conference on Advanced Computer Theory and Engineering, 20-22 August, 2012, Beijing, China.
2. Brown, Eric (20 September 2016). "21 Open Source Projects for IoT". Linux.com. Retrieved 23 October 2016.
3. "Internet of Things Global Standards Initiative". ITU. Retrieved 26 June 2015.
4. http://www.faz.net/aktuell/wirtschaft/diginomics/grosse-internationale-allianz-gegen-cyber-attacken-15451953-p2.html?printPagedArticle=true#pageIndex_1.
5. Nordrum, Amy (18 August 2016). "Popular Internet of Things Forecast of 50 Billion Devices by 2020 Is Outdated". IEEE.
6. Hsu, Chin-Lung; Lin, Judy Chuan-Chuan (2016). "An empirical examination of consumer adoption of Internet of Things services: Network externalities and concern for information privacy perspectives". Computers in Human Behavior. 62: 516–527. doi:10.1016/j.chb.2016.04.023.

7. "Internet of Things: Science Fiction or Business Fact?" (PDF). Harvard Business Review. November 2014. Retrieved 23 October 2016.
8. Vermesan, Ovidiu; Friess, Peter (2013). Internet of Things: Converging Technologies for Smart Environments and Integrated Ecosystems (PDF). Aalborg, Denmark: River Publishers. ISBN 978-87-92982-96-4.
9. Santucci, Gérald. "The Internet of Things: Between the Revolution of the Internet and the Metamorphosis of Objects" (PDF). European Commission Community Research and Development Information Service. Retrieved 23 October 2016.
10. Mattern, Friedemann; Floerkemeier, Christian. "From the Internet of Computers to the Internet of Things" (PDF). ETH Zurich. Retrieved 23 October 2016.
11. Lindner, Tim (13 July 2015). "The Supply Chain: Changing at the Speed of Technology". Connected World. Retrieved 18 September 2015.
12. "Molluscan eye". Retrieved 26 June 2015.
13. Erlich, Yaniv (2015). "A vision for ubiquitous sequencing". Genome Research. 25 (10): 1411–1416. doi:10.1101/gr.191692.115. ISSN 1088-9051. PMC 4579324/. PMID 26430149.
14. Wigmore, I. (June 2014). "Internet of Things (IoT)". TechTarget.
15. Noto La Diega, Guido; Walden, Ian (1 February 2016). "Contracting for the 'Internet of Things': Looking into the Nest". Queen Mary School of Law Legal Studies Research Paper No. 219/2016. SSRN 2725913/.
16. Nordrum, Amy (18 August 2016). "Popular Internet of Things Forecast of 50 Billion Devices by 2020 Is Outdated". IEEE.
17. ohammadi, Mehdi; Al-Fuqaha, Ala; Sorour, Sameh; Guizani, Mohsen (2017). "Deep Learning for IoT Big Data and Streaming Analytics: A Survey". arXiv:1712.04301/ [cs.NI].
18. Mohammadi, Mehdi; Al-Fuqaha, Ala (2018). "Enabling cognitive smart cities using big data and machine learning: Approaches and challenges". IEEE Communications Magazine.
19. Alippi, C. (2014). Intelligence for Embedded Systems. Springer Verlag. ISBN 978-3-319-05278-6.
20. Rafiullah Khan, Sarmad Ullah Khan, Rifaqat Zaheer, and Shahid Khan, "Future Internet: The Internet of Things Architecture,Possible Applications and Key Challenges", in the proceedings of 10th International Conference on Frontiers of Information Technology, Islamabad, Pakistan, 17-19 December, 2012.
21. https://www.linkedin.com/pulse/why-iot-needs-fog-computing-ahmed-banafa?trk=mp-author-card.
22. http://iot.ieee.org/newsletter/january-2017/iot-and-blockchain-convergence-benefits-and-challenges.html.

23. Y. Shi, G. Ding, H. Wang, H.E. Roman, S. Lu The fog computing service for healthcare Future Information and Communication Technologies for Ubiquitous HealthCare (Ubi-HealthTech), 2015 2nd International Symposium on, IEEE (2015), pp. 1-5 CrossRefView Record in Scopus.
24. F. Ramalho, A. Neto, K. Santos, N. Agoulmine, et al. Enhancing ehealth smart applications: a fog-enabled approach 2015 17th International Conference on E-health Networking, Application & Services (HealthCom), IEEE (2015), pp. 323-328 CrossRefView Record in Scopus.
25. A. Joakar, A Methodology for Solving Problems with Datascience for Internet of Things, DataScience for Internet of Things.
26. Shuai Zhang et. al., "Cloud Computing Research and Development Trend", in the proceedings of International Conference on Future Networks, 22-24 Jan., 2010, Sanya, China.
27. Y. Jadeja, et. al., "Cloud Computing — Concepts, Architecture and Challenges", in the proceedings of International Conference on Computing Electronics and Electrical Technologies, 21-22 March, 2012, Nagercoil, India.
28. L. Wang, R. Ranjan Processing distributed internet of things data in clouds.

    IEEE Cloud Comput., 2 (1) (2015), pp. 76-80 CrossRefView Record in Scopus.
29. Minqi Zhou et. al., "Services in the Cloud Computing Era: A Survey", in the proceedings of 4th International Universal Communications Symposium, 18-19 October, 2010, Beijing, China.
30. W Ma et. al., "The Survey and Research on Application of Cloud Computing", in the proceedings of 7th International Conference on Computerl Science and Education, 02-04 November, 2012, Wuyishan Mountain, China.
31. Jayavardhana Gubbi, Rajkumar Buyya, Slaven Marusic, and Marimuthu Palaniswami, "Internet of Things (IoT): A Vision, Architectural Elements, and Future Directions", Technical Report CLOUDS-TR-2012-2, July 2012.
32. A. Papageorgiou, M. Zahn, E. Kovacs.

    Efficient auto-configuration of energy-related parameters in cloud-based iot platforms
33. Cloud Networking (CloudNet), 2014 IEEE 3rd International Conference on, IEEE (2014), pp. 236-241, CrossRefView Record in Scopus.
34. Gerd Kortuem, Fahim Kawsar, Daniel Fitton, and Vasughi Sundramoorthi, "Smart Objects and Building Blocks of Internet of Things", IEEE Internet Computing Journal, volume 14, issue 1, pp. 44-51, Jan.-Feb., 2010.
35. Dieter Uckelamann, Mark Harrison, and Floria Michahelles, "Architecting the Internet of Things," Springer-Verlag Berlin Heidelberg, 2011.
36. D. Barber, Bayesian Reasoning and Machine Learning, Cambridge University Press (2012).

37. C.M. Bishop, Pattern Recognition and Machine Learning, Springer (2006).

38. K.P. Murphy, Machine Learning: a Probabilistic Perspective, MIT press (2012).

39. I.G.Y. Bengio, A. Courville, Deep Learning, Book in Preparation for MIT Press (2016).

40. T. Cover, P. Hart, Nearest neighbor pattern classification,IEEE Trans. Inf. Theory, 13 (1) (1967), pp. 21-27.

41. CrossRefView Record in Scopus39] H.V. Jagadish, B.C. Ooi, K.-L. Tan, C. Yu, R. Zhang, Idistance: an adaptive b+-tree based indexing method for nearest neighbor search ACM Trans. Database Syst. (TODS), 30 (2) (2005), pp. 364-397.
CrossRefView Record in Scopus.

42. H. Zhang, The optimality of naive bayes, AA, 1 (2) (2004), p. 3, ArticleDownload PDFCrossRefView Record in Scopus.

43. C. Cortes, V. Vapnik, Support-vector networks,Mach. Learn., 20 (3) (1995), pp. 273-297, CrossRefView Record in Scopus.

Annexure 1

WOKING WITH R PROGRAMMING LANGUAGE

1. THE R ENVIRONMENT

R is a programming language and software environment for statistical analysis, graphics representation and reporting. The name is partly based on the (first) names of the first two R authors (Robert Gentleman and Ross Ihaka), and partly a play on the name of the Bell Labs language 'S'

R is an integrated suite of software facilities for data manipulation, calculation and graphical display. Among other things it has

- an effective data handling and storage facility,
- a suite of operators for calculations on arrays, in particular matrices,
- a large, coherent, integrated collection of intermediate tools for data analysis,
- graphical facilities for data analysis and display either directly at the computer or on hardcopy, and
- a well developed, simple and effective programming language (called 'S') which includes conditionals, loops, user defined recursive functions and input and output facilities. (Indeed most of the system supplied functions are themselves written in the S language.)

R can be regarded as an implementation of the S language which was developed at Bell Laboratories by Rick Becker, John Chambers and Allan Wilks, and also forms the basis of the S-Plus systems.

2. R AND STATISTICS

Many people use R as a *statistics system*. We prefer to think of it of an environment within which many classical and modern statistical techniques have been implemented. A few of these are built into the base R environment, but many are supplied as packages. There are about 25 packages supplied with R (called "standard" and "recommended" packages) and many more are available through the CRAN family of Internet sites (via https://CRAN.R-project.org) and elsewhere

2.1 Getting Help with Functions and Features

R has an inbuilt help facility similar to the man facility of UNIX. To get more information on any specific named function, for example solve, the command is

```
> help(solve)
```

An alternative is

```
> ?solve
```

On most R installations help is available in HTML format by running

```
> help.start()
```

which will launch a Web browser that allows the help pages to be browsed with hyperlinks. On UNIX, subsequent help requests are sent to the HTML-based help system.

R Console

```
> help.start()
starting httpd help server ... done
If nothing happens, you should open
'http://127.0.0.1:15160/doc/html/index.html' yourself
>
```

At beginning the R console shall look like :

R Console

```
R version 3.4.3 (2017-11-30) -- "Kite-Eating Tree"
Copyright (C) 2017 The R Foundation for Statistical Computing
Platform: i386-w64-mingw32/i386 (32-bit)

R is free software and comes with ABSOLUTELY NO WARRANTY.
You are welcome to redistribute it under certain conditions.
Type 'license()' or 'licence()' for distribution details.

R is a collaborative project with many contributors.
Type 'contributors()' for more information and
'citation()' on how to cite R or R packages in publications.

Type 'demo()' for some demos, 'help()' for on-line help, or
'help.start()' for an HTML browser interface to help.
Type 'q()' to quit R.

>
```

It ends with a command prompt > after which you can enter command linewise. Aftereach line you have to press Enter key.To start learning programming for statistical experience, first clear the screen by using clear screen command from **Edit** menu of console and by clicking the **Clear Screen** option.

Interacting with R. Unlike languages like C, Fortran, or Java, R is an interactive programming langauge. This means that R works interactively, using a question-and-answer model:

- Start R
- Type a command and press Enter
- R executes this command (often printing the result)
- R then waits for more input
- Type q() to exit

Here are some simple examples:

```
> 2 + 2
[1] 4
```

This means that you have asked R to add two constants 2 and two, and R has given the answer as [1] 4 . [1] indicates line # 1 and 4 is the answer.

```
> exp(-3) ## exponential function
[1] 0.04978707
> log(100, base = 10)
```

R Console

```
> 2+2
[1] 4
> exp(-3) ## exponential function
[1] 0.04978707
>  log(100, base = 10)
[1] 2
>  log(1000, base = 10)
[1] 3
> |
```

Enter Following Command

```
➤ Runif(10)
```

The last command generates ten random variables; the result (which is printed) is a vector of 10 numbers. exp(), log(), and runif() are functions.

R features very strong graphics capabilities. The simplest way to produce plots is to use the plot() function. We will learn more about graphics in a different tutorial.

Enter following at command prompt.

```
> plot(runif(10))
```

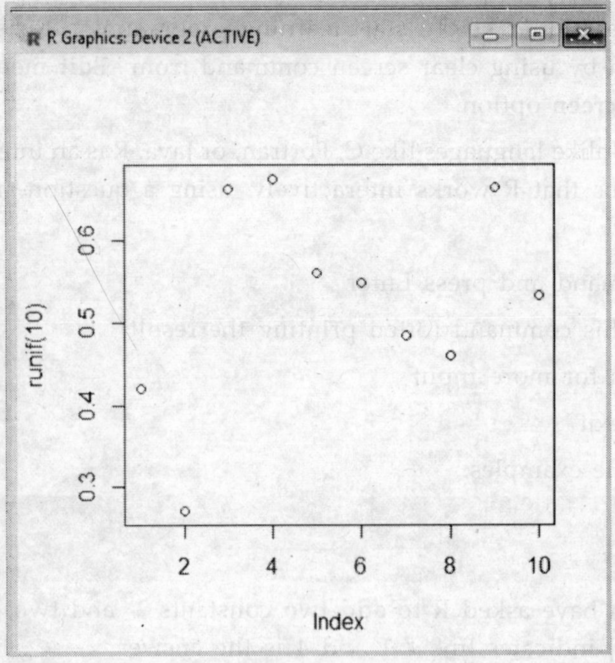

2.2 Variables

As in other programming languages, R has symbolic variables which can be assigned values. Assignment is done using the '<-' operator. The more C-like '=' also works (with some exceptions).

We can write

```
> x = 2 or
> x <- 2
```

Both have the same meaning

```
> x + x
[1] 4
> y = x + 3
> y
[1] 5
```

Entering strings

```
> s <- "this is a character string"
> s [1] "this is a character string"
```

R Console

```
> x=2
> x^2
[1] 4
> x+x
[1] 4
> x^.5
[1] 1.414214
> y =x+3
> y
[1] 5
> s <- "this is a character string"
> s
[1] "this is a character string"
> s = "this is a character string"
> s
[1] "this is a character string"
> |
```

2.3 Vectors and Assignment

R operates on named data structures. The simplest such structure is the numeric vector, which is a single entity consisting of an ordered collection of numbers. To set up a vector named x, say, consisting of five numbers, namely 10.4, 5.6, 3.1, 6.4 and 21.7, use the R command

```
> x <- c(10.4, 5.6, 3.1, 6.4, 21.7)
```

This is an assignment statement using the function c() which in this context can take an arbitrary number of vector arguments and whose value is a vector got by concatenating its arguments end to end.A number occurring by itself in an expression is taken as a vector of length one. Notice that the assignment operator ('<-'), which consists of the two characters "<" i.e. less Than and '-' ("minus") occurring strictly side-by-side and it 'points' to the object receiving the value of the expression. In most contexts the '=' operator can be used as an alternative.

Assignment can also be made using the function assign(). An equivalent way of making the same assignment as above is with:

```
> assign("x", c(10.4, 5.6, 3.1, 6.4, 21.7))
```

The usual operator, <-, can be thought of as a syntactic short-cut to this. Assignments can also be made in the other direction, using the obvious change in the assignment operator. So the same assignment could be made using

```
> c(10.4, 5.6, 3.1, 6.4, 21.7) -> x
```

The further assignment

```
> y <- c(x, 0, x)
```

would create a vector y with 11 entries consisting of two copies of x with a zero in the middle place.

2.4 Vectorized Arithmetic

The elementary data types in R are all vectors; even the scalar variables we defined above are stored as vectors of length one. The c(...) construct can be used to create vectors:

```
> weight <- c(60, 72, 57, 90, 95, 72)
> weight [1] 60 72 57 90 95 72
```

To generate a vector of regularly spaced numbers, use

```
> seq(0, 1, length = 11) [1] 0.0 0.1 0.2 0.3 0.4 0.5 0.6 0.7 0.8 0.9 1.0
> 1:10 [1] 1 2 3 4 5 6 7 8 9 10
```

The c() function can be used to combine vectors as well as scalars, e.g.,

```
> x <- seq(0, 1, length = 6)
> c(x, 1:10, 100) [1] 0.0 0.2 0.4 0.6 0.8 1.0 1.0 2.0 3.0 4.0 5.0 6.0
[13] 7.0 8.0 9.0 10.0 100.0
```

Common arithmetic operations (including +, -, *, /, ^) and mathematical functions (e.g. sin(), cos(), log()) work element-wise on vectors, and produce another vector:

```
> height <- c(1.75, 1.80, 1.65, 1.90, 1.74, 1.91)
> height^2 [1] 3.0625 3.2400 2.7225 3.6100 3.0276 3.6481
> bmi <- weight / height^2
> bmi [1] 19.59184 22.22222 20.93664 24.93075 31.37799 19.73630
> log(bmi) [1] 2.975113 3.101093 3.041501 3.216102 3.446107 2.982460
```

When two vectors are not of equal length, the shorter one is recycled. For example, The following adds 0 to all the odd elements and 2 to all the even elements of 1:10:

```
> 1:10 + c(0, 2) [1] 1 4 3 6 5 8 7 10 9 12
```

These simple vectorized arithmetic rules are among the most powerful design features of the R language.

3. GENERATING REGULAR SEQUENCES

R has a number of facilities for generating commonly used sequences of numbers. For example 1:10 is the vector c(1, 2, ..., 9, 10). The colon operator has high priority within an expression, so, for example 2*1:10 is the vector c(2, 4, ..., 8, 10).

```
> 1:10
 [1]  1  2  3  4  5  6  7  8  9 10
> 10:1
 [1] 10  9  8  7  6  5  4  3  2  1
> 2*1:10
 [1]  2  4  6  8 10 12 14 16 18 20
> |
```

The function seq() is a more general facility for generating sequences. It has five arguments, only some of which may be specified in any one call. The first two arguments, if given, specify the beginning and end of the sequence, and if these are the only two arguments given the result is the same as the colon operator. That is seq(2,10) is the same vector as 2:10.

Arguments to seq(), and to many other R functions, can also be given in named form, in which case the order in which they appear is irrelevant. The first two arguments may be named from=value and to=value; thus seq(1,30), seq(from=1, to=30) and seq(to=30, from=1) are all the same as 1:30. The next two arguments to seq() may be named by=value and length=value, which specify a step size and a length for the sequence respectively. If neither of these is given, the default by=1 is assumed.

For example

```
> seq(-5, 5, by=.2) -> s3
```

generates in s3 the vector c(-5.0, -4.8, -4.6, ..., 4.6, 4.8, 5.0).

```
R Console
> seq(-5, 5, by=.2) -> s3
> s3
 [1] -5.0 -4.8 -4.6 -4.4 -4.2 -4.0 -3.8 -3.6 -3.4 -3.2 -3.0 -2.8 -2.6 -2.4 -2.2
[16] -2.0 -1.8 -1.6 -1.4 -1.2 -1.0 -0.8 -0.6 -0.4 -0.2  0.0  0.2  0.4  0.6  0.8
[31]  1.0  1.2  1.4  1.6  1.8  2.0  2.2  2.4  2.6  2.8  3.0  3.2  3.4  3.6  3.8
[46]  4.0  4.2  4.4  4.6  4.8  5.0
> |
```

Similarly

```
> s4 <- seq(length=51, from=-5, by=.2)
```

We can generate a series of square roots by a command like

```
>sqrt(5:10)
```

```
> sqrt(5)
[1] 2.236068
> sqrt(5:10)
[1] 2.236068 2.449490 2.645751 2.828427 3.000000 3.162278
> |
```

A related function is rep() which can be used for replicating an object in various complicated ways. The simplest form is

```
> s5 <- rep(x=5, times=5)
```

which will put five copies of x end-to-end in s5. Another useful version is > s6 <- rep(x, each=5) which repeats each element of x five times before moving on to the next.

```
> s5 <- rep(x=5, times=5)
> s5
[1] 5 5 5 5 5
> |
```

Scalars from Vectors.

Many functions summarize a data vector by producing a scalar from a vector, e.g.,

```
> sum(weight)
[1] 446
> length(weight)
[1] 6
> avg.weight <- mean(weight)
> avg.weight
[1] 74.33333
```

Quantiles can be computed using the quantile() function. IQR() computes the inter-quartile range.

```
> xquants <- quantile(x)
> xquants
```

```
R Console
> x <- rnorm(100)
> xquants <- quantile(x)
> xquants
         0%         25%         50%         75%        100%
-2.35449065 -0.61522700  0.07212228  0.64554498  2.22899007
> xquants[4] - xquants[2]
     75%
1.260772
> IQR(x)
[1] 1.260772
>  quantile(x, probs = c(0.2, 0.4, 0.6, 0.8))
       20%        40%        60%        80%
-0.7398870 -0.2850785  0.2325715  0.7730473
> |
```

SQL

SQL stands for structured query language. It is one of the most widely used languages for extracting data from databases in traditional data warehouses and big data technologies. In order to demonstrate the basics of SQL we will be working with examples. In order to focus on the language itself, we will be using SQL inside R. In terms of writing SQL code this is exactly as would be done in a database.

The core of SQL are three statements: SELECT, FROM and WHERE. The following examples make use of the most common use cases of SQL. Navigate to the folder **bda/part2/SQL_introduction** and open the **SQL_introduction.Rproj** file. Then open the 01_select.R script. In order to write SQL code in R we need to install the **sqldf** package as demonstrated in the following code.

```
# Install the sqldf package
install.packages('sqldf')
# load the library
library('sqldf')
library(nycflights13)
# We will be working with the fligths dataset in order to introduce SQL
# Let's take a look at the table
str(flights)
# Classes 'tbl_d', 'tbl' and 'data.frame': 336776 obs. of  16 variables:
# $ year     : int  2013 2013 2013 2013 2013 2013 2013 2013 2013 2013 ...
# $ month    : int  1 1 1 1 1 1 1 1 1 1 ...
# $ day      : int  1 1 1 1 1 1 1 1 1 1 ...
# $ dep_time : int  517 533 542 544 554 554 555 557 557 558 ...
# $ dep_delay: num  2 4 2 -1 -6 -4 -5 -3 -3 -2 ...
# $ arr_time : int  830 850 923 1004 812 740 913 709 838 753 ...
# $ arr_delay: num  11 20 33 -18 -25 12 19 -14 -8 8 ...
# $ carrier  : chr  "UA" "UA" "AA" "B6" ...
# $ tailnum  : chr  "N14228" "N24211" "N619AA" "N804JB" ...
# $ flight   : int  1545 1714 1141 725 461 1696 507 5708 79 301 ...
# $ origin   : chr  "EWR" "LGA" "JFK" "JFK" ...
# $ dest     : chr  "IAH" "IAH" "MIA" "BQN" ...
# $ air_time : num  227 227 160 183 116 150 158 53 140 138 ...
# $ distance : num  1400 1416 1089 1576 762 ...
# $ hour     : num  5 5 5 5 5 5 5 5 5 5 ...
# $ minute   : num  17 33 42 44 54 54 55 57 57 58 ...
```

The select statement is used to retrieve columns from tables and do calculations on them. The simplest SELECT statement is demonstrated in **ej1**. We can also create new variables as shown in **ej2**.

```
### SELECT statement
ej1 = sqldf("
  SELECT
  dep_time
  ,dep_delay
  ,arr_time
  ,carrier
  ,tailnum
  FROM
  flights
")
head(ej1)
#     dep_time  dep_delay   arr_time   carrier  tailnum
# 1      517        2           830        UA     N14228
# 2      533        4           850        UA     N24211
# 3      542        2           923        AA     N619AA
# 4      544       -1          1004        B6     N804JB
# 5      554       -6           812        DL     N668DN
# 6      554       -4           740        UA     N39463
# In R we can use SQL with the sqldf function. It works exactly the same as in
a database
# The data.frame (in this case flights) represents the table we are querying
and goes in the FROM statement
# We can also compute new variables in the select statement using the
syntax:
# old_variables as new_variable
ej2 = sqldf("
  SELECT
  arr_delay - dep_delay as gain,
  carrier
  FROM
  flights
")
ej2[1:5, ]
```

cont.

```
#       gain    carrier
# 1     9       UA
# 2     16      UA
# 3     31      AA
# 4     -17     B6
# 5     -19     DL
```

One of the most common used features of SQL is the group by statement. This allows to compute a numeric value for different groups of another variable. Open the script 02_group_by.R.

```
### GROUP BY
# Computing the average
ej3 = sqldf("
  SELECT
   avg(arr_delay) as mean_arr_delay,
   avg(dep_delay) as mean_dep_delay,
   carrier
   FROM
   flights
   GROUP BY
   carrier
")
#     mean_arr_delay   mean_dep_delay      carrier
# 1        7.3796692        16.725769         9E
# 2        0.3642909         8.586016         AA
# 3       -9.9308886         5.804775         AS
# 4        9.4579733        13.022522         B6
# 5        1.6443409         9.264505         DL
# 6       15.7964311        19.955390         EV
# 7       21.9207048        20.215543         F9
# 8       20.1159055        18.726075         FL
# 9       -6.9152047         4.900585         HA
# 10      10.7747334        10.552041         MQ
# 11      11.9310345        12.586207         OO
# 12       3.5580111        12.106073         UA
                                                        cont.
```

```
# 13     2.1295951          3.782418        US
# 14     1.7644644         12.869421        VX
# 15     9.6491199         17.711744        WN
# 16    15.5569853         18.996330        YV
# Other aggregations
ej4 = sqldf("
  SELECT
  avg(arr_delay) as mean_arr_delay,
  min(dep_delay) as min_dep_delay,
  max(dep_delay) as max_dep_delay,
  carrier
  FROM
  flights
  GROUP BY
  carrier
")
# We can compute the minimun, mean, and maximum values of a numeric value
ej4

#     mean_arr_delay   min_dep_delay max_dep_delay   carrier
# 1       7.3796692         -24            747          9E
# 2       0.3642909         -24           1014          AA
# 3      -9.9308886         -21            225          AS
# 4       9.4579733         -43            502          B6
# 5       1.6443409         -33            960          DL
# 6      15.7964311         -32            548          EV
# 7      21.9207048         -27            853          F9
# 8      20.1159055         -22            602          FL
# 9      -6.9152047         -16           1301          HA
# 10     10.7747334         -26           1137          MQ
# 11     11.9310345         -14            154          OO
# 12      3.5580111         -20            483          UA
# 13      2.1295951         -19            500          US
# 14      1.7644644         -20            653          VX
```

cont.

```
# 15      9.6491199          -13            471            WN
# 16     15.5569853          -16            387            YV
 ### We could be also interested in knowing how many observations each
carrier has
ej5 = sqldf("
  SELECT
  carrier, count(*) as count
  FROM
  flights
  GROUP BY
  carrier
")
ej5
#      carrier    count
# 1       9E      18460
# 2      AA       32729
# 3      AS       714
# 4      B6       54635
# 5      DL       48110
# 6      EV       54173
# 7      F9       685
# 8      FL       3260
# 9       HA      342
# 10      MQ      26397
# 11      OO      32
# 12      UA      58665
# 13      US      20536
# 14      VX      5162
# 15      WN      12275
# 16      YV      601
```

The most useful feature of SQL are joins. A join means that we want to combine table A and table B in one table using one column to match the values of both tables. There are different types of joins, in practical terms, to get started these will be the most useful ones: inner join and left outer join.

```
# Let's create two tables: A and B to demonstrate joins.
A = data.frame(c1 = 1:4, c2 = letters[1:4])
B = data.frame(c1 = c(2,4,5,6), c2 = letters[c(2:5)])
A
#        c1       c2
#         1        a
#         2        b
#         3        c
#         4        d
B
#        c1       c2
#         2        b
#         4        c
#         5        d
#         6        e
### INNER JOIN
 # This means to match the observations of the column we would join the
tables by.
inner = sqldf("
  SELECT
  A.c1, B.c2
  FROM
  A INNER JOIN B
  ON A.c1 = B.c1
")
# Only the rows that match c1 in both A and B are returned
inner
# c1 c2
#  2  b
#  4  c
### LEFT OUTER JOIN
# the left outer join, sometimes just called left join will return the
# first all the values of the column used from the A table
                                                                   cont.
```

```
left = sqldf("
  SELECT
   A.c1, B.c2
  FROM
   A LEFT OUTER JOIN B
   ON A.c1 = B.c1
")
# Only the rows that match c1 in both A and B are returned
left
#   c1   c2
#    1 <NA>
#    2    b
#    3 <NA>
#    4    c
```

4. CHARTS AND GRAPHS

The first approach to analyzing data is to visually analyze it. The objectives at doing this are normally finding relations between variables and univariate descriptions of the variables. We can divide these strategies as—

- Univariate analysis
- Multivariate analysis

5. UNIVARIATE GRAPHICAL METHODS

Univariate is a statistical term. In practice, it means we want to analyze a variable independently from the rest of the data. The plots that allow to do this efficiently are "

Box-Plots

Box-Plots are normally used to compare distributions. It is a great way to visually inspect if there are differences between distributions. We can see if there are differences between the price of diamonds for different cut.

```
 # We will be using the ggplot2 library for plotting
 library(ggplot2)
 data("diamonds")
  # We will be using the diamonds dataset to analyze distributions of numeric
variables
                                                                        cont.
```

```
head(diamonds)
#   carat cut       color clarity depth table  price    x     y     z
# 1 0.23  Ideal       E   SI2     61.5   55    326    3.95  3.98  2.43
# 2 0.21  Premium     E   SI1     59.8   61    326    3.89  3.84  2.31
# 3 0.23  Good        E   VS1     56.9   65    327    4.05  4.07  2.31
# 4 0.29  Premium     I   VS2     62.4   58    334    4.20  4.23  2.63
# 5 0.31  Good        J   SI2     63.3   58    335    4.34  4.35  2.75
# 6 0.24  Very Good   J   VVS2    62.8   57    336    3.94  3.96  2.48
### Box-Plots
p = ggplot(diamonds, aes(x = cut, y = price, fill = cut)) +
  geom_box-plot() +
  theme_bw()
print(p)
```

We can see in the plot there are differences in the distribution of diamonds price in different types of cut.

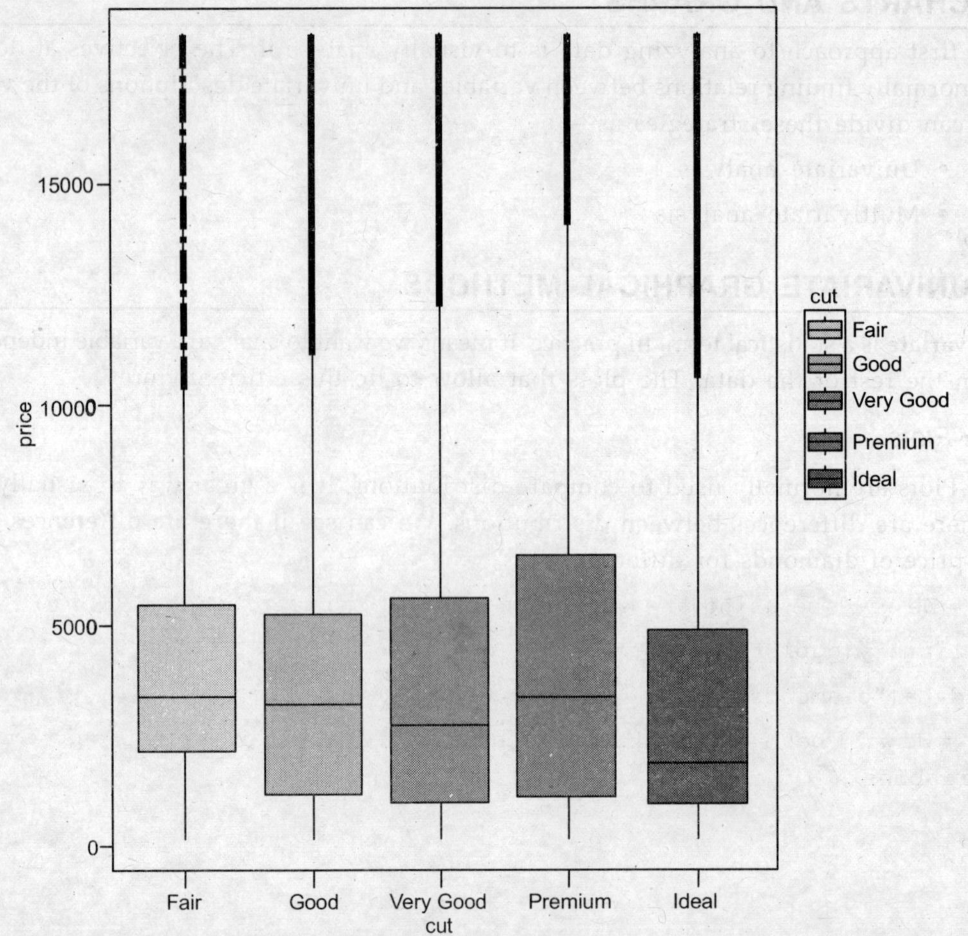

6. PLOTTING HISTOGRAMS

```
source('01_box_plots.R')

# We can plot histograms for each level of the cut factor variable using
facet_grid
p = ggplot(diamonds, aes(x = price, fill = cut)) +
  geom_histogram() +
  facet_grid(cut ~ .) +
  theme_bw()

p
# the previous plot doesn't allow to visuallize correctly the data because
of
the differences in scale
# we can turn this off using the scales argument of facet_grid

p = ggplot(diamonds, aes(x = price, fill = cut)) +
  geom_histogram() +
  facet_grid(cut ~ ., scales = 'free') +
  theme_bw()
p

png('02_histogram_diamonds_cut.png')
print(p)
dev.off()
The output of the above code will be as follows "
```

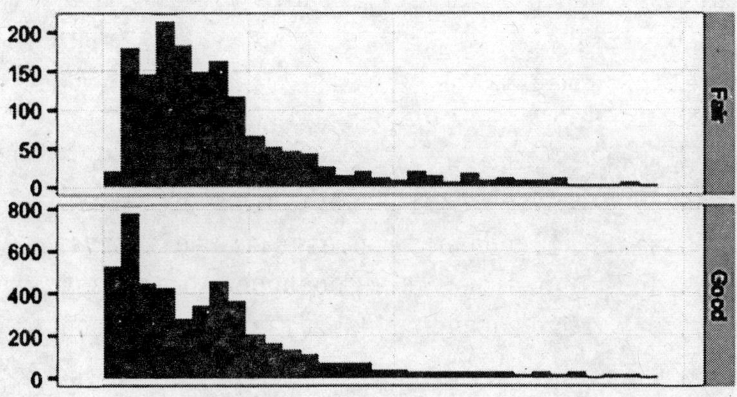

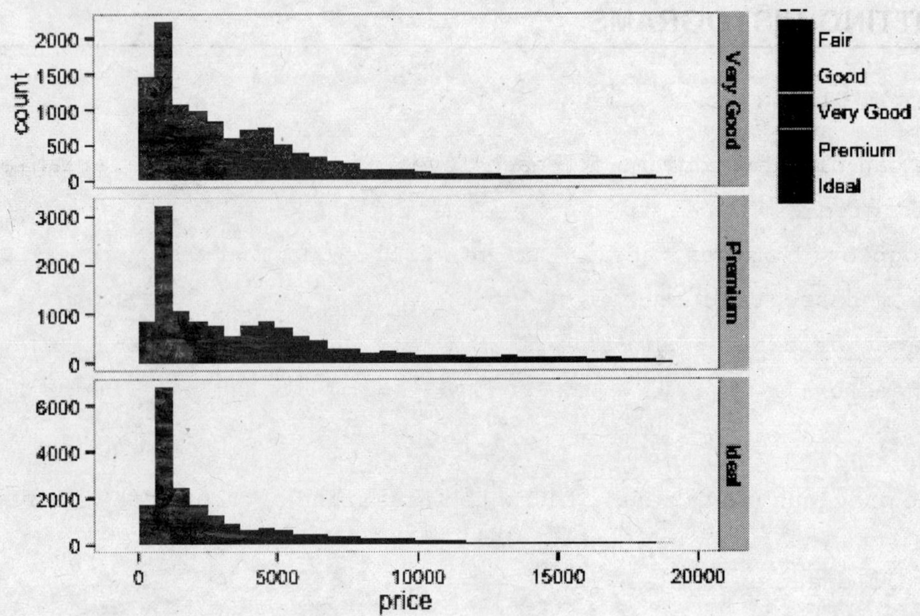

7. MULTIVARIATE GRAPHICAL METHODS

Multivariate graphical methods in exploratory data analysis have the objective of finding relationships among different variables. There are two ways to accomplish this that are commonly used: plotting a correlation matrix of numeric variables or simply plotting the raw data as a matrix of scatter plots.

In order to demonstrate this, we will use the diamonds dataset. To follow the code, open the script **bda/part2/charts/03_multivariate_analysis.R**.

```
library(ggplot2)
data(diamonds)
# Correlation matrix plots
keep_vars = c('carat', 'depth', 'price', 'table')
df = diamonds[, keep_vars]
# compute the correlation matrix
M_cor = cor(df)
#            carat        depth      price      table
# carat   1.00000000   0.02822431  0.9215913  0.1816175
# depth   0.02822431   1.00000000 -0.0106474 -0.2957785
# price   0.92159130  -0.01064740  1.0000000  0.1271339
# table   0.18161755  -0.29577852  0.1271339  1.0000000
# plots
heat-map(M_cor)
```

The code will produce the following output—

This is a summary, it tells us that there is a strong correlation between price and caret, and not much among the other variables.

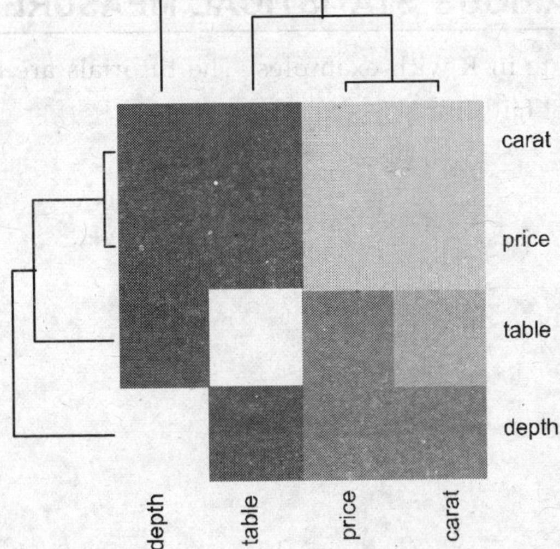

A correlation matrix can be useful when we have a large number of variables in which case plotting the raw data would not be practical. As mentioned, it is possible to show the raw data also—

```
library(GGally)
ggpairs(df)
```

We can see in the plot that the results displayed in the heat-map are confirmed, there is a 0.922 correlation between the price and carat variables.

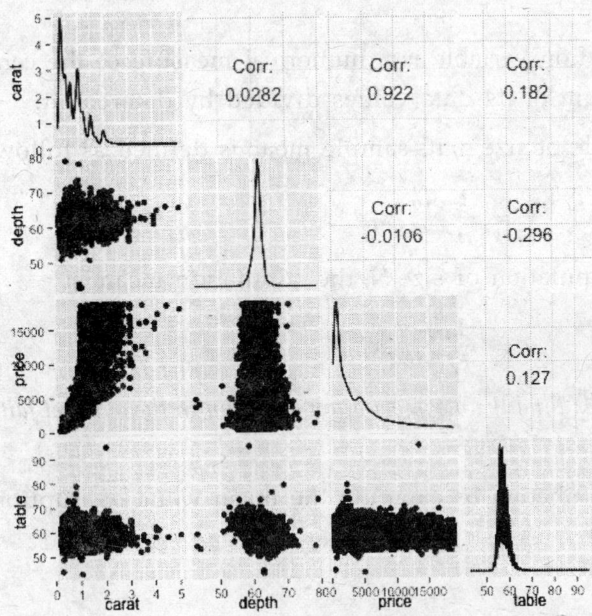

It is possible to visualize this relationship in the price-carat scatterplot located in the (3, 1) index of the scatterplot matrix.

8. CALCULATING VARIOUS STATISTICAL MEASURES USING R

We explain how to compute in R with examples. The tutorials are based on the previously discussed built-in data set faithful.

- Mean
- Median
- Quartile
- Percentile
- Range
- Interquartile Range
- Box Plot
- Variance
- Standard Deviation
- Covariance
- Correlation Coefficient
- Central Moment
- Skewness
- Kurtosis

8.1 Mean

The mean of an observation variable is a numerical measure of the central location of the data values. It is the sum of its data values divided by data count.

Hence, for a data sample of size n, its sample mean is defined as follows:

$$x = \frac{1}{n}\sum_{i=1}^{n} x_i$$

Similarly, for a data population of size N, the population mean is:

$$\mu = \frac{1}{N}\sum_{i=1}^{N} x_i$$

Example Annexure 1: *Find the mean eruption duration in the data set faithful.*

Solution:

We apply the mean function to compute the mean value of eruptions.

```
> duration = faithful$eruptions          # the eruption durations
> mean(duration)                         # apply the mean function
[1] 3.4878
> mean(waiting)                          # apply the mean function
[1] 3.4878
```

Answer

The mean eruption duration is 3.4878 minutes.

```
> mean(duration)                         # apply the mean function
[1] 3.487783
> mean(waiting)
[1] 70.89706
> |
```

8.2 Median

The median of an observation variable is the value at the middle when the data is sorted in ascending order. It is an ordinal measure of the central location of the data values.

Example Annexure 2: *Find the median of the eruption duration in the data set faithful.*

Solution:

We apply the median function to compute the median value of eruptions.

```
> duration = faithful$eruptions       # the eruption durations
> median(duration)                    # apply the median function
[1] 4
```

Answer

The median of the eruption duration is 4 minutes.

```
> median(duration)                    # apply the median function
[1] 4
>  median(waiting)                    # apply the median function
[1] 76
> |
```

8.3 Quartile

There are several quartiles of an observation variable. The first quartile, or lower quartile, is the value that cuts off the first 25% of the data when it is sorted in ascending order. The second quartile, or median, is the value that cuts off the first 50%. The third quartile, or upper quartile, is the value that cuts off the first 75%.

Example Annexure 3: *Find the quartiles of the eruption durations in the data set faithful.*

Solution:

We apply the quantile function to compute the quartiles of eruptions.

```
> duration = faithful$eruptions      # the eruption durations
>
   0%     25%     50%     75%    100%
1.6000 2.1627 4.0000 4.4543 5.1000
```

Answer

```
> quantile(duration)                    # apply the quantile function
     0%       25%      50%      75%     100%
1.60000 2.16275 4.00000 4.45425 5.10000
> quantile(waiting)                     # apply the quantile function
  0%  25%  50%  75% 100%
  43   58   76   82   96
> |
```

The first, second and third quartiles of the eruption duration are 2.1627, 4.0000 and 4.4543 minutes respectively.

```
> mean(duration)                        # apply the mean function
[1] 3.487783
> mean(waiting)
[1] 70.89706
> median(duration)                      # apply the median function
[1] 4
>  median(waiting)                      # apply the median function
[1] 76
> quantile(duration)                    # apply the quantile function
     0%      25%      50%      75%     100%
1.60000 2.16275 4.00000 4.45425 5.10000
> quantile(waiting)                     # apply the quantile function
  0%  25%  50%  75% 100%
  43   58   76   82   96
> quantile(duration, c(.31, .56, .95))
    31%      56%      95%
2.35017 4.11292 4.81700
```

8.4 Range

The range of an observation variable is the difference of its largest and smallest data values. It is a measure of how far apart the entire data spreads in value.

Range =Largest Value – Smallest Value

Example Annexure 4: *Find the range of the eruption duration in the data set faithful.*

Solution:

We apply the max and min function to compute the largest and smallest values of eruptions, then take the difference.

```
> duration = faithful$eruptions          # the eruption durations
> max(duration) ″ min(duration)         # apply the max and min functions
[1] 3.5
```

Answer

The range of the eruption duration is 3.5 minutes.

8.5 Box Plot

The box plot of an observation variable is a graphical representation based on its quartiles, as well as its smallest and largest values. It attempts to provide a visual shape of the data distribution.

Example Annexure 5: *Find the box plot of the eruption duration in the data set faithful.*

Solution:

We apply the boxplot function to produce the box plot of eruptions.

```
> duration = faithful$eruptions          # the eruption durations
> boxplot(duration, horizontal=TRUE)    # horizontal box plot
```

Answer

The box plot of the eruption duration is:

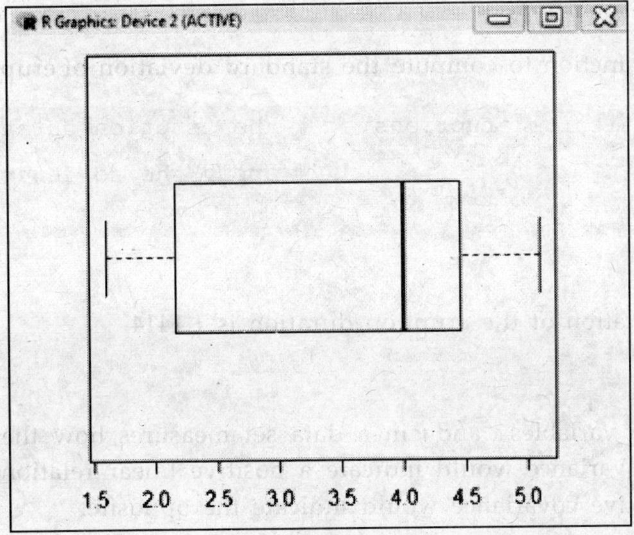

8.6 Variance

The variance is a numerical measure of how the data values is dispersed around the mean. In particular, the sample variance is defined as:

$$s^2 = \frac{1}{n-1}\sum_{i=1}^{n}(x_i - x)^2$$

Similarly, the population variance is defined in terms of the population mean ì and population size N:

$$\sigma^2 = \frac{1}{N}\sum_{i=1}^{N}(x_i - \mu)^2$$

Example Annexure 6: *Find the variance of the eruption duration in the data set faithful.*

Solution:

We apply the var function to compute the variance of eruptions.

```
> duration = faithful$eruptions     # the eruption durations
> var(duration)                     # apply the var function
[1] 1.3027
```

Answer

The variance of the eruption duration is 1.3027.

8.7 Standard Deviation

The standard deviation of an observation variable is the square root of its variance.

Example Annexure 7: *Find the standard deviation of the eruption duration in the data set faithful.*

Solution

We apply the sd function to compute the standard deviation of eruptions.

```
> duration = faithful$eruptions     # the eruption durations
> sd(duration)                      # apply the sd function
[1] 1.1414
```

Answer

The standard deviation of the eruption duration is 1.1414.

8.8 Covariance

The covariance of two variables *x* and *y* in a data set measures how the two are linearly related. A positive covariance would indicate a positive linear relationship between the variables, and a negative covariance would indicate the opposite.

The sample covariance is defined in terms of the sample means as:

$$s_{xy} = \frac{1}{n-1}\sum_{i=1}^{n}(x_i - \bar{x})(y_i - \bar{y})$$

Similarly, the population covariance is defined in terms of the population mean μ_x, μ_y as:

$$\sigma_{xy} = \frac{1}{N}\sum_{i=1}^{N}(x_i - \mu_x)(y_i - \mu_y)$$

Example Annexure 8: *Find the covariance of eruption duration and waiting time in the data set faithful. Observe if there is any linear relationship between the two variables.*

Solution:

We apply the cov function to compute the covariance of eruptions and waiting.

```
> duration = faithful$eruptions    # eruption durations
> waiting = faithful$waiting       # the waiting period
> cov(duration, waiting)           # apply the cov function
[1] 13.978
```

Answer

The covariance of eruption duration and waiting time is about 14. It indicates a positive linear relationship between the two variables.

8.9 Correlation Coefficient

The correlation coefficient of two variables in a data set equals to their covariance divided by the product of their individual standard deviations. It is a normalized measurement of how the two are linearly related.

Formally, the sample correlation coefficient is defined by the following formula, where s_x and s_y are the sample standard deviations, and s_{xy} is the sample covariance.

$$r_{xy} = \frac{s_{xy}}{s_x s_y}$$

Similarly, the population correlation coefficient is defined as follows, where σ_x and σ_y are the population standard deviations, and σ_{xy} is the population covariance.

$$p_{xu} = \frac{\sigma_{xy}}{\sigma_x \sigma_y}$$

If the correlation coefficient is close to 1, it would indicate that the variables are positively linearly related and the scatter plot falls almost along a straight line with positive slope. For –1, it indicates that the variables are negatively linearly related and the scatter plot almost falls along a straight line with negative slope. And for zero, it would indicate a weak linear relationship between the variables.

Example Annexure 9: *Find the correlation coefficient of eruption duration and waiting time in the data set faithful. Observe if there is any linear relationship between the variables.*

Solution:

We apply the cor function to compute the correlation coefficient of eruptions and waiting.

```
> duration = faithful$eruptions    # eruption durations
> waiting = faithful$waiting       # the waiting period
> cor(duration, waiting)           # apply the cor function
[1] 0.90081
```

Answer

The correlation coefficient of eruption duration and waiting time is 0.90081. Since it is rather close to 1, we can conclude that the variables are positively linearly related.

8.10 Central Moment

The kth central moment (or moment about the mean) of a data population is:

$$\mu_k = \frac{1}{N}\sum_{i=1}^{N}(x_i - \mu_x)^k$$

Similarly, the kth central moment of a data sample is:

$$m_k = \frac{1}{n}\sum_{i=1}^{n}(x_i - \bar{x})^k$$

In particular, the second central moment of a population is its variance.

Example Annexure 10: *Find the third central moment of eruption duration in the data set faithful.*

Solution:

We apply the function moment from the e1071 package. As it is not in the core R library, the package has to be installed and loaded into the R workspace.

```
> library(e1071)                        # load e1071
> duration = faithful$eruptions         # eruption durations
> moment(duration, order=3, center=TRUE)
[1] -0.6149
```

Answer

The third central moment of eruption duration is -0.6149.

8.11 Skewness

The skewness of a data population is defined by the following formula, where μ_2 and μ_3 are the second and third central moments.

$$\gamma_1 = \mu_3 / \mu_2^{3/2}$$

Intuitively, the skewness is a measure of symmetry. As a rule, negative skewness indicates that the mean of the data values is less than the median, and the data distribution is *left-skewed*. Positive skewness would indicate that the mean of the data values is larger than the median, and the data distribution is *right-skewed*.

Example Annexure 11: *Find the skewness of eruption duration in the data set faithful.*

Solution:

We apply the function skewness from the e1071 package to compute the skewness coefficient of eruptions. As the package is not in the core R library, it has to be installed and loaded into the R workspace.

```
> library(e1071)                          # load e1071
> duration = faithful$eruptions           # eruption durations
> skewness(duration)                      # apply the skewness function
[1] -0.41355
```

Answer

The skewness of eruption duration is -0.41355. It indicates that the eruption duration distribution is skewed towards the left.

8.12 Kurtosis

The kurtosis of a univariate population is defined by the following formula, where ì$_2$ and ì$_4$are respectively the second and fourth central moments.

$$\gamma_2 = \mu_4 / \mu_2^2 - 3$$

Intuitively, the *kurtosis* describes the *tail shape* of the data distribution. The normal_distribution has zero kurtosis and thus the standard tail shape. It is said to be mesokurtic. Negative kurtosis would indicate a *thin-tailed* data distribution, and is said to be platykurtic. Positive kurtosis would indicate a *fat-tailed* distribution, and is said to be leptokurtic.

Example Annexure 12: Find the kurtosis of eruption duration in the data set faithful.

Solution:

We apply the function kurtosis from the e1071 package to compute the kurtosis of eruptions. As the package is not in the core R library, it has to be installed and loaded into the R workspace.

```
> library(e1071)                          # load e1071
> duration = faithful$eruptions           # eruption durations
> kurtosis(duration)                      # apply the kurtosis function
[1] -1.5116
```

Answer

The kurtosis of eruption duration is -1.5116, which indicates that eruption duration distribution is platykurtic. This is consistent with the fact that its histogram is not bell-shaped.

Note : The default algorithm of the function kurtosis is based on the formula $g_2 = m_4/s^4 - 3$, where m_4 and s are the fourth central moment and sample standard deviation respectively.

```
> library(e1071)                        # load e1071
> help(kurtosis)
```

8.13 Examining the Distribution of a set of data

Given a (univariate) set of data we can examine its distribution in a large number of ways. The simplest is to examine the numbers. Two slightly different summaries are given by summary and fivenum and a display of the numbers by stem (a "stem and leaf" plot).

```
> attach(faithful)
> summary(eruptions)
```

Summary will be displayed on console. Now enter

```
> fivenum(eruptions)
[1] 1.6000 2.1585 4.0000 4.4585 5.1000
```

If you enter

```
> stem(eruptions)
```

Following shall be displayed on console.

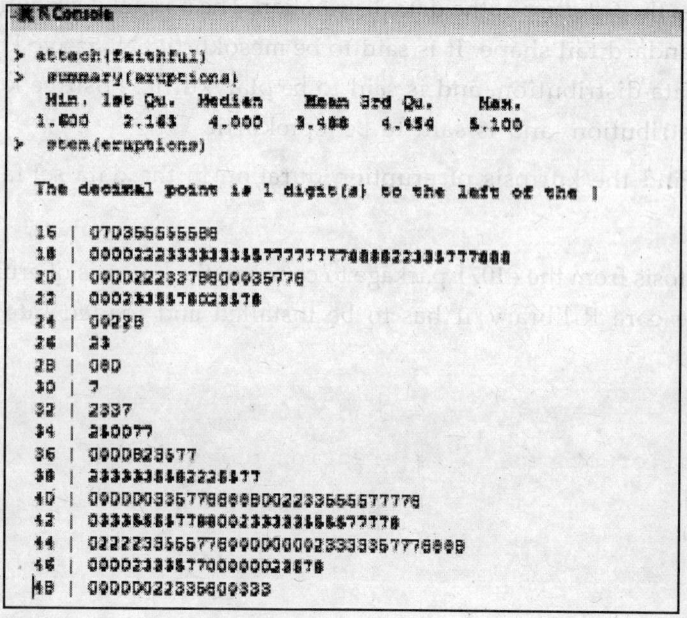

```
R Console
> attach(faithful)
>  summary(eruptions)
   Min. 1st Qu.  Median    Mean 3rd Qu.    Max.
  1.600   2.163   4.000   3.488   4.454   5.100
>  stem(eruptions)

  The decimal point is 1 digit(s) to the left of the |

  16 | 070355555588
  18 | 000022233333335577777777888822335777888
  20 | 00002223378800035778
  22 | 0002335578023578
  24 | 00228
  26 | 23
  28 | 080
  30 | 7
  32 | 2337
  34 | 250077
  36 | 0000823577
  38 | 2333335582225577
  40 | 0000003357788888002233555577778
  42 | 03335555778800233333555577778
  44 | 02222335557780000000023333357778888
  46 | 0000233357700000023578
  48 | 00000022335800333
```

A stem-and-leaf plot is like a histogram, and R has a function hist to plot histograms. Enter

```
> hist(eruptions)
#make the bins smaller,
```

We can write the remarks in our program after entering ##. To make make a plot of density

```
> hist(eruptions, seq(1.6, 5.2, 0.2), prob=TRUE)
```

A histogram shall appear in a separate window as shown below:

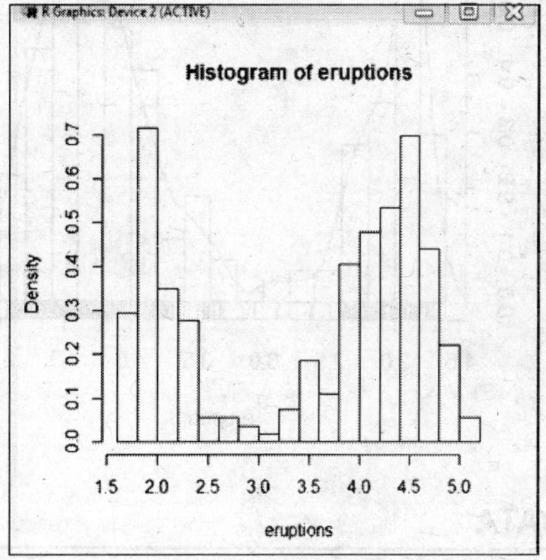


```
> lines(density(eruptions, bw=0.1))
```

Another histogram shall appear in a separate window showing the density lines linearly as below:

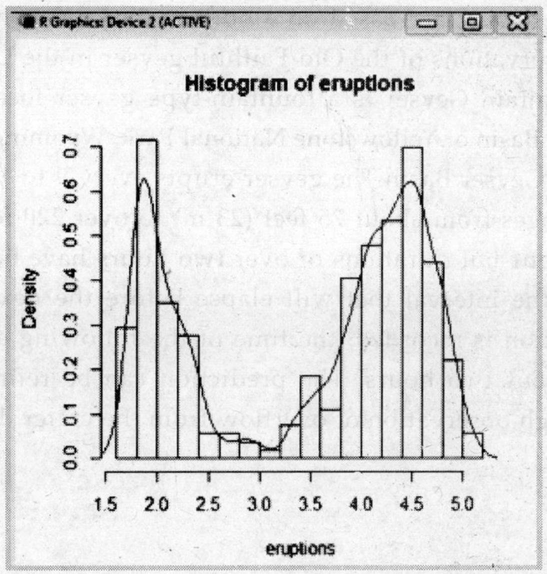

```
> rug(eruptions)
# show the actual data points
```

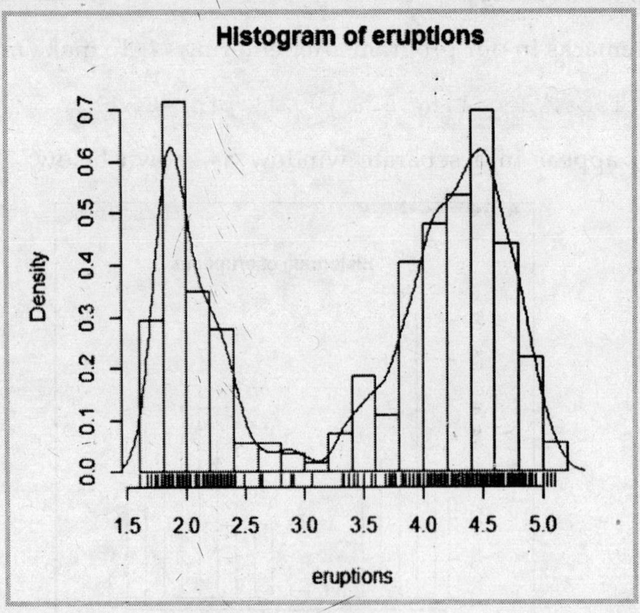

9. QUANTITATIVE DATA

Quantitative data, also known as continuous data, consists of numeric data that support arithmetic operations. This is in contrast with qualitative data, whose values belong to pre-defined classes with no arithmetic operation allowed. We will explain how to apply some of the R tools for quantitative data analysis with examples.

The tutorials in this section are based on a built-in data frame named faithful. It consists of a collection of observations of the Old Faithful geyser in the USA Yellowstone National Park. The Great Fountain Geyser is a fountain-type geyser located in the Firehole Lake area of Lower Geyser Basin of Yellowstone National Park, Wyoming. It is the only predictable geyser in the Lower Geyser Basin.The geyser erupts every 9 to 15 hours. Great Fountain's maximum height ranges from about 75 feet (23 m) to over 220 feet (67 m). Its duration is usually about one hour but durations of over two hours have been seen. The duration of an eruption affects the interval that will elapse before the next eruption, so that if the duration of an eruption is recorded, the time of the following eruption can be predicted to a precision of about two hours. The prediction can be refined, to plus or minus 15 minutes or so, through observation of overflow from the crater during the period between eruptions.

The following is a preview via the head function

Enter following at the command prompt in the R console to see the preview of head function of faithful dataframe :

```
> head(faithful)
```

R Console

```
> head(faithful)
  eruptions waiting
1     3.600      79
2     1.800      54
3     3.333      74
4     2.283      62
5     4.533      85
6     2.883      55
>
```

10. SCATTER PLOT

A scatter plot pairs up values of two quantitative variables in a data set and display them as geometric points inside a Cartesian diagram.

In the data set faithful, we pair up the eruptions and waiting values in the same observation as (x,y) coordinates. Then we plot the points in the Cartesian plane.

Example Annexure 13: *Find the scatter plot of the eruption durations and waiting intervals in faithful. Does it reveal any relationship between the variables?*

Solution:

We apply the plot function to compute the scatter plot of eruptions and waiting.Enter following code snipett at command prompt :

```
> duration = faithful$eruptions          # the eruption durations
> waiting = faithful$waiting             # the waiting interval
> plot(duration, waiting,                # plot the variables
+   xlab="Eruption duration",            # x"axis label
+   ylab="Time waited")                  # y"axis label
```

R Console

```
> duration = faithful$eruptions          # the eruption durations
> waiting = faithful$waiting             # the waiting interval
> plot(duration, waiting,                # plot the variables
+   xlab="Eruption duration",            # x-axis label
+   ylab="Time waited")                  # y-axis label
> |
```

The following scatter data plot shall appear in the separate window. It reveals a positive linear relationship between them.

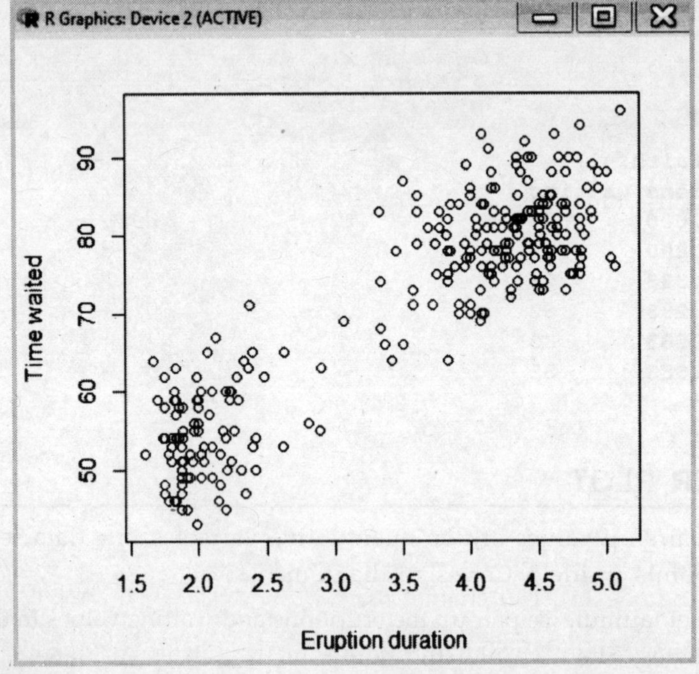

Enhanced Solution

We can generate a linear regression model of the two variables with the lm function, and then draw a trend line with abline.

```
> abline(lm(waiting ~ duration))
```

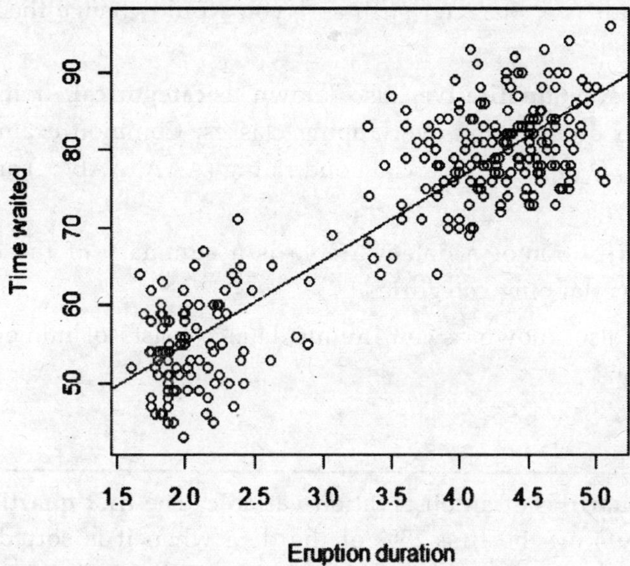

11. EXISTING LOCAL DATA

R has a function dedicated to reading comma-separated files. To import a local CSV file named filename.txt and store the data into one R variable named mydata, the syntax would be:

```
mydata <- read.csv("filename.txt")
```

(Aside: What's that ← where you expect to see an equals sign? It's the R assignment operator. I said R syntax was a bit quirky. More on this in the section on R syntax quirks.)

And if you're wondering what kind of object is created with this command, mydata is an extremely handy data type called a data frame — basically a table of data. A data frame is organized with rows and columns, similar to a spreadsheet or database table.

The read.csv function assumes that your file has a header row, so row 1 is the name of each column. If that's *not* the case, you can add header=FALSE to the command:

```
mydata <- read.csv("filename.txt", header=FALSE)
```

In this case, R will read the first line as data, not column headers (and assigns default column header names you can change later).

If your data use another character to separate the fields, not a comma, R also has the more general read.table function. So if your separator is a tab, for instance, this would work:

```
mydata <- read.table("filename.txt", sep="\t", header=TRUE)
```

The command above also indicates there's a header row in the file with header=TRUE.

If, say, your separator is a character such as | you would change the separator part of the command to sep="|"

A data sample is called **qualitative**, also known as **categorical**, if its values belong to a collection of known defined non-overlapping classes. Common examples include student letter grade (A, B, C, D or F), commercial bond rating (AAA, AAB, ...) and consumer clothing shoe sizes (1, 2, 3, ...).

The **frequency distribution** of a data variable is a summary of the data occurrence in a collection of non-overlapping categories.

Quantitative data, also known as **continuous** data, consists of numeric data that support arithmetic operations.

12. QUARTILE

There are several **quartiles** of an observation variable. The **first quartile**, or **lower quartile**, is the value that cuts off the first 25% of the data when it is sorted in ascending order. The **second quartile**, or **median**, is the value that cuts off the first 50%. The **third quartile**, or **upper quartile**, is the value that cuts off the first 75%

Percentile

The nth **percentile** of an observation variable is the value that cuts off the first *n* percent of the data values when it is sorted in ascending order.

Interquartile Range

The **interquartile range** of an observation variable is the difference of its upper and lower quartiles. It is a measure of how far apart the middle portion of data spreads in value.

$$\text{Inter quartile Range} = \text{Upper Quartile} - \text{Lower Quartile}$$

13. VARIANCE

The **variance** is a numerical measure of how the data values is dispersed around the mean. In particular, the **sample variance** is defined as:

$$s^2 = \frac{1}{n}\sum_{i=1}^{n}(x_i - \bar{x})^2$$

Similarly, the **population variance** is defined in terms of the population mean *i* and population size *N*:

$$\sigma^2 = \frac{1}{N}\sum_{i=1}^{N}(x_i - \mu)^2$$

14. COVARIANCE

The **covariance** of two variables *x* and *y* in a data set measures how the two are linearly related. A positive covariance would indicate a positive linear relationship between the variables, and a negative covariance would indicate the opposite.

The **sample covariance** is defined in terms of the sample means as:

$$s_{xy} = \frac{1}{n-1}\sum_{i=1}^{n}(x_i - \bar{x})(y_i - \bar{y})$$

Similarly, the **population covariance** is defined in terms of the population mean ì$_x$, ì$_y$ as:

$$\sigma_{xy} = \frac{1}{N}\sum_{i=1}^{N}(x_i - \mu_x)(y_i - \mu_y)$$

15. Correlation Coefficient

The **correlation coefficient** of two variables in a data set equals to their covariance divided by the product of their individual standard deviations. It is a normalized measurement of how the two are linearly related.

Formally, the **sample correlation coefficient** is defined by the following formula, where s_x and s_y are the sample standard deviations, and s_{xy} is the sample covariance.

$$r_{xy} = \frac{s_{xy}}{s_x s_y}$$

Similarly, the **population correlation coefficient** is defined as follows, where σ_x and σ_y are the population standard deviations, and σ_{xy} is the population covariance.

$$p_{xu} = \frac{\sigma_{xy}}{\sigma_x \sigma_y}$$

If the correlation coefficient is close to 1, it would indicate that the variables are positively linearly related and the scatter plot falls almost along a straight line with positive slope. For -1, it indicates that the variables are negatively linearly related and the scatter plot almost falls along a straight line with negative slope. And for zero, it would indicate a weak linear relationship between the variables.

16. SKEWNESS

The **skewness** of a data population is defined by the following formula, where ì$_2$ and ì$_3$ are the second and third central moments.

$$\gamma_1 = \mu_3 / \mu_2^{3/2}$$

Intuitively, the skewness is a measure of symmetry. As a rule, negative skewness indicates that the mean of the data values is less than the median, and the data distribution is *left-skewed*. Positive skewness would indicate that the mean of the data values is larger than the median, and the data distribution is *right-skewed*.

17. KURTOSIS

The **kurtosis** of a univariate population is defined by the following formula, where μ_2 and $\mu_4$are respectively the second and fourth central moments.

$$\gamma_2 = \mu_4 / \mu_2^2 - 3$$

Intuitively, the *kurtosis* describes the *tail shape* of the data distribution. The normal distribution has zero kurtosis and thus the standard tail shape. It is said to be **mesokurtic**. Negative kurtosis would indicate a *thin-tailed* data distribution, and is said to be **platykurtic**. Positive kurtosis would indicate a *fat-tailed* distribution, and is said to be **leptokurtic**.

18. PROBABILITY DISTRIBUTIONS

A **probability distribution** describes how the values of a random variable is distributed. For example, the collection of all possible outcomes of a sequence of coin tossing is known to follow the binomial distribution. Whereas the means of sufficiently large samples of a data population are known to resemble the normal distribution. Since the characteristics of these theoretical distributions are well understood, they can be used to make statistical inferences on the entire data population as a whole.

In the following tutorials, we demonstrate how to compute a few well-known probability distributions that occurs frequently in statistical study. We reference them quite often in other sections.

- Binomial Distribution
- Poisson Distribution
- Continuous Uniform Distribution
- Exponential Distribution
- Normal Distribution
- Chi-squared Distribution
- Student t Distribution
- F Distribution

19. BINOMIAL DISTRIBUTION

The **binomial distribution** is a discrete probability distribution. It describes the outcome of n independent trials in an experiment. Each trial is assumed to have only two outcomes, either success or failure. If the probability of a successful trial is p, then the probability of having x successful outcomes in an experiment of n independent trials is as follows.

$$f(x) = \binom{n}{x} p^x (1-p)^{(n-x)} \qquad \text{where } x = 0,1,2,\ldots,n$$

Example Annexure 13: *Suppose there are twelve multiple choice questions in an English class quiz. Each question has five possible answers, and only one of them is correct. Find the probability of having four or less correct answers if a student attempts to answer every question at random.*

Solution:

Since only one out of five possible answers is correct, the probability of answering a question correctly by random is 1/5=0.2. We can find the probability of having exactly 4 correct answers by random attempts as follows.

```
> dbinom(4, size=12, prob=0.2)
[1] 0.1329
```

To find the probability of having four or less correct answers by random attempts, we apply the function dbinom with $x = 0,\ldots,4$.

```
> dbinom(0, size=12, prob=0.2) +
+ dbinom(1, size=12, prob=0.2) +
+ dbinom(2, size=12, prob=0.2) +
+ dbinom(3, size=12, prob=0.2) +
+ dbinom(4, size=12, prob=0.2)
[1] 0.9274
```

Alternatively, we can use the cumulative probability function for binomial distribution pbinom.

```
> pbinom(4, size=12, prob=0.2)
[1] 0.92744
```

Answer

The probability of four or less questions answered correctly by random in a twelve question multiple choice quiz is 92.7%.

20. POISSON DISTRIBUTION

The **Poisson distribution** is the probability distribution of independent event occurrences in an interval. If ë is the mean occurrence per interval, then the probability of having x occurrences within a given interval is:

$$f(x) = \frac{\lambda^2 e^{-\lambda}}{x\,|} \qquad \textbf{where } x = 0,1,2,3,\ldots.$$

Example Annexure 14: *If there are twelve cars crossing a bridge per minute on average, find the probability of having seventeen or more cars crossing the bridge in a particular minute.*

Solution:

The probability of having *sixteen or less* cars crossing the bridge in a particular minute is given by the function ppois.

```
> ppois(16, lambda=12)     # lower tail
[1] 0.89871
```

Hence the probability of having seventeen or more cars crossing the bridge in a minute is in the *upper tail* of the probability density function.

```
> ppois(16, lambda=12, lower=FALSE)   # upper tail
[1] 0.10129
```

Answer

If there are twelve cars crossing a bridge per minute on average, the probability of having seventeen or more cars crossing the bridge in a particular minute is 10.1%.

21. CONTINUOUS UNIFORM DISTRIBUTION

The **continuous uniform distribution** is the probability distribution of random number selection from the continuous interval between *a* and *b*. Its density function is defined by the following.

$$f(x) = \begin{cases} \dfrac{1}{b-a} & \text{when } a \le x \le b \\ 0 & \text{when } x < a \text{ or } x > b \end{cases}$$

Here is a graph of the continuous uniform distribution with $a = 1$, $b = 3$.

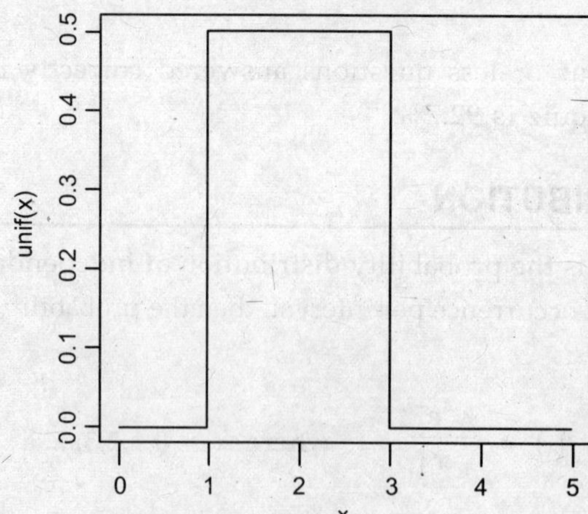

Example Annexure 15: *Select ten random numbers between one and three.*

Solution:

We apply the generation function runif of the uniform distribution to generate ten random numbers between one and three.

```
> runif(10, min=1, max=3)
[1] 1.6121 1.2028 1.9306 2.4233 1.6874 1.1502 2.7068
[8] 1.4455 2.4122 2.2171
```

22. EXPONENTIAL DISTRIBUTION

The **exponential distribution** describes the arrival time of a randomly recurring independent event sequence. If *ì* is the <u>mean</u> waiting time for the next event recurrence, its probability density function is:

$$f(x) = \begin{cases} \frac{1}{\mu} e^{-x/\mu} & \textbf{when } x \le 0 \\ 0 & \textbf{when } x < 0 \end{cases}$$

Here is a graph of the exponential distribution with $\mu = 1$.

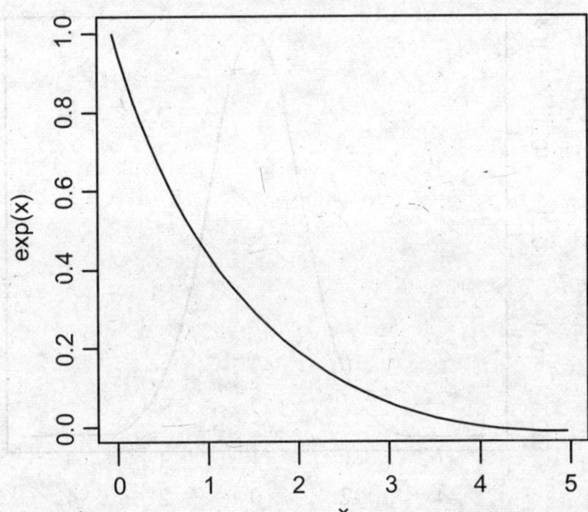

Example Annexure 16: *Suppose the mean checkout time of a supermarket cashier is three minutes. Find the probability of a customer checkout being completed by the cashier in less than two minutes.*

Solution:

The checkout processing rate is equals to one divided by the mean checkout completion time. Hence the processing rate is 1/3 checkouts per minute. We then apply the function pexp of the exponential distribution with rate=1/3.

```
> pexp(2, rate=1/3)
[1] 0.48658
```

Answer

The probability of finishing a checkout in under two minutes by the cashier is 48.7%

23. NORMAL DISTRIBUTION

The **normal distribution** is defined by the following probability density function, where ì is the population mean and ó^2 is the variance.

$$f(x) = \frac{1}{\alpha\sqrt{2\pi}} e^{-(x-\mu)^2/2\alpha^2}$$

If a random variable X follows the normal distribution, then we write:

$$\mathbf{X = N(\mu,\alpha^2)}$$

In particular, the normal distribution with ì = 0 and ó = 1 is called the *standard normal distribution,* and is denoted as $N(0,1)$. It can be graphed as follows.

In particular, the normal distribution with ì = 0 and ó = 1 is called the *standard normal distribution,* and is denoted as $N(0,1)$. It can be graphed as follows.

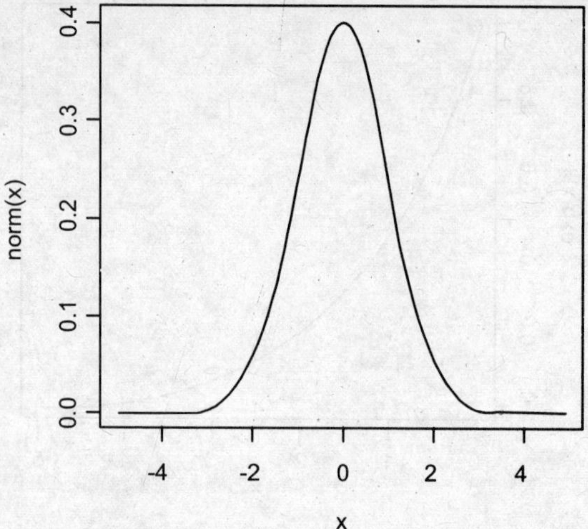

The normal distribution is important because of the **Central Limit Theorem**, which states that the population of all possible samples of size n from a population with mean ì and variance ó^2 approaches a normal distribution with mean ì and ó^2"n when n approaches infinity.

Example Annexure 17: *Assume that the test scores of a college entrance exam fits a normal distribution. Furthermore, the mean test score is 72, and the standard deviation is 15.2. What is the percentage of students scoring 84 or more in the exam?*

Solution:

We apply the function pnorm of the normal distribution with mean 72 and standard deviation 15.2. Since we are looking for the percentage of students scoring higher than 84, we are interested in the *upper tail* of the normal distribution.

```
> pnorm(84, mean=72, sd=15.2, lower.tail=FALSE)
[1] 0.21492
```

Answer

The percentage of students scoring 84 or more in the college entrance exam is 21.5%.

24. CHI-SQUARED DISTRIBUTION

If $X_1, X_2, \ldots, X_m$ are *m* independent random variables having the standard normal distribution, then the following quantity follows a **Chi-Squared distribution** with *m degrees of freedom*. Its mean is *m*, and its variance is 2*m*.

$$V = X_1^2 + X_1^2 + \ldots.. + X_m^2 \sim X_{(m)}^2$$

Here is a graph of the Chi-Squared distribution 7 degrees of freedom.

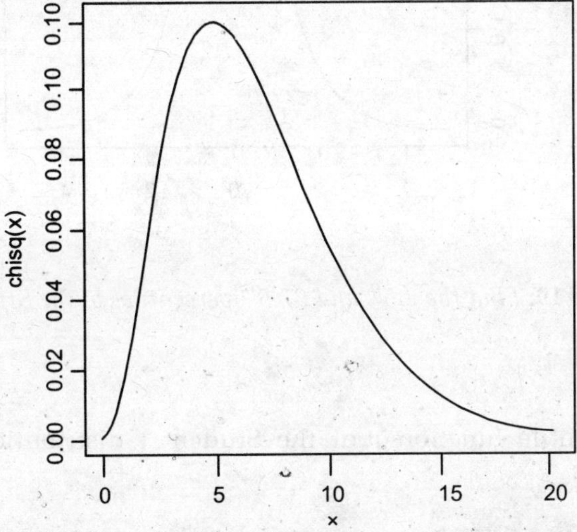

Example Annexure 18: *Find the 95*th *percentile of the Chi-Squared distribution with 7 degrees of freedom.*

Solution:

We apply the quantile function qchisq of the Chi-Squared distribution against the decimal values 0.95.

```
> qchisq(.95, df=7)          # 7 degrees of freedom
[1] 14.067
```

Answer

The 95th percentile of the Chi-Squared distribution with 7 degrees of freedom is 14.067.

Student t Distribution

Assume that a random variable Z has the standard normal distribution, and another random variable V has the Chi-Squared distribution with *m degrees of freedom*. Assume further that *Z* and *V* are independent, then the following quantity follows a **Student t distribution** with *m* degrees of freedom.

$$t = \frac{Z}{\sqrt{V/m}} - t_{(m)}$$

Here is a graph of the Student t distribution with 5 degrees of freedom.

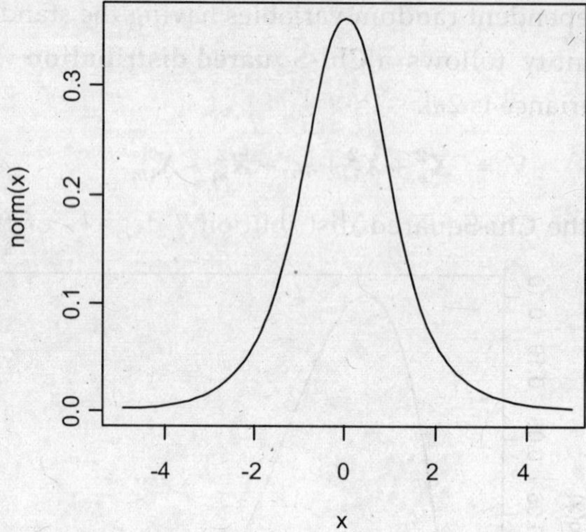

Example Annexure 19: *Find the 2.5^{th} and 97.5^{th} percentiles of the Student t distribution with 5 degrees of freedom.*

Solution:

We apply the quantile function qt of the Student t distribution against the decimal values 0.025 and 0.975.

```
> qt(c(.025, .975), df=5)   # 5 degrees of freedom
[1] -2.5706  2.5706
```

Answer:

The 2.5^{th} and 97.5^{th} percentiles of the Student t distribution with 5 degrees of freedom are -2.5706 and 2.5706 respectively.

MACHINE LEARNING

V.K. JAIN

FEEDBACK FORM

1. Which topics from your examination point of view are inadequately or not covered in this book?

___

___

2. Is there any misprints/mistakes/factual inaccuracy in this book? If so, please specify.

___

___

3. What is your assessment of this book as regards the presentation of the subject-matter, expression, precision and price in relation to the other recommended books available on this subject?

___

___

4. Which competing books you regard as better than this? Please mention their author and publishers.

___

___

5. Any further suggestions/comments you would like to make for the improvement of the book?

___

___

PS: If needed, please attach a separate sheet.

Name : ___

College : ___

Address : ___

Email : ___

Mobile : ___

Please mail the feedback form at:

KHANNA BOOK PUBLISHING CO. (P) LTD.

4C/4344, Ansari Road, Daryaganj, New Delhi-110002

You can also email this feedback form at contact@khannabooks.com or Whatsapp at +91 – 99109 09320

BEST FEEDBACK WILL BE REWARDED SUITABLY